CliffsAP™
Biology

2ND EDITION

by

By Phillip E. Pack, Ph.D.

Consultant

Jerry Bobrow, Ph.D.

Wiley Publishing, Inc.

About the Author

Phillip E. Pack has taught AP Biology and gifted programs for eleven years. He is currently an assistant professor of math and science at Woodbury University in Burbank, California.

Author's Dedication

To Mary and Megan

Publisher's Acknowledgments

Editorial

Project Editor: Michael Cunningham

Acquisitions Editor: Roxane Stanfield

Technical Editor: Kelly Schweitzer

Production

Proofreader: Mary Lagu

Wiley Indianapolis Composition Services

CliffsAP™ Biology, 2nd Edition

Published by:
Wiley Publishing, Inc.
909 Third Avenue
New York, NY 10022
www.wiley.com

Copyright © 2001 Phillip E. Pack.

Library of Congress Control Number: 00-112069

ISBN: 0-7645-8682-3

Printed in the United States of America

10

2B/RT/RR/QS/IN

Published simultaneously in Canada

Answers to Multiple-Choice Questions 95
Free-Response Questions 97
Some Typical Answers to Free-Response Questions 98
    Question 1 98
    Question 2 99

Heredity 101

Review 101
  Monohybrid Crosses 104
  Test Crosses 105
  Dihybrid Crosses 106
  Incomplete Dominance 107
    Codominance 107
  Multiple Alleles 108
  Epistasis 108
  Pleiotropy 109
  Polygenic Inheritance 109
  Linked Genes 109
  Sex-Linked Inheritance 111
  X-Inactivation 111
  Nondisjunction 112
  Human Genetic Defects 112
Sample Questions and Answers 114
  Multiple-Choice Questions 114
    Questions 7–9 115
    Questions 10–11 115
    Questions 17–19 116
  Answers to Multiple-Choice Questions 118
  Free-Response Questions 122
  A Typical Answer to the Free-Response Question 123
    Question 1 123

Molecular Genetics 125

Review 125
  DNA Replication 125
  Mutations 128
  Protein Synthesis 128
  Transcription 131
  RNA Processing 132
  Translation 132
  DNA Organization 134
  The Molecular Genetics of Viruses 135
  The Molecular Genetics of Bacteria 136
  Regulation of Gene Expression 137
  Recombinant DNA 138
Sample Questions and Answers 139
  Multiple-Choice Questions 139
    Questions 9–15 141
  Answers to Multiple-Choice Questions 143
  Free-Response Questions 145
  Some Typical Answers to Free-Response Questions 146
    Question 1 146
    Question 2 147
    Question 3 147

Evolution 149
Review 149
Evidence for Evolution 150
Natural Selection 151
Sources of Variation 154
Causes of Changes in Allele Frequencies 156
Genetic Equilibrium 157
Speciation 158
Maintaining Reproductive Isolation 159
Patterns of Evolution 160
Macroevolution 162
The Origin of Life 162
Sample Questions and Answers 165
Multiple-Choice Questions 165
Questions 10–14 167
Answers to Multiple-Choice Questions 168
Free-Response Questions 170
Some Typical Answers to Free-Response Questions 171
Question 1 171
Question 2 172
Question 3 172
Question 4 173
Question 5 173

A Five-Kingdom Survey 175
Review 175
Kingdom Monera 175
Kingdom Protista 177
Kingdom Fungi 179
Kingdom Plantae 181
Kingdom Animalia 186
Sample Questions and Answers 190
Multiple-Choice Questions 190
Questions 3–7 190
Answers to Multiple-Choice Questions 193
Free-Response Questions 195
Some Typical Answers to Free-Response Questions 196
Question 1 196
Question 2 196
Question 3 197
Question 4 197

Plants 199
Review 199
Plant Tissues 199
The Seed 200
Germination and Development 201
Primary Growth Versus Secondary Growth 202
Primary Structure of Roots 202
Primary Structure of Stems 204
Secondary Structure of Stems and Roots 205
Structure of the Leaf 206
Transport of Water 207

Control of Stomata 208
Transport of Sugars 209
Plant Hormones 210
Plant Responses to Stimuli 211
Photoperiodism 212
Sample Questions and Answers 214
Multiple-Choice Questions 214
Answers to Multiple-Choice Questions 217
Free-Response Questions 219
Some Typical Answers to Free-Response Questions 220
Question 1 220
Question 2 220

Animal Structure and Function 221
Review 221
Thermoregulation 222
The Respiratory System 222
The Circulatory System 224
The Excretory System 227
The Digestive System 231
The Nervous System 233
The Muscular System 237
The Immune System 239
The Endocrine System 243
Sample Questions and Answers 246
Multiple-Choice Questions 246
Answers to Multiple-Choice Questions 250
Free-Response Questions 252
Some Typical Answers to Free-Response Questions 253
Question 1 253
Question 2 254
Questions 3–6 254
Question 7 255

Animal Reproduction and Development 257
Review 257
Characteristics That Distinguish the Sexes 257
Human Reproductive Anatomy 257
Gametogenesis in Humans 259
Hormonal Control of Human Reproduction 259
Embryonic Development 261
Factors That Influence Development 265
Sample Questions and Answers 267
Multiple-Choice Questions 267
Questions 3–7 267
Questions 9–12 268
Answers to Multiple-Choice Questions 269
Free-Response Questions 270
Some Typical Answers to Free-Response Questions 271
Question 1 271
Question 2 271
Question 3 272
Question 4 272

Animal Behavior **273**
  Review 273
    Genetic Basis of Behavior 273
    Kinds of Animal Behavior 273
    Animal Movement 275
    Communication in Animals 276
    Foraging Behaviors 277
    Social Behavior 278
  Sample Questions and Answers 280
    Multiple-Choice Questions 280
      Questions 2–3 280
      Questions 4–7 281
    Answers to Multiple-Choice Questions 282
    Free-Response Questions 283
    Some Typical Answers to Free-Response Questions 284
      Question 1 284
      Question 2 284

Ecology **285**
  Review 285
    Population Ecology 285
    Human Population Growth 291
    Community Ecology 291
    Coevolution 293
    Ecological Succession 294
    Ecosystems 296
    Biogeochemical Cycles 297
    Biomes 299
    Human Impact on the Biosphere 299
  Sample Questions and Answers 301
    Multiple-Choice Questions 301
      Questions 2–4 301
      Questions 6–7 302
      Questions 8–13 303
      Question 19 305
      Question 20 308
    Answers to Multiple-Choice Questions 306
    Free-Response Questions 308
    Some Typical Answers to Free-Response Questions 309
      Question 1 309
      Question 2 309
      Question 3 310
      Question 4 310

PART III: LABORATORY REVIEW

Laboratory Review **313**
  Review 313
    Graphing Data 313
    Designing an Experiment 314
    Laboratory 1: Diffusion and Osmosis 315
    Laboratory 2: Enzyme Catalysis 317
    Laboratory 3: Mitosis and Meiosis 318
    Laboratory 4: Plant Pigments and Photosynthesis 319

Laboratory 5: Cell Respiration 321
Laboratory 6: Molecular Biology 323
Laboratory 7: Genetics of Drosophila 325
Laboratory 8: Population Genetics and Evolution 327
Laboratory 9: Transpiration 328
Laboratory 10: Physiology of the Circulatory System 330
Laboratory 11: Animal Behavior 331
Laboratory 12: Dissolved Oxygen and Aquatic Primary Productivity 332
Sample Questions and Answers 334
Multiple-Choice Questions 334
Questions 2–3 335
Questions 4–6 336
Question 7 337
Question 9 338
Questions 10–11 338
Question 13 339
Question 14 340
Question 17 341
Questions 19–20 342
Answers to Multiple-Choice Questions 343
Free-Response Questions 346
Some Typical Answers to Free-Response Questions 347
Question 1 347
Question 2 348

PART IV: AP BIOLOGY PRACTICE TEST

Answer Sheet for the Practice Test 351

AP Biology Practice Test 353
Section I (Multiple-Choice Questions) 353
Questions 23–24 357
Question 30 358
Questions 75–76 367
Questions 77–79 367
Questions 80–83 367
Question 84 368
Questions 85–87 369
Questions 88–89 369
Questions 90–91 370
Questions 92–93 370
Questions 94–96 371
Questions 97–99 372
Question 100 373
Questions 101–103 374
Questions 104–106 375
Questions 107–108 376
Questions 109–110 377
Questions 111–112 378
Question 113 379
Questions 114–117 380
Questions 118–120 382
Section II (Free-Response Questions) 383

Answer Key for the Practice Test 386
    Section I (Multiple-Choice Questions) 386
    Section II (Free-Response Questions) 388
Scoring Your Practice Test 389
    Section I (Multiple-Choice Questions) 389
    Section II (Free-Response Questions) 389
    Combined Score (Sections I + II) 389
Answers and Explanations for The Practice Test 390
    Section I (Multiple-Choice Questions) 390
    Section II (Free-Response Questions) 400
        Scoring Standards for the Essay Questions 400
        Question 1 (10 points maximum) 400
        Question 2 (10 points maximum) 401
        Question 3 (10 points maximum) 402
        Question 4 (10 points maximum) 403

PART I

INTRODUCTION

How You Should Use This Book

The Advanced Placement Program is designed to encourage students to take challenging courses in high school and receive college credit for their efforts. Many high schools offer classes especially designed for the AP program, but any course or program of study, whatever it is called, is appropriate if the content is college level. This book helps you to prepare for the Advanced Placement Examination in Biology. It does this in three ways:

- First, it reviews the important material that you need to know for the exam. These reviews are detailed but written in an organized and condensed format, making them especially useful for studying.

- Second, after each section review, the book provides you with questions that reinforce the review. These questions are typical of AP exam questions, and many of them, like those on the AP exam, require considerable thought to determine the correct answer. In addition, some of the review questions ask you to apply the reviewed material to new situations and, as a result, increase your breadth of understanding. Complete explanations of the answers are given.

- Third, a complete sample test is provided, giving you the opportunity to evaluate your knowledge and your test-taking skills. Complete explanations are given for each question, and a scoring worksheet is provided to determine your score.

Have you ever wished that you had a copy of your teacher's lecture notes? The review sections in this book are very much like lecture notes. Each section contains all the important terminology with brief descriptions. All the important biological processes are outlined with a key word or phrase, listed in an easy-to-remember sequence. After each key word or phrase, a short explanation is given. When you study the material the first time, you can read the key words and the short explanations. When you review, you can just study the key words, rereading the explanations only as needed.

You should consider this book, however, as a supplement to your textbook, your laboratory exercises, and your teacher's lectures. Much of the excitement and adventure of biology can be obtained only through hands-on activities and discussions with teachers. In addition, textbooks provide background information, extensive examples, and thought-provoking questions that add depth to your study of biology.

Each time you study a topic in class, after listening to the lectures and reading the textbook, use this book to review. Underline or highlight material to help you remember it. Write in the margins any additional material that you heard in lectures or read in your textbook that you or your teacher thinks is important. Then, answer the questions and read the answers at the end of each section. This will reinforce your learning.

At the end of your biology course, this book will be a single, condensed source of material to review before the AP exam. Begin your final preparation several weeks before the AP exam by reviewing the material in each section. Then take the practice AP exam at the end of the book.

The AP Exam in Biology

Format

The AP exam in biology consists of two parts. The first part consists of 120 multiple-choice questions. You have 90 minutes to complete this section. The second part of the exam consists of four free-response, or essay, questions. You must answer all four questions in 90 minutes. The multiple-choice section counts for 60% of the exam, and the essay section counts for the remaining 40%. The exam is administered in May of each year along with AP exams in other subjects.

| Section I: Multiple Choice | 120 questions | 90 minutes | 60% |
| Section II: Essay | 4 questions | 90 minutes | 40% |

Grading

Exams are graded on a scale of 1 to 5, with 5 being best. Most colleges will accept a score of 3 or better as a passing score. If you receive a passing score, colleges will give you college credit (applied toward your bachelor's degree), advanced placement (you can skip the college's introductory course in biology and take an advanced course), or both. You should check with the biology departments at the colleges you're interested in to determine their policy.

The distribution of student scores for some recent AP exams in biology is as follows:

		Percentage of Students		
	Exam Grade	1998	1999	2000
Extremely well qualified	5	18.9	19.7	18.5
Well qualified	4	18.4	22.0	20.7
Qualified	3	23.8	23.5	25.3
Possibly qualified	2	22.8	21.8	22.1
No recommendation	1	16.1	13.0	13.4
Mean Score		3.01	3.14	3.09

The multiple-choice section is designed with a balance of easy and difficult questions to produce a mean score of about 60 out of 120 (50%). Essay questions are also designed to obtain a 50% mean score, but scores vary significantly with individual questions. On the 1999 exam, mean scores ranged from 2.51 to 3.82 (out of a possible 10 points) for each of the four questions. Clearly, both sections of the exam are difficult. They are deliberately written that way so that the full range of student ability can be measured. In spite of the exam difficulty, however, 64.5% of the students taking the exam in 2000 received a score of 3 or better. Therefore, the AP exam is difficult, but most (prepared) people do well.

What's On The Exam

Each AP exam is written with a certain number of questions from each area in biology. Each section in Part II of this book is represented on the multiple-choice and the essay sections of the AP exam with approximately the following percentages:

I. Molecules and Cell	25%
Section 1: Chemistry	7%
Section 2: Cells	6%
Section 3: Photosynthesis	4%
Section 4: Respiration	4%
Section 5: Cell Division	4%
II. Genetics and Evolution	25%
Section 6: Heredity	8%
Section 7: Molecular Genetics	9%
Section 8: Evolution	8%
III. Organisms and Populations	50%
Section 9: Five-Kingdom Survey	8%
Section 10: Plants	10%
Section 11: Animal Structure and Function	14%
Section 12: Animal Reproduction and Development	5%
Section 13: Animal Behavior	1%
Section 14: Ecology	10%

In order to make your review as easy as possible, the sections in this book are organized in the same order used in most college textbooks. For this reason, the percentages given above differ somewhat from those given in the official *AP Course Description in Biology* (called the "Acorn Book" for its acorn logo) because its content outline is organized differently.

Laboratory experience contributes a very important component to the AP biology course. So that all students taking the AP exam will have appropriate laboratory preparation, the College Board provides a laboratory manual with twelve laboratory exercises. The exercises accompanying these labs provide valuable skills in experimental design and collecting and analyzing data. About 10% of the multiple-choice questions and usually one essay question are devoted to evaluating your laboratory knowledge. To help you review for the AP exam, Part III in this book reviews all twelve of the AP laboratory exercises.

Hints for Taking the Multiple-Choice Section

In the AP exam, questions for the multiple-choice section are provided in a booklet. While reading the questions in the booklet, feel free to cross out answers you know are wrong or underline important words. After you've selected the answer from the various choices, you carefully fill bubbles, labeled A, B, C, D, or E, on an answer sheet. Mark only your answers on the answer sheet. Since unnecessary marks can produce machine-scoring errors, be sure to fill the bubbles carefully and erase errors and stray marks thoroughly.

Some specific strategies for answering the multiple-choice questions follow:

1. **Don't let easy questions mislead you.** The multiple-choice questions range from easy to difficult. On one exam, 97% of the candidates got the easiest question right, while only 20% got the hardest question right. Don't let the easy questions mislead you. If you come across what you think is an easy question, it probably is. Don't suspect that it's a trick question.

2. **Budget your time by skipping hard questions.** You have 90 minutes to answer 120 questions, about 45 seconds per question. If you come across a hard question that you can't answer quickly, skip it, and mark the question to remind you to return to it if time permits. If you can eliminate some of the answer choices, mark those also so that you can save time when you return. It's important to skip a difficult question, even if you think you can eventually figure it out, because for each difficult question you spend three minutes on, you could have answered three easy questions. If you have time at the end of the test, you can always go back. If you don't have time, at least you will have had the opportunity to try all the questions. Also, if you never finish the test, don't be overly concerned. Since the test is designed to obtain a mean score of 50%, it is not unusual for a student to leave some answers blank.

3. **Make only "educated" guesses.** You make an educated guess when you can reduce the answer to two or three choices. If you get an answer right, you receive one point. If you leave it blank, you receive no points. *However, for each wrong answer, $\frac{1}{4}$ point is deducted from your score.*

4. **Avoid wrong answer penalties.** One-fourth point is deducted for each wrong answer. The $\frac{1}{4}$ point deduction for wrong answers adjusts for random guessing. Since each question has five choices, there is a one-in-five chance that you can *randomly* select the correct answer. If you choose five answers randomly for five questions, probability predicts that you will guess one correct answer and four wrong answers. Your total score for the five

guesses would be $1 - \frac{1}{4} - \frac{1}{4} - \frac{1}{4} - \frac{1}{4} = 0$. By deducting $\frac{1}{4}$ point for each of the wrong answers, your total score would be zero. That's reasonable because you really didn't know any of the answers. But if you can reduce your choices to two or three, the odds are in your favor that the number of questions you get right will exceed the number of points deducted. That's also reasonable because you knew some of the answer choices were wrong.

5. **Carefully answer reverse multiple-choice questions**. In a typical multiple-choice question you need to select the choice that is true. On the AP exam, you will find many "reverse" multiple-choice questions where you need to select the *false* choice. These questions usually use the word "EXCEPT" in sentences such as "All of the following are true EXCEPT:" or "All of the following occur EXCEPT:" A reverse multiple-choice question is more difficult to answer than regular multiple-choice questions because it requires you to know four true pieces of information about a topic before you can eliminate the false choice. It is equivalent to correctly answering five true-false questions correctly to get one point; and if you get one of the five wrong, you get them all wrong. Reverse multiple-choice questions are also difficult because half way through the question you can forget that you're looking for the false choice. To avoid confusion, do the following. After reading the opening part of the question, *read each choice and mark a T or an F next to each one to identify whether it is true or false*. If you're able to mark a T or an F for each one, then the correct answer is the choice marked with an F. Sometimes you won't be sure about one or more choices, or sometimes you'll have two choices marked F. In these cases, you can concentrate on the uncertain choices until you can make a decision.

Hints for Taking the Essay Section

There are four questions on the essay test. One of the questions is taken from Area I (molecules and cells), one from Area II (genetics and evolution), and two from Area III (organisms and populations). One of the questions specifically evaluates your laboratory knowledge.

The essay questions are provided in a green booklet. There's room on each page to make notes. Read the question thoroughly, circling key words. Next, write a brief outline using key words to organize your thoughts. Then begin writing your answer on the answer sheets that are provided separately. If for some reason you don't write an outline, go back and reread the question half way through writing your answer. Make sure you're still answering the question. It's easy to get carried away, and by the end of your response, you may be answering a different question.

Strategies for answering the essay questions follow:

1. **Don't approach the essay section with apprehension**. Most students approach the essay section of the exam with more anxiety than they have when approaching the multiple-choice section. However, in terms of the amount of detail in the knowledge required, the essay section is easier. On essay questions, *you* get to choose what to write. You can get an excellent score without writing every relevant piece of information. Besides, you don't have time to write an entire book on the subject. A general answer that addresses the question with a limited number of specifics will get a good score. Additional details may or *may not* (see below) improve your score, but the basic principles are the most important

elements for a good score. In contrast, a multiple-choice question focuses on a very narrow body of knowledge. The question doesn't let you select from a range of correct information. This isn't true for the essay questions.

2. **Give specific information in your answer.** You need to give specific information for each essay question. Don't be so general that you don't really say anything. Give more than just terminology with definitions. You need to use the terminology to explain biological processes. It's the combination of using the proper terminology and explaining processes that will convince an AP exam reader that you understand the answer. Give some detail when you know it—names of processes, names of structures, names of molecules—and then tell how they're related. The reader is looking for specific information. If you say it, you get the points. You don't have to say everything, however, to get the full 10 points.

3. **Answer each part of an essay question separately.** Many of the AP essay questions ask several related questions. A single question, for example, may have two or three parts, each requesting specific information. You should answer each part of the question in a separate paragraph. This will help the reader recognize each part of your answer. Some questions are formally divided into parts, such as a, b, c, d. Again, answer these questions in separate paragraphs labeled a, b, c, and d.

4. **Answer all parts of an essay question.** When you answer the essay questions, it is extremely important that you give a response for each part of the question. Don't overload the detail on one part at the expense of saying nothing in another part because you ran out of time. Each part of the question is apportioned a specific number of points. If you give abundant information on one part, and nothing on the remaining parts, you receive only the maximum number of points allotted to the part you completed. In a four-part question, that's often only 2.5 points. You won't get any extra points above the maximum 2.5, even if what you write is Nobel-prize quality.

5. **Budget your time.** You have 90 minutes for four questions, about 23 minutes each. Just as it's more important to answer all parts of a question, it's best to respond to all the essay questions rather than to answer two or even three of them extremely well, with no response on the last one or two. You'll probably know *something* about every question, so be sure you get that information written for each question. If you reach the last question with five minutes remaining, for example, use that time to write as much information as possible. One or two points is a lot better than zero.

6. **Don't worry if you make a factual error.** What if you write something that is incorrect? The AP exam readers look for correct information. They search for key words and phrases and award points when they find them. If you use the wrong word to describe a process, or identify a structure with the wrong name, there is no formal penalty (unlike the deduction for guessing on the multiple-choice test). If you're going to get any points, however, you need to write correct information.

7. **Don't be overly concerned about grammar, spelling, punctuation, or penmanship.** The AP exam readers don't penalize for incorrect grammar, spelling, or punctuation or for poor penmanship. They are interested in *content*. However, if your grammar, spelling, or penmanship impairs your ability to communicate, then the readers cannot recognize the content, and your score will suffer.

8. **Don't write a "standard" essay.** Don't spend your time writing a "standard" essay with introduction, support paragraphs, and conclusion. Just dive right into your outline and answer the question directly.

9. **Pay attention to direction words.** A direction word is the first word in an essay question that tells you how to answer the question. The direction word tells you what you need to say about the subject matter that follows. Here are the most common direction words found on the AP exam.

   - *Discuss* means to consider or examine various aspects of a subject or problem.
   - *Describe* means to characterize, or give an account in words.
   - *Define* means to give a precise meaning for a word or phrase.
   - *Explain* means to clarify or make understandable.
   - *Compare* means to discuss two or more items with an emphasis on their similarities.
   - *Contrast* means to discuss two or more items with an emphasis on their differences.

There are also specialized direction words for the laboratory essays. These words include *design* (an experiment), *calculate* (a value), and *construct* and *label* (a graph). These words have specific meanings for laboratory analyses and are discussed in the lab section later in this book.

Must-Know Essay Questions

Some AP Biology teachers try to predict which essay questions will be on the next AP test. For example, reviewing old AP exams may reveal some questions that haven't been asked in awhile. A new scientific discovery, or research that receives a Nobel Prize, might suggest an AP question. Unfortunately, guessing questions in this way is very unreliable.

Here is a better way. Questions on the essay section of the AP exam generally address fundamental principles or processes in biology. Here is a list of the most important principles—the ones on which questions keep reappearing on AP exams. Being able to answer these questions is an absolute requirement for being prepared. So, at the very least, know this material. Sample responses to questions on these topics appear at the end of the appropriate subject area review.

1. Section 2: Cells: Cell structure, especially structure and function of the plasma membrane
2. Section 3: Photosynthesis: Photosynthesis and chloroplasts
3. Section 4: Respiration: Respiration and mitochondria
4. Section 5: Cell Division: Mitosis and meiosis
5. Section 7: Molecular Genetics: DNA structure and replication
6. Section 7: Molecular Genetics: Protein synthesis
7. Section 8: Evolution: Natural selection
8. Section 8: Evolution: Speciation

9. Section 10: Plants: Reproduction in flowering plants

10. Section 10: Plants: Plant tropisms and hormones (especially auxin)

11. Section 11: Animal Structure and Function: Nerve transmission

12. Section 11: Animal Structure and Function: Muscle contraction

13. Section 12: Animal Reproduction and Development: Menstrual cycle

14. Section 14: Ecology: Succession

15. Section 14: Ecology: Biogeochemical cycles

There's no guarantee that questions on these topics will appear on your AP exam, but these topics appear so often that you should be prepared. In any case, the multiple-choice section of the exam will certainly include questions on these topics. So you can't lose by focusing on these areas.

PART II

SUBJECT AREA REVIEWS WITH SAMPLE QUESTIONS AND ANSWERS

Chemistry

Review

A major difference between an AP biology course and a regular high school biology course is the emphasis on detail. In many cases that detail derives from a description of the molecular structure of molecules and the chemistry of metabolic reactions. It is the understanding of biological processes at the molecular level that provides you with a more thorough understanding of biology. The AP examiners want to know whether you have this kind of understanding. With that in mind, your studying should begin with a brief review of chemistry and the characteristics of major groups of biological molecules.

Atoms, Molecules, Ions, and Bonds

Atoms consist of a nucleus of positively charged protons and neutrally charged neutrons. Negatively charged electrons are arranged outside the nucleus. **Molecules** are groups of two or more atoms held together by **chemical bonds**. Chemical bonds between atoms form because of the interaction of their electrons. The **electronegativity** of an atom, or the ability of an atom to attract electrons, plays a large part in determining the kind of bond that forms.

1. **Ionic** bonds form between two atoms when one or more electrons are *transferred* from one atom to the other. This bond occurs when the electronegativities of the atoms are very different and one atom has a much stronger pull on the electrons (high electronegativity) than the other atom in the bond. The atom that gains electrons has an overall negative charge, and the atom that loses electrons has an overall positive charge. Because of their positive or negative charges, these atoms are **ions**. The attraction of the positive ion to the negative ion constitutes the ionic bond. Sodium and chlorine form ions (Na^+ and Cl^-), and the bond formed in a molecule of sodium chloride ($NaCl$) is an ionic bond.

2. **Covalent** bonds form when electrons between atoms are *shared*, which means that neither atom completely retains possession of the electrons (as happens with atoms that form strong ionic bonds). Covalent bonds occur when the electronegativities of the atoms are similar.

   - **Nonpolar covalent** bonds form when electrons are *shared equally*. When the two atoms sharing electrons are identical, such as in oxygen gas (O_2), the electronegativities are identical and both atoms pull equally on the electrons.

   - **Polar covalent** bonds form when electrons are *shared unequally*. Atoms in this kind of bond have electronegativities that are different and an unequal distribution of the electrons results. The electrons forming the bond are closer to the atom with the greater electronegativity and produce a negative charge, or **pole**, near that atom. The area around the atom with the weaker pull on the electrons produces a positive pole. In a molecule of water (H_2O), for example, electrons are shared between the oxygen atom and each hydrogen atom. Oxygen, with a greater electronegativity, exerts a stronger pull on the shared electrons than does each hydrogen atom. This unequal distribution of electrons creates a negative pole near the oxygen and positive poles near each hydrogen atom.

- **Single covalent**, **double covalent**, and **triple covalent** bonds form when two, four, and six electrons are shared, respectively.

3. **Hydrogen** bonds are weak bonds between *molecules*. They form when a positively charged *hydrogen* atom in one covalently bonded molecule is attracted to a negatively charged area of another covalently bonded molecule. In water, the positive pole around a hydrogen atom forms a hydrogen bond to the negative pole around the oxygen atom of *another* water molecule (Figure 1-1).

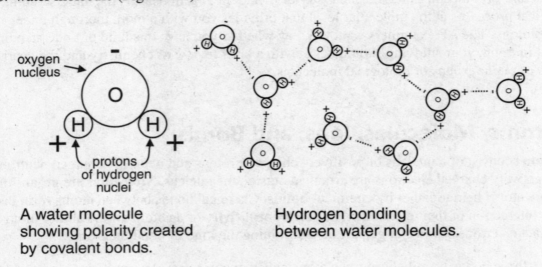

oxygen
nucleus

protons
of hydrogen
nuclei

A water molecule
showing polarity created
by covalent bonds.

Hydrogen bonding
between water molecules.

Figure 1-1

When you think of chemical bonds, imagine a continuum based on the differences of electronegativities (Figure 1-2). The left end represents bonds that form when there are no differences in the electronegativities of the atoms. Electrons are shared equally and nonpolar bonds form. The right end represents bonds that form when there are very large differences in electronegativities. Electrons are transferred from one atom to another and ionic bonds form. When the electronegativities of the atoms are different, but not strongly so, the electrons are shared unequally and polar covalent bonds form. This occurs in the center of Figure 1-2. The kind of bond that forms between two atoms and the strength of that bond depend upon the difference of electronegativities of the atoms and may occur any place along the line in Figure 1-2.

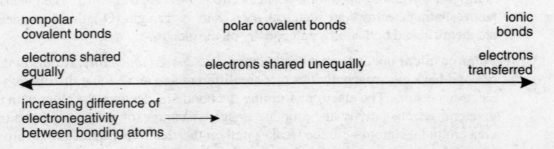

nonpolar covalent bonds	polar covalent bonds	ionic bonds
electrons shared equally	electrons shared unequally	electrons transferred

increasing difference of
electronegativity
between bonding atoms

Figure 1-2

Properties of Water

The hydrogen bonds among water molecules contribute to some very special properties for water.

1. *Water is an excellent* **solvent**. Ionic substances are soluble (they dissolve) in water because the poles of the polar water molecules interact with the ionic substances and separate them into ions. Substances with polar covalent bonds are similarly soluble because of the interaction of their poles with those of water. Substances that dissolve in water are called **hydrophilic** ("water loving"). Because they lack charged poles, nonpolar covalent substances do not dissolve in water and are called **hydrophobic** ("water fearing").

2. *Water has a high* **heat capacity**. Heat capacity is the degree to which a substance changes temperature in response to a gain or loss of heat. Water has a high heat capacity, changing temperature very slowly with changes in its heat content. Thus, the temperatures of large bodies of water are very stable in response to the temperature changes of the surrounding air. You must add a relatively large amount of energy to warm (and boil) water or remove a relatively large amount of energy to cool (and freeze) water. When sweat evaporates from your skin, a large amount of heat is taken with it and you are cooled.

3. *Ice floats*. Unlike most substances that contract and become more dense when they freeze, water *expands* as it freezes, becomes less dense than its liquid form, and, as a result, floats in liquid water. Hydrogen bonds are typically weak, constantly breaking and reforming, allowing molecules to periodically approach one another. In the solid state of water, the weak hydrogen bonds between water molecules become rigid and form a crystal that keeps the molecules separated and less dense that its liquid form. If ice did not float, it would sink and remain frozen due to the insulating protection of the overlaying water.

4. *Water has strong* **cohesion** *and high* **surface tension**. Cohesion, or the attraction between *like* substances, occurs in water because of the hydrogen bonding between water molecules. The strong cohesion between water molecules produces a high surface tension, creating a water surface that is firm enough to allow many insects to walk upon without sinking.

5. *Water adheres to other molecules*. **Adhesion** is the attraction of *unlike* substances. When water adheres to the walls of narrow tubing or to absorbent solids like paper, it demonstrates **capillary action** by rising up the tubing or creeping through the paper.

Organic Molecules

Organic molecules are those that have carbon atoms. In living systems, large organic molecules, called **macromolecules**, may consist of hundreds or thousands of atoms. Most macromolecules are **polymers**, molecules that consist of a single unit (**monomer**) repeated many times.

Four of carbon's six electrons are available to form bonds with other atoms. Thus, you will always see four lines connecting a carbon atom to other atoms, each line representing a pair of shared electrons (one electron from carbon and one from another atom). Complex molecules can be formed by stringing carbon atoms together in a straight line or by connecting carbons together to form rings. The presence of nitrogen, oxygen, and other atoms adds additional variety to these carbon molecules.

Many organic molecules share similar properties because they have similar clusters of atoms, called **functional groups**. Each functional group gives the molecule a particular property, such as acidity or polarity. The more common functional groups with their properties are listed in Figure 1-3.

Functional Group		Class Name	Examples	Characteristics
— OH	hydroxyl	alcohols	ethanol, glycerol, sugars	polar hydrophilic
$-C\overset{O}{\underset{OH}{<}}$	carboxyl	carboxylic acids	aceticacid, aminoacids, fattyacids, sugars	polar, hydrophilic, weakacid
$-N\overset{H}{\underset{H}{<}}$	amino	amines	aminoacids	polar, hydrophilic, weakbase
$-\overset{O}{\overset{\|}{P}}-O^-$ with O^- below	phosphate	organic phosphates	DNA, ATP, phospholipids	polar, hydrophilic, acid
$-\overset{O}{\overset{\|}{C}}-$	carbonyl	ketones	acetone, sugars	polar, hydrophilic
$-\overset{O}{\overset{\|}{C}}-H$	carbonyl	aldehydes	formaldehyde, sugars	polar, hydrophilic
$-\overset{H}{\underset{H}{C}}-H$	methyl	—	fatty acids, oils, waxes	nonpolar, hydrophobic

Figure 1-3

Four important classes of organic molecules—carbohydrates, lipids, proteins, and nucleic acids—are discussed below.

Carbohydrates

Carbohydrates are classified into three groups according to the number of sugar (or saccharide) molecules present.

1. A **monosaccharide** is the simplest kind of carbohydrate. It consists of a single sugar molecule, such as fructose or glucose (Figure 1-4). (Note that the symbol C for carbon may be omitted in ring structures; a carbon exists wherever four bond lines meet.) Sugar molecules have the formula $(CH_2O)_n$, where n is any number from 3 to 8. For **glucose**, n is 6, and its formula is $C_6H_{12}O_6$. The formula for **fructose** is also $C_6H_{12}O_6$, but as you can see in Figure 1-4, the placement of the carbon atoms is different. Two forms of glucose, α-**glucose** and β-**glucose**, differ simply by a reversal of the H and OH on the first carbon (clockwise, after the oxygen). As you will see below, even very small changes in the position of certain atoms may dramatically change the chemistry of a molecule.

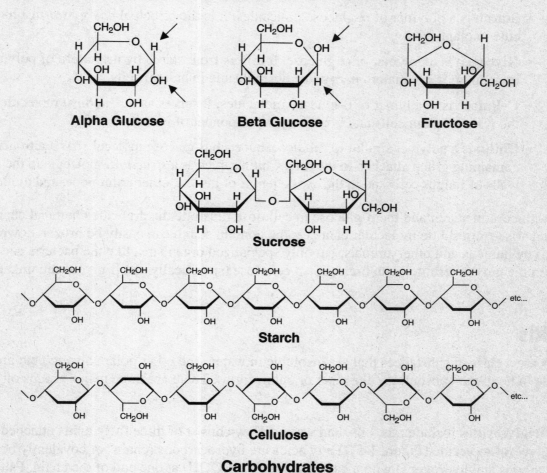

Alpha Glucose   **Beta Glucose**   **Fructose**

Sucrose

Starch

Cellulose

Carbohydrates

Figure 1-4

2. **A disaccharide** consists of two sugar molecules joined by a **glycosidic linkage**. During the process of joining, a water molecule is lost. Thus, when glucose and fructose link to form sucrose, the formula is $C_{12}H_{22}O_{11}$ (not $C_{12}H_{24}O_{12}$). This type of chemical reaction, where a simple molecule is lost, is generally called a **condensation** reaction (or specifically, a **dehydration** reaction, if the lost molecule is water). Some common disaccharides follow:

   - glucose + fructose = **sucrose** (common table sugar)

   - glucose + galactose = **lactose** (the sugar in milk)

   - glucose + glucose = **maltose**

3. **A polysaccharide** consists of a series of connected monosaccharides. Thus, a polysaccharide is a polymer because it consists of repeating units of a monosaccharide. The following examples of polysaccharides may contain thousands of glucose monomers:

   - **Starch** is a polymer of α-glucose molecules. It is the principal *energy storage* molecule in plant cells.

   - **Glycogen** is a polymer of α-glucose. It differs from starch by its pattern of polymer branching. It is a major *energy storage* molecule in animal cells.

   - **Cellulose** is a polymer of β-glucose molecules. It serves as a *structural* molecule in the walls of plant cells and is the major component of wood.

   - **Chitin** is a polymer similar to cellulose, but each β-glucose molecule has a nitrogen-containing group attached to the ring. Chitin serves as a *structural* molecule in the walls of fungus cells and in the exoskeletons of insects, other arthropods, and mollusks.

The α-glucose in starch and the β-glucose in cellulose illustrate the dramatic chemical changes that can arise from subtle molecular changes: the bond in starch can easily be broken down (digested) by humans and other animals, but only specialized organisms, like the bacteria and protozoa in the guts of termites, can break down cellulose (specifically, the β-glycosidic linkage).

Lipids

Lipids are a class of substances that are insoluble in water (and other polar solvents) but are soluble in nonpolar substances (like ether or chloroform). There are three major groups of lipids:

1. **Triglycerides** include fats, oils, and waxes. They consist of three **fatty acids** attached to a **glycerol** molecule (Figure 1-5). Fatty acids are hydrocarbons (chains of covalently bonded carbons and hydrogens) with a carboxyl group (–COOH) at one end of the chain. Fatty acids vary in structure by the number of carbons and by the placement of single and double covalent bonds between the carbons, as follows:

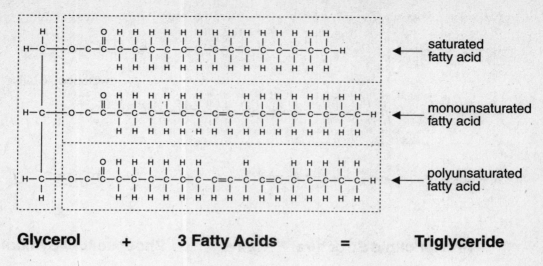

Glycerol   +   3 Fatty Acids   =   Triglyceride

Figure 1-5

- A **saturated** fatty acid has a single covalent bond between each pair of carbon atoms, and each carbon has two hydrogens bonded to it (three hydrogens bonded to the last carbon). You can remember this by thinking that each carbon is "saturated" with hydrogen.

- A **monounsaturated** fatty acid has *one double* covalent bond and each of the two carbons in this bond has only one hydrogen atom bonded to it.

- A **polyunsaturated** fatty acid is like a monounsaturated fatty acid except that there are *two or more double* covalent bonds.

2. **A phospholipid** looks just like a lipid except that one of the fatty acid chains is replaced by a phosphate group ($-PO_3^{2-}$) (Figure 1-6). An additional chemical group (indicated by R in Figure 1-6) is usually attached to the phosphate group. The two fatty acid "tails" of the phospholipid are nonpolar and hydrophobic and the phosphate "head" is polar and hydrophilic. A phospholipid is termed an **amphipathic** molecule because it has both polar (hydrophilic) and nonpolar (hydrophobic) regions. Phospholipids are often found oriented in sandwichlike formations with the hydrophobic tails grouped together on the inside of the sandwich and the hydrophilic heads oriented toward the outside and facing an aqueous environment. Such formations of phospholipids provide the structural foundation of cell membranes.

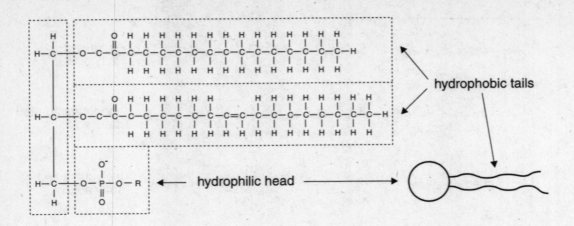

Phospholipid Structural Formula   **Phospholipid Symbol**

Figure 1-6

3. **Steroids** are characterized by a backbone of four linked carbon rings (Figure 1-7). Examples of steroids include cholesterol (a component of cell membranes) and certain hormones, including testosterone and estrogen.

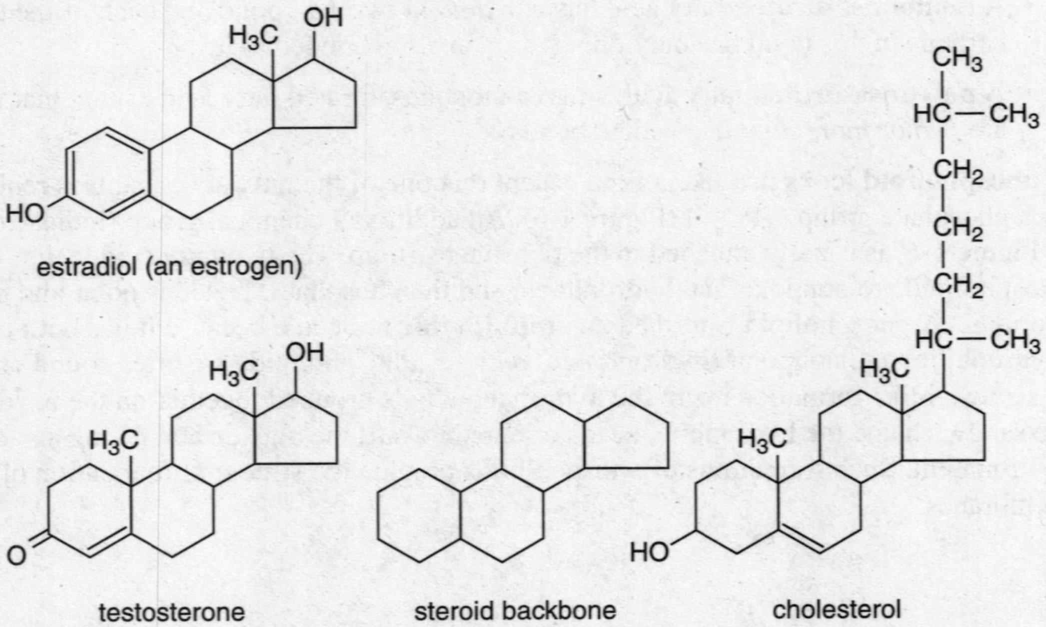

estradiol (an estrogen)

testosterone   steroid backbone   cholesterol

Steroids

Figure 1-7

Proteins

Proteins can be grouped according to their functions. Some major categories follow:

1. **Structural proteins** such as keratin in the hair and horns of animals, collagen in connective tissues, and silk in spider webs.

2. **Storage proteins** such as casein in milk, ovalbumin in egg whites, and zein in corn seeds.

3. **Transport proteins** such as those in the membranes of cells that transport materials into and out of cells and as oxygen-carrying hemoglobin in red blood cells.

4. **Defensive proteins** such as the antibodies that provide protection against foreign substances that enter the bodies of animals.

5. **Enzymes** that regulate the rate of chemical reactions.

Although the functions of proteins are diverse, their structures are similar. All proteins are polymers of **amino acids**, that is, they consist of a chain of amino acids covalently bonded. The bonds between the amino acids are called **peptide bonds**, and the chain is a **polypeptide**, or **peptide**. One protein differs from another by the number and arrangement of the twenty different amino acids. Each amino acid consists of a central carbon bonded to an amino group ($-NH_2$), a carboxyl group ($-COOH$), and a hydrogen atom (Figure 1-8). The fourth bond of the central carbon is shown with the letter R (for radical), which indicates an atom or group of atoms that varies from one kind of amino acid to another. For the simplest amino acid, glycine, the R is a hydrogen atom. For serine, R is CH_2OH. For other amino acids, R may contain sulfur (as in cysteine) or a carbon ring (as in phenylalanine).

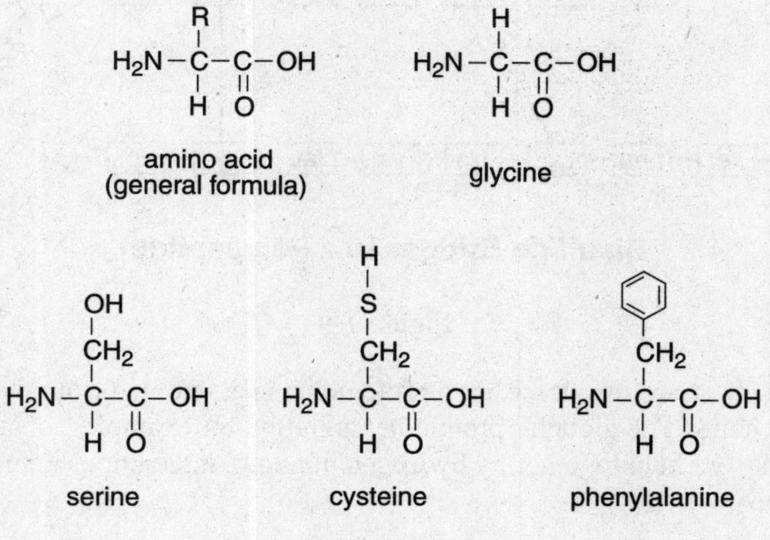

Amino Acids

Figure 1-8

There are four levels that describe the structure of a protein:

1. The **primary structure** of a protein describes the order of amino acids. Using three letters to represent each amino acid, the primary structure for the protein antidiuretic hormone (ADH) can be written as Cys-Tyr-Phe-Gln-Asn-Cys-Pro-Arg-Gly.

2. The **secondary structure** of a protein is a three-dimensional shape that results from hydrogen bonding between the amino and carboxyl groups of adjacent amino acids. The bonding produces a spiral (**alpha helix**) or a folded plane that looks much like the pleats on a skirt (**beta pleated sheet**). Proteins whose shape is dominated by these two patterns often form **fibrous proteins**.

3. The **tertiary structure** of a protein includes additional three-dimensional shaping and often dominates the structure of **globular proteins**. The following factors contribute to the tertiary structure:

   - **Hydrogen bonding** between R groups of amino acids.

   - **Ionic bonding** between R groups of amino acids.

   - The **hydrophobic effect** that occurs when hydrophobic R groups move toward the center of the protein (away from the water in which the protein is usually immersed).

   - The formation of **disulfide bonds** when the sulfur atom in the amino acid cysteine bonds to the sulfur atom in another cysteine (forming cystine, a kind of "double" amino acid). This disulfide bridge helps maintain turns of the amino acid chain (Figure 1-9).

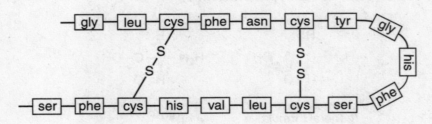

Disulfide Bridges in a Polypeptide

Figure 1-9

4. The **quaternary structure** describes a protein that is assembled from two or more separate peptide chains. The globular protein hemoglobin, for example, consists of four peptide chains that are held together by hydrogen bonding, interactions among R groups, and disulfide bonds.

Nucleic Acids

The genetic information of a cell is stored in molecules of deoxyribonucleic acid (DNA). The DNA, in turn, passes its genetic instructions to ribonucleic acid (RNA) for directing various metabolic activities of the cell.

DNA is a polymer of **nucleotides**. A DNA nucleotide consists of three parts—a **nitrogen base,** a five-carbon sugar called **deoxyribose,** and a **phosphate group**. There are four DNA nucleotides, each with one of the four nitrogen bases, as follows (see Figure 1-10):

1. Adenine—a double-ring base (purine).

2. Thymine—a single-ring base (pyrimidine).

3. Cytosine— a single-ring base (pyrimidine).

4. Guanine— a double-ring base (purine).

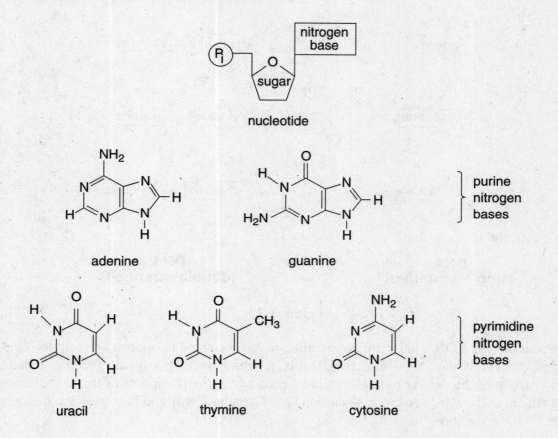

Nitrogen Bases

Figure 1-10

Pyrimidines are single-ring nitrogen bases, and purines are double-ring bases. You can remember which bases are purines because only the two purines end with *nine*. The first letter of each of these four bases is often used to symbolize the respective nucleotide (A for the adenine nucleotide, for example).

Figure 1-11 shows how two strands of nucleotides, paired by weak hydrogen bonds between the bases, form a double-stranded DNA. When bonded in this way, DNA forms a two-stranded spiral, or double helix. *Note that adenine always bonds with thymine and guanine always bonds with cytosine.*

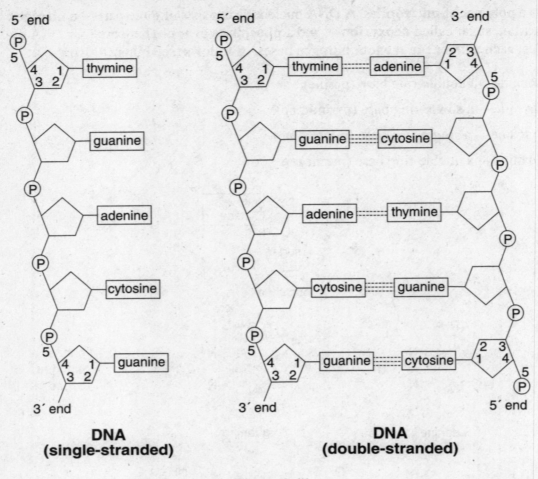

Figure 1-11

The two strands of a DNA helix are antiparallel, that is, oriented in opposite directions. One strand is arranged in the 5' → 3' direction; that is, it begins with a phosphate group attached to the *fifth* carbon of the deoxyribose (5' end) and ends where the phosphate of the next nucleotide would attach, at the *third* deoxyribose carbon (3'). The adjacent strand is oriented in the opposite, or 3' → 5' direction.

RNA differs from DNA in the following ways:

1. The sugar in the nucleotides that make an RNA molecule is **ribose,** not deoxyribose as it is in DNA.

2. The thymine nucleotide does not occur in RNA. It is replaced by **uracil.** When pairing of bases occurs in RNA, uracil (instead of thymine) pairs with adenine.

3. RNA is usually single-stranded and does not form a double helix as it does in DNA.

Chemical Reactions in Metabolic Processes

In order for a chemical reaction to take place, the reacting molecules (or atoms) must first collide and then have sufficient energy (**activation energy**) to trigger the formation of new bonds.

Although many reactions can occur spontaneously, the presence of a **catalyst** accelerates the rate of the reaction because it lowers the activation energy required for the reaction to take place. A catalyst is any substance that accelerates a reaction but does not undergo a chemical change itself. Since the catalyst is not changed by the reaction, it can be used over and over again.

Chemical reactions that occur in biological systems are referred to as **metabolism**. Metabolism includes the breakdown of substances (**catabolism**), the formation of new products (**synthesis** or **anabolism**), or the transferring of energy from one substance to another. Metabolic processes have the following characteristics in common:

1. The net direction of metabolic reactions, that is, whether the overall reaction proceeds in the forward direction or in the reverse direction, is determined by the concentration of the reactants and the end products. Chemical **equilibrium** describes the condition where the rate of reaction in the forward direction equals the rate in the reverse direction and, as a result, there is no net production of reactants or products.

2. **Enzymes** are globular proteins that act as catalysts (activators or accelerators) for metabolic reactions. Note the following characteristics of enzymes:

   - *The **substrate** is the substance or substances upon which the enzyme acts.* For example, amylase catalyzes the breakdown of the substrate amylose (starch).

   - *Enzymes are substrate specific.* The enzyme amylase, for example, catalyzes the reaction that breaks the α-glycosidic linkage in starch but cannot break the β-glycosidic linkage in cellulose.

   - *The **induced-fit model** describes how enzymes work.* Within the protein (the enzyme), there is an **active site** with which the reactants readily interact because of the shape, polarity, or other characteristics of the active site. The interaction of the reactants (substrate) and the enzyme causes the enzyme to change shape. The new position places the substrate molecules into a position favorable to their reaction. Once the reaction takes place, the product is released.

   - *An enzyme is unchanged as a result of a reaction.* It can perform its enzymatic function repeatedly.

   - *The efficiency of an enzyme is affected by temperature and pH.* The human body, for example, is maintained at a temperature of 98.6°, near the optimal temperature for most human enzymes. Above 104°, these enzymes begin to lose their ability to catalyze reactions as they become **denatured**, that is, they lose their three-dimensional shape as hydrogen bonds and peptide bonds begin to break down. The enzyme pepsinogen, which digests proteins in the stomach, becomes active only at a low pH (very acidic).

   - *The standard suffix for enzymes is "ase,"* so it is easy to identify enzymes that use this ending (some do not).

3. **Cofactors** are nonprotein molecules that assist enzymes. A **holoenzyme** is the union of the cofactor and the enzyme (called an **apoenzyme** when part of a holoenzyme).

   - **Coenzymes** are *organic* cofactors that usually function to donate or accept some component of a reaction, often electrons. Some vitamins are coenzymes or components of coenzymes.

   - **Inorganic cofactors** are often metal ions, like Fe^{2+}.

4. **ATP** (adenosine triphosphate) is a common source of activation energy for metabolic reactions (Figure 1-12). ATP is essentially an RNA adenine nucleotide with two additional phosphate groups. The wavy lines between these two phosphate groups indicate high-energy bonds. When ATP supplies energy to a reaction, it is usually the energy in the last bond that is delivered to the reaction. In the process of giving up this energy, the last phosphate bond is broken and the ATP molecule is converted to ADP (adenosine diphosphate) and a phosphate group (indicated by P_i). In contrast, new ATP molecules are assembled by **phosphorylation** when ADP combines with a phosphate group using energy obtained from some energy-rich molecule (like glucose).

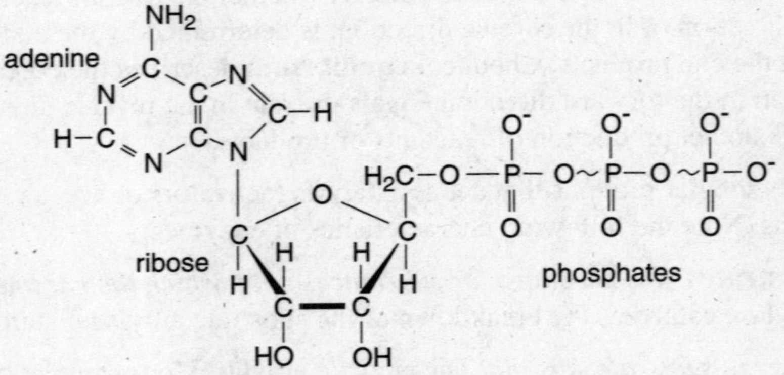

Adenosine Triphosphate (ATP)

Figure 1-12

How do living systems regulate chemical reactions? How do they know when to start a reaction and when to shut it off? One way of regulating a reaction is by regulating its enzyme. Here are four common ways in which this is done:

1. **Allosteric enzymes** have two kinds of binding sites—one an active site for the substrate and one an allosteric site for an **allosteric effector**. There are two kinds of allosteric effectors:

   - An **allosteric activator** binds to the enzyme and induces the enzyme's *active* form.
   - An **allosteric inhibitor** binds to the enzyme and induces the enzyme's *inactive* form.

   In **feedback inhibition**, an end product of a series of reactions acts as an allosteric inhibitor, shutting down one of the enzymes catalyzing the reaction series.

2. In **competitive inhibition**, a substance that mimics the substrate inhibits an enzyme by occupying the active site. The mimic displaces the substrate and prevents the enzyme from catalyzing the substrate.

3. A **noncompetitor inhibitor** binds to an enzyme at locations other than an active or allosteric site. The inhibitor changes the shape of the enzyme which disables its enzymatic activity.

4. In **cooperativity**, an enzyme becomes more receptive to additional substrate molecules after one substrate molecule attaches to an active site. This occurs, for example, in enzymes that consist of two or more subunits (quaternary structure), each with its own active site. A common example of this process (though not an enzyme) is hemoglobin, whose binding capacity to additional oxygen molecules increases after the first oxygen binds to an active site.

Sample Questions and Answers

Multiple-Choice Questions

Directions: Each of the following questions or statements is followed by five possible answers or sentence completions. Choose the one best answer or sentence completion.

1. Which of the following molecules orient themselves into sandwichlike membranes because of hydrophobic components within the molecule?

   A. Amylose

   B. Glycogen

   C. Cellulose

   D. Phospholipid

   E. Protein

$$A \xrightarrow{A'} B \xrightarrow{B'} C \xrightarrow[C_2']{C_1'} \begin{array}{l} D \xrightarrow{D'} E \\ J \xrightarrow{J'} K \xrightarrow{K'} L \end{array}$$

2. In the series of metabolic reactions shown above, C' catalyzes the conversion of C to D, and C_2' catalyzes the conversion of C to J. Assume that product E is an allosteric effector that inhibits enzyme D'. Normally, products E and L are consumed by other reactions. Which of the following would likely happen if product E were not consumed by other reactions?

   A. The net rate of production of product B would decrease.

   B. The net rate of production of product C would decrease.

   C. The net rate of production of product D would decrease.

   D. The net rate of production of product J would decrease.

   E. The net rate of production of product K would decrease.

$$A \xrightarrow{A'} B \xrightarrow{B'} C \xrightarrow{C_1'} \begin{array}{l} D \xrightarrow{D'} E \\ J \xrightarrow{J'} K \xrightarrow{K'} L \end{array}$$

3. In the series of metabolic reactions shown above, C' catalyzes the splitting of C into D and J. Assume that product E is an allosteric effector that inhibits enzyme C'. If product E were not consumed in a subsequent reaction, which of the following would likely happen?

   A. The rate of production of product D would increase.

   B. The rate of production of product E would increase.

   C. The rate of production of product J would increase.

   D. The rate of production of product L would increase.

   E. The rate of production of all products D, E, J, K, and L would decrease.

4. Each of the following molecules is a polymer EXCEPT:

    A. protein

    B. glucose

    C. cellulose

    D. starch

    E. glycogen

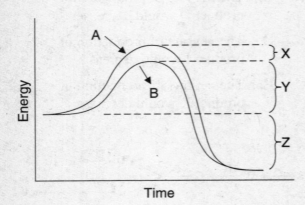

5. For the graph given above, the two curves describe the potential energy of substances during the progress of a chemical reaction. All of the following items could apply to this graph EXCEPT:

    A. Curve B could be showing the influence of an enzyme.

    B. The sum of energy in the products of the reaction is less than the sum of energy in the reactants.

    C. The activation energy of this reaction could be given by $X + Y + Z$.

    D. This reaction graph could describe the reaction $ATP \rightarrow ADP = P_i$.

    E. This is an exergonic reaction.

Questions 6–10

Questions 6–10 refer to the molecules below.

6. A monosaccharide

7. A polysaccharide

8. A polypeptide

9. An amino acid

10. A major component of cell membranes

11. Hydrophilic properties are characteristic of all of the following EXCEPT:

    A. polar molecules

    B. molecules soluble in water

    C. molecules that readily ionize in water

    D. the long hydrocarbon chain components of some molecules

    E. the hydroxyl group

12. All of the following are carbohydrates EXCEPT:

    A. polypeptide

    B. glycogen

    C. amylose

    D. glucose

    E. polysaccharide

Answers to Multiple-Choice Questions

1. **D.** Phospholipids are composed of glycerol molecules bonded to two fatty acids and one phosphate group. The phosphate group is a hydrophilic "head" and the long hydrocarbon chains of fatty acids are hydrophobic "tails". In cell membranes, phospholipids orient themselves into two layers, with the hydrophobic tails pointing to the inside of the "sandwich."

2. **C.** When product E is no longer consumed by other reactions, it is available to inactivate enzyme D'. As quantities of product E accumulate, more and more of D' will be inactivated. As a result, the rate of production of E will decrease and quantities of product D will accumulate. As product D accumulates, the rate of the reverse reaction, of D to C, increases. Now, more of C is available for conversion to J (and then to K and L), and as C increases, the rate of production of J increases. Eventually, the rate of production of D will equal the rate of the reverse reaction (of D to C), and chemical equilibrium between C and D will be reached. The *net* rate of production of D will become zero.

3. **E.** The effect of the allosteric effector E is to inhibit enzyme C'. As quantities of product E accumulate, increasing amounts of C' would become inactivated. As a result, fewer and fewer quantities of C would be converted to products D and J. Thus, quantities of C increase, which, in turn, increase the rate of the reverse reaction of C to B (and then to A). In the end, A, B, and C would be in chemical equilibrium, and the rate of production of products D, E, J, K, and L would be zero.

4. **B.** Glucose is a monomer consisting of a single glucose molecule. Starch, glycogen, and cellulose are polymers consisting of repeating units of glucose. Protein is a polymer of amino acids.

5. **C.** The activation energy is given by X + Y for curve A or Y for curve B. Curve B shows how the activation energy would be lowered if an enzyme were present. Since the products (right side of the curve) have less energy than the reactants, energy is released. This kind of reaction, where energy is released, is called an exergonic reaction. If the products had more energy than the reactants, it would be an endergonic reaction. The reaction ATP → ADP = P_i is an exergonic reaction where the energy released is used as activation energy for other metabolic reactions.

6. **A.** This is the ring structure of glucose.

7. **C.** This is amylose, a starch found in plants.

8. **E.** This polypeptide contains five amino acids.

9. **B.** This is the amino acid histidine. Note the amino group (NH_2) at the left side of the molecule and the carboxyl group (COOH) on the right side. Between these two groups is a carbon with a hydrogen below. Above the carbon is the R group with a carbon-nitrogen ring.

10. **D.** This is a phospholipid.

11. **D.** Long hydrocarbon chains are nonpolar and, therefore, hydrophobic. Any polar molecule (or polar group of atoms like the hydroxyl group) is hydrophilic. When a substance ionizes in water, it dissolves; thus, it is hydrophilic.

12. **A.** A polypeptide is a protein. Amylose is a starch and, therefore, a carbohydrate.

Free-Response Questions

Free-response questions on the AP exam may require you to provide information from a narrow area of biology, or they may consist of parts that require you to assemble information from diverse areas of biology. The questions that follow are typical of either an entire AP exam question or merely that part of a question that is related to this section.

Directions: Answer the questions below as completely and as thoroughly as possible. Answer the question in essay form (NOT outline form), using complete sentences. You may use diagrams to supplement your answers, but a diagram alone without appropriate discussion is inadequate.

1. Discuss each of the following:

   (a.) The structure of an enzyme

   (b.) How enzymes function

   (c.) How enzymes are regulated

2. Describe why water is an ideal medium for living things.

3. When you hard-boil an egg, the clear liquid part surrounding the yolk becomes white and solid. Discuss why this happens.

Some Typical Answers to Free-Response Questions

Question 1

(a.) Enzymes are globular proteins. Proteins, in turn, are polymers of amino acid—chains of amino acids, bonded to each other by peptide bonds. The general formula for an amino acid is a central carbon atom bonded to an amino group (NH_2^+), a carboxyl group (COOH), and a hydrogen atom. A fourth bond is made with a group of atoms that varies with each of the twenty amino acids. This variable group can be a single hydrogen atom (as in the amino acid glycine) or a group of many atoms sometimes including sulfur, nitrogen, or carbon rings. The individual amino acids in a protein interact with one another, giving the protein special spatial and functional characteristics. These characteristics impart to an enzyme unique attributes that allow it to catalyze specific reactions of specific substrates. The characteristics of proteins (and, therefore, enzymes) are derived from four features of the protein's structure. The first, described by the primary structure, is the kind and arrangement of amino acids in the protein. A secondary structure originates from hydrogen bonding between amino and carboxyl groups of amino acids. This secondary structure is the three-dimensional shape of a helix or a pleated sheet. Further interactions between amino acids give proteins a tertiary structure. These interactions include hydrogen bonding and ionic bonding between R groups, the "hiding" of hydrophobic R groups into the interior of the protein, and a disulfide bridge between two cysteine amino acids. The summation of all of the interactions gives enzymes a globular shape.

(b.) The function of an enzyme is to speed up the rate of, or catalyze, a reaction. The induced-fit model describes how enzymes work. In this model, there are specific active sites within the enzyme to which substrate molecules weakly bond. When substrate molecules bond to the active sites, the enzyme changes shape in such a way as to reduce the activation energy required for a bond to form between the substrate molecules. With less energy required, bonding proceeds at a faster rate.

Many enzymes require a cofactor to catalyze a reaction. Cofactors include coenzymes (nonprotein, organic molecules) and metal ions (like Fe^{2+} or Mg^{2+}).

(c.) There are several ways that enzymes are regulated. Allosteric enzymes are controlled by allosteric effectors, substances that bind to the enzyme and inhibit (or activate) the enzyme. Sometimes an allosteric inhibitor is a product of a series of reactions partly catalyzed by the allosteric enzyme. This is an example of feedback inhibition. Allosteric effectors bind to special sites in the enzyme. In competitive inhibition, however, an inhibitor binds to the active site, competing with substrate molecules. As a result, the activity of the enzyme is inhibited. Environmental factors also contribute to the activity of enzymes. Enzymes operate best at specific temperatures and pH. Enzymes in the stomach, for example, are active only when the pH is low.

This answer provides quite a bit of detail on the structure of proteins. Although the material is relevant, you may be able to condense it to save time for your other questions. On the other hand, if time were available, you could give examples of some specific enzymes or coenzymes (both of which you'll learn about in subsequent sections).

Question 2

For this question, you should describe the properties of water and then explain why these properties are valuable to living systems. All of the properties listed in this section (capacity to act as a solvent, temperature stability, decrease in density during freezing, cohesion, surface tension, capillary action) originate from the polarity of an H2O molecule and the resulting hydrogen bonding that occurs among H2O molecules and between H2O and other kinds of molecules. Thus, it is important to discuss polar covalent bonds and hydrogen bonds and then hydrophobic and hydrophilic responses to water. Relating these characteristics to living things follows.

Cellular activities depend upon chemical reactions. Water is an ideal medium for chemical reactions. As a liquid, water provides a medium in which substances can easily mix, make contact, and readily react. The solvent properties of water allow easy mixing because when substances dissolve they mix by random motion. Also, dissolved substances can be transported by a liquid medium. On the other hand, substances that do not dissolve separate from the liquid by the pull of gravity and cannot be easily transported, nor do they remain mixed. If they do not remain mixed, they cannot react.

Because hydrophobic substances resist dissolving in water, they are able to create barriers. Plasma membranes, nuclear envelopes, and the membranes to cellular organelles are barriers that allow diverse and incompatible biosynthetic processes to occur without interference. Without a plasma membrane, cells could not exist.

The temperature stability of water is favorable to the evolution of living systems. In temperature-stable environments, structurally important substances, like enzymes, can evolve to operate with great sensitivity to specific reactions. In a temperature-unstable environment, enzymes would be unreliable and, as a result, incapable of regulating the chemical reactions that maintain living systems.

Other temperature-related features of water are also important. Because liquid water requires a relatively large amount of energy to change into water vapor, water that evaporates helps maintain the temperature of the surrounding medium. Thus, sweat has a cooling effect when it evaporates. Furthermore, because freezing water is less dense than liquid water, ice floats and provides thermal insulation for the water below it, thus reducing further freezing. Again, the qualities of water help maintain a temperature-constant environment for living things. If ice did not float, it would sink and continue to accumulate until the entire body of water was frozen. It is not likely that living things, as we know them, could be maintained in such an environment.

The cohesion of water molecules allows water to flow through small openings. Water movement through plant vessels and animal capillaries is possible because of this characteristic. The movement of water to the upper parts of tall trees occurs because of the strong cohesion among water molecules.

Question 3

The white of an egg is mostly the protein albumin. When a protein is heated above a critical temperature, it begins to lose its structure. Secondary, tertiary, and quaternary structures begin to break down. If temperatures are high enough, and applied for a long enough time, the structure of the protein is permanently destroyed.

To answer this question, you would need to discuss the structure of proteins first. A complete answer would include discussion of the primary, secondary, tertiary, and quaternary structure of proteins, as well as a discussion of amino acids (see answer to free-response Question 1, above). Once protein structure is described, you could provide the information given in the preceding paragraph about the breakdown of albumin during cooking.

Review

Structure and Function of the Cell

The **cell** is the basic functional unit of all living things. The **plasma membrane (cell membrane)** bounds the cell and encloses the **nucleus** and **cytoplasm.** The **cytoplasm** consists of specialized bodies called **organelles** suspended in a fluid matrix, the **cytosol**, which consists of water and dissolved substances such as proteins and nutrients.

The **plasma membrane** separates internal metabolic events from the external environment and controls the movement of materials into and out of the cell. The plasma membrane is a double phospholipid membrane (**lipid bilayer**) with the polar hydrophilic heads forming the two outer faces and the nonpolar hydrophobic tails pointing toward the inside of the membrane (Figure 2-1).

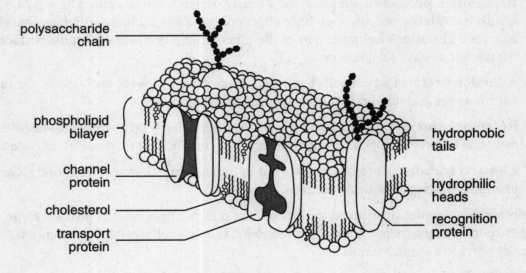

The Plasma Membrane

Figure 2-1

Proteins are scattered throughout the flexible phospholipid membrane. Proteins may attach loosely to the inner or outer surface of the membrane (**peripheral proteins**), or they may extend into the membrane (**integral proteins**). Integral proteins may span across the membrane, appearing at both surfaces (**transmembrane proteins**). Like phospholipids, integral proteins are amphipathic, with the hydrophobic regions embedded in the membrane and the hydrophilic regions exposed to the aqueous solutions bordering the membrane. The mosaic nature of scattered proteins within a flexible matrix of phospholipid molecules describes the **fluid mosaic model** of the cell membrane. Additional features of the plasma membrane follow:

1. The **phospholipid membrane** is selectively permeable. Only small, uncharged, polar molecules (such as H_2O and CO_2) and hydrophobic molecules (nonpolar molecules like O_2 and lipid-soluble molecules such as hydrocarbons) freely pass across the membrane. In contrast, large polar molecules (such as glucose) and all ions are impermeable.

2. **Proteins** in the plasma membrane provide a wide range of functions and include the following:

   - **Channel proteins** provide passageways through the membrane for certain hydrophilic (water-soluble) substances such as polar and charged molecules.

   - **Transport proteins** spend energy (ATP) to transfer materials across the membrane. When energy is used for this purpose, the materials are said to be *actively* transported, and the process is called **active transport**.

   - **Recognition proteins** distinguish the identity of neighboring cells. These proteins are **glycoproteins** because they have short polysaccharide chains (oligosaccharides) attached. The oligosaccharide part of the glycoprotein protrudes from the surface of the membrane like an antenna.

   - **Adhesion proteins** attach cells to neighboring cells or provide anchors for the internal filaments and tubules that give stability to the cell.

   - **Receptor proteins** provide binding sites for hormones or other trigger molecules. In response to the hormone or trigger molecule, a specific cell response is activated.

   - **Electron transfer proteins** are involved in transferring electrons from one molecule to another during chemical reactions.

3. **Cholesterol** molecules distributed throughout the phospholipid bilayer provide some rigidity to the plasma membranes of *animal cells*. In plant cells, related substances (sterols) provide a similar function.

4. The **glycocalyx** is a carbohydrate "coat" covering the outer face of the plasma membrane. It consists of various oligosaccharides that are attached to membrane phospholipids (**glycolipids**) and proteins (such as the **glycoproteins** of recognition proteins). The glycocalyx provides markers for cell-cell recognition.

Organelles are bodies within the cytoplasm that serve to physically separate the various metabolic reactions that occur within cells. A description of these organelles as well as other structures in the cell follows (Figure 2-2).

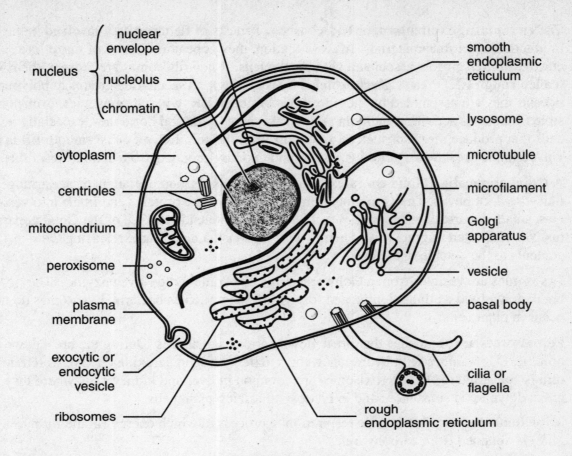

An Animal Cell

Figure 2-2

1. The **nucleus** is bounded by the **nuclear envelope**, a phospholipid bilayer similar to the plasma membrane. The nucleus contains DNA (deoxyribonucleic acid), the hereditary information of the cell. Normally, the DNA is spread out within the nucleus as a threadlike matrix called **chromatin**. When the cell begins to divide, the chromatin condenses into rod-shaped bodies called **chromosomes**, each of which, before dividing, is made up of two long DNA molecules and various histone (protein) molecules. The histones serve to organize the lengthy DNA, coiling it into bundles called **nucleosomes.** Also visible within the nucleus are one or more **nucleoli**, concentrations of DNA in the process of manufacturing the components of **ribosomes.** The nucleus also serves as the site for the separation of chromosomes during cell division.

2. **Ribosome** subunits are manufactured in the nucleus and consist of RNA molecules and proteins. The two subunits, labeled 60S and 40S, move across the nuclear envelope and into the cytoplasm where they are assembled into a single 80S ribosome. (An S value, or Svedberg unit, expresses how readily a product forms a sediment in a centrifuge, with larger values representing larger and heavier products). In the cytoplasm, ribosomes assist in the assembly of amino acids into proteins.

3. The **endoplasmic reticulum,** or **ER,** consists of stacks of flattened sacs involved in the production of various materials. In cross section, they appear as a series of maze-like channels, often closely associated with the nucleus. When ribosomes are present, the ER (called **rough ER**) creates **glycoproteins** by attaching polysaccharide groups to polypeptides as they are assembled by the ribosomes. **Smooth ER,** without ribosomes, is responsible for various activities, including the synthesis of lipids and hormones, especially in cells that produce these substances for export from the cell. In liver cells, smooth ER is involved in the breakdown of toxins, drugs, and toxic by-products from cellular reactions.

4. A **Golgi apparatus** (**Golgi complex** or **Golgi body**) is a group of flattened sacs arranged like a stack of bowls. They function to modify and package proteins and lipids into **vesicles,** small, spherically shaped sacs that bud from the outside surface of the Golgi apparatus. Vesicles often migrate to and merge with the plasma membrane, releasing their contents to the outside of the cell.

5. **Lysosomes** are vesicles from a Golgi apparatus that contain digestive enzymes. They break down food, cellular debris, and foreign invaders such as bacteria. Lysosomes do not occur in plant cells.

6. **Peroxisomes** are organelles that break down various substances. During the breakdown process, O_2 combines with hydrogen to form toxic hydrogen peroxide (H_2O_2), which in turn is converted to H_2O. Peroxisomes are common in liver and kidney cells where they break down toxic substances and in photosynthesizing plant cells.

7. **Mitochondria** carry out aerobic respiration, a process in which energy (in the form of ATP) is obtained from carbohydrates.

8. **Chloroplasts** carry out photosynthesis, the plant process of incorporating energy from sunlight into carbohydrates.

9. **Microtubules, intermediate filaments,** and **microfilaments** are three protein fibers of decreasing diameter, respectively. All are involved in establishing the shape of or in coordinating movements of the **cytoskeleton**, the internal structure of the cytoplasm.

   • **Microtubules** are made of the protein **tubulin** and provide support and motility for cellular activities. They are found in the **spindle apparatus** (which guides the movement of chromosomes during cell division), and in flagella and cilia (described in the following section), structures that project from the plasma membrane to provide motility to the cell.

   • **Intermediate filaments** provide support for maintaining the shape of the cell.

   • **Microfilaments** are made of the protein **actin** and are involved in cell motility. They are found in muscle cells and in cells that move by changing shape, such as phagocytes (white blood cells that wander throughout the body attacking bacteria and other foreign invaders).

10. **Flagella** and **cilia** are structures that protrude from the cell membrane and make wavelike movements. Flagella and cilia are classified by their lengths and by their numbers per cell: flagella are long and few; cilia are short and many. A single flagellum propels sperm, while the numerous cilia that line the respiratory tract sweep away debris. Structurally, both flagella and cilia consist of microtubules arranged in a "9 + 2" array–nine pairs (doublets) of microtubules arranged in a circle surrounding a pair of microtubules (Figure 2-3).

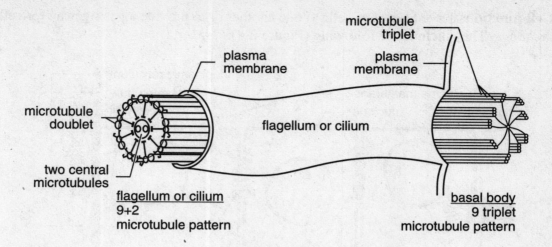

microtubule triplet

plasma membrane

plasma membrane

microtubule doublet

flagellum or cilium

two central microtubules

flagellum or cilium
9+2
microtubule pattern

basal body
9 triplet
microtubule pattern

Flagella, Cilia, and Basal Bodies

Figure 2-3

11. **Centrioles** and **basal bodies** act as **microtubule organizing centers** (**MTOCs**). A pair of centrioles (enclosed in a **centrosome**) located outside the nuclear envelope gives rise to the microtubules that make up the spindle apparatus used during cell division. Basal bodies are at the base of each flagellum and cilium and appear to organize their development. Both centrioles and basal bodies are made up of nine triplets arranged in a circle (Figure 2-3). Plant cells lack centrioles and only "lower" plants (such as mosses and ferns) with motile sperm have flagella and basal bodies.

12. **Cell walls** are found in plants, fungi, protists, and bacteria. They develop outside the plasma membrane and provide support for the cell. In plants, the cell wall consists mainly of **cellulose,** a polysaccharide made from β-glucose. The cell walls of fungi are usually made of cellulose or chitin. **Chitin** is a modified polysaccharide differing from cellulose in that one of the hydroxyl groups is replaced by a group containing nitrogen.

13. **Vacuoles and vesicles** are fluid-filled, membrane-bound bodies.

   • **Transport vesicles** move materials between organelles or between organelles and the plasma membrane.

   • **Food vacuoles** are temporary receptacles of nutrients. Food vacuoles often merge with lysosomes, whose digestive enzymes break down the food.

   • **Storage vacuoles** in plants store starch, pigments, and toxic substances (nicotine, for example).

   • **Central vacuoles** are large bodies occupying most of the interior of certain plant cells. When fully filled, they exert **turgor,** or pressure, on the cell walls, thus maintaining rigidity in the cell. They also store nutrients and carry out functions otherwise assumed by lysosomes in animal cells.

   • **Contractile vacuoles** are specialized organelles in single-celled organisms that collect and pump excess water out of the cell.

14. **Cell junctions** serve to *anchor* cells to one another or to provide a passageway for cellular *exchange*. They include the following (Figure 2-4):

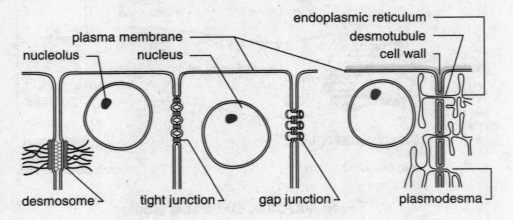

Cell Junctions

Figure 2-4

- **Desmosomes** are protein attachments between adjacent *animal* cells. Inside the plasma membrane, a desmosome bears a disk-shaped structure from which protein fibers extend into the cytoplasm. Desmosomes act like spot welds to hold together tissues that undergo considerable stress (such as skin or heart muscle).

- **Tight junctions** are tightly stitched seams between *animal* cells. The junction completely encircles each cell, preventing the movement of material between the cells. Tight junctions are characteristic of cells lining the digestive tract where materials are required to pass through cells (rather than intercellular spaces) to penetrate the blood stream.

- **Gap junctions** are narrow tunnels between *animal* cells that consist of proteins called **connexons**. The proteins prevent the cytoplasms of each cell from mixing, but allow the passage of ions and small molecules. In this manner, gap junctions allow communication between cells through the exchange of materials or through the transmission of electrical impulses.

- **Plasmodesmata** (singular, plasmodesma) are narrow channels between *plant* cells. A narrow tube of endoplasmic reticulum, called a **desmotubule**, surrounded by cytoplasm and the plasma membrane, passes through the channel. Material exchange through a plasmodesma apparently occurs through the cytoplasm surrounding the desmotubule.

Note that plant cells can *generally* be distinguished from animal cells by:

1. the *presence* of cell walls, chloroplasts, and central vacuoles in *plants* and their absence in animals, and

2. the *presence* of lysosomes and centrioles in *animals* and their absence in plants.

Prokaryotes and Eukaryotes

The cells described so far are those of **eukaryotic** organisms. Eukaryotic organisms include all living things except for bacteria and cyanobacteria. Bacteria and cyanobacteria are **prokaryotes** and lack all the organelles described above. They generally consist of only a plasma membrane, a DNA molecule, ribosomes, cytoplasm, and often a cell wall. In addition, they differ in the following respects:

1. Prokaryotes do not have a nucleus.

2. The hereditary material in prokaryotes exists as a single "naked" DNA molecule without the proteins that are associated with the DNA in eukaryotic chromosomes.

3. Prokaryotic ribosomes are smaller (70S, with 50S and 30S subunits) than those of eukaryotes (80S, with 60S and 40S subunits).

4. The cell walls of bacteria, when present, are constructed from peptidoglycans, a polysaccharide-protein molecule.

5. Flagella, when present in prokaryotes, are not constructed of microtubules.

Movement of Substances

Various terms are used to describe the movement of substances between cells and into and out of a cell. These terms differ in the following respects.

1. The movement of substances may occur across a **selectively permeable membrane** (such as the plasma membrane). A selectively permeable membrane allows only specific substances to pass.

2. The substance whose movement is being described may be *water* (the *solvent*) or it may be the substance dissolved in the water (the *solute*).

3. Movement of substances may occur from higher to lower concentrations (*down* the concentration gradient) or the reverse (*up* or *against* the gradient).

4. Solute concentrations between two areas may be compared. A solute may be **hypertonic** (a higher concentration of *solutes*), **hypotonic** (a lower concentration of *solutes*), or **isotonic** (an equal concentration of *solutes*) relative to another region.

5. The movement of substances may be *passive* or *active*. Active movement requires the expenditure of energy and usually occurs up a gradient.

Bulk flow is the collective movement of substances in the same direction in response to a force or pressure. Blood moving through a blood vessel is bulk flow.

Passive transport processes describe the movement of substances from regions of higher to lower concentrations (*down* a concentration gradient) and do not require expenditure of energy.

1. **Simple diffusion**, or **diffusion**, is the *net* movement of substances from an area of higher concentration to an area of lower concentration. This movement occurs as a result of the random and constant motion characteristic of all molecules (atoms or ions), motion that is independent from the motion of other molecules. Since, at any one time, some molecules may be moving against the gradient and some molecules may be moving down the gradient (remember, the motion is random), the word "net" is used to indicate the overall, eventual result of the movement. Eventually, a state of **equilibrium** is attained where molecules are uniformly distributed but continue to move randomly.

2. **Osmosis** is the diffusion of *water* molecules across a selectively permeable membrane. When water moves into a body by osmosis, hydrostatic pressure (**osmotic pressure**) may build up inside the body. **Turgor pressure** is the osmotic pressure that develops when water enters the cells of plants and microorganisms.

3. **Dialysis** is the diffusion of *solutes* across a selectively permeable membrane. The term dialysis is usually used when different solutes are separated by a selectively permeable membrane.

4. **Plasmolysis** is the movement of water out of a *cell* (osmosis) that results in the collapse of the cell (especially plant cells with central vacuoles).

5. **Facilitated diffusion** is the diffusion of *solutes* through channel proteins in the plasma membrane. Note that *water* can pass through the plasma membrane without the aid of specialized proteins.

6. **Countercurrent exchange** describes the diffusion of substances between two regions in which substances are moving by bulk flow in opposite directions. For example, the direction of water flow through the gills of a fish is opposite to the flow of blood in the blood vessels. Diffusion of oxygen from water to blood is maximized because the relative motion of the molecules between the two regions is increased and because the concentration gradients between the two regions remain constant along their area of contact.

Active transport is the movement of *solutes against* a gradient and requires the expenditure of *energy* (usually ATP). Transport proteins in the plasma membrane transfer solutes such as small ions (Na^+, K^+, Cl^-, H^+), amino acids, and monosaccharides across the membrane.

Vesicular transport uses vesicles or other bodies in the cytoplasm to move macromolecules or large particles across the plasma membrane. Types of vesicular transport are described below.

- **Exocytosis** describes the process of vesicles fusing with the plasma membrane and releasing their contents to the outside of the cell. This is common when a cell produces substances for export.

- **Endocytosis** describes the capture of a substance outside the cell when the plasma membrane merges to engulf it. The substance subsequently enters the cytoplasm enclosed in a vesicle. There are three kinds of endocytosis.

  - **Phagocytosis** ("cellular eating") occurs when *undissolved* material enters the cell. The plasma membrane wraps around the solid material and engulfs it, forming a phagocytic vesicle. Phagocytic cells (such as certain white blood cells) attack and engulf bacteria in this manner.

- **Pinocytosis** ("cellular drinking") occurs when *dissolved* substances enter the cell. The plasma membrane folds inward to form a channel allowing the liquid to enter. Subsequently, the plasma membrane closes off the channel, encircling the liquid inside a vesicle.

- **Receptor-mediated endocytosis** occurs when *specific molecules* in the fluid surrounding the cell bind to specialized receptors that concentrate in coated pits in the plasma membrane. The membrane pits, the receptors, and their specific molecules (called **ligands**) fold inward and the formation of a vesicle follows. Proteins that transport cholesterol in blood (low-density lipoproteins, or LDLs) and certain hormones target specific cells by receptor-mediated endocytosis.

Sample Questions and Answers

Multiple-Choice Questions

Directions: Each of the following questions or statements is followed by five possible answers or sentence completions. Choose the one best answer or sentence completion.

1. The cellular structure that is involved in producing ATP during aerobic respiration is the

   A. nucleus

   B. nucleolus

   C. chloroplast

   D. mitochondrion

   E. endoplasmic reticulum

2. Which of the following cellular structures are common to both prokaryotes and eukaryotes?

   A. Ribosomes

   B. Nucleoli

   C. Chloroplasts

   D. Mitochondria

   E. Golgi bodies

3. The plasma membrane consists principally of

   A. proteins embedded in a carbohydrate bilayer

   B. phospholipids embedded in a protein bilayer

   C. proteins embedded in a phospholipid bilayer

   D. proteins embedded in a nucleic acid bilayer

   E. proteins embedded in a polymer of glucose molecules

4. When the concentration of solutes differs on the two sides of a membrane permeable only to water,

   A. water will move across the membrane by osmosis

   B. water will move across the membrane by active transport

   C. water will move across the membrane by plasmolysis

   D. water will move across the membrane by facilitated diffusion

   E. solutes will move across the membrane from the region of higher concentration to the region of lower concentration

5. All of the following characterize microtubules EXCEPT:

   A. They are made of the protein tubulin.

   B. They are involved in providing motility.

   C. They are organized by basal bodies or centrioles.

   D. They develop from the plasma membrane.

   E. They make up the spindle apparatus observed during cell division.

6. Lysosomes are

    A. involved in the production of fats

    B. involved in the production of proteins

    C. involved in the production of polysaccharides

    D. often found near areas requiring a great deal of energy (ATP)

    E. involved in the degradation of cellular substances

7. Mitochondria

    A. are found only in animal cells

    B. produce energy (ATP) with the aid of sunlight

    C. are often more numerous near areas of major cellular activity

    D. originate from centrioles

    E. are microtubule organizing centers

Questions 8–12

Use the following key for the next five questions. Each answer in the key may be used once, more than once, or not at all.

    A. Active transport

    B. Bulk flow

    C. Osmosis

    D. Facilitated diffusion

    E. Plasmolysis

8. Movement of solutes across a plasma membrane from a region of higher solute concentration to a region of lower solute concentration with the aid of proteins.

9. Movement of water across a membrane from a region of higher concentration of water to a region of lower concentration of water.

10. Movement of water out of a cell resulting in the collapse of the plasma membrane.

11. Movement of urine through the urinary tract.

12. Movement of solutes across a plasma membrane requiring the addition of energy.

13. The movement of molecules during diffusion can be described by all of the following EXCEPT:

    A. Molecular movements are random.

    B. Net movement of solute molecules is from a region of higher concentration to a region of lower concentration.

    C. Each molecule moves independently of other molecules.

    D. Solute molecules always move down the concentration gradient.

    E. Net movement of gas molecules is from a region of higher concentration to a region of lower concentration.

14. Plant and animal cells differ mostly in that

    A. only animal cells have mitochondria.

    B. only animal cells have flagella and cilia with a "9 + 2" microtubule arrangement.

    C. only plant cells have plasma membranes with cholesterol.

    D. only plant cells have cell walls.

    E. only plant cells have ribosomes attached to the endoplasmic reticulum.

15. A smooth endoplasmic reticulum exhibits all of the following activities EXCEPT:

    A. assembling amino acids to make proteins

    B. manufacturing lipids

    C. manufacturing hormones

    D. breaking down toxins

    E. breaking down toxic cellular by-products

16. All of the following are known to be components of cell walls EXCEPT:

    A. actin

    B. chitin

    C. polysaccharides

    D. cellulose

    E. peptidoglycans

17. A saturated suspension of starch is enclosed in a bag formed from dialysis tubing, a material through which water can pass, but starch cannot. The bag with the starch is placed into a beaker of distilled water. All of the following are expected to occur EXCEPT:

    A. There will be a net movement of water from a hypotonic region to a hypertonic region.

    B. There will be a net movement of solute from a hypertonic region to a hypotonic region.

    C. There will be a net movement of water from a region of higher concentration of water to a region of lower concentration of water.

    D. The dialysis bag with its contents will gain weight.

    E. No starch will be detected outside the dialysis bag.

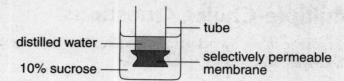

distilled water
10% sucrose
tube
selectively permeable membrane

18. As shown above, a tube covered on one end by a membrane impermeable to sucrose is inverted and half filled with distilled water. It is then placed into a beaker of 10% sucrose to a depth equal to the midpoint of the tube. Which of the following statements is true?

A. The water level in the tube will rise to a level above the water in the beaker.

B. The water level in the tube will drop to a level below the water in the beaker.

C. There will be no change in the water level of the tube, and the water in the tube will remain pure.

D. There will be no change in the water level of the tube, but sucrose will enter and mix with the water in the tube.

E. The concentration of the sucrose solution will increase.

Answers to Multiple-Choice Questions

1. **D.** Respiration takes place in the mitochondrion. ATP is also produced in the chloroplast, but that is from photosynthesis.

2. **A.** Prokaryotes lack nucleoli, chloroplasts, mitochondria, and Golgi bodies.

3. **C.** The plasma membrane consists principally of proteins embedded a phospholipid bilayer.

4. **A.** When there is a concentration gradient, water will move across a membrane unassisted by ATP or channel proteins. In contrast, solutes (the dissolved substances) cannot cross the membrane unassisted.

5. **D.** Microtubules originate from basal bodies or centrioles (microtubule organizing centers, or MTOCs), not from the plasma membrane.

6. **E.** Fats usually originate from smooth ER; proteins originate from ribosomes or rough ER; polysaccharides have various origins; answer **D** would be appropriate for mitochondria.

7. **C.** Since mitochondria produce ATP, they are often found near areas of major cellular activity, areas that require large amounts of energy.

8. **D.** Note that this question asks about *solutes* moving *down* a concentration gradient across a plasma membrane and without ATP.

9. **C.** Note that this question asks about *water* moving down a gradient.

10. **E.** If the solute concentration is higher outside than inside the cell, water moves out of the cell (by osmosis), resulting in the collapse of the cell.

11. **B.** The movement of urine through the urinary tract is by bulk flow, a collective movement of all substances moving in the same general direction. This is in contrast to diffusion, osmosis, and other molecular motions, in which the motion of particular molecules with respect to other molecules is being described.

12. **A.** The energy requirement indicates active transport.

13. **D.** Since the motion of the molecules is random, at any particular moment there are sure to be some molecules moving against the concentration gradient. It is only the *net* movement of molecules that moves down the gradient.

14. **D.** Animal cells, not plant cells, have plasma membranes that contain cholesterol. Both animals and plants have cells with mitochondria and have ribosomes attached to ER. The flagella of all eukaryotic cells (including plants such as ferms and mosses) contain microtubules with the 9+2 arrangement.

15. **A.** Ribosomes assemble amino acids into proteins.

16. **A.** Microfilaments are made up of the protein actin; chitin is often found in the cell walls of fungi; cellulose is the main constituent of plant cell walls; peptidoglycans are found in the cell walls of bacteria.

17. B. The solute, starch, cannot pass through the dialysis tubing. The dialysis bag will gain weight because water will diffuse into it. Note that **A** refers to the movement of water and **B** refers to the movement of the solute and that both describe the gradient relative to the solute (hypotonic and hypertonic refer to *solute* concentrations).

18. B. Since sucrose cannot pass through the membrane, no sucrose will enter the tube. However, since there is a concentration gradient, water will diffuse down the gradient. The beginning concentrations of water in the tube and in the beaker are 100% and 90%, respectively. Therefore, water will move from the tube and into the beaker. The water level in the tube will drop (and the beaker level will rise), and the concentration of sugar in the beaker will decrease.

Free-Response Questions

Free-response questions on the AP exam may require you to provide information from a narrow area of biology, or they may consist of parts that require you to assemble information from diverse areas of biology. The questions that follow are typical of either an entire AP exam question or merely that part of a question that is related to this section.

Directions: Answer the questions below as completely and as thoroughly as possible. Answer the question in essay form (NOT outline form), using complete sentences. You may use diagrams to supplement your answers, but a diagram ALONE without appropriate discussion is inadequate.

1. Describe the structure of the plasma membrane and the various ways in which the plasma membrane permits interactions with the outside environment.

2. Compare and contrast the cellular characteristics of prokaryotes and eukaryotes.

3. Describe the various activities that occur within cells and the methods which cells use to separate these activities from one another.

Some Typical Answers to Free-Response Questions

Question 1

(a.) Structure of the plasma membrane:

The plasma membrane is composed of a bilayer of phospholipids. A molecule of phospholipid consists of two fatty acids and a phosphate group attached to a glycerol component. The fatty acid tails represent a hydrophobic region of the molecule, while the glycerol-phosphate head is hydrophilic. The phospholipids are arranged into a bilayer formation with the hydrophilic heads pointing to the outside and the hydrophobic tails pointing toward the inside. As a result, the plasma membrane is a barrier to most molecules. In plants, fungi, and bacteria, the membrane deposits cellulose or other polysaccharides on the outside of the membrane to create a cell wall. The cell wall provides support to the cell.

Embedded in the phospholipid bilayer are cholesterol molecules and various proteins. This mixture of molecules accounts for the fluid mosaic model of the plasma membrane, that is, a highly flexible lipid boundary impregnated with various other molecules.

(b.) Interactions of plasma membrane with the outside environment:

The plasma membrane is a selectively permeable membrane. Small molecules, like H_2, O_2, and CO_2, readily diffuse through the membrane. The movement of larger molecules is regulated by proteins in the plasma membrane. There are several kinds of these proteins. Channel proteins provide passage for certain dissolved substances. Transport proteins actively transport substances against a concentration gradient. The glycocalyx, consisting of the oligosaccharides from glycolipids, recognition proteins, and other glycoproteins, participates in cell-to-cell interactions. Receptor proteins recognize hormones and transmit their signals to the interior of the cell.

Various substances can be exported into the external environment by exocytosis. In exocytosis, substances are packaged in vesicles that merge with the plasma membrane. Once they merge with the membrane, their contents are released to the outside. In an opposite kind of procedure, food and other substances can be imported by endocytosis. In endocytosis, the plasma membrane encircles the substance and encloses it in a vesicle.

When a question has two or more parts, you should separate your answers and identify the parts.

Question 2

You should separate your answer into two distinct parts. The first part should compare prokaryotes and eukaryotes that is, describe characteristics they have in common For example, they both have a plasma membrane, ribosomes, and DNA. Also, many prokaryotes have a cell wall, a structure they have in common with the eukaryotic cells of plants and fungi.

In the second part of your answer, contrast prokaryotes and eukaryotes that is, describe how they are different. Indicate that the DNA is packaged differently (naked DNA molecules in prokaryotes compared to DNA associated with proteins in eukaryotes), that prokaryotic ribosomes are smaller than those of eukaryotes, that the prokaryotic flagella do not contain microtubules, and that prokaryotic cells lack a nuclear membrane and the various eukaryotic organelles. Also, the cell walls of bacteria contain peptidoglycans, unlike the cellulose and chitin of plants and fungi.

Question 3

This is a two-part question. In the first part, describe each cell organelle and its function. In the second part, explain that partitioning metabolic functions into organelles serves primarily to separate the biochemical activities. In addition, describe how the channels among layers of endoplasmic reticulum serve to create compartments as well. Last, describe the packaging relationship between the ER and Golgi bodies.

Review

Photosynthesis is the first major topic for which you will apply your knowledge of chemistry. For the most part, however, the chemistry is descriptive, that is, you won't have to solve chemical equations or even memorize structural formulas. Instead, you will need to provide names of molecules, describe their sequence in a metabolic process, and most important, describe how the process accomplishes its metabolic objective. Photosynthesis is extremely important; free-response questions about photosynthesis frequently appear on the AP exam.

Photosynthesis is the process of converting energy from sunlight to energy in chemical bonds. The general equation describing photosynthesis is

$$\text{light} + 6\,H_2O + 6\,CO_2 \rightarrow C_6H_{12}O_6 + 6\,O_2$$

$C_6H_{12}O_6$ is glucose. Sometimes you will see CH_2O or $(CH_2O)_n$. These are general formulas for glucose or any carbohydrate.

The process of photosynthesis begins with light-absorbing pigments in plant cells. A pigment molecule is able to absorb the energy from light only within a narrow range of wavelengths. In order to absorb as much of the entire bandwidth from sunlight as possible, different pigments, capable of absorbing different wavelengths, act together to optimize energy absorption. These pigments include the green chlorophyll *a* and chlorophyll *b* and the carotenoids, which are red, orange, or yellow. When the light is absorbed into one of these pigments, the energy from the light is incorporated into electrons within the atoms that make up the molecule. These energized electrons (or **"excited" electrons**) are unstable and almost immediately re-emit the absorbed energy. The energy is then reabsorbed by electrons of a nearby pigment molecule. The process of energy absorption, followed by re-emission of energy, continues, with the energy bouncing from one pigment molecule to another. The process ends when the energy is absorbed by one of two special chlorophyll *a* molecules, P_{680} and P_{700}. These two chlorophyll molecules, named with numbers that represent the wavelengths at which they absorb their maximum amounts of light (680 and 700 nanometers), are different from other chlorophyll molecules because of their association with various nearby pigments. Together with these other pigments, chlorophyll P_{700} forms a pigment cluster called photosystem I (PS I). Chlorophyll P_{680} forms photosystem II (PS II).

The chemical reactions that now take place are illustrated in Figure 3-1. Refer to the figure as you read the following descriptions of the metabolic processes.

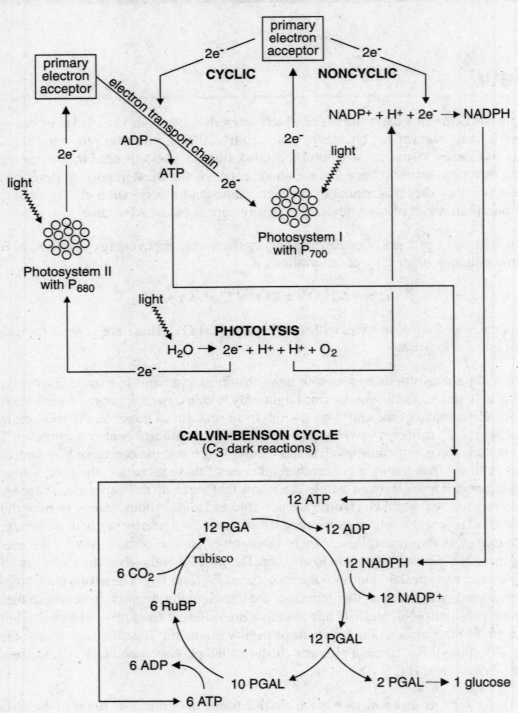

Figure 3-1

Noncyclic Photophosphorylation

Photophosphorylation is the process of making ATP from ADP and P_i (phosphorylation) using energy derived from light (photo). Noncyclic photophosphorylation begins with PS II and follows the steps:

1. **Photosystem II.** Electrons trapped by P_{680} in photosystem II are energized by light. In Figure 3-1, two electrons are shown "moving" up, signifying an increase in their energy.

2. **Primary electron acceptor.** Two energized electrons are passed to a molecule called the primary electron acceptor. This electron acceptor is called "primary" because it is the first in a chain of electron acceptors.

3. **Electron transport chain.** Electrons pass through an electron transport chain. This chain consists of proteins that pass electrons from one carrier protein to the next. Some carrier proteins, like **ferredoxin** and **cytochrome,** include nonprotein parts containing iron.

4. **Phosphorylation.** As the two electrons move "down" the electron transport chain, they lose energy. The energy lost by the electrons as they pass along the electron transport chain is used to phosphorylate, on average, about 1.5 ATP molecules.

5. **Photosystem I.** The electron transport chain terminates with PS I (with P_{700}). Here the electrons are again energized by sunlight and passed to a primary electron acceptor (different from the one associated with PS II).

6. **NADPH.** The two electrons pass through a short electron transport chain. At the end of the chain, the two electrons combine with $NADP^+$ and H^+ to form NADPH. NADPH is a coenzyme. Since the electrons have a considerable amount of energy left, NADPH is an energy-rich molecule.

7. **Photolysis.** The two electrons that originated in PS II are now incorporated into NADPH. The loss of these two electrons from PS II is replaced when H_2O is split into two electrons, $2 H^+$ and $\frac{1}{2} O_2$. The process is called photolysis and literally means decomposition (lysis) by light (photo). A manganese-containing protein complex catalyzes the reaction. The two electrons from H_2O replace the lost electrons from PS II. One of the H^+ provides the H in NADPH.

In summary, photophosphorylation takes the energy in light and the electrons in H_2O to make the energy-rich molecules ATP and NADPH. Because the reactions require light, they are often called the **light-dependent reactions** or, simply, light reactions. The following equation informally summarizes the process:

$$H_2O + ADP + P_i + NADP^+ + light \rightarrow ATP + NADPH + O_2 + H^+$$

Cyclic Photophosphorylation

A second photophosphorylation sequence occurs when the electrons energized in PS I are "recycled." In this sequence, energized electrons from PS I join with protein carriers and generate ATP as they pass along the electron transport chain. In contrast to noncyclic photophosphorylation where electrons become incorporated into NADPH, electrons in cyclic photophosphorylation return to PS I. Here they can be energized again to participate in cyclic or noncyclic photophosphorylation. Cyclic photophosphorylation is considered a primitive form of photosynthesis but occurs simultaneously with noncyclic photophosphorylation.

Calvin-Benson Cycle

The Calvin-Benson cycle "fixes" CO_2. That is, it takes chemically unreactive, inorganic CO_2 and incorporates it into an organic molecule that can be used in biological systems. The biosynthetic pathway involves over a dozen products. The function of the pathway is to produce a single molecule of glucose ($C_6H_{12}O_6$). In order to accomplish this, the Calvin-Benson cycle must repeat six times, and use 6 CO_2 molecules. Thus, in Figure 3-1 and the discussion that follows, all the molecules involved have been multiplied by 6. Only the most important molecules are discussed.

1. **Carboxylation: 6 CO_2 combine with 6 RuBP to produce 12 PGA.** The enzyme RuBP carboxylase, or rubisco, catalyzes the merging of CO_2 and RuBP (ribulose bisphosphate). The Calvin-Benson cycle is referred to as C_3 photosynthesis because the first product formed, PGA (phosphoglycerate), contains three carbon atoms. Other names are the Calvin cycle and the carbon reduction cycle.

2. **Reduction: 12 ATP and 12 NADPH are used to convert 12 PGA to 12 PGAL.** The energy in the ATP and NADPH molecules is incorporated into PGAL (glyceride 3-phosphate), thus making PGAL a very energy-rich molecule. ADP, P_i, and NADP$^+$ are released and then re-energized in noncyclic photophosphorylation.

3. **Regeneration: 6 ATP are used to convert 10 PGAL to 6 RuBP.** Regenerating the 6 RuBP originally used to combine with 6 CO_2 allows the cycle to repeat.

4. **Carbohydrate synthesis.** Note that 12 PGAL were created in step 2, but only 10 were used in step 3. What happened to the remaining two? These two remaining PGAL are used to build glucose, a common energy-storing molecule. Other monosaccharides like fructose and maltose can also be formed. In addition, glucose molecules can be combined to form disaccharides like sucrose and polysaccharides like starch and cellulose.

You should recognize that no light is directly used in the Calvin-Benson cycle. Thus, these reactions are often called the **light-independent reactions** or even the **dark reactions.** But be careful—the process cannot occur in the dark. This is because it is dependent upon the energy from ATP and NADPH, and these two energy-rich molecules can be created only during photophosphorylation, which can occur only in light.

In summary, the Calvin-Benson cycle takes CO_2 from the atmosphere and the energy in ATP and NADPH to create a glucose molecule. Of course, the energy in ATP and NADPH represents energy from the sun captured during photophosphorylation. The Calvin-Benson cycle can be informally summarized as follows:

$$6\,CO_2 + 18\,ATP + 12\,NADPH + H^+ \rightarrow 18\,ADP + 18\,P_i + 12\,NADP^+ + 1\,glucose$$

Keep in mind that the reactions that occur during photosynthesis (and in any biosynthetic pathway) do not occur spontaneously. Every product formed in every reaction is catalyzed by an enzyme. In some reactions, coenzymes or metal-ion cofactors may also be involved.

Chloroplasts

Chloroplasts are the sites where both the light-dependent and light-independent reactions of photosynthesis occur. Chloroplasts consist of an outside phospholipid bilayer membrane enclosing a fluid called the **stroma** (Figure 3-2). Suspended within the stroma are stacks of pancakelike membranes. Individual membrane layers (the "pancakes") are **thylakoids**; an entire stack of thylakoids is a **granum** (plural, **grana**). Within the thylakoids are the light-absorbing pigments and enzymes for the light-dependent reactions. In the surrounding stroma are the enzymes for the Calvin-Benson cycle. Thus, the light reactions occur on the thylakoid membranes, and the dark reactions occur in the stroma.

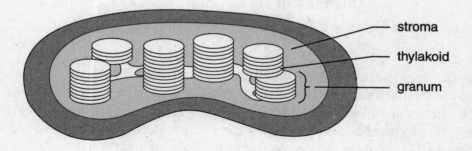

Chloroplast

Figure 3-2

Chemiosmotic Theory

Chemiosmotic theory describes the mechanism by which ADP is phosphorylated to ATP. The process illustrated in Figure 3-3 follows the steps listed below.

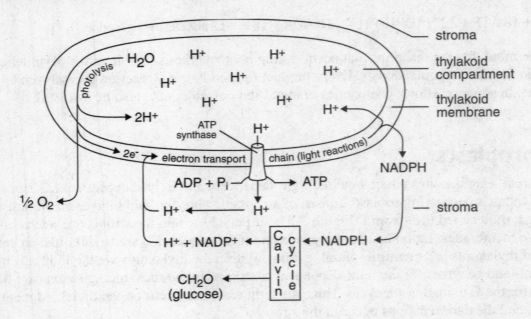

Chemiosmosis in Chloroplasts

Figure 3-3

1. **H^+ ions (protons) accumulate inside thylakoids.** The light reactions of photosynthesis occur in the membranes of the thylakoids. As photolysis occurs, H^+ are created and released to the inside of the thylakoids (the oxygen is released to the outside). Also, H^+ accompany the electrons as they pass along the electron transport chain between PS II and PS I. These H^+ come from the stroma (outside the thylakoids) and are released to the inside of the thylakoids.

2. **A pH and electrical gradient across the thylakoid membrane is created.** As H^+ accumulate inside the thylakoid, the pH decreases. Since some of these H^+ come from outside the thylakoids (from the stroma), the H^+ concentration decreases in the stroma and its pH increases. This creates a pH gradient consisting of differences in the concentration of H^+ across the thylakoid membrane from a stroma pH 8 to a thylakoid pH 5 (a factor of 1000). Since H^+ are positively charged, their accumulation on the inside of the thylakoid creates an electric gradient (or voltage) as well.

3. **ATP synthases generate ATP.** The pH and electrical gradient represent potential energy like water behind a dam. Similar to a dam, **channel proteins,** called **ATP synthases,** allow the H^+ to flow through the thylakoid membrane and out to the stroma. The energy generated by the passage of the H^+ (like the water through turbines in a dam) provides the energy for the ATP synthases to phosphorylate ADP to ATP. The passage of about three H^+ is required to generate one ATP.

Photorespiration

Because of its critical function in catalyzing the fixation of CO_2 in all photosynthesizing plants, rubisco is the most common protein on earth. However, it is not a particularly efficient molecule. In addition to its CO_2-fixing capabilities, it is also able to fix oxygen. The biosynthetic pathway that leads to the fixation of oxygen is called **photorespiration.** Photorespiration leads to two problems. The first is that the CO_2-fixing efficiency is reduced because, instead of fixing only CO_2, rubisco fixes some O_2 as well. The second problem is that the products formed when O_2 is combined with RuBP do not lead to the production of useful, energy-rich molecules like glucose. Instead, specialized cellular organelles, the **peroxisomes,** are found near chloroplasts, where they function to break down photorespiration products. Thus, considerable effort is made by plants to rid the cell of the products of photorespiration. Since the early atmosphere in which primitive plants originated contained very little oxygen, it is hypothesized that the early evolution of rubisco was not influenced by its O_2-fixing handicap.

C₄ Photosynthesis

Improving upon photosynthetic efficiency, some plants have evolved a special "add-on" feature to C_3 photosynthesis. When CO_3 enters the leaf, it is absorbed by the usual photosynthesizing cells, the mesophyll cells. Instead of being fixed by rubisco into PGA, the CO_2 combines with **PEP** (phosphoenolpyruvate) to form **OAA** (oxaloacetate or oxaloacetic acid) (Figure 3-4). The fixing enzyme is **PEP carboxylase.** OAA, the first product of this pathway, has 4 carbon atoms, thus the name **C₄ photosynthesis.** OAA is then converted to **malate,** and the malate is shuttled to specialized cells within the leaf, the **bundle sheath cells.** Here malate is converted to **pyruvate** and CO_2. The pyruvate is then shuttled back to the mesophyll cells where one ATP (broken down to AMP, instead of ADP) is required to convert the pyruvate back to PEP. Then the process repeats. The overall effect is to move CO_2 from mesophyll cells to the bundle sheath cells.

The purpose for moving CO_2 to bundle sheath cells is to increase the efficiency of photosynthesis. The bundle sheath cells surround the leaf veins and are themselves surrounded by densely packed mesophyll cells. Since bundle sheath cells rarely make contact with an intercellular space, very little oxygen reaches them. When malate delivers CO_2 to a bundle sheath cell, rubisco begins the Calvin-Benson cycle (C_3 photosynthesis). Because little oxygen is present, rubisco can fix CO_2 without competition from O_2. Thus, little photorespiration takes place, and photosynthesis is more efficient.

In order for photosynthesis to occur, the stomata must be open to allow CO_2 to enter. However, when the stomata are open, H_2O can escape. The higher rate of photosynthesis among C_4 plants allows them to reduce the time that the stomata are open, thereby, reducing H_2O loss. Thus, C_4 plants are found in hot, dry climates, where they possess an adaptive advantage over C_3 plants. This advantage apparently compensates for the additional energy requirement (1 ATP to AMP) for C_4 photosynthesis.

C_4 photosynthesis occurs in about a dozen plant families. Sugarcane and crab grass are two examples.

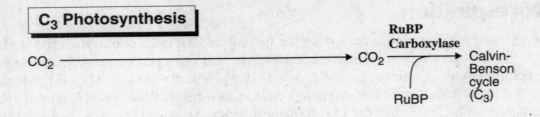

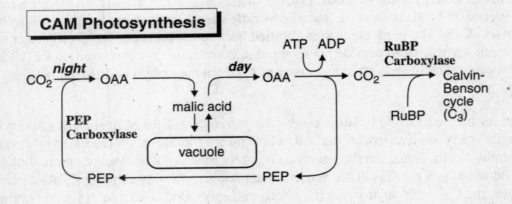

Figure 3-4

CAM Photosynthesis

Another "add-on" feature to C_3 photosynthesis is **crassulacean acid metabolism (CAM)** (Figure 3-4). The physiology of this pathway is almost identical to C_4 photosynthesis, with the changes that follow:

1. PEP carboxylase still fixes CO_2 to OAA, as in C_4. Instead of malate, however, OAA is converted to **malic acid.** (This is a minor difference, since malate is merely the ionized form of malic acid).

2. Malic acid is shuttled to the vacuole of the cell (not moved out of the cell to bundle sheath cells as in regular C_4).

3. Stomata are open at night. During the night, PEP carboxylase is active and malic acid accumulates in the cell's vacuole.

4. Stomata are closed during the day (the reverse of other plants). At this time, malic acid is shuttled out of the vacuole and converted back to OAA (requiring 1 ATP to ADP), releasing CO_2. The CO_2 is now fixed by rubisco, and the Calvin-Benson cycle proceeds.

The advantage of CAM is that photosynthesis can proceed during the day while the stomata are closed, greatly reducing H_2O loss. As a result, CAM provides an adaptation for plants that grow in hot, dry environments with cool nights (such as deserts). The name crassulacean acid metabolism comes from the early discovery of CAM in the succulent plants of the family Crassulaceae and the discovery of the accumulation of malic acid in vacuoles during the night. In addition to the Crassulaceae, CAM is found among plants in over a dozen different families, including cacti.

Sample Questions and Answers

Multiple-Choice Questions

Directions: Each of the following questions or statements is followed by five possible answers or sentence completions. Choose the one best answer or sentence completion.

1. Which of the following is the original source of all energy used by nearly all organisms on earth?

   A. ATP

   B. Plants

   C. Heat

   D. The sun

   E. Water

2. Which of the following statements about photosynthetic pigments is true?

   A. There is only one kind of chlorophyll.

   B. Chlorophyll absorbs mostly green light.

   C. Chlorophyll is required in the Calvin-Benson cycle.

   D. Chlorophyll is found in the membranes of thylakoids.

   E. P_{700} is a carotenoid pigment.

3. When deciduous trees drop their leaves in the fall, the leaves turn to various shades of red, orange, and yellow. The source of these colors is

   A. chlorophyll

   B. carotenoids

   C. ATP

   D. fungal growth

   E. natural decay of cell walls

4. A product of noncyclic photophosphorylation is

   A. NADPH

   B. H_2O

   C. CO_2

   D. ADP

   E. AMP

5. Which of the following molecules contains the most stored energy?

   A. ADP

   B. ATP

   C. NADPH

   D. Glucose

   E. Starch

6. All of the following occur in cyclic photophosphorylation EXCEPT:

   A. Electrons move along an electron transport chain.

   B. Electrons in chlorophyll become excited.

   C. ATP is produced.

   D. Light energy is absorbed.

   E. NADPH is produced.

Questions 7–11

Questions 7–11 refer to the lettered answer choices below. Each answer may be used once, more than once, or not at all.

A. Cyclic photophosphorylation

B. Noncyclic photophosphorylation

C. Photolysis

D. Calvin-Benson cycle

E. C_4 photosynthesis

7. Releases oxygen

8. Stores energy obtained from light into NADPH

9. A metabolic pathway that involves movement of substances between two kinds of cells

10. Occurs in the stroma of a chloroplast

11. The ultimate source of electrons used in making a molecule of glucose

Questions 12–15

Questions 12–15 refer to the diagram below. The two boxes represent the two major biosynthetic pathways in C_3 photosynthesis. Arrows represent reactants or products.

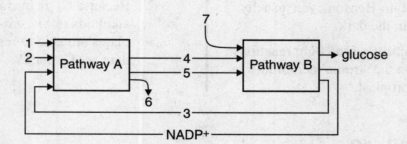

12. Arrow 1 could represent

A. ATP

B. H_2O

C. NADPH

D. O_2

E. CO_2

13. Arrow 3 could represent

A. NADPH

B. ADP

C. glucose

D. O_2

E. electrons

14. Arrow 4 could represent

   A. NADPH

   B. ADP

   C. glucose

   D. O_2

   E. electrons

15. Arrow 7 represents

   A. ATP

   B. glucose

   C. NADPH

   D. light

   E. CO_2

16. All of the following are true about photosynthesis EXCEPT:

   A. The Calvin-Benson cycle usually occurs in the dark.

   B. The majority of the light reactions occur on the stroma membranes in the chloroplast.

   C. Light energy is stored in ATP.

   D. A proton gradient drives the formation of ATP from ADP + P_i.

   E. Glucose (or another 6-carbon sugar) is made during the photosynthetic process.

17. How is C_4 photosynthesis different from C_3 photosynthesis?

   A. C_4 plants require less water for photosynthesis than do C_3 plants.

   B. C_4 plants can photosynthesize better in lower levels of light than can C_3 plants.

   C. C_4 plants are more efficient CO_2 fixers than are C_3 plants.

   D. In C_4 plants, chlorophyll P_{680} is more efficient than it is in C_3 plants.

   E. Because C_4 plants have special alkaloids (toxic substances), C_4 plants are able to resist pests better than are C_3 plants.

Questions 18–19

Questions 18–19 refer to the graph below that reports measurements of pH in plant leaves during a 36-hour period.

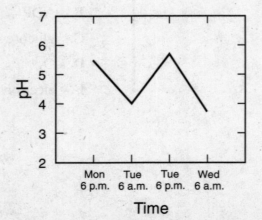

18. The changes in pH over the 36-hour period could indicate that acid products were being

A. produced at night

B. produced during the day

C. produced at night and degraded during the day

D. produced during the day and degraded at night

E. produced during the night and day but degraded only at night

19. The graph could be illustrating which of the following processes?

A. CAM

B. Calvin-Benson cycle

C. C_4 photosynthesis

D. Noncyclic photophosphorylation

E. Photolysis

Questions 20–21

The graph below shows the relationship between CO_2 uptake by leaves and the concentrations of O_2 (percent of atmosphere in growth chambers) and CO_2 (ppm in growth chambers).

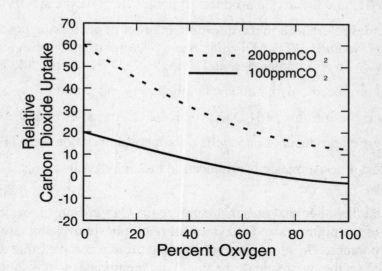

20. The relative CO_2 uptake is a measure of

A. photosynthetic rate

B. light intensity

C. water stress

D. leaf size

E. leaf temperature

21. According to the graph, the relative CO_2 uptake is best under which of the following conditions?

A. 100 ppm CO_2, 20% O_2

B. 100 ppm CO_2, 40% O_2

C. 100 ppm CO_2, 80% O_2

D. 200 ppm CO_2, 20% O_2

E. 200 ppm CO_2, 80% O_2

Answers to Multiple-Choice Questions

1. **D.** The sun supplies the energy for photosynthesis. It is the sun's energy that becomes stored in ATP and NADPH and ultimately glucose and starch. In turn, these and other photosynthetic products supply the energy to nearly all the nonphotosynthetic living things on earth when plants get eaten.

2. **D.** All of the light-absorbing pigments and most of the enzymes for the light reactions are found in the thylakoid membranes. There are several kinds of chlorophyll, including chlorophyll a and b (and c and d in certain algae). P_{700} and P_{680} are special chlorophyll a molecules differing from other chlorophyll a molecules because of their special arrangement among nearby proteins and thylakoid membrane constituents. Chlorophyll is green because it *reflects* green light, not absorbs it. It looks green because the green light it reflects is the light we see. Similarly, carotenoids look orange or yellow because they reflect those colors.

3. **B.** The leaves turn to these colors because, as the leaves age, the tree begins to break the chlorophyll down (to extract its valuable components, like magnesium). In the absence of chlorophyll, the carotenoids are visible. As the various carotenoids break down, different colors from different carotenoids become visible.

4. **A.** NADPH, ATP, and O_2 are the products of noncyclic photophosphorylation.

5. **E.** The molecules referenced in the question, in order of decreasing potential energy, are starch, glucose, NADPH, ATP, ADP. Starch is a polymer of glucose. A single glucose molecule can provide 36 ATP molecules, and a single NADPH can provide 3 ATP molecules.

6. **E.** NADPH is produced only by noncyclic photophosphorylation.

7. **C.** Photolysis is the splitting of H_2O to produce 2 electrons, 2 H^+, and ½ O_2.

8. **B.** The energy-rich products of noncyclic photophosphorylation are ATP and NADPH.

9. **E.** In C_4 photosynthesis, malate is produced in mesophyll cells and is shuttled to the bundle sheath cells.

10. **D.** Rubisco and the other enzymes that catalyze the Calvin-Benson cycle occur in the stroma. Most of the pigments and enzymes for photophosphorylation are embedded in the thylakoid membranes. The manganese-containing protein complex that catalyzes photolysis is embedded on the inner side of the thylakoid membrane, so the splitting of water occurs there inside the thylakoid. PEP carboxylase, the CO_2-fixing enzyme for C_4 photosynthesis operates in the cytoplasm (outside the chloroplast).

11. **C.** Photolysis splits H_2O to provide the electrons for photophosphorylation, which are incorporated in NADPH. These electrons in NADPH eventually find their way into glucose during the Calvin-Benson cycle.

12. **B.** It could also be light, but that is not a choice. You should test yourself on all aspects of this diagram: Pathway A is noncyclic photophosphorylation and photolysis, and Pathway B is the Calvin-Benson cycle. Arrows 1 and 2: H_2O and light; 3: ADP; 4 and 5: ATP and NADPH; 6: O_2; 7: CO_2.

13. **B.** ADP is recycled. ADP is used in photophosphorylation to produce ATP. In the Calvin-Benson cycle, the energy in ATP is used, releasing ADP and P_i. The answer could also be $NADP^+$, but that choice is not given.

14. **A.** It could also be ATP, but that is not a choice.

15. **E.** Pathway B is the Calvin-Benson cycle and requires CO_2.

16. **A.** Although the Calvin-Benson cycle is light-independent, it requires ATP and NADPH from photophosphorylation, which occurs only in light.

17. **C.** Answer **A** is incorrect because C_4 photosynthesis requires the same amount of water to produce a single molecule of glucose as does C_3. It is true, however, that C_4 reduces water loss because the stomata are open for a shorter length of time. Answer **B** is incorrect because C_4 plants are usually found in relatively high levels of light because of the additional ATP requirement of the C_4 pathway.

18. **C.** Remember that *lower* pH means more acidic.

19. **A.** This graph describes what happens in CAM. Malic acid is produced during the night and then degraded during the day. Thus, pH levels decrease (become more acidic) during the night as malic acid accumulates and increase during the day as the malic acid is broken down to release CO_2.

20. **A.** CO_2 uptake is a measure of Calvin-Benson cycle activity.

21. **D.** According to this graph, CO_2 uptake is greater when there is more CO_2 in the growth chamber (the 200 ppm curve), and when O_2 is minimum (the left side of the graph). Lower concentrations of O_2 minimize photorespiration.

Free-Response Questions

Free-response questions on the AP exam may require you to provide information from a narrow area of biology, or they may consist of parts that require you to assemble information from diverse areas of biology. The questions that follow are typical of either an entire AP exam question or merely that part of a question that is related to this section.

Directions: Answer the questions below as completely and as thoroughly as possible. Answer the question in essay form (NOT outline form), using complete sentences. You may use diagrams to supplement your answers, but a diagram alone without appropriate discussion is inadequate.

1. Describe the biochemical pathways of the light and dark reactions in C_3 photosynthesis. Begin with a molecule of H_2O and CO_2 and end with a molecule of glucose.

2. Discuss how C_4 and CAM photosynthesis improve upon C_3 photosynthesis. Include both advantages and disadvantages of the processes. Describe appropriate leaf anatomy to complete your discussion.

Some Typical Answers to Free-Response Questions

Question 1

Photosynthesis is the process by which water and light energy are used to fix inorganic carbon dioxide into glucose. The complete equation is

$$6\,CO_2 + 6\,H_2O + light \rightarrow C_6H_{12}O_6 + 6\,O_2$$

Various pigments exist in the photosynthetic membranes of plants. These include chlorophyll *a* and *b* and various carotenoids. The purpose of a variety of pigments is to absorb light energy (photons) of different wavelengths. The absorption spectrums of the pigments overlap so that they maximize the energy absorbed. When light energy is absorbed, the pigment becomes energized. The energy is then bounced around among pigments until it is absorbed by either of two special kinds of chlorophyll *a*, P_{700} and P_{680}.

P_{700} and P_{680} are organized into separate photosystems (pigment systems) I and II. Cyclic photophosphorylation involves photosystem I. This process is a more primitive form of photosynthesis. In cyclic photophosphorylation, the energy absorbed by the pigment system is captured by the P_{700}. As a result, two electrons are excited to a higher energy level, where they are absorbed by a primary electron acceptor. From here, the electrons are passed through an electron transport chain from electron acceptor to electron acceptor (some of which are cytochromes). During this transit, the energy loss of the electrons is used to bond a phosphate group to ADP, making it ATP (adenosine triphosphate). The process is called phosphorylation, and the result is that energy (originally from light) from the two electrons is trapped in an ATP molecule. The cycle is completed when the two electrons return to the photosystem pigments.

Noncyclic photophosphorylation is a more advanced system involving both photosystems I and II. It begins when chlorophyll P_{680} in photosystem II traps photon energy and energizes two electrons. These two electrons are passed to a primary electron acceptor, then through an electron transport chain producing on average, 1.5 ATP, and are then finally returned to photosystem I. Here the electrons are energized again (by light), and are received by another primary electron acceptor. These two electrons then combine with $2\,H^+$ to form NADPH.

Meanwhile, a water molecule is split (photolysis) producing 2 electrons, $2\,H^+$ and $\tfrac{1}{2}O_2$. The 2 electrons replace the electrons energized from photosystem II. The oxygen is released. One of the H^+ is used to make the $NADPH + H^+$.

The dark reaction (Calvin-Benson cycle) combines CO_2, NADPH, and ATP to form PGAL and RuBP. It takes $6\,CO_2$ to create 2 PGAL, so the cycle repeats 6 times to produce 2 PGAL. The 2 PGAL form glucose. Glucose can then be used to make various other carbohydrates such as sucrose and starch, or it can be broken down to release its store of energy in the form of ATP to drive metabolic activities.

This is a good general answer. To improve the answer, you could name a few more important molecules (for example, rubisco, manganese protein, etc.). The answer could also have included a description of chemiosmotic theory. Although the question does not request it, you *could also discuss the structure of the chloroplast and the locations where each part of photosynthesis occurs. If time permitted, you could include additional information about photosynthesis, such as C_4 and CAM. Illustrations such as those in this section would also get you points.*

Question 2

For this question you would describe the biochemical pathways for C_4 and CAM. For advantages to C_4, you would discuss the problems with rubisco (it fixes O_2 as well as CO_2) and how, with the aid of PEP carboxylase, C_4 avoids this problem. Describe how CO_2, incorporated into malate, is shuttled from mesophyll cells to the bundle sheath cells, and how, in the absence of O_2, rubisco is more efficient fixing CO_2 in bundle sheath cells. For CAM, discuss the diurnal (daily) build up of malic acid in the vacuole and how that prevents water loss in hot climates. For both CAM and C_4, a disadvantage is that these pathways require additional energy (ATP).

Review

Photosynthesis is the process of incorporating energy from light into energy-rich molecules like glucose. **Respiration** is the opposite process extracting that stored energy from glucose to form ATP (from ADP and P_i). The chemical equation describing this process is

$$C_6H_{12}O_6 + 6O_2 \rightarrow 6CO_2 + 6H_2O + energy$$

If you replace the energy with light and reverse the equation, it will describe photosynthesis.

Respiration in the presence of O_2 is called **aerobic respiration.** Aerobic respiration is divided into three components: glycolysis, the Krebs cycle, and oxidative phosphorylation. The steps are illustrated in Figure 4-1.

Glycolysis

Glycolysis is the decomposition (lysis) of **glucose** (glyco) to **pyruvate** (or **pyruvic acid**). Nine intermediate products are formed, and, of course, each one is catalyzed by an enzyme. In six of the steps, magnesium ions (Mg^{2+}) are cofactors that promote enzyme activity. The steps are summarized as follows.

1. **2 ATP are added.** The first several steps require the input of energy. This changes glucose in preparation for subsequent steps.

2. **2 NADH are produced.** NADH is a coenzyme, accepting 2 electrons from the substrate molecule. Like NADPH in photosynthesis, it is an energy-rich molecule. (You can keep the two coenzymes NADH and NADPH associated with the correct processes by using the P in NADPH as a reminder of the P in photosynthesis. The P in NADPH, however, actually represents phosphorus.)

3. **4 ATP are produced**.

4. **2 pyruvate are formed.**

In summary, glycolysis takes 1 glucose and turns it into 2 pyruvate, 2 NADH, and a *net* of 2 ATP (made 4 ATP, but used 2 ATP).

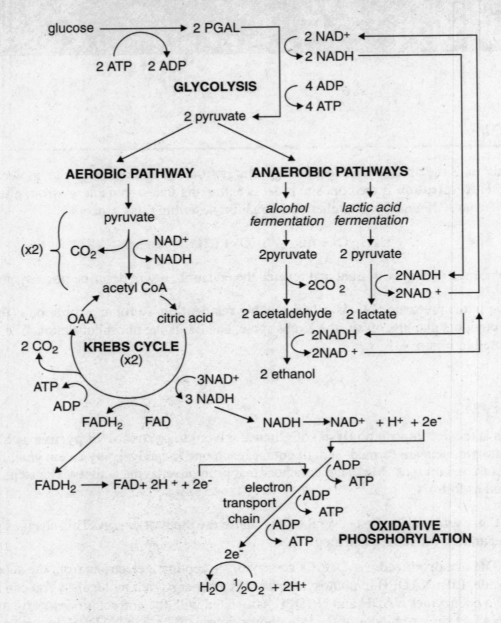

Respiration

Figure 4-1

The Krebs Cycle

The Krebs cycle details what happens to the pyruvate end product of glycolysis. Although the Krebs cycle is described for 1 pyruvate, remember that glycolysis produces 2 pyruvate. In Figure 4-1, the "× 2" next to the pyruvate and the Krebs cycle is a reminder to multiply the products of this cycle by 2 to account for the products of a single glucose.

1. **Pyruvate to acetyl CoA.** In a step leading up to the actual Krebs cycle, pyruvate combines with **coenzyme A (CoA)** to produce **acetyl CoA.** In that reaction 1 NADH and 1 CO_2 are also produced.

2. **Krebs Cycle: 3 NADH, 1 FADH$_2$, 1 ATP, CO$_2$.** The Krebs cycle begins when acetyl CoA combines with OAA (oxaloacetic acid) to form citric acid. There are 7 intermediate products. Along the way, 3 NADH and 1 $FADH_2$ are made and CO_2 is released. $FADH_2$, like NADH, is a coenzyme, accepting electrons during a reaction. Because the first product made from acetyl CoA is the 3-carbon citric acid, the Krebs cycle is also known as the **citric acid cycle** or the **tricarboxylic acid (TCA) cycle.**

The CO_2 produced by the Krebs cycle is the CO_2 animals exhale when they breathe.

Oxidative Phosphorylation

Oxidative phosphorylation is the process of extracting ATP from NADH and $FADH_2$. Electrons from NADH and $FADH_2$ pass along an electron transport chain analogous to electron transport chains in photophosphorylation. These electrons pass from one carrier protein to another along the chain, losing energy at each step. **Cytochromes** and various other modified proteins participate as carrier proteins in this chain. One of these cytochromes, **cytochrome c,** is often compared among species to assess genetic relatedness. The last electron acceptor at the end of the chain is **oxygen.** The $\frac{1}{2} O_2$ accepts the two electrons and, together with 2 H^+, forms water. NADH provides electrons that have enough energy to phosphorylate 3 ADP to 3 ATP. $FADH_2$ produces 2 ATP.

How Many ATP?

How many ATP are made from the energy released from the breakdown of 1 glucose? Glycolysis produces 2 ATP and 2 NADH. When 2 pyruvate (from 1 glucose) are converted to 2 acetyl CoA, 2 more NADH are produced. From 2 acetyl CoA, the Krebs cycle produces 6 NADH, 2 FADH$_2$, and 2 ATP. If each NADH produces 3 ATP during oxidative phosphorylation, and FADH$_2$ produces 2 ATP, the total ATP count from 1 original glucose appears to be 38 (Table 4-1). The actual number, however, is 36. This is because glycolysis occurs in the cytoplasm and each NADH produced there must be transported into the mitochondria for oxidative phosphorylation. The transport of NADH across the mitochondrial membrane reduces the yield of these NADH to only 2 ATP.

Table 4-1				
Source	**FADH₂ Produced**	**NADH Produced**		**ATP Yield**
glycolysis				2 ATP
glycolysis		2 NADH	=	4 ATP
pyruvate to acetyl CoA		2 NADH	=	6 ATP
Kreb's Cycle				2 ATP
Kreb's Cycle		6 NADH	=	18 ATP
Kreb's Cycle	2 FADH₂		=	4 ATP
Total				**36 ATP**

A balance sheet accounting for ATP production from glucose by aerobic respiration. Total ATP production is 36 ATP for each glucose processed.

Mitochondria

The Krebs cycle and the conversion of pyruvate to acetyl CoA occur in the mitochondrial **matrix** (the fluid part) (Figure 4-2). The electron transport chain proteins are embedded in the **cristae** (singular, **crista**). The cristae are internal convoluted membranes that separate the mitochondrion into an inner compartment that contains the matrix and an outer compartment between the cristae and the outer mitochondrial membrane. Note how the spatial arrangement of the respiratory processes in the mitochondrion is similar to the spatial arrangement of photosynthetic processes in the chloroplasts. In chloroplasts, the carrier proteins of electron transport chains are embedded in the inner membranes, the thylakoids, while the enzymes for the Calvin-Benson cycle are in the stroma.

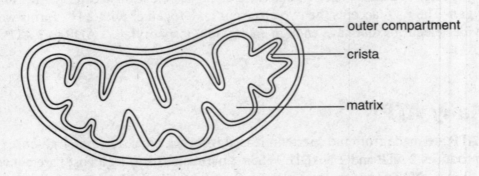

Mitochondrion

Figure 4-2

In the cytoplasm, glycolysis produces 2 pyruvate, 2 NADH, and 2 ATP. In order for ATP to be extracted from the pyruvate and NADH, these molecules must be shipped across the mitochondrial membrane and into the matrix. Within the mitochondria, pyruvate (after conversion to acetyl CoA) enters the Krebs cycle. The 2 NADH begin oxidative phosphorylation with the electron transport chain in the cristae. These NADH, however, to produce a net of only 2 ATP each because 1 ATP is required to move each of them into the mitochondria.

Chemiosmotic Theory

Electrons from NADH and FADH$_2$ lose energy as they pass along the electron transport chain in oxidative phosphorylation. That energy is used to phosphorylate ADP to ATP. Chemiosmotic theory describes how that phosphorylation occurs. The process is analogous to ATP generation in chloroplasts (Figure 4-3).

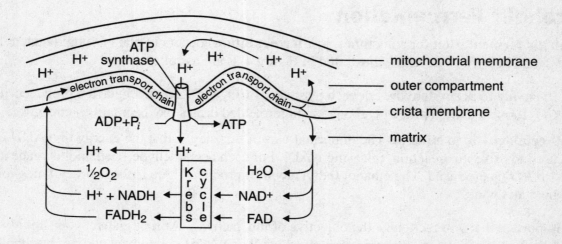

Chemiosmosis in Mitochondria

Figure 4-3

1. **H$^+$ accumulate in the outer compartment.** The Krebs cycle produces NADH and FADH$_2$ in the matrix. As these two molecules move through the electron transport chain, H$^+$ (which is only a proton) are pumped from the matrix across the cristae and into the outer compartment (between the cristae and the mitochondrial outer membrane).

2. **A pH and electrical gradient across the crista membrane is created.** The accumulation of H$^+$ in the outer compartment creates a proton gradient (equivalent to a pH gradient) and an electric charge (or voltage) gradient. These gradients are potential energy reserves in the same manner as water behind a dam is stored energy.

3. **ATP synthases generate ATP.** Channel proteins (ATP synthases) in the cristae allow the protons in the outer compartment to flow back into the matrix. The protons moving through the channel generate the energy for these channel proteins to produce ATP. It is similar to how turbines in a dam generate electricity when water flows through them.

Anaerobic Respiration

What if oxygen is not present? If oxygen is not present, there is no electron acceptor to accept the electrons at the end of the electron transport chain. If this occurs, then NADH accumulates. Once all the NAD$^+$ has been converted to NADH, the Krebs cycle and glycolysis both stop (both need NAD$^+$ to accept electrons). Once this happens, no new ATP is produced, and the cell soon dies.

Anaerobic respiration is a method cells use to escape this fate. The pathways in plants and animals, **alcoholic** and **lactate fermentation,** respectively, are slightly different, but the objective of both processes is to replenish NAD^+ so that glycolysis can proceed once again. Anaerobic respiration occurs in the cytoplasm alongside glycolysis.

Alcoholic Fermentation

Alcoholic fermentation (or sometimes, just **fermentation**) occurs in plants, fungi (such as yeasts), and bacteria. The steps, illustrated in Figure 4-1, are as follows:

1. **Pyruvate to acetaldehyde.** For each pyruvate, 1 CO_2 and 1 acetaldehyde are produced. The CO_2 formed is the source of carbonation in fermented drinks like beer and champagne.

2. **Acetaldehyde to ethanol.** The important part of this step is that the energy in NADH is used to drive this reaction, releasing NAD^+. For each acetaldehyde, 1 ethanol is made and 1 NAD^+ is produced. The ethanol (ethyl alcohol) produced here is the source of alcohol in beer and wine.

It is important that you recognize the objective of this pathway. At first glance, you should wonder why the energy in an energy-rich molecule like NADH is removed and put into the formation of ethanol, essentially a waste product that eventually kills the yeast (and other organisms) that produce it. The goal of this pathway, however, does not really concern ethanol, but the task of freeing NAD^+ to allow glycolysis to continue. Recall that in the absence of O_2, all the NAD^+ is bottled up in NADH. This is because oxidative phosphorylation cannot accept the electrons of NADH without oxygen. The purpose of the fermentation pathway, then, is to release some NAD^+ for use by glycolysis. The reward for this effort is 2 ATP from glycolysis for each 2 converted pyruvate. This is not much, but it's better than the alternative—0 ATP.

Lactate Fermentation

There is only one step in lactate fermentation. A pyruvate is converted to lactate (or lactic acid) and in the process, NADH gives up its electrons to form NAD^+. As in alcoholic fermentation, the NAD^+ can now be used for glycolysis. When O_2 again becomes available, lactate can be broken down and its store of energy can be retrieved. Because O_2 is required to do this, lactate fermentation creates what is often called an **oxygen debt.**

Sample Questions and Answers

Multiple-Choice Questions

Directions: Each of the following questions or statements is followed by five possible answers or sentence completions. Choose the one best answer or sentence completion.

1. What is the value of the alcoholic fermentation pathway?

   A. It produces ATP.

   B. It produces lactate (or lactic acid).

   C. It produces ADP for the electron transport chain.

   D. It replenishes CO_2 for the dark reaction.

   E. It replenishes NAD^+ so that glycolysis can produce ATP.

2. What is the purpose of oxygen in aerobic respiration?

   A. Oxygen accepts electrons at the end of an electron transport chain.

   B. Oxygen is necessary to carry away the waste CO_2.

   C. Oxygen is used in the formation of sugar molecules.

   D. The oxygen molecule becomes part of the ATP molecule.

   E. Oxygen donates H^+ used in the formation of NADH.

Questions 3–7

Questions 3–7 refer to the diagram below. The three boxes represent the three major biosynthetic pathways in aerobic respiration. Arrows represent net reactants or products.

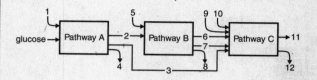

3. Arrow 2 is

   A. O_2

   B. ATP

   C. H_2O

   D. $FADH_2$

   E. pyruvate

4. Arrows 4, 8, and 12 could all be

   A. NADH

   B. ATP

   C. H_2O

   D. FAD^+

   E. $FADH_2$

5. Arrows 3 and 7 could both be

   A. NADH

   B. ATP

   C. H_2O

   D. FAD^+

   E. $FADH_2$

6. Arrow 9 could be

   A. O_2

   B. ATP

   C. H_2O

   D. FAD^+

   E. $FADH_2$

7. Pathway B is

   A. oxidative phosphorylation

   B. photophosphorylation

   C. the Calvin-Benson cycle

   D. the Krebs cycle

   E. glycolysis

8. Which of the following sequences correctly indicates the potential ATP yield of the indicated molecules from greatest ATP yield to least ATP yield?

   A. Pyruvate, ethanol, glucose, acetyl CoA

   B. Glucose, pyruvate, acetyl CoA, NADH

   C. Glucose, pyruvate, NADH, acetyl CoA

   D. Glucose, $FADH_2$, acetyl CoA, pyruvate

   E. Glucose, $FADH_2$, NADH, pyruvate

Questions 9–10

Questions 9–10 refer to the graph below that shows the amount of CO_2 that is produced by plant cells at various levels of atmospheric oxygen.

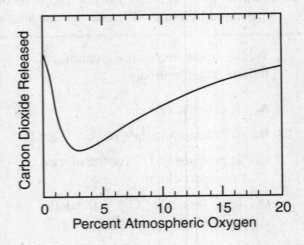

9. At levels of atmospheric O_2 below 1%, the amount of CO_2 released is relatively high. This is probably because

   A. the Krebs cycle is very active

   B. O_2 is being converted to H_2O

   C. alcoholic fermentation is occurring

   D. there are insufficient amounts of coenzyme A

   E. photosynthesis cannot function at night

10. As levels of atmospheric O_2 increase beyond 5%, the amounts of CO_2 released increase. This is probably a direct result of

   A. an increase in glycolytic activity

   B. a greater availability of appropriate enzymes

   C. an increase in Krebs cycle activity

D.   an increase in atmospheric temperature

E.   a decrease in the pH of the cytoplasm

11. All of the following processes produce ATP EXCEPT:

A.   glycolysis

B.   the Krebs cycle

C.   lactate fermentation

D.   oxidative phosphorylation

E.   photophosphorylation

12. Chemiosmotic theory describes how ATP is generated from ADP. All of the following statements conform to the principles of the theory EXCEPT:

A. H^+ accumulate in the area between the membrane of the cristae and the outer membrane of the mitochondrion.

B.   A pH gradient is created across the cristae membranes.

C.   A voltage gradient is created across the cristae membranes.

D.   A proton gradient is created across the cristae membranes.

E.   Electrons flowing through the ATP synthase channel protein provide the energy to phosphorylate ADP to ATP.

13. After strenuous exercise, a muscle cell would contain increased amounts of all of the following EXCEPT:

A.   ADP

B. CO_2

C.   lactate

D.   glucose

E. P_i

14. All of the following statements about respiration are true EXCEPT:

A.   Some of the products in the breakdown of proteins enter the Krebs cycle.

B.   Some of the products in the breakdown of lipids enter the Krebs cycle.

C.   Anaerobic respiration is probably a more primitive energy-yielding pathway than is aerobic respiration.

D.   The purpose of oxygen in aerobic respiration is to donate the electrons that transform $NAD^+ + H^+$ to NADH.

E.   Oxygen is required to break down lactate.

15. All of the following processes release CO_2 EXCEPT:

A.   the Krebs cycle

B.   alcoholic fermentation

C.   oxidative phosphorylation

D.   the conversion of pyruvate to ethanol

E.   the conversion of pyruvate to acetyl CoA

Answers to Multiple-Choice Questions

1. **E.** In the absence of oxygen, all of the NAD^+ gets converted to NADH. With no NAD^+ to accept electrons from the glycolytic steps, glycolysis stops. By replenishing NAD^+, alcoholic fermentation allows glycolysis to continue.

2. **A.** At the end of the electron transport chain in oxidative phosphorylation, $\frac{1}{2} O_2$ combines with 2 electrons and $2 H^+$ to form water.

3. **E.** You should review aerobic respiration by identifying each arrow: Pathway A is glycolysis, Pathway B is the Krebs cycle, and Pathway C is oxidative phosphorylation. Arrow 1: ADP or NAD^+; 2: pyruvate; 3: NADH; 4: ATP; 5: ADP, NAD^+, or FAD; 6 and 7: $FADH_2$ and NADH (either one can be 6 or 7); 8: ATP or CO_2; 9 and 10: O_2 and ADP (either one can be 9 or 10); 11 and 12: H_2O and ATP (either one can be 11 or 12).

4. **B.** ATP is produced in the glycolytic pathway (glycolysis), the Krebs cycle, and by oxidative phosphorylation.

5. **A.** Arrow 3 represents the NADH produced in glycolysis (Pathway A) and used in oxidative phosphorylation (Pathway C). In addition, NADH could also be represented by arrow 7, a product of the Krebs cycle (Pathway B). Arrow 7 could also represent $FADH_2$, but $FADH_2$ cannot be represented by arrow 3. Thus, only NADH can be represented by both arrows 3 and 7. If arrow 7 represents NADH, then arrow 6 represents $FADH_2$.

6. **A.** Arrow 9 could represent the O_2 that accepts the electrons after they pass through the electron transport chain in oxidative phosphorylation. Arrow 9 could also be ADP, but ADP is not among the answers.

7. **D.** Pathway B represents the Krebs cycle. The Krebs cycle uses the energy in pyruvate (arrow 2) to generate $FADH_2$ and NADH (arrows 6 and 7).

8. **B.** These molecules each have the potential to produce the following amounts of ATP: glucose, 36 ATP; pyruvate, 15 ATP; acetyl CoA, 12 ATP; NADH, 3 ATP (or 2 ATP if they originate in glycolysis); $FADH_2$, 2 ATP. The metabolic pathway that breaks down ethanol to H_2O and CO_2 in the human liver is variable. However, answer **A** can be eliminated without knowing how many ATP molecules ethanol can yield because glucose produces more ATP than does pyruvate.

9. **C.** When O_2 is absent (or very low), anaerobic respiration (alcoholic fermentation) is initiated. Alcoholic fermentation releases CO_2.

10. **C.** CO_2 is produced in the Krebs cycle.

11. **C.** Lactate fermentation, the conversion of pyruvate to lactate, removes electrons from NADH to make NAD^+. No ATP is generated by this step.

12. **E.** Protons, not electrons, pass through ATP synthase as they move down the proton gradient. A proton gradient is the same as a pH gradient, and an electrical gradient or voltage is produced by the greater number of positive charges (from the protons) in the outer compartment relative to the number of positive charges inside the crista membrane.

13. D. During strenuous exercise, glucose is broken down to pyruvate. Aerobic respiration produces CO_2. Anaerobic respiration, which would occur during strenuous exercise, would increase lactate formation. Exercise would also consume ATP, producing ADP and P_i.

14. D. The purpose of O_2 is to accept the electrons at the end of the electron transport chain in oxidative phosphorylation. Lipid and protein breakdown products produce pyruvate, acetyl CoA, or intermediate carbon compounds used in the Krebs cycle. An oxygen debt is generated during lactate fermentation because O_2 is required to break down lactate to H_2O and CO_2.

15. C. Note that answers **B** and **D** describe the same process.

Free-Response Questions

Free-response questions on the AP exam may require you to provide information from a narrow area of biology, or they may consist of parts that require you to assemble information from diverse areas of biology. The questions that follow are typical of either an entire AP exam question or merely that part of a question that is related to this section.

Directions: Answer the questions below as completely and as thoroughly as possible. Answer the question in essay form (NOT outline form), using complete sentences. You may use diagrams to supplement your answers, but a diagram alone without appropriate discussion is inadequate.

1. Discuss the Krebs cycle and oxidative phosphorylation. Specifically address ATP and coenzyme production, the location where these biosynthetic pathways occur, and chemiosmotic theory.

2. Describe, at the molecular level, how cells extract energy from starches, proteins, and lipids by the process of aerobic respiration.

3. **(a.)** Explain, at the molecular level, why many organisms need oxygen to maintain life.

   (b.) Explain, at the molecular level, how some organisms can sustain life in the absence of oxygen.

Some Typical Answers to Free-Response Questions

Question 1

(a.) The Krebs cycle and oxidative phosphorylation are the oxygen-requiring processes involved in obtaining ATP from pyruvate. Pyruvate is derived from glucose through glycolysis, a process that does not require oxygen.

Before pyruvate enters the Krebs cycle, it combines with coenzyme A. During this initial reaction with coenzyme A, 2 electrons and 2 H^+ removed from pyruvate combine with NAD^+ to form 1 NADH + H^+. NADH is a coenzyme storing enough energy to generate 3 ATP in oxidative phosphorylation. A CO_2 molecule is also released. The end product of this reaction is acetyl CoA. To begin the Krebs cycle, acetyl CoA combines with oxaloacetic acid (OAA) to form citric acid, releasing the coenzyme A component. A series of reactions then occurs that generates 3 molecules of the coenzyme NADH (from NAD^+), 1 molecule of the coenzyme $FADH_2$ (from FAD), and 1 ATP (from ADP + P_i) for each molecule of acetyl CoA that enters the Krebs cycle. The last product in the series of reactions, OAA, is the substance that reacts with acetyl CoA; thus, the Krebs reactions sustain a cycle.

Energy from the coenzymes NADH and $FADH_2$ is extracted to make ATP in oxidative phosphorylation. For each of these coenzymes, 2 electrons pass through an electron transport chain, passing through a series of protein carriers (some are cytochromes, such as cytochrome c). During this passage, 3 ATP are generated for each NADH originating in the Krebs cycle. $FADH_2$ generates 2 ATP. At the end of the electron transport chain, O_2 accepts the electrons (and 2 H^+) to form water. NAD^+ and FAD can be used again to receive electrons in the Krebs cycle. The total number of ATP generated from a single pyruvate is 15 ATP.

(b.) The Krebs cycle and oxidative phosphorylation occur in the mitochondria. The Krebs cycle occurs in the matrix of the mitochondria. The protein carriers for the electron transport chain are embedded in the inner mitochondrial membranes, called the cristae. Thus, oxidative phosphorylation occurs in these cristae membranes.

(c.) Chemiosmotic theory describes how ATP is generated from ADP + P_i. During oxidative phosphorylation, H^+ (protons) are deposited on the outside of the cristae, between the cristae and the outer membrane. The excess number of protons in this outer compartment creates a pH and electric gradient. The gradient provides the energy to generate ATP as protons pass back into the matrix through ATP synthase, a channel protein in the cristae.

Note that the answer to each part of the question is labeled (a.), (b.), or (c.). Answering each part separately helps you organize your answer and helps the grader recognize that you addressed each part of the question.

Question 2

This question is similar to question 1. One major difference is that you need to discuss glycolysis in detail. You also need to correctly connect glycolysis with the Krebs cycle and ATP production because glycolysis produces 2 pyruvate. The answer to question 1 is for only 1 pyruvate. The second major difference is that you need to include a discussion of how starches, proteins, and lipids are tied to respiration. That part of the answer follows.

Starches are polymers of glucose. Various enzymes break down starches to glucose, which in turn enter the glycolytic pathway. Disaccharides like sucrose are catalyzed to glucose and fructose. The glucose enters the glycolytic pathway at the beginning, but the fructose undergoes some intermediate steps and enters the glycolytic pathway after a couple of steps.

Lipids are broken down to glycerol and fatty acids. Both of these components undergo enzymatic reactions that eventually produce acetyl CoA.

Proteins are broken down to amino acids. Each of the various amino acids produces different products when broken down. Some of these products are converted to acetyl CoA; others are converted to OAA or other Krebs cycle intermediates. NH_3 is a toxic waste product from amino acid breakdown and is exported from the cell.

Question 3

The first part of this question is the same as question 2, except there is an additional focus on the function of O_2. For this question, then, it is especially important that you state that the purpose of O_2 is to accept electrons at the end of the electron transport chain in oxidative phosphorylation. Then describe the consequences if oxygen is not present—no ATP, no oxidative phosphorylation, and no Krebs cycle. For (b.), you would describe lactate fermentation and alcoholic fermentation, specifically indicating that the function of these two processes is to regenerate NAD^+ so that glycolysis can continue and produce 2 ATP for each glucose.

Review

Cell division consists of two phases, nuclear division followed by **cytokinesis.** Nuclear division divides the genetic material in the nucleus, while cytokinesis divides the cytoplasm. There are two kinds of nuclear division—**mitosis** and **meiosis.** Mitosis divides the nucleus so that both daughter cells are genetically identical. In contrast, meiosis is a reduction division, producing daughter cells that contain half the genetic information of the parent cell.

The first step in either mitosis or meiosis begins with the condensation of the genetic material, **chromatin,** into tightly coiled bodies, the **chromosomes.** Each chromosome is made of two identical halves called **sister chromatids** joined at the **centromere** (Figure 5-1). Each chromatid consists of a single, tightly coiled molecule of DNA, the genetic material of the cell. In **diploid cells,** there are two copies of every chromosome, forming a pair, called **homologous chromosomes.** In a homologous pair of chromosomes, one homologue originated from the maternal parent, the other from the paternal parent. Humans have 46 chromosomes, 23 homologous pairs, consisting of a total of 92 chromatids.

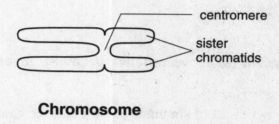

Chromosome

Figure 5-1

When a cell is not dividing, the chromatin is enclosed within a clearly defined nuclear envelope. Within the nucleus, one or more **nucleoli** are visible. Outside the nucleus, two **microtubule organizing centers** (**MTOCs,** also called **centrosomes** in animals) lie adjacent to one another. In animals, each MTOC contains a pair of **centrioles.** These features are characteristic of **interphase,** the nondividing period of the **cell cycle** (Figure 5-2). When cell division begins, these features change, as described below.

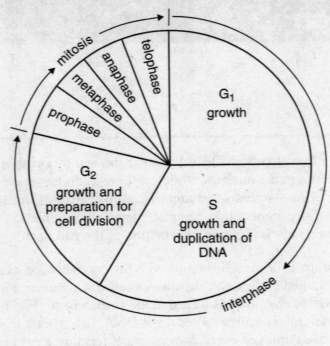

The Cell Cycle

Figure 5-2

Mitosis

There are four phases in **mitosis** (adjective, **mitotic**): **prophase, metaphase, anaphase,** and **telophase** (Figure 5-3).

1. In **prophase,** three activities occur simultaneously. First, the nucleoli disappear and the chromatin condenses into chromosomes. Second, the nuclear envelope breaks down. Third, the **mitotic spindle** is assembled. The development of the mitotic spindle begins as the MTOCs move apart to opposite ends (or poles) of the nucleus. As they move apart, microtubules develop from each MTOC, increasing in length by the addition of tubulin units to the microtubule ends away from the MTOC. Microtubules from each MTOC connect to a specialized region in the centromere called a **kinetochore.** Microtubules tug on the kinetochore, moving the chromosomes back and forth, toward one pole, then the other. In addition to these microtubules, the completed spindle also includes other microtubules from each MTOC that overlap at the center of the spindle and do not attach to the chromosomes.

2. **Metaphase** begins when the chromosomes are distributed across the **metaphase plate,** a plane lying between the two poles of the spindle. Metaphase ends when the microtubules, still attached to the kinetochores, pull each chromosome apart into two chromatids. Each chromatid is complete with a centromere and a kinetochore. Once separated from its sister chromatid, each chromatid is called a chromosome. (To count the number of chromosomes at any one time, count the number of centromeres.)

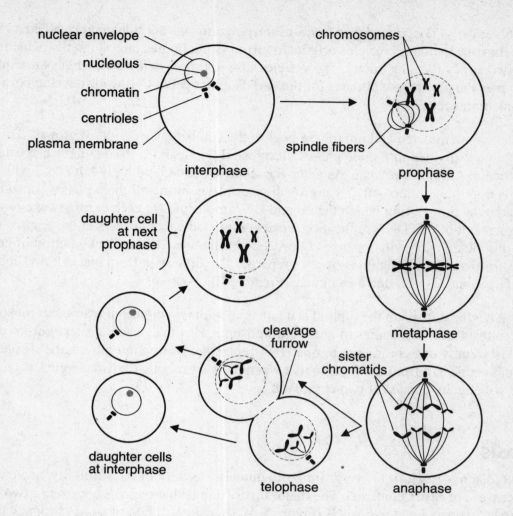

Mitosis in an Animal Cell

Figure 5-3

3. **Anaphase** begins after the chromosomes are separated into chromatids. During anaphase, the microtubules connected to the chromatids (now chromosomes) shorten, effectively pulling the chromosomes to opposite poles. The microtubules shorten as tubulin units are uncoupled at their chromosome ends. Overlapping microtubules originating from opposite MTOCs, but not attached to chromosomes, interact to push the poles farther apart. At the end of anaphase, each pole has a complete set of chromosomes, the same number of chromosomes as the original cell. (Since they consist of only one chromatid, each chromosome contains only a single copy of the DNA molecule.)

4. **Telophase** concludes the nuclear division. During this phase, a nuclear envelope develops around each pole, forming two nuclei. The chromosomes within each of these nuclei disperse into chromatin, and the nucleoli reappear. Simultaneously, cytokinesis occurs, dividing the cytoplasm into two cells. In animals, microfilaments form a ring inside the plasma membrane between the two newly forming nuclei. As the microfilaments shorten, they act like purse strings to pull the plasma membrane into the center, dividing the cell into two

daughter cells. The groove that forms as the purse strings are tightened is called a **cleavage furrow.** In plants, vesicles originating from Golgi bodies migrate to the plane between the two newly forming nuclei. The vesicles fuse to form a **cell plate,** which subsequently becomes the plasma membranes for the two daughter cells. Cell walls develop between the membranes.

Once mitosis is completed and interphase begins, the cell begins a period of growth. This growth period is divided into three phases, designated G_1, S, and G_2 to distinguish special activities that occur. Although you can associate the labels G_1 and G_2 with growth and S with synthesis, it is important to recognize that growth takes place during all three phases. In addition, S phase marks the time during which the second DNA molecule for each chromosome is synthesized. As a result of this DNA replication, each chromosome that appears at the beginning of the next mitotic division will appear as two sister chromatids. During the G_2 period of growth, materials for the next mitotic division are prepared. The time span from one cell division through G_1, S, and G_2 is called a **cell cycle** (Figure 5-2).

A cell that begins mitosis in the diploid state, that is, with two copies of every chromosome, will end mitosis with two copies of every chromosome. However, each of these chromosomes will consist of only one chromatid, or one DNA molecule. During interphase, the second DNA molecule is replicated from the first, so that when the next mitotic division begins, each chromosome will, again, consist of two chromatids.

Meiosis

Meiosis (adjective, **meiotic**) is very similar to mitosis. Because of the similarity, however, the two processes are easily confused. The major distinction is that meiosis consists of two groups of divisions, meiosis I and meiosis II (Figure 5-4). In meiosis I, homologous chromosomes pair at the metaphase plate, and then the homologues migrate to opposite poles. In meiosis II, chromosomes spread across the metaphase plate and sister chromatids separate and migrate to opposite poles. Thus, meiosis II is analogous to mitosis. A summary of each meiotic stage follows:

1. **Prophase I** begins like prophase of mitosis. The nucleolus disappears, chromatin condenses into chromosomes, the nuclear envelope breaks down, and the spindle apparatus develops. Unlike mitosis, however, once the chromosomes are condensed, homologous chromosomes pair, a process called **synapsis.** These pairs of homologous chromosomes are variously referred to as **tetrads** (a group of four chromatids) or **bivalents.** During synapsis, corresponding regions along nonsister chromatids form close associations called **chiasmata** (singular, **chiasma**). Chiasmata are sites where genetic material is exchanged between nonsister homologous chromatids, a process called **crossing over.** A tetrad together with chiasmata and crossover events is referred to as a **synaptonemal complex.**

2. At **metaphase I,** homologous pairs of chromosomes are spread across the metaphase plate. Microtubules extending from one pole are attached to the kinetochore of one member of each homologous pair. Microtubules from the other pole are connected to the second member of each homologous pair.

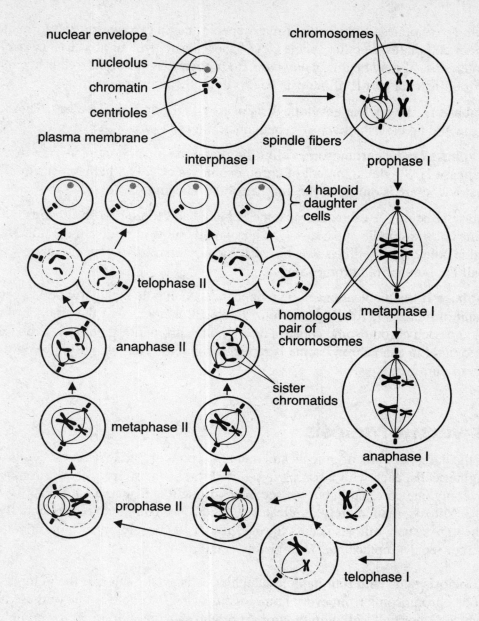

Meiosis in an Animal Cell

Figure 5-4

3. **Anaphase I** begins when homologues within tetrads uncouple as they are pulled to opposite poles.

4. In **telophase I,** the chromosomes have reached their respective poles, and a nuclear membrane develops around them. Note that each pole will form a new nucleus that will have half the number of chromosomes, but each chromosome will contain two chromatids. Since daughter nuclei will have half the number of chromosomes, cells that they eventually form will be **haploid.**

Beginning in telophase I, the cells of many species begin cytokinesis and form cleavage furrows or cell plates. In other species, cytokinesis is delayed until after meiosis II. Also, a short interphase II may begin. In any case, no replication of chromosomes occurs during this period. Instead, part II of meiosis begins in both daughter nuclei.

5. In **prophase II,** the nuclear envelope disappears and the spindle develops. There are no chiasmata and no crossing over of genetic material as in prophase I.

6. In **metaphase II,** the chromosomes align singly on the metaphase plate (not in tetrads as in metaphase I). Single alignment of chromosomes is exactly what happens in mitosis except that now there is only half the number of chromosomes.

7. **Anaphase II** begins as each chromosome is pulled apart into two chromatids by the microtubules of the spindle apparatus. The chromatids (now chromosomes) migrate to their respective poles. Again, this is exactly what happens in mitosis except that now there is only half the number of chromosomes.

8. In **telophase II,** the nuclear envelope reappears at each pole and cytokinesis occurs. The end result of meiosis is four haploid cells. Each cell contains half the number of chromosomes, and each chromosome consists of only one chromatid. Later in interphase, a second chromatid in each chromosome is replicated, but the cell will still have only half the number of chromosomes.

Mitosis versus Meiosis

Comparing the daughter cells of mitosis and meiosis, you will find that mitosis ends with two diploid daughter cells, each with a complete set of chromosomes. True, each chromosome is composed of only one chromatid, but the second chromatid is regenerated during the S phase of interphase. Mitosis, then, merely duplicates cells, the two daughter cells essentially clones of the original cell. As such, mitosis occurs during growth and development of multicellular organisms and for repair (replacement) of existing cells.

In contrast, meiosis ends with four haploid daughter cells, each with half the number of chromosomes (one chromosome from every homologous pair). In order for one of these haploid cells to produce a "normal" cell with the full set of chromosomes, it must first combine with a second haploid cell to create a diploid cell. Thus, meiosis produces **gametes,** that is, eggs and sperm, for sexual reproduction. The fusing of an egg and a sperm, **fertilization** (or **syngamy**), gives rise to a diploid cell, the **zygote.** The single-celled zygote then divides by mitosis to produce a multicellular organism. Note that one copy of each chromosome in the zygote originates from one parent, and the second copy from the other parent. Thus, a pair of homologous chromosomes in the diploid zygote represents both maternal and paternal heritage.

The **life cycle** of a human illustrates the production of gametes by meiosis and subsequent growth by mitosis (Figure 5-5). Note that the number of chromosomes in diploid and haploid cells is indicated by $2n$ and n, respectively. Human cells (except gametes) contain 46 chromosomes (23 homologous pairs). Thus $2n = 46$. For human gametes, $n = 23$. In humans, gametes are produced in the reproductive organs, the ovaries and the testes.

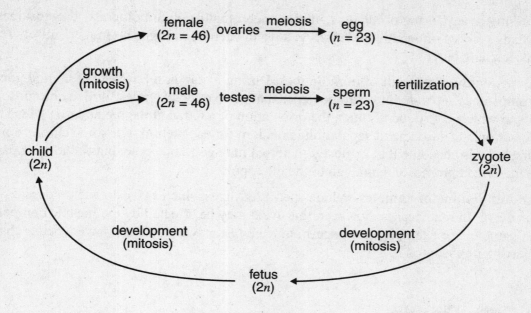

The Human Life Cycle

Figure 5-5

In other organisms, such as plants, meiosis produces **spores.** Spores are haploid cells that divide by mitosis to become a multicellular haploid structure, the **gametophyte.** Gametes are produced by the gametophyte by mitosis since the organism is already haploid. The gametes then fuse and produce a diploid cell that grows by mitosis to become the **sporophyte.** Specialized cells in the sporophyte divide by meiosis to produce haploid spores, which germinate to repeat the life cycle. The fern illustrates this type of reproductive cycle (Figure 5-6).

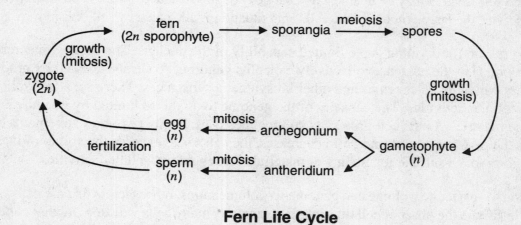

Fern Life Cycle

Figure 5-6

Genetic Variation

In mitosis, every daughter cell is exactly like the parent cell. Meiosis and sexual reproduction, however, result in a reassortment of the genetic material. This reassortment, called **genetic recombination,** originates from three events during the reproductive cycle:

1. **Crossing over.** During prophase I, nonsister chromatids of homologous chromosomes exchange pieces of genetic material. As a result each homologue no longer entirely represents a single parent.

2. **Independent assortment of homologues.** During metaphase I, tetrads of homologous chromosomes separate into chromosomes that go to opposite poles. Which chromosome goes to which pole depends upon the orientation of a tetrad at the metaphase plate. This orientation and subsequent separation is random for each tetrad. For some chromosome pairs, the chromosome that is mostly maternal may go to one pole, but for another pair, the maternal chromosome may go to the other pole.

3. **Random joining of gametes.** Which sperm fertilizes which egg is to a large degree a random event. In many cases, however, this event may be affected by the genetic composition of a gamete. For example, some sperm may be faster swimmers and have a better chance of fertilizing the egg.

Why Cells Divide

There are two important factors that limit the size of a cell and motivate its division. The first is the relative size of the surface area of the plasma membrane and the volume of the cell. When a cell grows, the volume of a cell increases faster than the surface area enclosing it. This is because volume increases by the *cube* of the radius (volume of a sphere = $(4/3)\pi r^3$, where r is the radius), whereas the surface area increases by only the *square* of the radius (surface area = $4\pi r^2$). When the **surface-to-volume ratio** (S/V) is large, there is a large surface area relative to volume. Under these conditions, the cell can efficiently react with the outside environment. For example, adequate amounts of oxygen (for respiration) can diffuse into the cell, and waste products can be rapidly eliminated. When the S/V is small, the surface area is small compared to the volume. When this occurs, the surface area may be unable to exchange enough substances with the outside environment to service the large volume of the cell. This situation is alleviated by cell division.

A second reason for dividing is the limited capability of the nucleus. The genetic material (chromosomes) in the nucleus, collectively called its **genome,** "controls" the cell by producing substances which make enzymes and other biosynthetic substances. These substances, in turn, regulate cellular activities. The capacity of the genome to do this is limited by its finite amount of genetic material. As the cell grows, its volume increases, but its genome size remains constant. As the **genome-to-volume ratio** decreases, the cell's size exceeds the ability of its genome to produce sufficient amounts of materials for regulating cellular activities.

In addition to surface-to-volume and genome-to-volume ratios, other factors that are cell-specific influence the onset of cell division. For example, many cells will stop dividing when the surrounding cell density reaches a certain maximum (**density-dependent inhibition**). Other cells, such as nerve cells, will rarely divide once they have matured. When the cell cycle is interrupted and the cell stops dividing, the cell remains in an extended G_1 phase (or G_0 phase), never beginning the S or G_2 phases until some internal or external cue initiates a resumption of the cell cycle.

Sample Questions and Answers

Multiple-Choice Questions

Directions: Each of the following questions or statements is followed by five possible answers or sentence completions. Choose the one best answer or sentence completion.

1. If a cell has 46 chromosomes at the beginning of mitosis, then at anaphase there would be a total of

    A. 23 chromatids

    B. 23 chromosomes

    C. 46 chromosomes

    D. 46 chromatids

    E. 92 chromosomes

2. If a cell has 46 chromosomes at the beginning of meiosis, then at anaphase I there would be a total of

    A. 23 chromatids

    B. 23 chromosomes

    C. 46 chromosomes

    D. 46 chromatids

    E. 92 chromosomes

3. All of the following statements are true EXCEPT:

    A. Spindle fibers are composed largely of microtubules.

    B. Centrioles consist of nine triplets of microtubules arranged in a circle.

    C. All eukaryotic cells have centrioles.

    D. All eukaryotic cells have a spindle apparatus.

    E. Many of the microtubules in a spindle apparatus attach to kinetochores of chromosomes.

Questions 4–7

Questions 4–7 refer to a mitotically dividing cell and to the lettered answer choices below. Each answer may be used once, more than once, or not at all.

    A. Anaphase

    B. Telophase

    C. Metaphase

    D. Prophase

    E. Interphase

4. Cytokinesis begins.

5. Chromosomes begin migrating to opposite poles.

6. MTOCs migrate to opposite poles.

7. Chromosomes replicate.

Questions 8–9

Questions 8–9 refer to the following figures. Figure (A) represents a normal diploid cell with 2n = 8.

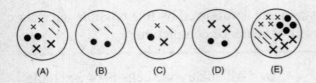

(A)   (B)   (C)   (D)   (E)

8. A zygote

9. A gamete

10. Crossing over occurs during

   A. prophase of mitosis

   B. prophase I of meiosis

   C. prophase II of meiosis

   D. prophase I and II of meiosis

   E. prophase of mitosis and prophase I of meiosis

11. In typical cell divisions by mitosis and meiosis, all of the following contribute to genetic variation EXCEPT:

   A. anaphase of mitosis

   B. anaphase of meiosis I

   C. fertilization

   D. crossing over

   E. random union of egg and sperm

Questions 12–16

Questions 12–16 refer to the cell illustrations below. The normal diploid number for the cells illustrated is four chromosomes. Each answer may be used once, more than once, or not at all.

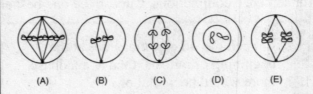

(A)   (B)   (C)   (D)   (E)

12. Anaphase II

13. Telophase II

14. Metaphase II

15. Metaphase of mitosis

16. Metaphase I

Answers to Multiple-Choice Questions

1. E. Metaphase ends when each chromosome separates into a pair of chromatids. During anaphase, chromatids from each pair move to opposite poles. Each chromatid is now considered a complete chromosome, since it consists of a complete DNA molecule. To count the number of chromosomes at any point during the cell cycle, count the centromeres.

2. C. During metaphase I, homologous chromosomes pair at the metaphase plate. One member of each pair migrates to opposite poles during anaphase I. If the cell started with 46 chromosomes, 23 chromosomes move to each pole during anaphase II, so the total is still 46 chromosomes.

3. C. Most plants do not have centrioles.

4. B. During telophase, cytokinesis begins, chromosomes uncoil into chromatin, and the nuclear membrane and nucleolus reappear.

5. A. At metaphase, the chromosomes are arranged on the metaphase plate. The end of metaphase and the beginning of anaphase is defined by the separation of the chromosomes into chromatids (which are now considered chromosomes by themselves).

6. D. During prophase, the two MTOCs (and centrioles, if present) migrate to opposite poles as the spindle apparatus develops between them. Also during prophase, the nucleolus and nuclear membrane disappear, and the chromatin condenses into chromosomes.

7. E. Chromosomes replicate during the S phase of interphase.

8. A. Since the zygote consists of the union of two haploid gametes, the zygote would have the same number of chromosomes as the parent. The eight chromosomes would consist of four homologous pairs.

9. C. A gamete would possess four chromosomes, half the number of chromosomes as the parent cell. Also, these four chromosomes would consist of one member of each pair of homologous chromosomes. Answers **B** and **D** also have four chromosomes, but they do not represent one homologue of each homologous pair.

10. B. Chromosomes pair during prophase I (synapsis) forming tetrads with chiasmata. Exchanges of genetic material occur within chiasmata.

11. A. There are generally no events during normal mitosis that would produce genetic differences between the two daughter cells. The daughter cells are clones, genetically identical. In contrast, the independent assortment of homologues during anaphase I, the random union of egg and sperm during fertilization, and crossing over during prophase I all contribute to genetic variation.

12. C. At the end of meiosis I, each daughter cell would have two chromosomes, each comprised of two chromatids. At metaphase II, these two chromosomes would line up on the metaphase plate, and at anaphase II, each would split into two chromatids (now called chromosomes).

13. D. This figure is late telophase II. The nuclear membrane is reappearing. Only one daughter cell is shown, suggesting that cytokinesis has been completed.

14. **B.** If the cell began with four chromosomes, then after meiosis I, each daughter cell would have two complete chromosomes. At metaphase II, the two chromosomes would align on the metaphase plate.

15. **A.** Only in mitosis would you see four chromosomes spread out, unpaired, on the metaphase plate. If this were metaphase I, the chromosomes would be paired in tetrads; if metaphase II, there would be only two chromosomes.

16. **E.** The pairing of homologous chromosomes occurs only in meiosis and at metaphase I.

Free-Response Questions

Free-response questions on the AP exam may require you to provide information from a narrow area of biology, or they may consist of parts that require you to assemble information from diverse areas of biology. The questions that follow are typical of either an entire AP exam question or merely that part of a question that is related to this section.

Directions: Answer the questions below as completely and as thoroughly as possible. Answer the question in essay form (NOT outline form), using complete sentences. You may use diagrams to supplement your answers, but a diagram alone without appropriate discussion is inadequate.

1. Describe the process of cell division in plants and animals giving specific attention to the following:

   (a.) The stages of mitosis, cytokinesis, and other phases of the cell cycle (do not include meiosis)

   (b.) Factors that induce cells to divide

   (c.) Factors that might contribute to abnormal cell divisions such as cancer

2. Describe meiosis in animal and plant cells giving special attention to the following:

   (a.) The stages of meiosis

   (b.) The function of meiotic daughter cells and the organs where meiosis takes place

   (c.) Contributions to genetic variation

Some Typical Answers to Free-Response Questions

Question 1

(a.) Mitosis consists of four phases—prophase, metaphase, anaphase and telophase. In prophase, the chromatin condenses into chromosomes and the nuclear envelope and nucleolus disappear. As centrioles (or MTOCs, in plants) migrate to opposite poles, microtubules develop between them to form the spindle apparatus. The microtubules attach to the kinetochores in the centromeres of the chromosomes and pull on the chromosomes. At metaphase, the microtubules have pulled the chromosomes so that they are all lined up on the metaphase plate. In anaphase, the sister chromatids of each chromosome are separated and are pulled to opposite poles by the microtubules of the spindle apparatus. In telophase, the chromatids are well segregated to opposite poles. Nuclear membranes appear around each pole and chromosomes diffuse into chromatin. Cytokinesis, the dividing of the cytoplasm, begins during telophase. The cell is divided by a cleavage furrow in animals, or a cell plate in plants. If the mother cell began with a diploid number of chromosomes, then the two nuclei that form at each pole will also both be diploid, though at this point, each chromosome would consist of only a single chromatid.

The entire cell cycle includes both mitosis and interphase. Interphase is a period of growth and is divided into three stages, identified G_1, S, and G_2. The G_1 phase describes the first period of growth following mitosis. During the S phase, a second DNA molecule (chromatid) is replicated from each chromosome. During the G_2 phase, the cell prepares for mitosis.

(b.) There are two major factors that induce a cell to divide. The first is surface-to-volume ratio. As the surface-to-volume ratio becomes progressively smaller as the cell grows, the ability of the plasma membrane to provide a surface large enough to meet the import and export requirements of the cell diminishes. The second major factor is the genome-to-volume ratio. When the cell increases in size, the amount of genetic material remains the same. As a result, the ability of the nucleus to control the cell decreases.

(c.) If and when a cell divides are determined much like other metabolic activities by enzymes. Enzymes are produced at specific points of the cell cycle that induce specific activities that prepare the cell for division. The production of these enzymes is affected by environmental factors (such as carcinogens or cell density), by internal conditions (such as genome-to-volume ratio), and by genetic factors. When the genetic machinery for making these growth enzymes becomes distorted, the production of these enzymes may go out of control. Once the production of growth enzymes becomes unregulated, cells become cancerous and divide uncontrollably.

As was done in this response, you should write your answer in sections, responding separately to each part of the question and labeling each response with the appropriate letter. Also, since your time is very limited, you should not spend too much of it defining words, unless specifically requested to do so. The free-response section of the exam is not a vocabulary test. Rather, these questions are designed to evaluate your understanding of biological processes. Thus, you should focus on describing the process, using (but not defining) as much of the appropriate vocabulary as you can. By doing so, you demonstrate both an understanding of the meaning of the words and the biological process.

Question 2

(a.) Meiosis consists of two groups of divisions, meiosis I and II. In prophase I, the nuclear membrane breaks down, the nucleolus disappears, and chromatin condenses into chromosomes. The MTOCs (which contain centrioles in animals) migrate to opposite poles, developing microtubules and the spindle apparatus between them. Synapsis occurs when homologous chromosomes pair, forming tetrads. During synapsis, crossing over between nonsister chromatids of homologous pairs results in an exchange of genetic material. The microtubules connect to the kinetochores in the centromeres of the chromosomes and pull on the chromosomes, as tetrads, to the metaphase plate. Metaphase I occurs when the tetrads are aligned on the metaphase plate. Anaphase I begins as each member of a homologous pair of chromosomes is pulled by the microtubules to opposite poles. Telophase I follows when nuclear membranes appear. Cytokinesis and a short interphase II may occur at this point. Prophase II begins in each daughter cell in the same manner as prophase I. However, synapsis does not occur, and at metaphase II, the chromosomes are spread over the metaphase plate without any kind of pairing. Anaphase II begins as each chromosome is separated into two chromatids (now called chromosomes) and pulled by the microtubules of the spindle apparatus to opposite poles. During telophase II, meiosis is concluded as cytokinesis separates the nuclei into four haploid cells, each containing half the number of chromosomes of the original parent cell.

(b.) Meiosis is a reduction division that occurs in sexual reproduction. It halves the number of chromosomes so that daughter cells are haploid. In humans, the daughter cells are the gametes, sperm and eggs, formed in the testes and ovaries. Gametes fuse to form a diploid zygote, which then grows into a multicellular organism by mitotic divisions. In other organisms, meiosis may produce haploid spores, which divide by mitosis to grow into multicellular haploid organisms.

(c.) There are three points during meiosis and sexual reproduction where genetic material is rearranged to create genetic variation. First, crossing over during metaphase I results in an exchange of genetic material between nonsister chromatids of homologous chromosomes. Chromosomes, previously of either paternal or maternal origin, now contain genetic material from both parents. Second, chromosome tetrads randomly align across the metaphase plate in metaphase I. As a result, chromosomes migrating to one pole are a random mixture of paternal and maternal chromosomes. Third, the zygote is a combination of a randomly selected egg and a sperm. As a result of these random arrangements of chromosomes, daughter cells are genetically variable.

Review

Most of the material in this section prepares you for solving genetics problems. A genetics problem is an analysis of the characteristics (traits) of parents and offspring (progeny). Given the traits of one of these generations, you are required to determine the traits of the other generation.

Genetics problems require the application of probability rules. If a coin is tossed, there is a ½ (50%) chance, or probability, that it will be heads. If a coin is tossed again, there is, again, a ½ chance that it will be heads. The first toss does not affect the second toss; that is, the two tosses are independent. To determine the probability of two or more independent events occurring together, you merely multiply the probabilities of each event happening separately. This is the **multiplication rule** of probability. For two consecutive tosses of a coin, the probability of getting two heads is ½ × ½ = ¼. For three tosses, the probability of three heads would be ½ × ½ × ½ = ⅛.

The following terms are used in genetics:

1. A **gene** represents the genetic material on a chromosome that contains the instructions for creating a particular trait. Since the formula for carrying out these instructions is described by a genetic code, a gene is often said to **code** for a trait. In pea plants, for example, there is a gene that codes for purple flowers.

2. An **allele** is one of several varieties of a gene. In pea plants, there are two alleles of the gene for flower color—the purple allele, which codes for purple flowers, and the white allele, which codes for white flowers.

3. A **locus** refers to the location on a chromosome where a gene is located. Every gene has a unique locus on a particular chromosome.

Every cell contains two copies of each chromosome, one inherited from each parent (Figure 6-1). This pair of chromosomes is called a **homologous pair,** and each chromosome in the pair contains a gene for the same trait at exactly the same loci. At any one particular locus, the two genes on a pair of homologous chromosomes (a **gene pair**) may represent two different alleles for that gene because they originated from different parents. For example, the allele for flower color on one pea plant chromosome (inherited from one parent) may code for purple flowers, while a different allele for flower color on the other chromosome (inherited from the second parent) may code for white flowers.

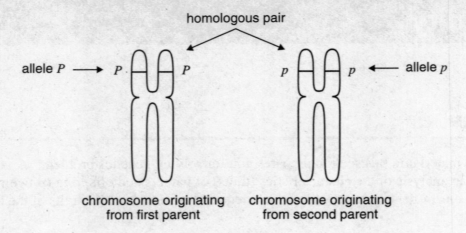

Homologous Pair of Chromosomes

Figure 6-1

4. If the two alleles inherited for a gene are different, one allele may be **dominant,** while the other is **recessive.** The trait coded by the dominant allele is the actual trait expressed. In pea plants, the purple flower allele is dominant and the white allele is recessive. Therefore, if a pea plant inherits one of each of these alleles, only the dominant allele is expressed, producing purple flowers. In genetics problems, a dominant allele is represented by a capital letter, while the recessive allele is represented by the lower-case form of the *same* letter. In addition, it is common convention to use the first letter of the dominant allele to represent the gene. Thus, P and p represent the dominant (purple) and recessive (white) alleles, respectively, of the same gene. (It is easiest to read these two alleles as "big" P and "small" p.)

5. **Homozygous dominant** refers to the inheritance of two dominant alleles (PP). In this condition, the dominant trait is expressed. In the **homozygous recessive** condition, two recessive alleles are inherited (pp) and the recessive trait is expressed. **Heterozygous** refers to the condition where the two inherited alleles are different (Pp—it is normal convention to write a pair of alleles with the dominant allele first). In this condition, only the dominant allele is expressed.

6. The **phenotype** is the actual expression of a gene. Purple flowers, blue eyes, and brown hair each represent the phenotype of their respective genes. On the other hand, the **genotype** represents the actual alleles. For example, PP describes the genotype for the homozygous dominant condition. If P represents the allele for purple flowers and p is the allele for white flowers, the *genotype Pp* would express the *phenotype* of purple flowers.

During meiosis I, the two members (homologues) of each pair of homologous chromosomes migrate to opposite poles (Figure 6-2). As a result, each gamete will contain one allele for each gene. Thus, the **law of segregation** refers to the random segregation of alleles (and their chromosomes) to separate gametes.

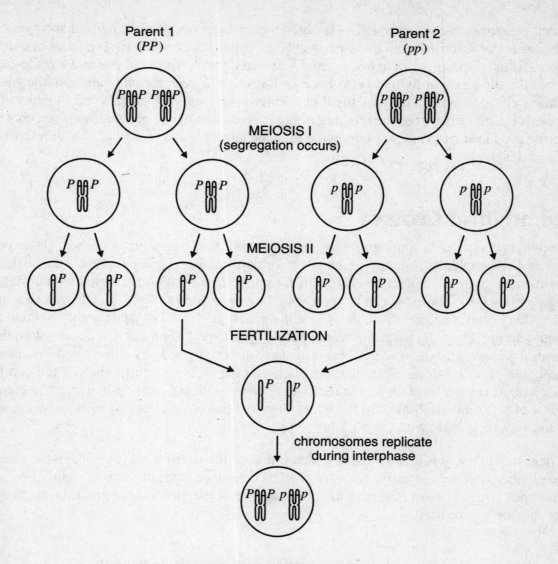

Meiosis and Fertilization

Figure 6-2

In addition, the migration of homologues within one pair of homologous chromosomes to opposite poles does not influence the migration of homologues of another homologous pair. Thus, homologous chromosomes, and the genes they carry, segregate independently of the segregation of other chromosome pairs. This is referred to as the **law of independent assortment.**

Because both the laws of segregation and independent assortment are random processes, the rules of probability can be used to describe how the different chromosomes (and their alleles) in parents assemble in gametes and offspring.

Mendel, a nineteenth-century monk, is credited with the discovery of the laws of segregation and independent assortment. In his experiments, he mated, or **crossed,** two varieties of pea plants to form offspring, or **hybrids.** A cross between a purple-flowered pea and a white-flowered pea is called a **monohybrid cross** because it involves a gene for only one trait, the gene for flower color. In genetic crosses, the **P generation** represents the parents, the **F$_1$ generation** represents the offspring from the crossing of the parents, and the **F$_2$ generation** represents the offspring produced from crosses among the F$_1$. (The letter F stands for *filial,* which refers to sons and daughters.)

Monohybrid Crosses

In monohybrid crosses, a single trait (originating from a single gene) is examined. Using pea plants as an example, let *P* represent the allele for purple flowers and *p* represent the allele for white flowers. Suppose a plant heterozygous for purple flowers (*Pp*) is crossed with a white-flowered plant (*pp*). The cross can be represented by genotypes as *Pp* × *pp*. The first step in analyzing this genetics problem is to determine the genotypes for all possible gametes produced by both parents. Thus, the purple-flowered parent (genotype *Pp*) produces a gamete with the *P* allele or a gamete with the *p* allele. This is because the genotype *Pp* is represented by a pair of homologous chromosomes, one with the *P* allele and the other with the *p* allele. Each chromosome (with its respective allele) migrates to an opposite pole and ends up in a separate gamete (the law of segregation). Similarly, the white-flowered parent produces a gamete with the *p* allele and another gamete with the *p* allele.

The next step in the genetic analysis is to determine all the possible ways in which the gametes can combine. This is most easily accomplished by creating a Punnett square (Figure 6-3). (Sometimes you may see a Punnett square rotated so that it appears in the shape of diamond; either method can be used.)

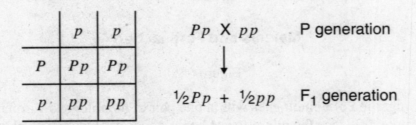

Monohybrid Cross (F$_1$ Generation)

Figure 6-3

In a Punnett square for a monohybrid cross, the gametes from one parent are represented in two spaces at the top of the diagram (*p* and *p* in Figure 6-3). The gametes of the second parent are represented at the left side (*P* and *p* in Figure 6-3). In the middle are four boxes, each box combining the allele found at the top with the allele found to the left. The four boxes represent all of the possibilities of combining the two gametes from one parent with the two gametes from the second parent. In Figure 6-3, the results of the cross $Pp \times pp$ are $\frac{1}{2} Pp$ and $\frac{1}{2} pp$. These results represent the genotypic frequencies of the offspring. The phenotypic results are $\frac{1}{2}$ purple-flowered and $\frac{1}{2}$ white-flowered plants. Results can be given as frequencies (fractions), as percents ($\frac{1}{2} = 50\%$), or as ratios (the ratio of white to purple flowers is 1:1).

Suppose you were asked to find the frequencies of the F_2 generation for the cross $PP \times pp$. Following the procedures above, all of the F_1 progeny would have the genotype Pp.

To find the F_2 generation, cross the F_1 offspring with themselves, $Pp \times Pp$ (Figure 6-4). The genotypic results of this cross would produce $\frac{1}{4} PP$, $\frac{1}{2} Pp$, and $\frac{1}{4} pp$, while the phenotypic frequencies would be $\frac{3}{4}$ purple and $\frac{1}{4}$ white because both PP and Pp genotypes produce purple flowers.

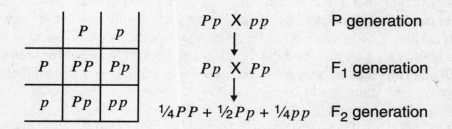

Monohybrid Cross (F_2 Generation)

Figure 6-4

Test Crosses

Suppose you wanted to know the genotype of a white-flowered pea plant. That would easily be identified as pp because white flowers must have two copies of the recessive allele. Suppose, however, you wanted to know the genotype of a plant with the dominant trait, purple flowers. Would it be PP or Pp? To determine which genotype is correct, you would perform a **test cross**. A test cross is a mating of an individual whose genotype you are trying to determine with an individual whose genotype is known. You will always know the genotype of the individual that expresses the recessive trait (white flowers). So the cross is $P\_\_ \times pp$. Since you do not know the second allele for the first individual, represent it with an underscore, leaving a blank space for the unknown allele. The next step is to perform both possible crosses, $PP \times pp$ and $Pp \times pp$. For the first cross, all F_1 will be purple flowered (Pp). For the second cross, $\frac{1}{2}$ will be purple (Pp) and $\frac{1}{2}$ will be white (pp). A farmer would perform a test cross if he or she wanted to know if the purple flower in question was Pp or pp. If there were any white-flowered offspring, the farmer could be sure that the purple parent was Pp, since you cannot obtain white-flowered offspring unless both parents contribute the white allele (p). In contrast, if all offspring were purple, the farmer could reasonably conclude that the purple parent was PP. It is possible, though not likely, that the purple-flowered parent could be Pp, but due to chance, no white-flowered offspring were produced.

A coin toss presents an analogous situation. If you toss a coin six times, the prediction is that half the time it will be tails. However, there is a small chance, $\frac{1}{64}$ ($\frac{1}{2} \times \frac{1}{2} \times \frac{1}{2} \times \frac{1}{2} \times \frac{1}{2} \times \frac{1}{2}$), that all six tosses will be tails. As the number of coin tosses increases, though, the probability of obtaining all tails gets smaller and smaller. For the farmer who finds all purple offspring in the test cross, there is a small possibility that the purple parent will be Pp. However, the identification of the genotype as PP will become more conclusive as the number of offspring observed increases.

Dihybrid Crosses

In a **dihybrid** cross, genes for two different traits are observed at the same time. A cross observing the traits of flower color (purple or white) and plant height (short or tall) is a dihybrid cross. Another example of a dihybrid cross might involve two characteristics of seeds, color and texture. In peas, seed color can be yellow (Y) or green (y) and seed texture can be round (R) or wrinkled (r). Thus, Y and y are used to represent the two alleles (yellow and green) for the gene for seed color, and R (round) and r (wrinkled) are used for the gene for seed texture. A cross between one pea plant homozygous dominant for both traits and a second plant homozygous recessive for both traits would be given as $YYRR \times yyrr$.

The first step in analyzing this cross is to determine the alleles of all possible gametes. The $YYRR$ plant can produce only one kind of gamete, YR. This is determined by the law of segregation; that is, one allele of each allele pair migrates to opposite poles and ends up in separate gametes. Thus one Y and one R end up in a single gamete. All segregation possibilities produce gametes that are YR. For the second plant, there is also only one kind of gamete produced, yr. The next step is to determine the different ways that the gametes from one parent can combine with the gametes of the second parent. Usually you would make a Punnett square for this, but since each parent has only one kind of gamete, you can quickly conclude, without a Punnett square, that all the F_1 offspring will result from the union of a YR gamete and a yr gamete. The result of that union produces individuals that have the genotype $YyRr$, which bears the phenotype yellow and round.

Now, analyze the F_2 generation produced by $YyRr \times YyRr$. Each parent can produce four kinds of gametes: YR, Yr, yR, yr. The Punnett square, illustrated in Figure 6-5, shows the gametes of one parent in spaces on the top line and the gametes of the second parent in spaces along the left margin. In the sixteen boxes of the square, alleles from gametes at the top and left are combined. By convention, both alleles from the color gene are arranged together (for example, Y and y), and both alleles of the texture gene are arranged together (for example, R and r). The next step is to list each kind of genotype and count the number of times each genotype appears. This information is shown at the bottom of Figure 6-5. The final step is to identify the phenotype of each genotype and to count how many times each phenotype appears. You will see that some phenotypes have more than one genotype. For example, $YYRR$, $YYRr$, $YyRR$, and $YyRr$ all code for a yellow and round seed. The conclusion is that the F_2 progeny consist of nine plants with yellow and round seeds, three plants with green and round seeds, three plants with yellow and wrinkled seeds, and one plant with green and wrinkled seeds. This ratio, 9:3:3:1, is the same ratio Mendel observed in his experiments for this dihybrid cross.

P $\qquad$ $YYRR$ X $yyrr$

↓

F_1 $\qquad$ $YyRr$ X $YyRr$

↓

	YR	Yr	yR	yr
YR	$YYRR$	$YYRr$	$YyRR$	$YyRr$
Yr	$YYRr$	$YYrr$	$YyRr$	$Yyrr$
yR	$YyRR$	$YyRr$	$yyRR$	$yyRr$
yr	$YyRr$	$Yyrr$	$yyRr$	$yyrr$

F_2

genotypic frequencies	phenotypic frequencies

$YYRR$ = 1
$YYRr$ = 2
$YyRR$ = 2
$YyRr$ = 4 $\Big\}$ 9 yellow round

$yyRR$ = 1
$yyRr$ = 2 $\Big\}$ 3 green round

$YYrr$ = 1
$Yyrr$ = 2 $\Big\}$ 3 yellow wrinkled

$yyrr$ = 1 } 1 green wrinkled

Dihybrid Cross

Figure 6-5

Incomplete Dominance

Sometimes, the alleles for a gene do not exhibit the dominant and recessive behaviors discussed above. Instead, the combined expression of two different alleles in the heterozygous condition produces a blending of the individual expressions of the two alleles called **incomplete dominance.** In snapdragons, for example, the heterozygous condition consisting of one allele for red flowers (R) and one allele for white flowers (r) is pink (Rr). Sometimes, both alleles are written with the same upper-case or lower-case letter but with a prime or a superscript number or letter to differentiate the two. As an example, R and R' might represent red and white alleles for snapdragons. As another example, H and H_1 might represent straight and curly hair alleles in humans. The HH_1 phenotype is expressed as an intermediate trait, wavy hair. In still other cases there may be no apparent rationale, except perhaps historical, for the notation used to indicate different alleles.

Codominance

Another kind of inheritance pattern is termed **codominance.** In this pattern, both inherited alleles are completely expressed. For example, the M and N blood types produce two molecules that appear on the surface of human red blood cells. The M (or sometimes written as L^M) allele produces a certain blood molecule. The N (or L^N) allele produces another molecule. Individuals who are MM ($L^M L^M$) produce one kind of molecule; those who are NN ($L^N L^N$) produce a second kind of molecule; and those who are MN ($L^M L^N$) produce both kinds of molecules.

To help you distinguish the three kinds of inheritance, imagine a continuum. At one extreme, there is complete dominance by a dominant allele over a recessive allele. At the other extreme, both alleles are expressed (codominance). Between the two extremes, a blending of two different alleles produces an intermediate phenotype (incomplete dominance).

Multiple Alleles

In the blood group that produces A, B, and O blood types, there are three possible alleles, represented by I^A, I^B, or i. Superscripts are used because the two alleles, A and B, are codominant. A lower-case i is used for the third allele because it is recessive when expressed with I^A or I^B. There are six possible genotypes representing all possible combinations of two alleles: $I^A I^A$ and $I^A i$ (A blood type), $I^B I^B$ and $I^B i$ (B blood type), $I^A I^B$ (AB blood type), and ii (O blood type). The four phenotypes (A, B, AB, and O types) correspond to the presence or absence of an A or B carbohydrate component of a glycoprotein on the surface of red blood cells. Thus, the $I^A I^A$ and $I^A i$ genotypes produce the A type carbohydrate, the $I^B I^B$ and $I^B i$ genotypes produce the B type carbohydrate, and the $I^A I^B$ genotype produces both carbohydrates. The ii genotype produces a carbohydrate with no effect.

You should be aware of why blood transfusions must be made between individuals of like phenotypes. If an individual with $I^B I^B$, $I^B i$, or ii blood is given type A blood, then the immune system of the recipient will identify the A carbohydrate on the introduced red blood cells as a foreign substance. The immune system responds to foreign substances (**antigens**) by producing **antibodies** that attack the antigens. The result is clumping, or **agglutination,** of the blood and possibly death. Individuals with AB type blood can accept any blood type because both A and B carbohydrates are recognized as "self." Also, anyone can accept O type blood because it contains neither A or B carbohydrates. Thus, a person with O type blood is a universal donor.

Epistasis

Epistasis occurs when one gene affects the phenotypic expression of a second gene. This frequently occurs in the expression of pigmentation. One gene turns on (or off) the production of pigment, while a second gene controls either the amount of pigment produced or the color of the pigment. If the first gene codes for no pigment, then the expression of the second gene has no effect, regardless of the kind of pigmentation it encodes.

Epistasis occurs in the pigmentation of fur in mice. One gene codes for the presence or absence of pigmentation. A second gene codes for the color of pigmentation, black or brown. Thus, C and c represent the alleles for the presence and absence of color, and B and b represent the alleles for black and brown pigments. As the allele notation indicates, both genes are expressed by the complete dominance inheritance pattern. The phenotypic expressions of $CCBB$, $CCBb$, $CcBB$, and $CcBb$ are all black, and the expressions of $CCbb$ and $Ccbb$ are both brown. However, whenever cc is inherited, no pigment is produced and the fur is white regardless of the color encoded by the B allele.

Pleiotropy

Pleiotropy occurs when a single gene has more than one phenotypic expression. For example, the gene in pea plants that expresses the round or wrinkled texture of seeds also influences the phenotypic expressions of starch metabolism and water absorption. The allele for round seeds codes for a greater conversion of glucose to starch than does the allele for wrinkled seeds. In wrinkled seeds, then, there is more unconverted glucose. A higher concentration of glucose increases the osmotic gradient, which increases the absorption of water (by osmosis). Immature wrinkled seeds thus contain more water. When these seeds mature and dehydrate, however, the water is lost, which results in the wrinkling pattern observed. In contrast, round seeds absorb less water, lose less water during dehydration, and, as a result, wrinkle less, giving the seeds a smoother, rounder texture. As you can see, the gene for seed texture influences not only seed texture, but also starch production and water absorption.

Many disease-causing genes exhibit pleiotropy. Sickle-cell anemia, a human blood disease, is caused by an allele that incorrectly codes for hemoglobin. As a result, the abnormal hemoglobin molecule causes the red blood cell, usually circular, to become sickle shaped. In response, red blood cells do not flow through capillaries freely and oxygen is not adequately delivered throughout the body. As a result, there is a general breakdown throughout the entire body, including damage to the heart, lungs, kidneys, brain, and other organs, which in turn promotes various disorders including anemia, pneumonia, heart and kidney failure, bone abnormalities, and impaired mental functioning.

Polygenic Inheritance

Many traits are not expressed in just two or three varieties, such as yellow and green pea seeds or A, B, and O blood types, but as a range of varieties. The heights of humans, for example, are not just short or tall but are displayed as a **continuous variation** from very short to very tall. Continuous variation usually results from **polygenic inheritance,** the interaction of many genes to shape a single phenotype. Polygenic inheritance (many genes shaping one phenotype) is the opposite of pleiotropy (one gene influencing many phenotypes).

Linked Genes

If two genes are on different chromosomes, such as the seed color and seed texture genes of pea plants, the genes segregate independently of one another (law of independent assortment). **Linked genes** are genes that reside on the *same* chromosome and thus cannot segregate independently because they are physically connected. Genes that are linked are usually inherited together.

In the fruit fly *Drosophila melanogaster,* flies reared in the laboratory have occasionally been found to exhibit abnormal traits. These traits originate from gene mutations, or molecular changes in the DNA. Two such mutations, affecting body color and wing structure, are linked. The normal, or wild, body color is gray (*B*), while the mutant allele is expressed as black (*b*). The second mutation, for wing structure, results in vestigial wings (*v*) (small, underdeveloped, and nonfunctional). (Note that for *Drosophila* mutations, the gene notation uses letters that denote the name for the mutation.) Since these two genes are linked, a fly heterozygous for a gray body and normal wings (called gray-normal), indicated by *BbVv*, would have the *BV* on one chromosome and the *bv* on the homologous chromosome. If the linkage between these genes were not known, then the expected results from a cross between this gray-normal fly (*BbVv*) and a black fly with vestigial wings (called black-vestigial, *bbvv*) would be ¼ *BbVv*, ¼ *bbvv*, ¼ *Bbvv*, and ¼ *bbVv* (Figure 6-6). However, since the two genes are on the same chromosome and cannot assort independently, the gray-normal fly produces only two kinds of gametes, *BV* and *bv*. *Bv* and *bV* gametes are not produced. Taking linkage into consideration, the expected offspring would be ½ *BbVv* and ½ *bbvv* (Figure 6-6). If this cross were actually carried out, however, the results would produce a ratio among the four offspring *BbVv:bbvv:Bbvv:bbVv* closer to 41:41:9:9. This is because linked genes cross over (recombine) during prophase I—in this case, about 18% of the time. Instead of 50% of the gametes being *BV* and 50% *bv*, an 18% crossover rate would produce 41% *BV* and 41% *bv* (which sum to 82%) and 9% *Bv* and 9% *bV* (which sum to 18%)(Figure 6-6).

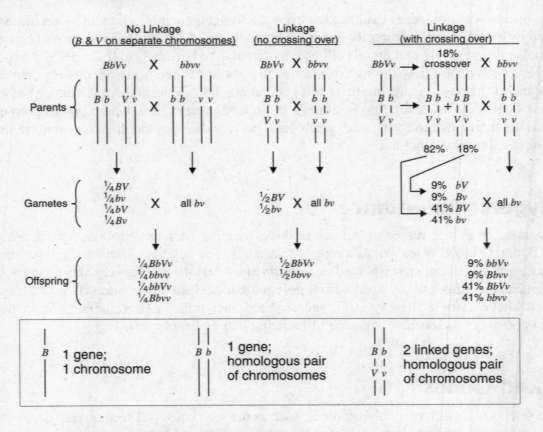

Dihybrid Cross with Linked Genes and Crossing Over

Figure 6-6

The greater the distance between two genes on a chromosome, the more places between the genes that the chromosome can break and thus the more likely the two genes will cross over during synapsis. As a result, recombination frequencies are used to give a picture of the arrangement of genes on a chromosome. Suppose you knew that for a fly with genotype *BBVVAA* (where *A* is the apterous, or wingless, mutant) the crossover frequency between *B* and *V* was 18%, between *A* and *V* was 12%, and between *B* and *A* was 6%. Since greater recombination frequencies indicate greater distances between genes, then B and V are separated by the greatest distance. Using the frequencies as a direct measure of distance, B and V are 18 map units apart, A and V are 12 map units apart, and B and A are 6 map units apart. This suggests that the three genes are arranged in the order B-A-V (or alternatively, V-A-B), with B and A separated by 6 units and A and V separated by 12 units. The sum of these two distances, 18 (or 6 + 12), is the map distance between B and V. A chromosome map created in this fashion is a **linkage map** and is a portrayal of the sequence of genes on a chromosome. A map portraying the true relative positions of the genes, a **cytological map,** requires additional experimental analyses.

Sex-Linked Inheritance

There is one pair of homologous chromosomes in animals that does not have exactly the same genes. These two chromosomes, the X and Y chromosomes, are called the **sex chromosomes.** All other chromosomes are called **autosomes**.

Sex-linked (or **X-linked**) genes are genes that reside on the X, or sex, chromosome. **Y-linked** genes are also possible, but since so few genes reside on the Y chromosome, Y-linkage is rarely encountered. In biology, the meaning of "linkage" in "sex-linkage" is different from its meaning when used alone. Used alone, the word *linkage* refers to two or more genes that reside on the same chromosome; *sex-linkage* refers to a single gene residing specifically on a sex chromosome.

There are additional considerations when working with sex-linked genes because when females (XX) inherit a sex-linked gene, they receive two copies of the gene, one on each X chromosome. This situation is similar to that for autosomal inheritance. In contrast, however, a male (XY) will inherit only one copy of the gene because only the X chromosome delivers the gene. There is no similar gene delivered by the Y chromosome. As a result, whichever allele is on the X chromosome of a male, regardless of whether it is dominant or recessive, is the allele whose trait expressed.

Hemophilia is caused by a sex-linked, recessive gene (h) in humans. Hemophiliacs cannot properly form blood clots and in the worst cases can die from minor injuries by bleeding to death. Females and males who inherit the normal allele (H) are $X^H X^H$ and $X^H Y$, respectively, and are both normal. In order for a female to be a hemophiliac, she must have two copies of the defective allele ($X^h X^h$). A male, however, need inherit only one copy of the defective allele ($X^h Y$) to be a hemophiliac. As a result, hemophilia, as well as other sex-linked genetic defects, are much more common in males. Females who are $X^H X^h$ have normal clotting abilities but are said to be carriers, since they can pass the defective allele to their offspring.

X-Inactivation

During embryonic development in female mammals, one of the two X chromosomes in each cell does not uncoil into chromatin. Instead, **X-inactivation** occurs, and one chromosome remains coiled as a dark, compact body, called a **Barr body.** Barr bodies are mostly inactive X chromosomes—most of the genes are not expressed nor do they interact (in a dominant/recessive or codominant manner) with their respective alleles on the X chromosome that is expressed. Thus, only the alleles of the genes on the one active X chromosome are expressed by that cell. When X-inactivation begins, one of the two chromosomes in each embryonic cell randomly becomes inactive. Subsequent daughter cells will have the same X chromosome inactivated as did the embryonic parent cell from which they originated. In the fully developed fetus, then, some groups of cells will have one X chromosome inactivated, while other groups will have the other X chromosome inactivated. Thus, all of the cells in a female mammal are not functionally identical.

A very visible example of X-inactivation can be seen in the different groups of cells producing different patches of color in an individual calico cat. Calico cats have yellow, black, and white hair, randomly arranged in patches over their bodies. The yellow and black colors are coded by a gene on the X chromosome (the white color is controlled by a different gene). When the X chromosome with the yellow allele is inactivated, the black color allele on the active chromosome is expressed, and the hair is black. In other patches, the chromosome with the black allele may be inactivated, and those patches will be yellow.

What does this mean for sex-linked genetic defects in humans, such as hemophilia? A carrier female ($X^H X^h$) should usually be normal with respect to this trait, because at least some cells will have the X^H active, will manufacture the appropriate clotting factor, and will secrete it into the blood for general circulation throughout the body. However, it is possible that all of the cells producing the clotting factor have X^H inactivated. In that case, the carrier female should express the same symptoms of hemophilia as a male.

Nondisjunction

In the normal process of meiosis, chromosomes pair at the metaphase plate and subsequently separate and migrate to opposite poles. When **nondisjunction** occurs, the chromosomes do not properly separate. Instead, *both* members of one homologous chromosome pair migrate to the same pole. As a result, half the gametes will have an extra chromosome, and half will be missing a chromosome. Gametes with missing or with extra chromosomes are usually sterile. However, sometimes, certain chromosome imbalances are fertile. These almost always lead to genetic defects.

Down syndrome occurs when an egg or sperm with an extra number 21 chromosome fuses with a normal gamete. The result is a zygote with three copies of chromosome 21 (**trisomy 21**). Down syndrome individuals bear various abnormalities, including mental retardation, heart defects, respiratory problems, and deformities in external features.

Turner syndrome results when there is nondisjunction of the sex chromosomes. Sperm will have either both chromosomes (XY) or no chromosome (O, used to indicate the absence of a chromosome). Similarly, eggs will be either XX or O. A Turner syndrome zygote (XO) is a female who has one X (from a normal egg or sperm) and no second chromosome (from nondisjunction in an egg or sperm). Individuals with Turner syndrome are physically abnormal and sterile.

Human Genetic Defects

Genetic defects can be caused by the inheritance of an allele (such as in hemophilia), or it can be caused by chromosomal abnormalities. Chromosomal abnormalities result when the inherited genome is missing a chromosome or has an extra chromosome (both from nondisjunction) or when one or more chromosomes have portions deleted (called a **deletion**), duplicated (**duplication**), moved to another chromosome (**translocation**), or rearranged in reverse orientation on the same chromosome (**inversion**).

The AP exam expects you to know the more common genetic defects in humans and their underlying causes. Some of these have been discussed above. These and others are summarized in Table 6-1.

Table 6-1		
Genetic Defect	*Pattern of Inheritance*	*Description of Defect*
Phenylketonuria	autosomal recessive	Inability to properly break down the amino acid phenylalanine. Accumulation of phenylalanine in untreated children causes mental retardation. Symptoms can be avoided with diets low in phenylalanine.
Sickle-cell anemia	autosomal recessive	Abnormal hemoglobin. Red blood cells of individuals with this defect are unable to effectively transport oxygen throughout the body.
Tay-Sachs disease	autosomal recessive	Inability to properly break down certain lipids. Accumulation of the lipids in brain cells causes progressive nervous system dysfunction and is usually fatal by age four.
Huntington's disease	autosomal dominant	Expression begins in middle age with mild mental illness and loss of motor control progressing to total physical and mental incapability.
Hemophilia	sex-linked recessive	Inability to code for a clotting factor required to form normal blood clots
Red-green color blindness	sex-linked recessive	Inability to distinguish red from green.
Duchenne's muscular	sex-linked dominant	Absence of an essential muscle protein. Results in dystrophy deteriorating muscles and loss of coordination.
Down syndrome	nondisjunction of chromosome 21	Trisomy 21 (three copies of chromosome 21). Physical abnormalities, mental retardation.
Turner syndrome	nondisjunction of sex chromosomes	XO and female. Union of a gamete missing the sex chromosome with a normal egg or sperm bearing an X chromosome.
Klinefelter syndrome	nondisjunction of sex chromosomes	XXY and male. Union of XX gamete and normal Y gamete. Sterile and often mentally retarded.
Cri du chat syndrome	deletion in chromosome 5	Physical and mental retardation and catlike cry (*cri du chat* is French for "cry of the cat").

Sample Questions and Answers

Multiple-Choice Questions

Directions: Each of the following questions or statements is followed by five possible answers or sentence completions. Choose the one best answer or sentence completion.

1. If you roll a pair of dice, what is the probability that they will both turn up a three?

   A. ½
   B. ¼
   C. ⅛
   D. ¹⁄₁₆
   E. ¹⁄₃₆

2. Which of the following best expresses the concept of the word "allele"?

   A. Genes for wrinkled and yellow
   B. Genes for wrinkled and round
   C. The expression of a gene
   D. Phenotypes
   E. Mutations

3. Some people are able to roll their tongues into a U-shape. The ability to do this is inherited as an autosomal dominant allele. What is the probability that children descendent from parents both heterozygous for this trait will be able to form a U-shape with their tongues?   *Uu × Uu*

   A. 0
   B. ¼

   C. ½
   D. ¾
   E. 1

   Dd

4. In fruit flies, dumpy wings are shorter and broader than normal wings. The allele for normal wings (*D*) is dominant to the allele for dumpy wings (*d*). Two normal-winged flies were mated and produced 300 normal-winged and 100 dumpy-winged flies. The parents were probably

   A. *DD* and *DD*
   B. *DD* and *Dd*
   C. *Dd* and *Dd*
   D. *Dd* and *dd*
   E. *dd* and *dd*

5. Which of the following is true of the gametes produced by an individual with genotype *Dd*?

   A. ½ *D* and ½ *D*
   B. ½ *D* and ½ *d*
   C. ½ *Dd* and ½ *dD*
   D. All *Dd*
   E. All *d*

6. Suppose that in sheep, a dominant allele (*B*) produces black hair and a recessive allele (*b*) produces white hair. If you saw a black sheep, you would be able to identify

   A. its phenotype for hair color

   B. its genotype for hair color

   C. the genotypes for only one of its parents

   D. the genotypes for both of its parents

   E. the phenotypes for both of its parents

Questions 7–9

Use the following key for the next three questions. Each answer in the key may be used once, more than once, or not at all.

   A. 0

   B. $\frac{1}{16}$

   C. $\frac{3}{16}$

   D. $\frac{9}{16}$

   E. 1

In fruit flies, the gene for curved wings (*c*) and the gene for spineless bristles (*s*) are on different chromosomes. The respective wild-type alleles for each of these genes produce normal wings and normal bristles.

7. From the cross *CCSS* × *ccss*, what is the probability of having an offspring that is *CcSs*?

8. From the cross *CcSs* × *CcSs*, what is the probability of having an offspring that is *ccss*?

9. From the cross *CcSs* × *CcSs*, what is the probability of having an offspring that is normal for both traits?

Questions 10–11

In snapdragons, the allele for tall plants (*T*) is dominant to the allele for dwarf plants (*t*), and the allele for red flowers (*R*) is codominant with the allele for white flowers (*R'*). The heterozygous condition for flower color is pink (*RR'*).

10. If a dwarf red snapdragon is crossed with a white snapdragon homozygous for tall, what are the probable genotypes and phenotypes of the F_1 generation?

    A. All *TtRR'* (tall and pink)

    B. All *TtRR* (tall and red)

    C. All *TtR'R'* (tall and white)

    D. All *ttRR* (dwarf and red)

    E. All *ttR'R'* (dwarf and white)

11. If *ttRR'* is crossed with *TtRR*, what would be the probable frequency for offspring that are dwarf and white?

    A. 0

    B. $\frac{1}{4}$

    C. $\frac{1}{2}$

    D. $\frac{3}{4}$

    E. 1

12. For the cross *AABBCCDd* × *AAbbCcDd*, what is the probability that an offspring will be *AABbCcDd*?

    A. $\frac{1}{16}$

    B. $\frac{1}{8}$

    C. $\frac{1}{4}$

    D. $\frac{3}{8}$

    E. $\frac{1}{2}$

13. The inheritance of skin color in humans is an example of which of the following?

    A. Pleiotropy

    B. Codominance

    C. Epistasis

    D. Polygenic inheritance

    E. Gene linkage

14. Red-headed people frequently have freckles. This is best explained by which of the following?

    A. The genes for these two traits are linked on the same chromosome.

    B. The genes for these two traits are sex-linked.

    C. Nondisjunction occurs frequently with chromosomes bearing these traits.

    D. Alleles for these two traits are codominant.

    E. Both parents have red hair and freckles.

15. Let A and a represent two alleles for one gene and B and b represent two alleles for a second gene. If for a particular individual, A and B were on one chromosome and a and b were on a second chromosome, then all of the following are true EXCEPT:

    A. The two genes are linked.

    B. The two chromosomes are homologous.

    C. All gametes would be either AB or ab.

    D. The genotype of this individual is $AaBb$.

    E. An offspring of this individual could have the genotype $AABB$.

16. Four genes, $J, K, L,$ and $M,$ reside on the same chromosome. Given that the crossover frequency between K and J is 3, between K and L is 8, between J and M is 12, and between L and M is 7, what is the order of the genes on the chromosome?

    A. $J\ K\ L\ M$

    B. $J\ K\ M\ L$

    C. $K\ J\ L\ M$

    D. $K\ J\ M\ L$

    E. $K\ L\ J\ M$

Questions 17–19

Questions 17–19 refer to the following pedigree. Circles indicate females, and squares indicate males. A horizontal line connecting a male and female indicate that these two individuals produced offspring. Offspring are indicated by a descending vertical line that branches to the offspring. A filled circle or filled square indicates that the individual has a particular trait, in this case, red-green color blindness. Color blindness is inherited as a sex-linked, recessive allele.

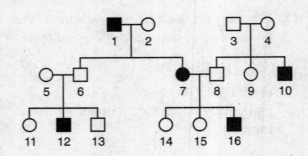

Use the following key for the next three questions. Each answer in the key may be used once, more than once, or not at all.

A. $X^N X^N$

B. $X^N X^n$

C. $X^n X^n$

D. $X^N Y$

E. $X^n Y$

17. Identify the genotype for individual 10.

18. Identify the genotype for individual 5.

19. Identify the genotype for individual 14.

20. In domestic cats, two alleles of a sex-linked (X-linked) gene code for hair color. One allele codes for yellow hair, and the other allele codes for black hair. Cats can be all yellow or all black, or they can be calico, a coat characterized by randomly arranged patches of yellow and black hair. With respect to this gene, all of the following are true EXCEPT:

A. A black female and a yellow male can produce a black male cat.

B. A black female and a yellow male can produce a female calico cat.

C. A calico female and a black male can produce a female calico cat.

D. A calico female and a yellow male can produce a female calico cat.

E. A calico female and a yellow male can produce a male calico cat.

21. From which parent(s) did a male with red-green color blindness inherit the defective allele?

A. *Only* the mother

B. *Only* the father

C. The mother or the father, but not both

D. *Both* the mother and the father

E. It is impossible to determine with certainty using only the given information.

22. A human genetic defect that is caused by nondisjunction of the sex chromosomes is

A. sickle-cell anemia

B. hemophilia

C. Down syndrome

D. Turner syndrome

E. red-green color blindness

23. Two genes, *A* and *B*, are linked. An individual who is *AaBb* produces equal numbers of four gametes *AB, Ab, aB,* and *ab*. The best explanation for this would be that

A. nondisjunction occurred

B. the genes are on homologous chromosomes

C. the genes are on nonhomologous chromosomes

D. the two genes are close together on the same chromosome

E. the two genes are separated by a large distance on the same chromosome

Answers to Multiple-Choice Questions

1. **E.** The chance that one die will turn up a three is 1 in 6, or $\frac{1}{6}$. For both dice to turn up a three, the probability is determined by multiplying the probability of each event happening independently, or $\frac{1}{6} \times \frac{1}{6} = \frac{1}{36}$.

2. **B.** Alleles refer to the various forms of a gene, or the various forms in which a particular gene can be expressed. Wrinkled and round are alleles that refer to two forms of a single gene (at a particular locus) that code for seed texture. Answer **A** is incorrect because wrinkled and yellow refer to two different genes (at different loci), one for seed texture, the other for seed color.

3. **D.** If you let R represent the dominant allele for tongue-rolling ability, then the cross would be $Rr \times Rr$. The Punnett square below shows that $\frac{3}{4}$ of the offspring have the tongue-rolling trait ($\frac{1}{4} RR + \frac{1}{2} Rr$).

	R	r
R	RR	Rr
r	Rr	rr

4. **C.** If both parents have normal wings (DD or Dd), there are three possible parent crosses: $DD \times DD$, $DD \times Dd$, or $Dd \times Dd$. All of the progeny of $DD \times DD$ and of $DD \times Dd$ would have normal wings. Only the progeny of $Dd \times Dd$ would consist of $\frac{3}{4}$ normal-winged flies. (Confirm this by constructing a Punnett square for each of the three possible parent combinations.)

5. **B.** At the end of meiosis I, the two homologous chromosomes, one with D and one with d, would separate and migrate to opposite poles which will form separate cells. During meiosis II, each chromosome separates into two chromatids (both of which will have exactly the same allele, assuming no crossing over) which migrate to opposite poles and become separate gametes. Thus, the cell containing the D chromosome, will produce two gametes, each with a D chromosome (previously a chromatid). Similarly, the cell containing the d chromosome will produce two gametes, both with a d chromosome. At the end of meiosis II, then, there will be two gametes with a D chromosome and two gametes with a d chromosome.

6. **A.** Black is the phenotype of the sheep. That is given to you in the question. Without further information, you cannot identify the genotype of a black sheep because it could be either BB or Bb. The possible genotypes of the parents of a black sheep could be $BB \times BB$, $BB \times Bb$, $BB \times bb$, or $Bb \times Bb$. Thus, there is no one single genotype for either parent. Answer **E** is incorrect because although one parent would always be black, you cannot be certain whether the second parent is black or white.

7. **E.** In the $CCSS \times ccss$, $CCSS$ produces only CS gametes, and $ccss$ produces only cs gametes. Thus, all offspring are $CcSs$.

8. B. The cross of *CcSs* × *CcSs* is the same kind of cross illustrated in Figure 6-5. Among the 16 genotypes given in the Punnett square, only one is *ccss*.

9. D. The cross of *CcSs* × *CcSs* is the same kind of cross illustrated in Figure 6-5. Among the sixteen genotypes given in the Punnett square, nine are normal for both traits (one of *CCSS*, two of *CCSs*, two of *CcSS*, and four of *CcSs*).

10. A. The question involves the progeny of the cross *ttRR* × *TTR'R'*. Since *ttRR* produces only *tR* gametes, and *TTR'R'* produces only *TR'* gametes, all progeny will be *TtRR'*. The *Tt* genotype codes for tall, and *RR'* codes for pink.

11. A. This is a trick question because there's a long way and a very short way to solve this problem. The long way would be to construct a Punnett square and sort and count all the offspring. The short, easy way is to recognize that a white flower has the genotype *R'R'*. Looking at only the color gene for each parent, the cross is *RR'* × *RR*. In order for a cross to produce a white-flowered offspring (*R'R'*), both parents must contribute *R'*. Since this is not the case, no offspring will be white flowered.

12. C. It is not usually practical to make a Punnett square for genotypes involving more than two genes. In this problem, you are asked about the frequency of one specific offspring, *AABbCcDd*. To solve this problem, look at each gene separately. Looking at the first gene, the parents are *AA* × *AA* and all offspring will be *AA* (frequency of 1). For the second gene, *BB* × *bb*, all offspring will be *Bb* (1). For the third gene, the parents are *CC* × *Cc*, which produces ½ *CC* and ½ *Cc* (do a Punnett square to confirm this). Finally, a cross of the fourth gene, *Dd* × *Dd*, produces ¼ *DD*, ½ *Dd*, and ¼ *dd*. To find the probability of *AABbCcDd*, find the product of the frequencies for each gene separately. The probability of *AA* is 1, of *Bb* is 1, of *Cc* is ½, and of *Dd* is ½. Thus, the frequency of *AABbCcDd* is $1 \times 1 \times \frac{1}{2} \times \frac{1}{2} = \frac{1}{4}$.

13. D. Since the range of skin colors in humans shows continuous variation from very pale to very dark, it is most likely coded by many genes (polygenic inheritance).

14. A. When two traits frequently occur together, then they are probably linked. Sometimes, a red-headed person may not have freckles, or a freckled person may not have red hair. In these cases, there was probably a crossover event, exchanging one of the two genes with an allele that did not code for freckles or red hair.

15. C. is the false statement. Since *A* and *B* are on one chromosome, then, by definition, they are linked and **A** is true. **B** is also true because the homologous chromosome would have the same genes but with possibly different alleles. In this case, both chromosomes carry the same genes, but the alleles are different (*A* and *B* on one chromosome and *a* and *b* on its homologue). Taking both chromosomes together, you get the genotype *AaBb*, and thus **D** is true. Since this individual can produce a gamete that is *AB*, it can have *AABB* offspring if it mates with an individual who can also donate an *AB* gamete (such as an *AABB*, *AABb*, *AaBB*, or *AaBb* individual). Thus, **E** is true. **C** is false because even though the chromosomes separate during meiosis to produce gametes that are *AB* and *ab*, crossing over can take place, producing some gametes that are *Ab* and *aB*.

16. C. Begin by drawing a horizontal line with about 30 tick marks. Since *K* and *J* have a crossover frequency of 3, write the letters *K* and *J* on two marks 3 ticks apart, near the middle. Next, add the letter *L* in two positions, 8 units to the right of *K* and 8 units to the left of K. At this point of the solution, both positions are possible. Next, add the letter M 12 units to the right of J and, again, 12 units to the left of J. Both are possible. Last, use the L-M frequency to determine which configuration of M and L are correct. Since the L-M frequency is 7, only the M and L positions at the right are correct. That leaves only one possible sequence, K-J-L-M.

17. **E.** In any pedigree problem, you should begin by first identifying genotypes for which there is only one possibility. For a sex-linked recessive pattern of inheritance, you can identify the genotypes of all males and of all females that express the trait that the pedigree is describing. In this case, color-blind males are $X^n Y$ (filled boxes, 1, 10, 12, 16), normal males are $X^N Y$ (open boxes, 3, 6, 8, 13), and color-blind females are $X^n X^n$ (filled circles, 7).

18. **B.** The next step in this pedigree problem is to identify the normal females (open circles). Are they $X^N X^N$ or $X^N X^n$? Note that box 12 is a color-blind son ($X^n Y$). Since a son can inherit only his Y chromosome from his father (box 6), box 12 must have inherited his X^n gene from his mother (circle 5). Thus, you can conclude that the mother, circle 5, is $X^N X^n$.

19. **B.** There are two possibilities for female 14, $X^N X^N$ or $X^N X^n$. The color-blind mother, 7, is $X^n X^n$. The normal father, 8, is $X^N Y$. A cross between these two individuals can produce only one kind of daughter, $X^N X^n$ (confirm this with a Punnett square). For practice, you should try to identify every female. Female 7 is color blind ($X^n X^n$), females 2, 4, 5, 14, and 15 are carriers ($X^N X^n$), and females 9 and 11 are either normal ($X^N X^N$) or carriers ($X^N X^n$) (there is not enough information to determine which genotype is correct).

20. **E.** To be a calico, a cat must have two X chromosomes, one with the yellow allele and one with the black allele. Since a male cat has only one X chromosome, it normally can be only yellow or black.

21. **A.** Since red-green color blindness is inherited as a sex-linked recessive, a color-blind male must be $X^n Y$. Because he is a male, he received the Y from his father. Therefore, he inherited the X^n from his mother.

22. **D.** Turner syndrome is caused by the nondisjunction of the sex chromosomes. The result is a sperm or egg that is missing a sex chromosome. The formation of a zygote from the union of one of these sperm or eggs with a normal egg or sperm (with an X chromosome) results in Turner syndrome (XO). It is also possible to form a OY zygote, but because this zygote is missing an X chromosome, a chromosome with many essential genes, the development of the zygote is aborted. Answer **C**, Down syndrome, is also caused by nondisjunction, but of chromosome 21, not the sex chromosomes. Sickle-cell anemia is inherited as an autosomal recessive allele, while hemophilia and red-green color blindness are inherited as sex-linked recessive alleles.

23. **E.** Since the genes A and B are on the same chromosome (linked), there are two possible allele arrangements for an $AaBb$ individual. The first is that AB is on one chromosome and ab is on the homologous chromosome. The second possibility is that Ab is on one chromosome and aB is on the homologous chromosome. Using the first possibility as an example, one would expect only two kinds of gametes in the absence of crossing over—AB and ab in equal quantities. Crossing over would produce gametes that are Ab and aB. If the two genes are very close together, there would be very few crossovers because there are few places between the genes that the chromosomes can break and cross over. If the

genes are far apart, there would be many crossovers because there are many places for chromosome breaks. When the genes are very far apart, they cross over so frequently that by observing the allele frequencies of the gametes the genes seem to assort independently as if they were on different chromosomes (not linked). That is exactly what has happened in this question. The observed frequencies are those that would have been expected had the genes been on different chromosomes. Since the question states that the genes are linked, they must be far apart to allow so large a number of crossovers.

Free-Response Questions

Free-response questions on the AP exam may require you to provide information from a narrow area of biology, or they may consist of parts that require you to assemble information from diverse areas of biology.

Directions: Answer the question below as completely and as thoroughly as possible. Answer the question in essay form (NOT outline form), using complete sentences. You may use diagrams to supplement your answers, but a diagram alone without appropriate discussion is inadequate.

1. Discuss Mendel's laws of segregation and independent assortment with respect to

    (a.) genes that are not linked

    (b.) genes that are linked

    (c.) crossing over

    (d.) sex-linkage

    (e.) Down syndrome

    (f.) Turner syndrome

A Typical Answer to the Free-Response Question

Question 1

(a.) When chromosomes align on the metaphase plate during meiosis I, homologous chromosomes are paired. Each homologue migrates to a separate pole and becomes a member of a separate gamete. The migration to separate poles is random—that is, either chromosome of a homologous pair can migrate to either pole (Mendel's law of segregation).

Different homologous pairs of chromosomes act independently of other homologous chromosome pairs. Thus, genes that are on different chromosomes (unlinked) migrate independently of genes on other chromosomes (Mendel's law of independent assortment).

(b.) When two genes are linked, they are on the same chromosome. If they are on the same chromosome, they migrate together to either pole (unless crossing over occurs). Thus, they violate Mendel's law of independent assortment and are inherited together as if they were a single gene in a monohybrid cross. If the dominant alleles *A* and *B* are on one chromosome and the recessive alleles *a* and *b* are on the homologous chromosome, they produce only two kinds of gametes, *AB* and *ab*. Then the dihybrid cross *AaBb* × *AaBb* would produce a 1:2:1 genotypic ratio for *AABB, AaBb,* and *aabb* with a phenotypic ratio of 3:1, not the typical 9:3:3:1 phenotypic ratio Mendel found when using unlinked genes. The 1:2:1 and 3:1 genotypic and phenotypic ratios are those expected from a typical *monohybrid* cross.

(c.) Crossing over occurs between linked genes. Instead of producing only two kinds of gametes—say *AB* and *ab*—exchanges occur between homologous chromosomes, producing some *Ab* and *aB* gametes, quantities of which depend on the frequency of crossing over. The frequency of crossing over increases as the distance between the gene loci increases.

(d.) Sex-linkage occurs when a gene is located on one of the sex chromosomes, usually the X chromosome. For example, in humans, hemophilia is inherited as a recessive allele on the X chromosome. Females receive two copies of the gene, one on each of their X chromosomes. If they receive two recessive alleles, they are hemophiliacs. If they receive two normal alleles, they are normal, but if they inherit one normal and one hemophilia allele, they will have normal clotting abilities (because the normal allele is dominant) but will be carriers of the disease. Males, on the other hand, inherit only one X chromosome and, thus, only one copy of the allele. If they receive the normal allele, they will have normal clotting; if they receive the hemophilia allele, they will be hemophiliacs. Because they need only one copy of the allele to express the trait, sex-linked diseases are more common in males than in females.

(e.) Down syndrome occurs as a result of the nondisjunction of the two number 21 chromosomes. As a result, the homologous pair does not separate and move to opposite poles (as the law of segregation implies), but rather both chromosomes end up at the same pole and in the same gamete. Two kinds of gametes are formed, one with two copies of chromosome 21 and one with no chromosome 21. Only the gamete with two copies of the chromosome is viable. The zygote formed between this gamete and a normal gamete will have three copies of chromosome 21, and the infant will express the Down syndrome phenotype, which consists of physical abnormalities and mental retardation.

(f.) Turner syndrome results from a nondisjunction of the sex chromosomes. This results in a gamete that has either two sex chromosomes or no sex chromosomes. If a gamete with no sex chromosomes (O) fuses with a normal gamete bearing the X chromosome, the resulting zygote will have only a single X chromosome (XO) and express the Turner syndrome phenotype. Turner syndrome individuals are female and exhibit physical abnormalities, including sterility.

Molecular Genetics

Review

In eukaryotes, chromosomes bear the genetic information that is passed from parents to off-spring. The genetic information is stored in molecules of DNA. The DNA, in turn, codes for enzymes, which, in turn, regulate chemical reactions that direct metabolism for cell development, growth, and maintenance. The underlying molecular mechanisms that interpret the information in DNA to generate these effects is the subject of this section.

The structure of DNA and RNA was presented earlier in the chapter on chemistry. As a review, both DNA and RNA are polymers of **nucleotides**. The nucleotide monomer consists of three parts—a nitrogen base, a sugar, and a phosphate. Figure 7-1 reviews the differences in the structures of DNA and RNA and summarizes their functions. Details of the functions of these molecules will be presented in this chapter.

	Nucleotide Components		Function	Structure
	Sugar	Nitrogen Bases	Function	Structure
DNA	deoxyribose	adenine, thymine, guanine cytosine	contains hereditary information (genes) of the cell	double helix
RNA (3 kinds)	ribose	adenine, uracil, guanine cytosine	mRNA—provides the instructions for assembling amino acids into a polypeptide chain	linear
			tRNA—delivers amino acids to a ribosome for their addition into a growing polypeptide chain	"clover-leaf" shaped
			rRNA—combines with proteins to form ribosomes	globular

Comparison of DNA and RNA

Figure 7-1

DNA Replication

During interphase of the cell cycle, a second chromatid containing a copy of the DNA molecule is assembled. The process, called **DNA replication,** involves separating ("unzipping") the DNA molecule into two strands, each of which serves as a template to assemble a new, complementary strand. The result is two identical double-stranded molecules of DNA. Because each of these double-stranded molecules of DNA consists of a single strand of old DNA (the template strand) and a single strand of new, replicated DNA (the complementary strand), the process is called **semiconservative replication.**

During DNA replication, the enzyme **helicase** unwinds the DNA helix, forming a Y-shaped **replication fork. Single-stranded DNA binding proteins** attach to each strand of the uncoiled DNA to keep them separate. As helicase unwinds the DNA, it forces the double-helix in front of it to twist. A group of enzymes, called **topoisomerases,** break and rejoin the double helix, allowing the twists to unravel and preventing the formation of knots.

Since a DNA double-helix molecule consists of two opposing DNA strands, the uncoiled DNA consists of a $3' \rightarrow 5'$ template strand and a $5' \rightarrow 3'$ template strand. The enzyme that assembles the new DNA strand, **DNA polymerase,** moves in the $3' \rightarrow 5'$ direction along each template strand. The new (complement) strands grow in the antiparallel, $5' \rightarrow 3'$ direction.

For the $3' \rightarrow 5'$ template strand, replication occurs readily as the DNA polymerase follows the replication fork, assembling a $5' \rightarrow 3'$ complementary strand. This complementary strand is called the **leading strand.**

For the $5' \rightarrow 3'$ template strand, however, the DNA polymerase moves away from the uncoiling replication fork. This is because it can assemble nucleotides only as it travels in the $3' \rightarrow 5'$ direction. As the helix is uncoiled, DNA polymerase assembles short segments of nucleotides along the template strand in the direction away from the replication fork. After each complement segment is assembled, the DNA polymerase must return back to the replication fork to begin assembling the next segment. These short segments of complementary DNA are called **Okazaki segments.** The Okazaki segments are connected by **DNA ligase,** producing a single complement strand. Because this complementary strand requires more time to assemble than the leading strand, it is called the **lagging strand.**

DNA polymerase can append nucleotides only to an already existing complementary strand. The first nucleotides of the leading strand and each Okazaki fragment are initiated by **RNA primase** and other proteins. RNA primase initiates each complementary segment with RNA (*not* DNA) nucleotides which serve as an **RNA primer** for DNA polymerase to append succeeding DNA nucleotides. Later, the RNA nucleotides are replaced with appropriate DNA nucleotides.

Figure 7-2 illustrates the growth of leading and lagging DNA complements. In the figure, the RNA primer that initiated the leading strand is not shown because it was replaced with DNA nucleotides earlier in its synthesis. The Okazaki fragment of the lagging strand, however, still have its RNA primer attached, because a primer must initiate each new fragment.

The details of DNA replication are summarized below. Numbers correspond to events illustrated in Figure 7-2.

1. **Helicase** unwinds the DNA, producing a **replication fork. Single-stranded DNA binding proteins** prevent the single strands of DNA from recombining. **Topoisomerase** removes twists and knots that form in the double-stranded template as a result of the unwinding induced by helicase. (See 1A, 1B, 1C and 1D in Figure 7-2.)

2. **RNA primase** initiates DNA replication at special nucleotide sequences (called **origins of replication**) with short segments of RNA nucleotides (called **RNA primers**) (see 2A and 2B in Figure 7-2).

3. **DNA polymerase** attaches to the RNA primers and begins **elongation,** the adding of DNA nucleotides to the complement strand.

4. The **leading complementary strand** is assembled continuously as the double-helix DNA uncoils.

5. The **lagging complementary strand** is assembled in short Okazaki fragments, which are subsequently joined by **DNA ligase** (see 5A, 5B, and 5C in Figure 7-2).

6. The RNA primers are replaced by DNA nucleotides.

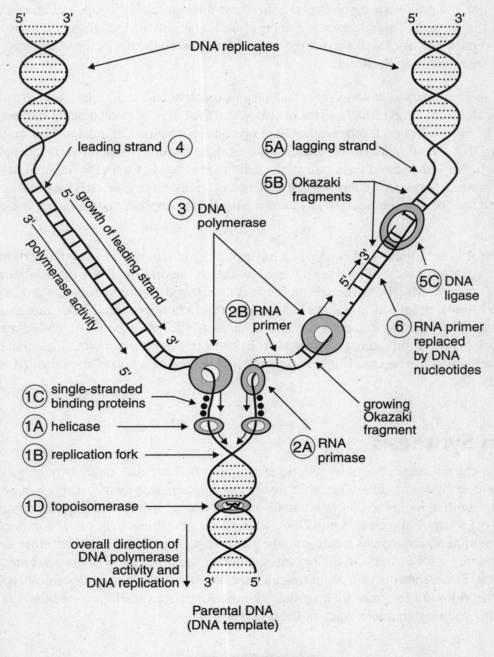

DNA Replication

Figure 7-2

127

Energy for elongation is provided by two additional phosphates that are attached to each new nucleotide (making a total of three phosphates attached to the nitrogen base). Breaking the bonds holding the two extra phosphates provides the chemical energy for the process.

Mutations

The replication process of DNA is extremely accurate. In bacteria, the DNA polymerase **proofreads** the pairing process by checking the newly attached nucleotide to confirm that it is correct. If it is not, the polymerase removes the incorrect nucleotide, backs up, and attaches a new nucleotide. If a mismatch should escape the proofreading ability of the DNA polymerase, other, **mismatch repair,** enzymes will correct the error. Repair mechanisms occur in eukaryotic cells as well but are not well understood.

Radiation (such as ultraviolet and x-ray) and various reactive chemicals can cause errors in DNA molecules. One kind of DNA error occurs when the bases of two adjacent nucleotides in one DNA strand bond to each other rather than make proper pairs with nucleotides in the complementary DNA strand. A **thymine dimer,** for example, originates when two adjacent thymine nucleotides in the same strand base-pair with each other instead of with the adenine bases in the complementary strand. Such errors can be fixed by **excision repair** enzymes that splice out the error and use the complementary strand as a pattern, or template, for replacing the excised nucleotides.

If a DNA error is not repaired, it becomes a **mutation.** A mutation is any sequence of nucleotides in a DNA molecule that does not exactly match the original DNA molecule from which it was copied. Mutations include an incorrect nucleotide (**substitution**), a missing nucleotide (**deletion**), or an additional nucleotide not present in the original DNA molecule (**insertion**). When an insertion mutation occurs, it causes all the subsequent nucleotides to be displaced one position, producing a **frameshift mutation.** Radiation or chemicals that cause mutations are called **mutagens. Carcinogens** are mutagens that activate uncontrolled cell growth (cancer).

Protein Synthesis

The DNA in chromosomes contains genetic instructions that regulate development, growth, and the metabolic activities of cells. The DNA instructions determine whether a cell will be that of a pea plant, a human, or some other organism, as well as establish specific characteristics of the cell in that organism. For example, the DNA in a cell may establish that it is a human cell. If, during development, it becomes a cell in the iris of an eye, the DNA will direct other information appropriate for its location in the organism, such as the production of brown, blue, or other pigmentation. DNA controls the cell in this manner because it contains codes for polypeptides. Many polypeptides are enzymes that regulate chemical reactions, and these chemical reactions influence the resulting characteristics of the cell.

In the study of heredity, the terms **gene** and **genotype** are used to represent the genetic information for a particular trait. From the molecular viewpoint, *traits are the end products of metabolic processes regulated by enzymes.* When this relationship between traits and enzymes was discovered, the gene was defined as the segment of DNA that codes for a particular enzyme (**one-gene-one-enzyme hypothesis**). Since many genes code for polypeptides that are not enzymes (such as structural proteins or individual components of enzymes), the gene has been redefined as the DNA segment that codes for a particular polypeptide (**one-gene-one-polypeptide hypothesis**).

The process that describes how enzymes and other proteins are made from DNA is called **protein synthesis.** There are three steps in protein synthesis: **transcription, RNA processing,** and **translation.** In transcription, RNA molecules are created by using the DNA molecule as a template. After transcription, RNA processing modifies the RNA molecule with deletions and additions. In translation, the processed RNA molecules are used to assemble amino acids into a polypeptide.

There are three kinds of RNA molecules produced during transcription, as follows:

1. **Messenger RNA (mRNA)** is a single strand of RNA that provides the template used for sequencing amino acids into a polypeptide. A triplet group of three adjacent nucleotides on the mRNA, called a **codon,** codes for one specific amino acid. Since there are 64 possible ways that four nucleotides can be arranged in triplet combinations ($4 \times 4 \times 4 = 64$), there are 64 possible codons. However, there are only 20 amino acids, and thus, some codons code for the same amino acid. The **genetic code,** given in Figure 7-3, provides the "decoding" for each codon. That is, it identifies the amino acid specified by each of the possible 64 codon combinations. For example, the codon composed of the three nucleotides cytosine-guanine-adenine (CGA) codes for the amino acid arginine. This can be found in Figure 7-3 by aligning the C found in the first column with the G in the center part of the table and the A in the column at the far right.

2. **Transfer RNA (tRNA)** is a short RNA molecule (consisting of about 80 nucleotides) that is used for transporting amino acids to their proper place on the mRNA template. Interactions among various parts of the tRNA molecule result in base-pairings between nucleotides, folding the tRNA in such a way that it forms a three-dimensional molecule. (In two dimensions, a tRNA resembles the three leaflets of a clover leaf.) The 3' end of the tRNA (ending with cytosine-cytosine-adenine, or C-C-A-3') attaches to an amino acid. Another portion of the tRNA, specified by a triplet combination of nucleotides, is the **anticodon.** During translation, the anticodon of the tRNA base pairs with the codon of the mRNA. Exact base-pairing between the third nucleotide of the tRNA anticodon and the third nucleotide of the mRNA codon is often not required. This "**wobble**" allows the anticodon of some tRNAs to base-pair with more than one kind of codon. As a result, about 45 different tRNAs base-pair with the 64 different codons.

First Letter	Second Letter				Third Letter
	U	C	A	G	
U	phenylalanine	serine	tyrosine	cysteine	U
	phenylalanine	serine	tyrosine	cysteine	C
	leucine	serine	STOP	STOP	A
	leucine	serine	STOP	tryptophan	G
C	leucine	proline	histidine	arginine	U
	leucine	proline	histidine	arginine	C
	leucine	proline	glutamine	arginine	A
	leucine	proline	glutamine	arginine	G
A	isoleucine	threonine	asparagine	serine	U
	isoleucine	threonine	asparagine	serine	C
	isoleucine	threonine	lysine	arginine	A
	methionine &ST ART	threonine	lysine	arginine	G
G	valine	alanine	aspartate	glycine	U
	valine	alanine	aspartate	glycine	C
	valine	alanine	glutamate	glycine	A
	valine	alanine	glutamate	glycine	G

The Genetic Code

Figure 7-3

3. **Ribosomal RNA (rRNA)** molecules are the building blocks of ribosomes. The nucleolus is an assemblage of DNA actively being transcribed into rRNA. Within the nucleolus, various proteins imported from the cytoplasm are assembled with rRNA to form large and small ribosome subunits. Together, the two subunits form a ribosome which coordinates the activities of the mRNA and tRNA during translation. Ribosomes have three binding sites—one for the mRNA, one for a tRNA that carries a growing polypeptide chain (P site, for "polypeptide"), and one for a second tRNA that delivers the next amino acid that will be inserted into the growing polypeptide chain (A site, for "amino acid").

Transcription

Transcription begins with **initiation,** continues with **elongation,** and ends with **termination.** The details follow, with numbers corresponding to events illustrated in Figure 7-4,

1. In **initiation,** the RNA polymerase attaches to promoter regions on the DNA and begins to unzip the DNA into two strands. A promoter region for mRNA transcriptions contains the sequence T-A-T-A (called the TATA box).

2. **Elongation** occurs as the RNA polymerase unzips the DNA and assembles RNA nucleotides using one strand of the DNA as a template. As in DNA replication, elongation of the RNA molecule occurs in the 5' → 3' direction. In contrast to DNA replication, new nucleotides are RNA nucleotides (rather than DNA nucleotides), and only one DNA strand is transcribed.

3. **Termination** occurs when the RNA polymerase reaches a special sequence of nucleotides that serve as a termination point. In eukaryotes, the termination region often contains the DNA sequence AAAAAAA.

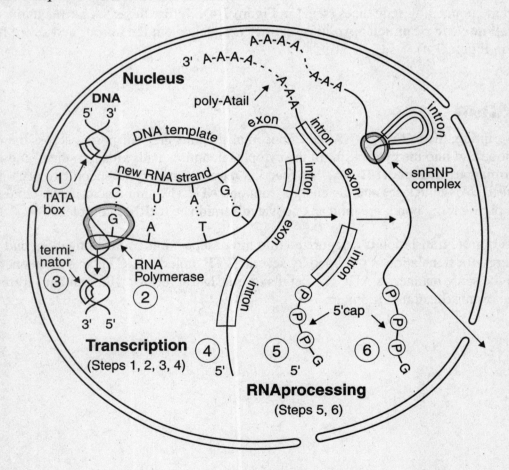

Transcription and RNAP rocessing

Figure 7-4

RNA Processing

Before a mRNA molecule leaves the nucleus, it undergoes two kinds of alterations. The first modification adds special nucleotide sequences to both ends of the mRNA (see 5 in Figure 7.4). A modified guanosine triphosphate (GTP) is added to the 5' end to form a **5' cap** (-P-P-P-G-5'). A GTP molecule is a guanine nucleotide with two additional phosphate groups (in the same way that ATP is an adenine nucleotide with two additional phosphates). The 5' cap provides stability to the mRNA and a point of attachment for the small subunit of the ribosome. To the 3' end of the mRNA, a sequence of 150 to 200 adenine nucleotides is added, producing a **poly-A tail** (-A-A-A . . . A-A-3'). The tail provides stability and also appears to control the movement of the mRNA across the nuclear envelope. By controlling its transport and subsequent expression, the poly-A tail may serve to regulate gene expression.

The second alteration of the mRNA occurs when some mRNA segments are removed. A transcribed DNA segment contains two kinds of sequences—**exons,** which are sequences that *ex*press a code for a polypeptide, and **introns,** *in*tervening sequences that are noncoding. The original unprocessed mRNA molecule, called **heterogenous nuclear RNA,** contains both the coding and the noncoding sequences (see 4 in Figure 7-4). Before the RNA moves to the cytoplasm, **small nuclear ribonucleoproteins,** or **snRNPs,** delete out the introns and splice the exons (see 6 in Figure 7-4).

Translation

After transcription, the mRNA, tRNA, and ribosomal subunits are transported across the nuclear envelope and into the cytoplasm. In the cytoplasm, amino acids attach to the 3' end of the tRNAs, forming an **aminoacyl-tRNA.** The reaction requires an enzyme specific to each tRNA (aminoacyl-tRNA synthetase) and the energy from one ATP. The amino acid-tRNA bond that results is a high-energy bond, creating an "activated" amino acid-tRNA complex.

As in transcription, translation is categorized into three steps—initiation, elongation, and termination. Energy for translation is provided by several **GTP** molecules. GTP acts as an energy supplier in the same manner as ATP. The details of translation follow, with numbers corresponding to events illustrated in Figure 7-5.

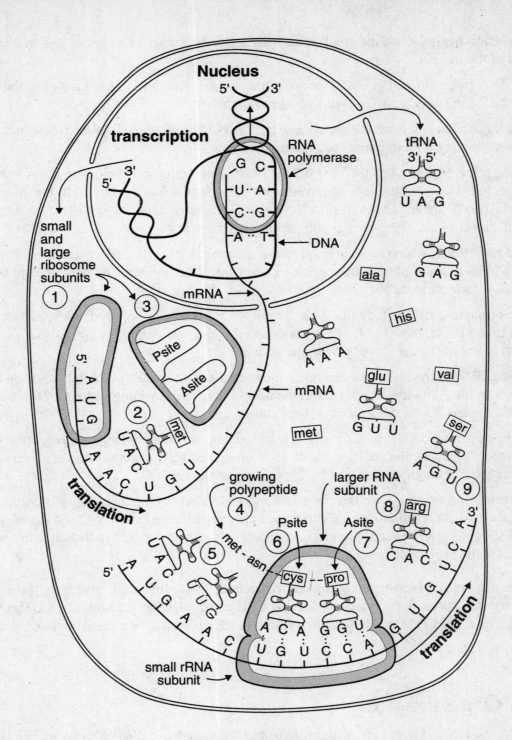

Protein Synthesis

Figure 7-5

1. **Initiation** begins when the small ribosomal subunit attaches to a special region near the 5' end of the mRNA.

2. A tRNA (with anticodon UAC) carrying the amino acid methionine attaches to the mRNA (at the "start" codon AUG) with hydrogen bonds.

3. The large ribosomal subunit attaches to the mRNA, forming a complete ribosome with the tRNA (bearing a methionine) occupying the P site.

4. **Elongation** begins when the next tRNA (bearing an amino acid) binds to the A site of the ribosome. The methionine is removed from the first tRNA and attached to the amino acid on the newly arrived tRNA. Figure 7-5 shows elongation after several tRNAs have delivered amino acids. The growing polypeptide is shown at 4.

5. The first tRNA, which no longer carries an amino acid, is released. After its release, the tRNA can again bind with its specific amino acid, allowing repeated deliveries to the mRNA during translation.

6. The remaining tRNA (together with the mRNA to which it is bonded) moves from the A site to the P site. Now the A site is unoccupied and a new codon is exposed. This is analogous to the ribosome moving over one codon.

7. A new tRNA carrying a new amino acid enters the A site. The two amino acids on the tRNA in the P site are transferred to the new amino acid, forming a chain of three amino acids. Figure 7-5 shows a chain of four amino acids.

8. As in step 5, the tRNA in the P site is released, and subsequent steps are repeated. As each new tRNA arrives, the polypeptide chain is elongated by one new amino acid, growing in sequence and length as dictated by the codons on the mRNA.

9. **Termination** occurs when the ribosome encounters one of the three "stop" codons (see Figure 7-3). At termination, the completed polypeptide, the last tRNA, and the two ribosomal subunits are released. The ribosomal subunits can now attach to the same or another mRNA and repeat the process.

Once the polypeptide is completed, interactions among the amino acids give it its secondary and tertiary structures. Subsequent processing by the endoplasmic reticulum or a Golgi body may make final modifications before the protein functions as a structural element or as an enzyme.

DNA Organization

In eukaryotes, DNA is packaged with proteins to form a matrix called *chromatin*. The DNA is coiled around bundles of eight or nine **histone** proteins to form DNA-histone complexes called **nucleosomes.** Through the electron microscope, the nucleosomes appear like beads on a string.

During cell division, DNA is compactly organized into chromosomes. In the nondividing cell, the DNA is arranged as either of two types of chromatin, as follows:

1. **Euchromatin** describes regions where the DNA is loosely bound to nucleosomes. DNA in these regions is actively being transcribed.

2. **Heterochromatin** represents areas where the nucleosomes are more tightly compacted, and where DNA is inactive. Because of its condensed arrangement, heterochromatin stains darker than euchromatin.

Some DNA segments within a DNA molecule are able to move to new locations. These transposable genetic elements, called **transposons** (or **"jumping genes"**) can move to a new location on the same chromosome or to a different chromosome. Some transposons consist only of DNA that codes for an enzyme that enables it to be transported. Other transposons contain genes that invoke replication of the transposon. After replication, the new transposon copy is transported to the new location. Wherever they are inserted, transposons have the effect of a mutation. They may change the expression of a gene, turn on or turn off its expression, or have no effect at all.

The Molecular Genetics of Viruses

Viruses are parasites of cells. A typical virus penetrates a cell, commandeers its metabolic machinery, assembles hundreds of new viruses that are copies of itself, then leaves the cell to infect other cells. In the process, the host cell is usually destroyed.

Viruses are specific for the kinds of cells they will parasitize. Some viruses will attack only one kind of cell within a single host species, while others will attack similar cells from a range of closely related species. **Bacteriophages,** or **phages,** for example, are viruses that attack only bacteria.

Viruses consist of a nucleic acid surrounded by a protein coat called a **capsid.** Viruses are categorized by the kind of nucleic acid they contain; that is, they are either DNA viruses or RNA viruses. The capsids of some viruses include an **envelope** that assists them in penetrating their hosts. Envelopes incorporate phospholipids and proteins obtained from the cell membrane of the host.

There are two basic replication cycles that viruses follow:

1. In the **lytic cycle,** a virus penetrates the cell membrane of the host, uses the enzymes of the host cell to replicate viral DNA, transcribes viral DNA into RNA, and translates the RNA into proteins. The proteins and DNA are then assembled into new viruses which subsequently erupt from the host cell, destroying the cell in the process. The new viruses then infect other cells, and the process repeats.

2. In the **lysogenic cycle,** the viral DNA is temporarily incorporated into the DNA of the host cell. A virus in this dormant state is called a **provirus** (or, if a bacteriophage, a **prophage**). The virus remains inactive until some trigger, usually an external environmental stimulus (such as radiation or certain chemicals), causes the virus to begin the destructive lytic cycle.

Since RNA viruses use RNA to carry genetic information, their reproductive cycles deviate from the lytic and lysogenic cycles described above. In some RNA viruses, the viral RNA is used directly as mRNA. Other viruses, such as **retroviruses,** use an enzyme called **reverse transcriptase** to make a DNA complement of their RNA. The DNA complement can then be transcribed immediately to manufacture mRNA, or it can begin the lysogenic cycle by becoming incorporated into the DNA of the host.

The Molecular Genetics of Bacteria

Bacteria are prokaryotes. They do not contain a nucleus, nor do they possess any of the specialized organelles of eukaryotes. The primary genetic material of a bacterium is a "chromosome" consisting of a single, circular DNA molecule. A bacterial chromosome is often called a "naked" chromosome because it lacks the histones and other proteins associated with eukaryotic chromosomes. A bacterial cell reproduces by **binary fission.** In binary fission, the chromosome replicates and the cell divides into two cells, each cell bearing one chromosome. The spindle apparatus, microtubules, and centrioles found in eukaryotic cell divisions are lacking, since in bacteria, there is no nucleus to divide.

Bacteria also contain **plasmids,** short, circular DNA molecules outside the chromosome. Plasmids carry genes that are beneficial but not normally essential to the survival of the bacterium. Plasmids replicate independently of the chromosome. Some plasmids, called **episomes,** can become incorporated into the bacterial chromosome.

There are several ways in which genetic variation is introduced into the genome of bacteria. Short descriptions follow.

1. **Conjugation** is a process of DNA exchange between bacteria. A donor bacterium produces a tube, or **pilus** (plural, **pili**), that connects to a recipient bacterium. Through the pilus, the donor bacterium sends chromosomal or plasmid DNA to the recipient. In some cases, copies of large portions of a donor's chromosome are sent, allowing recombination with the recipient's chromosome. One plasmid, called the **F plasmid,** contains the genes that enable a bacterium to produce pili. When a recipient bacterium receives the F plasmid, it too can become a donor cell. A group of plasmids, called **R plasmids,** provide bacteria with resistance against antibiotics.

2. **Transduction** occurs when new DNA is introduced into bacteria by a virus. When a virus is assembled during a lytic cycle, it is sometimes assembled with some bacterial DNA in place of some of the viral DNA. When this aberrant virus infects another cell, the bacterial DNA that it delivers can recombine with the resident DNA.

3. **Transformation** occurs when bacteria absorb DNA from their surroundings. Specialized proteins on the cell membranes of some bacteria facilitate this kind of DNA uptake.

Regulation of Gene Expression

Every cell in a human contains exactly the same sequences of DNA. Yet some cells become muscle cells, while other cells become nerve cells. One way in which cells with identical DNA become different is by regulating gene expression through the activation of only selected genes.

Gene regulation is best understood in the bacterium *E. coli,* a common bacterium that lives in the digestive tracts of humans. The DNA of this bacterium contain sequences of DNA, called **operons,** that direct particular biosynthetic pathways. There are four major components of an operon, as follows:

1. A **regulatory gene** produces a **repressor** protein, a substance that can prevent gene expression by blocking the action of RNA polymerase.

2. The **promoter** region is a sequence of DNA to which the RNA polymerase attaches to begin transcription.

3. The **operator** region can block the action of the RNA polymerase if the region is occupied by a repressor protein.

4. The **structural genes** contain DNA sequences that code for several related enzymes that direct the production of some particular end product.

The *lac* operon in *E. coli* controls the breakdown of lactose. The regulatory gene in the *lac* operon produces an active repressor that binds to the operator region. When the operator region is occupied by the repressor, RNA polymerase is unable to transcribe several structural genes that code for enzymes that control the uptake and subsequent breakdown of lactose. When lactose is available, however, some of the lactose (in a converted form) combines with the repressor to make it inactive. When the repressor is inactivated, RNA polymerase is able to transcribe the genes that code for the enzymes that break down lactose. Since a substance (lactose, in this case) is required to induce (turn on) the operon, the enzymes that the operon produces are said to be **inducible enzymes.**

Another operon in *E. coli,* the *trp* **operon,** produces enzymes for the synthesis of the amino acid tryptophan. The regulatory gene produces an inactive repressor that does not bind to the operator. As a result, the RNA polymerase proceeds to transcribe the structural genes necessary to produce enzymes that synthesize tryptophan. When tryptophan is available to *E. coli* from the surrounding environment, the bacterium no longer needs to manufacture its own tryptophan. In this case, rising levels of tryptophan induce some tryptophan to react with the inactive repressor and make it active. Here tryptophan is acting as a **corepressor.** The active repressor now binds to the operator region, which, in turn, prevents the transcription of the structural genes. Since these structural genes stop producing enzymes only in the presence of an active repressor, they are called **repressible enzymes.**

Recombinant DNA

Recombinant DNA is DNA that contains DNA segments or genes from different sources. DNA transferred from one part of a DNA molecule to another, from one chromosome to another chromosome, or from one organism to another all constitute recombinant DNA. The transfer of DNA segments can occur naturally through viral transduction, bacterial conjugation, or transposons or artificially through recombinant DNA technology.

Recombinant DNA technology uses **restriction enzymes** to cut up DNA. Restriction enzymes are obtained from bacteria that manufacture these enzymes to combat invading viruses. Restriction enzymes are very specific, cutting DNA at specific recognition sequences of nucleotides. The cut across a double-stranded DNA is usually staggered, producing fragments that have one strand of the DNA extending beyond the complementary strand. The unpaired extension is called a **sticky end.**

Fragments produced by a restriction enzyme are often inserted into a plasmid because plasmids can subsequently be introduced into bacteria by transformation. This is accomplished by first treating the plasmid with the same restriction enzyme as was used to create the DNA fragment. The restriction enzyme will cut the plasmid at the same recognition sequences, producing the same sticky ends carried by the fragments. Mixing the fragments with the cut plasmids allows base-pairing at the sticky ends. Application of DNA ligase stabilizes the attachment. The recombinant plasmid is then introduced into a bacterium by transformation. By following this procedure, the human gene for insulin has been inserted into *E. coli*. The transformed *E. coli* produce insulin which is isolated and used to treat diabetes.

Restriction fragments can be separated by **gel electrophoresis.** In this process, DNA fragments of different lengths are separated as they diffuse through a gelatinous material under the influence of an electric field. Since DNA is negatively charged (because of the phosphate groups), it moves toward the positive electrode. Shorter fragments migrate further through the gel than longer, heavier fragments. Gel electrophoresis is often used to compare DNA fragments of closely related species in an effort to determine evolutionary relationships.

When restriction fragments between individuals of the same species are compared, the fragments differ in length because of polymorphisms, which are slight differences in DNA sequences. These fragments are called **restriction fragment length polymorphisms,** or **RFLPs.** In **DNA fingerprinting,** RFLPs produced from DNA left at a crime scene are compared to RFLPs from the DNA of suspects.

When foreign genes are inserted into the genome of a bacterium with recombinant DNA technology, introns often prevent their transcription. To avoid this problem, the DNA fragment bearing the required gene is obtained directly from the mRNA that codes for the desired polypeptide. Reverse transcriptase (obtained from retroviruses) is used to make a DNA molecule directly from the mRNA. DNA obtained in this manner is called **complementary DNA,** or **cDNA,** and lacks the introns that suppress transcription.

Instead of using a bacterium to clone DNA fragments, some fragments can be copied millions of times by using DNA polymerase directly. This method, called **polymerase chain reaction,** or **PCR,** uses synthetic primers that initiate replication at specific nucleotide sequences.

Sample Questions and Answers

Multiple-Choice Questions

Directions: Each of the following questions or statements is followed by five possible answers or sentence completions. Choose the one best answer or sentence completion.

1. The two strands of a DNA molecule are connected by

   A. hydrogen bonds between the codons and anticodons

   B. hydrogen bonds between the bases of one strand and the bases of the second strand

   C. hydrogen bonds between deoxyribose sugar molecules of one strand and deoxyribose molecules of the second strand

   D. covalent bonds between phosphate groups

   E. covalent bonds between the nitrogen bases

2. All of the following combinations of nucleotides are examples of normal base-pairing EXCEPT:

   A. an adenine DNA nucleotide to a thymine DNA nucleotide

   B. a guanine DNA nucleotide to a cytosine DNA nucleotide

   C. a thymine RNA nucleotide to an adenine DNA nucleotide

   D. a cytosine RNA nucleotide to a guanine DNA nucleotide

   E. a uracil RNA nucleotide to a thymine DNA nucleotide

3. Which of the following is true?

   A. A messenger RNA molecule has the form of a double helix.

   B. Ribosomes contain RNA nucleotides and amino acids.

   C. The uracil nucleotide consists of the uracil nitrogen base, a deoxyribose sugar, and a phosphate group.

   D. When tRNA attaches to mRNA during translation, cytosine nucleotides base-pair with guanine nucleotides, and adenine nucleotides base-pair with thymine nucleotides.

   E. In eukaryotes, DNA is manufactured in the nucleus and RNA is manufactured in the cytoplasm

4. All of the following enzymes are involved in DNA replication EXCEPT:

   A. helicase

   B. DNA ligase

   C. DNA polymerases

   D. RNA polymerases

   E. primase

5. ATP, the common energy-carrying molecule, most resembles the

   A. adenine DNA nucleotide

   B. adenine RNA nucleotide

   C. adenine DNA nucleotide with two extra phosphates

   D. adenine RNA nucleotide with two extra phosphates

   E. adenine nitrogen base

6. The end products of translation are

   A. polypeptides

   B. amino acids

   C. lipids

   D. RNA

   E. DNA

7. Which of the following contains a code for a protein?

   A. DNA polymerase

   B. RNA polymerase

   C. rRNA

   D. tRNA

   E. mRNA

8. Which of the following would most likely cause a mutation with the greatest deleterious effect?

   A. An insertion of a nucleotide triplet into a DNA strand that codes for a mRNA

   B. A deletion of a nucleotide triplet from a DNA strand that codes for a mRNA

   C. A single substitution of a nucleotide in a DNA strand that, when transcribed, results in a change in the nucleotide occupying the third codon position in a mRNA

   D. A single substitution of a nucleotide in a DNA strand that, when transcribed, results in a change in the nucleotide occupying the first codon position in a mRNA

   E. A single addition of a nucleotide in a DNA strand that codes for a mRNA

Questions 9–15

Questions 9–15 refer to the following diagram of DNA and RNA segments. Boxes represent nucleotides. The letters A, G, and C refer to the names of the nucleotides that occupy a particular position.

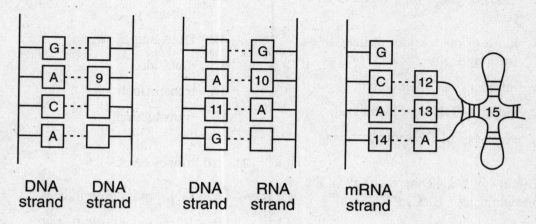

Use the following key for the next six questions. Each answer in the key may be used once, more than once, or not at all.

A.   Adenine nucleotide

B.   Cytosine nucleotide

C.   Guanine nucleotide

D.   Thymine nucleotide

E.   Uracil nucleotide

9. The nucleotide that would occupy box 9 would be the

10. The nucleotide that would occupy box 10 would be the

11. The nucleotide that would occupy box 11 would be the

12. The nucleotide that would occupy box 12 would be the

13. The nucleotide that would occupy box 13 would be the

14. The nucleotide that would occupy box 14 would be the

15. The segment identified by 15 is

A.   tRNA

B.   rRNA

C.   mRNA

D.   DNA

E.   ATP

16. The DNA of an elephant and the DNA of a cherry tree will probably differ in all of the following respects EXCEPT the

    A. kinds of genes for which the DNA codes

    B. kinds of nucleotides utilized in forming DNA

    C. number of DNA molecules

    D. length of DNA molecules

    E. sequence of DNA nucleotides

17. Protein synthesis consists of all of the following steps EXCEPT:

    A. replication

    B. transcription

    C. translation

    D. elongation

    E. initiation

18. The genetic instructions for forming a polypeptide chain are carried to the ribosome by the

    A. tRNA

    B. rRNA

    C. mRNA

    D. ATP

    E. DNA

19. In bacteria, a small circle of DNA found outside the main chromosome is called a

    A. plasmid

    B. cDNA

    C. RFLP

    D. PCR

    E. genetic fingerprint

20. Genetic recombination can occur in bacteria by all of the following methods EXCEPT:

    A. transfer of DNA between bacteria through pili

    B. DNA amplification

    C. mutation

    D. transformation

    E. transduction

21. All viruses consist of

    A. DNA and a protein coat

    B. RNA and a protein coat

    C. a nucleic acid and a protein coat

    D. a nucleic acid and a phospholipid bilayer membrane

    E. proteins and polysaccharides

22. A mRNA actively being translated in the cytoplasm would have all of the following EXCEPT:

    A. a poly-A tail

    B. a 5' cap

    C. exons

    D. introns

    E. RNA nucleotides

23. The *lac* operon in *E. coli* is involved in

    A. regulating the expression of a gene

    B. regulating the translation of mRNA

    C. controlling the formation of ribosomes

    D. controlling DNA replication

    E. preventing the transfer of the F plasmid

Answers to Multiple-Choice Questions

1. **B.** Weak hydrogen bonds form between bases of the two strands. In particular, a pyrimidine (a base with one nitrogen ring) in one strand bonds to a purine (a base with two nitrogen rings) in the second strand.

2. **C.** Thymine is not used as a base in any RNA nucleotide. Instead, RNA uses the uracil base, which base-pairs with the adenine DNA nucleotide during transcription.

3. **B.** RNA ribosome is a complex of rRNA molecules (RNA nucleotides) and proteins (amino acids). The remaining choices are incorrect because a messenger RNA molecule is single stranded (not a double helix), the uracil nucleotide contains a ribose sugar (not a deoxyribose sugar), adenine nucleotides base-pair with uracil nucleotides, and both DNA and RNA are produced in the nucleus.

4. **D.** RNA polymerases are involved in the transcription of DNA into RNA, not the replication of DNA.

5. **D.** Since ATP contains the adenine nitrogen base, the sugar ribose (not deoxyribose), and three phosphate groups, it is equivalent to the adenine RNA nucleotide with two extra phosphate groups. In contrast, an adenine DNA nucleotide with two extra phosphates contains a deoxyribose sugar and would be written as dATP.

6. **A.** Translation is the process in which ribosomes conduct the matching of tRNA with mRNA, producing an amino acid chain, or polypeptide.

7. **E.** The mRNA is a sequence of nucleotides. Each triplet of nucleotides codes for a particular amino acid. The sequence of triplets on the mRNA corresponds to the sequence of amino acids in an entire polypeptide, or protein.

8. **E.** An addition of a nucleotide in a DNA strand that codes for mRNA produces a frameshift mutation. As a result, the first nucleotide in every codon will become the second, the second nucleotide will become the third, and the third nucleotide will become the first nucleotide of the next codon. Such an arrangement is likely to change many of the amino acids in the sequence (depending upon where in the sequence the frameshift begins) and thus considerably affect the final sequence of the polypeptide. Answer **C** may have no effect at all because a change in the third position of a codon will often code for the same amino acid. (This results from the "wobble" of the third position of the tRNA anticodon.) Answers **A** and **B** will result in an additional amino acid and a missing amino acid, respectively, while answer **D** will change one amino acid to a different amino acid. These changes may change the effectiveness of the polypeptide, but not as severely as changing many amino acids, as would occur in answer **E**. The genetic disease sickle-cell anemia is caused by the replacement of one amino acid by another in two chains of the hemoglobin protein, severely reducing the effectiveness of hemoglobin in carrying oxygen. However, a frameshift in the mRNA coding for hemoglobin would certainly make it entirely ineffective.

9. **D.** In a DNA double helix, thymine base-pairs with adenine.

10. **E.** During transcription of DNA, the uracil RNA nucleotide base-pairs with the adenine DNA nucleotide.

11. **D.** During transcription of DNA, the adenine RNA nucleotide base-pairs with the thymine DNA nucleotide.

12. **C.** Guanine base-pairs with cytosine.

13. **E.** When base-pairing occurs between the anticodon nucleotides of the tRNA and the codon nucleotides of the mRNA, a uracil nucleotide base-pairs with an adenine nucleotide.

14. **E.** This is the same base-pair as in question 13.

15. **A.** The process illustrated here is translation. In particular, the anticodon of a tRNA is shown base-pairing with the codon of a mRNA.

16. **B.** The DNA of all cells uses the same DNA nucleotides—adenine, cytosine, guanine, and thymine nucleotides. On the other hand, the DNA of two unrelated species is likely to differ considerably in the genes produced as well as in the number of DNA molecules (that is, the number of chromosomes), the DNA lengths, and the DNA nucleotide sequences.

17. **A.** Replication is the process of copying DNA. Protein synthesis involves transcription and translation. Translation begins with initiation, continues with elongation, and ends with termination.

18. **C.** The genetic instructions originate on the DNA and are carried to the cytoplasm by the mRNA. The rRNA and tRNA operate together to translate the code on the mRNA into a polypeptide.

19. **A.** Plasmids are small circular DNA molecules that a bacterium contains in addition to their primary chromosome.

20. **B.** DNA amplification refers to a process, such as PCR, that generates multiple copies of DNA. DNA amplification can easily be confused with another process, gene amplification. In gene amplification, an organism produces an enormous number of rRNAs that enables an accelerated burst of protein synthesis. Gene amplification has been observed in unfertilized eggs in preparation for fertilization. Answer **A** is a description of conjugation, which, together with mutation, transformation, and transduction, is a mechanism that can introduce genetic variation into the genome of bacteria.

21. **C.** Viruses consist of a nucleic acid (DNA or RNA) surrounded by a protein coat. Some viruses contain an envelope made from lipids or glycoproteins obtained from the membranes of their hosts but that do not have the phospholipid bilayer membrane typical of cells.

22. **D.** Introns are intervening sequences in the mRNA that are cleaved from the mRNA by snRNPs before export to the cytoplasm and subsequent translation.

23. **A.** Operons are DNA segments that include a regulatory gene, a promoter region, an operator region, and a series of structural genes. The four parts work collectively to control transcription, which results in a regulation of gene expression.

Free-Response Questions

Free-response questions on the AP exam may require you to provide information from a narrow area of biology, or they may consist of parts that require you to assemble information from diverse areas of biology. The questions that follow are typical of either an entire AP exam question or merely that part of a question that is related to this section.

Directions: Answer the questions below as completely and as thoroughly as possible. Answer the question in essay form (NOT outline form), using complete sentences. You may use diagrams to supplement your answers, but a diagram alone without appropriate discussion is inadequate.

1. Describe the biochemical processes involved in transforming the information stored in a gene into the expression of a physical trait.

2. Contrast the ways in which bacteria and viruses cause disease.

3. Describe how gene regulation occurs in bacterial cells.

Some Typical Answers to Free-Response Questions

Question 1

Genes are segments of the DNA that contain instructions for producing a specific polypeptide. Many polypeptides are enzymes which regulate cellular reactions which, in turn, produce chemical end products that appear as traits. For example, white and black hair color in mice may be traits that are controlled by a single gene. One form of the gene may code for an enzyme that directs the production of a pigment. When the gene is present, the pigment is produced and hair color is black. When an alternative gene (an allele) is present which lacks the information for producing the enzyme for pigmentation, the hair color is white.

The process by which information is transferred from gene to enzyme is called protein synthesis. Protein synthesis consists of two parts, transcription and translation.

Transcription describes the process by which RNA is synthesized from DNA. RNA polymerase directs RNA nucleotides to base-pair with the DNA fragment that represents the gene. If a fragment of DNA contained the nucleotide sequence adenine, cytosine, guanine, and thymine, the RNA nucleotides that would base-pair with it are uracil, guanine, cytosine, and adenine, respectively.

Three kinds of RNA are made—rRNA, tRNA, and mRNA. The mRNA contains the code for the polypeptide. After the removal of noncoding intervening sequences, called introns, the mRNA moves to the cytoplasm. In the cytoplasm, ribosomes, consisting of rRNA and proteins, attach to the mRNA. There are three binding sites in the ribosome—one for the mRNA and two for tRNA.

There are various kinds of tRNA molecules. Each kind is specific for a particular amino acid which attaches to one end of the cloverleaf-shaped tRNA. Each tRNA has a special region of three nucleotides, called an anticodon.

In the process of translation, ribosomes direct the pairing of the anticodons of tRNAs with appropriate triplet regions of the mRNA, called codons. Each mRNA codon specifies a particular amino acid. The genetic code describes which amino acid is indicated by each of the 64 different mRNA codons. Some codons indicate a "stop" code. Another codon indicates methionine, the "start" amino acid.

During translation, the ribosome provides binding sites to incoming tRNAs. Each tRNA brings the appropriate amino acid as dictated by the codon sequence on the mRNA. As each new tRNA arrives, the growing polypeptide chain that is attached to the previous tRNA is transferred to the new tRNA. The old tRNA is released, the ribosome moves over one binding site, and the process repeats until the stop codon is encountered. At this point the ribosome separates into two subunits, and the polypeptide is released.

Once released, the amino acids in the polypeptide may interact with one another giving the polypeptide secondary and tertiary protein structures. In its final form, the polypeptide can enzymatically regulate a reaction that will produce some end product, or trait.

In the limited time you have available to answer this essay question, your goal should not be to discuss a single facet of protein synthesis in extreme detail. Rather, you should try to discuss every step in the entire process, pursuing detail only when you have available time. When your essay is evaluated, points are given for each step in the process. There is a maximum number of points given for each step, so pursuing detail in one step does not improve your score. Providing a few pieces of information for every part optimizes your time and maximizes your score. For example, you would not improve your score by discussing, in detail, the structure of an mRNA (such as the poly-A tail or 5' cap). However, if you omit an explanation of the genetic code, you would probably lose at least two points out of a maximum of ten.

Question 2

Viruses cause disease by destroying cells. Viruses consist of a nucleic acid core (either DNA or RNA) and a protein coat. In the lytic cycle of reproduction, a virus enters a cell and uses the metabolic machinery and raw materials of the cell to manufacture more viral DNA and viral protein coats. The viral DNA and protein assemble into hundreds of new viruses which burst from the cell, killing the cell in the process. In the lysogenic cycle, the virus may temporarily remain dormant as part of the host's genome, to become active only when exposed to radiation or other environmental disturbance. When activated, the viral DNA begins the lytic cycle.

Some viruses are RNA retroviruses. These viruses produce the enzyme reverse transcriptase to first manufacture DNA, which in turn, enters a lytic or lysogenic cycle.

Bacteria, in contrast, do not usually cause disease by direct destruction of host cells. Rather, most bacteria cause disease by producing toxins, usually waste products of their normal metabolism. When the toxins affect the normal metabolism of the host, disease results.

Some bacteria also cause disease by competing for the same resources as do the host cells. In other cases, the symptoms of a disease are the result of the host's response to invasion by foreign bodies. For example, in pneumonia, the mucus that accumulates in the lungs is produced by the lung cells in response to the presence of the bacteria.

Question 3

To answer this question, discuss operon theory. Describe the four parts of an operon and how the two kinds of operons operate.

Review

In general, **evolution** (or **organismic evolution**) is about changes in populations, species, or groups of species. More specifically, evolution occurs because populations vary by the frequency of heritable traits that appear from one generation to the next. These traits are represented by alleles for genes that modify morphology (form or structure), physiology, or behavior. Thus, evolution is changes in allele frequencies over time.

There are two areas of evolutionary study, as follows:

1. **Microevolution** describes the details of how populations of organisms change from generation to generation and how new species originate.

2. **Macroevolution** describes patterns of changes in groups of related species over broad periods of geologic time. The patterns determine **phylogeny,** the evolutionary relationships among species and groups of species.

One of the earliest advocates for evolutionary ideas was **Lamarck.** His theory included the following three important ideas:

1. **Use and disuse** described how body parts of organisms can develop with increased usage, while unused parts weaken. This idea was correct, as is commonly observed among athletes who train for competitions.

2. **Inheritance of acquired characteristics** described how body features acquired during the lifetime of an organism (such as muscle bulk) could be passed on to offspring. This, however, was incorrect. Only changes in the genetic material of cells can be passed on to offspring.

3. **Natural transformation of species** described how organisms produced offspring with changes, transforming each subsequent generation into a slightly different form toward some ultimate, higher order of complexity. Species did not become extinct nor did they split and change into two or more species. This idea was also incorrect.

Fifty years after Lamarck published his ideas, Darwin published The Origin of Species. Darwin's theory that **natural selection,** or "survival of the fittest," was the driving force of evolution is now called **Darwinism.** Later, genetics was incorporated into evolutionary thinking, creating a new, more comprehensive view of evolution, now variously called **neo-Darwinism,** the **synthetic theory of evolution,** or the **modern synthesis.**

There is abundant evidence that evolution occurs—that some species change over time, that other species diverge and become one or more new species, and that still other species become extinct. The question that evolutionists try to answer is *how* evolution occurs. For this they propose theories. Lamarck theorized, incorrectly, that evolution occurs through the inheritance of acquired characteristics. Darwin's theory was that evolution progresses through natural selection. The synthetic theory of evolution combines natural selection with the influence of genetics. These theories, together with others discussed below, propose mechanisms responsible for the evolutionary patterns unequivocally observed in nature.

Evidence for Evolution

Evidence for evolution is provided by the following five scientific disciplines:

1. **Paleontology** provides fossils that reveal the prehistoric existence of extinct species. As a result, changes in species and the formation of new species can be studied.

   - Fossil deposits are often found among sediment layers, where the deepest fossils represent the oldest specimens. For example, fossil oysters removed from successive layers of sediment show gradual changes in the size of the oyster shell alternating with rapid changes in shell size. Large, rapid changes produced new species.

2. **Biogeography** uses geography to describe the distribution of species. This information has revealed that unrelated species in different regions of the world look alike when found in similar environments. This provides strong evidence for the role of natural selection in evolution.

   - Rabbits did not exist in Australia until introduced by humans. A native Australian wallaby resembles a rabbit both in structure and habit. As similar as these two animals appear, they are not that closely related. The rabbit is a placental mammal, while the wallaby is a marsupial mammal. The fetus of a placental mammal develops in the female uterus, obtaining nourishment from the mother through the placenta. The fetus of a marsupial leaves the mother's uterus at an early stage of development and completes the remaining development while attached to a teat in the abdominal pouch. The great similarity of the rabbit and the wallaby is the result of natural selection.

3. **Embryology** reveals similar stages in development (**ontogeny**) among related species. The similarities help establish evolutionary relationships (**phylogeny**).

   - Gill slits and tails are found in fish, chicken, pig, and human embryos.

4. **Comparative anatomy** describes two kinds of structures that contribute to the identification of evolutionary relationships among species.

   - **Homologous structures** are body parts that resemble one another in different species because they have evolved from a common ancestor. Because anatomy may be modified for survival in specific environments, homologous structures may look different, but will resemble one another in pattern (how they are put together). The forelimbs of cats, bats, whales, and humans are homologous because they have all evolved from a common ancestral mammal.

   - **Analogous structures** are body parts that resemble one another in different species, not because they have evolved from a common ancestor, but because they evolved independently as adaptations to their environments. The fins and body shapes of sharks, penguins, and porpoises are analogous because they are adaptations to swimming.

5. **Molecular biology** examines the nucleotide and amino acid sequences of DNA and proteins from different species. Closely related species share higher percentages of sequences than species distantly related. In addition, all living things share the same genetic code. This data strongly favors evolution of different species through modification of ancestral genetic information.

   • More than 98% of the nucleotide sequences in humans and chimpanzees are identical.

Natural Selection

Natural selection is the differences in survival and reproduction among individuals in a population as a result of their interaction with the environment. In other words, some individuals possess alleles (genotypes) that generate traits (phenotypes) that enable them to cope more successfully in their environment than other individuals. The more successful individuals produce more offspring. Superior traits are **adaptations** to the environment and increase an individual's **fitness**, or relative ability to survive and leave offspring. When the environment favors a trait, that is, when a trait increases the survival of its bearer, selection is said to act for that trait. In contrast, selection is said to act against unfavorable traits. Favorable traits are adaptive, while unfavorable traits are maladaptive.

Darwin presented his theory for natural selection using the following arguments:

1. **Populations possess an enormous reproductive potential.** Darwin calculated that two elephants would produce a population of 19 million individuals after 750 years if all offspring survived to reproductive maturity and fostered their normal number of offspring.

2. **Population sizes remain stable.** Darwin observed that populations generally fluctuate around a constant size.

3. **Resources are limited.** Resources, such as food, water, or light, do not increase as populations grow larger.

4. **Individuals compete for survival.** Eventually, the needs of a growing population will exceed the available resources. As a result, individuals must compete for resources.

5. **There is variation among individuals in a population.** Most traits reveal considerable variety in their form. In humans, for example, skin, hair, and eye color occur as continuous variation from very dark to very light.

6. **Much variation is heritable.** Most traits are produced by the action of enzymes that are coded by DNA. DNA is the hereditary information that is passed from generation to generation. This contrasts with characteristics acquired during the life of an organism. The amputation of a limb, for example, is not heritable.

7. **Only the most fit individuals survive.** "Survival of the fittest" occurs because individuals with traits best adapted for survival in the environment are able to outcompete other individuals for resources.

8. **Evolution occurs as advantageous traits accumulate.** The best adapted individuals survive and leave offspring who inherit the traits of their parents. In turn, the best adapted of these offspring leave the most offspring. Over time, traits best adapted for survival in the environment and the alleles that generate them accumulate in the population.

Natural selection may act upon a population in a variety of ways. These are illustrated in Figure 8-1 and discussed below.

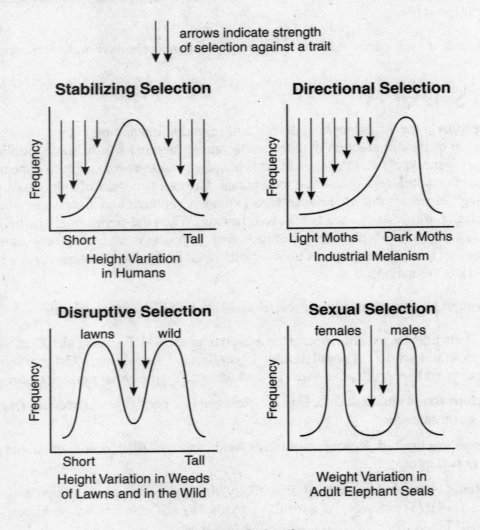

Kinds of Selection

Figure 8-1

1. **Stabilizing selection** eliminates individuals that have extreme or unusual traits. Under this condition, individuals with the most common trait are the best adapted, while individuals who differ from the common form are poorly adapted. As a result, stabilizing selection maintains the existing population frequencies of common traits while selecting against all other trait variations.

2. **Directional selection** favors traits that are at one extreme of a range of traits. Traits at the opposite extreme are selected against. If directional selection continues for many generations, favored traits become more and more extreme, leading to distinct changes in the allele frequencies of the population.

   - **Insecticide resistance** occurs as a result of directional selection. Because traits of individuals vary in a population, some individuals may possess some degree of resistance to the insecticide. These few individuals survive and produce offspring, most of whom will inherit the insecticide-resistance trait. After several generations of directional selection, the population will consist of nearly all insecticide-resistant individuals.

   - The **peppered moth** provides an example of directional selection of moth color from a light to a dark color. Before the industrial revolution, the light form of the moth was well camouflaged among the light-colored lichens that grew on tree barks around London. Since color variation is known to exist in other moths, the dark form of the moth probably existed but was never observed because it was so easily spotted and eaten by predator birds. With the advent of the industrial revolution, soot killed the pollution-sensitive lichens, exposing the dark tree bark below. As a result, the dark form of the moth became the better camouflaged of the two forms, and increased in frequency. A hundred years after the first dark moth was discovered in 1848, 90% of the moths were dark colored. Meanwhile, the light form of the moth continued to dominate populations in unpolluted areas outside London. The selection of dark-colored (melanic) varieties in various species of moths as a result of industrial pollution is called **industrial melanism.**

3. **Disruptive selection** (or **diversifying selection**) occurs when the environment favors extreme or unusual traits, while selecting against the common traits.

   - In the wild, many species of weeds occur in a range of heights, but tall forms predominate. Because of disruptive selection, however, only very short forms of these same weeds occur in lawns. On lawns, short weeds are selectively advantageous because they escape mowing. Weeds in the wild are primarily tall because tallness makes them better competitors for sunlight.

4. **Sexual selection** is the differential mating of males (sometimes females) in a population. Since females usually make a greater energy investment into producing offspring than males, they can increase their fitness by increasing the quality of their offspring by choosing superior males. Males, on the other hand, contribute little energy to the production of offspring and thus increase their fitness by maximizing the quantity of offspring produced. Thus, traits (physical qualities or behaviors) that allow males to increase their mating frequency have a selective advantage and, as a result, increase in frequency within the population. This leads to two kinds of sexual selection, as follows.

   - **Male competition** leads to contests of strength that award mating opportunities to the strongest males. The evolution of antlers, horns, and large stature or musculature are examples of this kind of sexual selection.

   - **Female choice** leads to traits or behaviors in males that are attractive to females. Colorful bird plumage (the peacock's tail is an extreme example) or elaborate mating behaviors are examples.

- Sexual selection often leads to **sexual dimorphism,** differences in the appearance of males and females. When this occurs, sexual selection is a form of disruptive selection.

5. **Artificial selection** is a form of directional selection carried out by humans when they sow seeds or breed animals that possess desirable traits. Since it is carried out by humans, it is not "natural" selection, but is given here for comparison.

  - The various breeds of dogs have originated as a result of humans breeding animals with specific desirable traits.

  - Brussels sprouts, broccoli, cabbage, and cauliflower have all originated from a single species of wild mustard after artificial selection of offspring possessing specific traits.

Sources of Variation

In order for natural selection to operate, there must be variation among individuals in a population. Indeed, considerable variation exists in nearly all populations. The variation arises from or is maintained by the following mechanisms:

1. **Mutations** provide the raw material for new variation. All other contributions to variation, listed below, occur by rearranging existing alleles into new combinations. Mutations, however, can invent alleles that never before existed in the gene pool.

2. **Sexual reproduction** creates individuals with new combinations of alleles. These rearrangements, or **genetic recombination,** originate from three events during the sexual reproductive process, as follows.

  - **Crossing over,** or exchanges of DNA between nonsister chromatids of homologous chromosomes, occurs during prophase I of meiosis.

  - **Independent assortment of homologues** during metaphase I creates daughter cells with random combinations of maternal and paternal chromosomes.

  - **Random joining of gametes** during fertilization contributes to the diversity of gene combinations in the zygote.

3. **Diploidy** is the presence of two copies of each chromosome in a cell. In the heterozygous condition (when two different alleles for a single gene locus are present), the recessive allele is hidden from natural selection. As a result, more variation is maintained in the gene pool.

4. **Outbreeding,** or mating with unrelated partners, increases the possibility of mixing different alleles and creating new allele combinations.

5. **Balanced polymorphism** is the maintenance of different phenotypes in a population. Often, a single phenotype provides the best adaptation, while other phenotypes are less advantageous. In these cases, the alleles for the advantageous trait increase in frequency,

while the remaining alleles decrease. However, examples of polymorphism (two or more different phenotypes) are observed in many populations. These polymorphisms can be maintained in the following ways:

- **Heterozygote advantage** occurs when the heterozygous condition bears a greater selective advantage than either homozygous condition. As a result, both alleles and all three phenotypes are maintained in the population by selection. For example, the alleles for normal and sickle-cell hemoglobins (*A* and *S*, respectively) produce three phenotypes, *AA*, *AS*, and *SS*. *AA* individuals are normal, while *SS* individuals suffer from sickle-cell anemia, because the sickle-cell allele produces hemoglobin with an impaired oxygen-carrying ability. Most *SS* individuals die before puberty. *AS* individuals are generally healthy, but their oxygen-carrying ability may be significantly reduced during strenuous exercise or exposure to low oxygen concentrations (such as at high altitudes). Despite fatal effects to homozygote *SS* individuals and reduced viability of heterozygote individuals, the frequency of the *AS* condition exceeds 14% in parts of Africa, an unusually high value for a deleterious phenotype. However, *AS* individuals have a selective advantage (in Africa) because the *AS* trait also provides resistance to malaria. When *AS* phenotypes are selected, both *A* and *S* alleles are preserved in the gene pool, and all three phenotypes are maintained.

- **Hybrid vigor** (or **heterosis**) describes the superior quality of offspring resulting from crosses between two different inbred strains of plants. The superior hybrid quality results from a reduction of loci with deleterious homozygous recessive conditions and an increase in loci with heterozygote advantage. For example, a hybrid of corn, developed by crossing two different corn strains that were highly inbred, is more resistant to disease and produces larger corn ears that either of the inbred strains.

- **Frequency-dependent selection** (or **minority advantage**) occurs when the least common phenotypes have a selective advantage. Common phenotypes are selected against. However, since rare phenotypes have a selective advantage, they soon increase in frequency and become common. Once they become common, they lose their selective advantage and are selected against. With this type of selection, then, phenotypes alternate between low and high frequencies, thus maintaining multiple phenotypes (polymorphism). For example, some predators form a "search image," or standard representation of their prey. By standardizing on the most common form of its prey, the predator optimizes its search effort. The prey that is rare, however, escapes predation.

Not all variation has selective value. Instead, much of the variation observed, especially at the molecular level in DNA and proteins, is **neutral variation.** For example, the differences in fingerprint patterns among humans represent neutral variation. In many cases, however, the environment to which the variation is exposed determines whether a variation is neutral or whether it has selective value.

Causes of Changes in Allele Frequencies

Natural selection was the mechanism that Darwin proposed for evolution. With the understanding of genetics, it became evident that factors other than natural selection can change allele frequencies and thus promote evolution. These factors, together with natural selection, are given here:

1. **Natural selection** is the increase or decrease in allele frequencies due to the impact of the environment.

2. **Mutations** introduce new alleles that may provide a selective advantage. In general, however, most mutations are **deleterious,** or harmful.

3. **Gene flow** describes the introduction or removal of alleles from the population when individuals leave (emigration) or enter (immigration) the population.

4. **Genetic drift** is a *random* increase or decrease of alleles. In other words, some alleles may increase or decrease for no other reason than by chance. When populations are small (usually less than 100 individuals) the effect of genetic drift can be very strong and can dramatically influence evolution.

   - An analogy of genetic drift can be made with the chances associated with flipping a coin. If a coin is flipped 100 times, the number of heads obtained would approach the expected probability of ½. However, if the coin is flipped only 5 times (analogous to a small population), one may obtain, by chance, all tails. Similarly, gene frequencies, especially in small populations, may change by chance.

   Two special kinds of genetic drift are commonly observed, as follows:

   - The **founder effect** occurs when allele frequencies in a group of migrating individuals are, by chance, not the same as that of their population of origin. For example, one of the founding members of the small group of Germans that began the Amish community in Pennsylvania possessed an allele for polydactylism (more than five fingers or toes on a limb). After 200 years of reproductive isolation, the number of cases of this trait among the 8,000 Amish exceed the number of cases occurring in the remaining world's population.

   - A **bottleneck** occurs when the population undergoes a dramatic decrease in size. Regardless of the cause of the bottleneck (natural catastrophe, predation, and disease, for example), the small population that results becomes severely vulnerable to genetic drift. Destructive geological or meteorological events such as floods, volcano eruptions, and ice ages have created bottlenecks for many populations of plants and animals.

5. **Nonrandom mating** occurs when individuals choose mates based upon their particular traits. For example, they may always choose mates with traits similar to their own or traits different from their own. Nonrandom mating also occurs when mates choose only nearby individuals. In all of these cases, mate selection is not random. The following two kinds of nonrandom mating are commonly observed.

   - **Inbreeding** occurs when individuals mate with relatives.

   - **Sexual selection** occurs when females choose males based upon their attractive appearance or behavior or their ability to defeat other males in contests.

Genetic Equilibrium

When the allele frequencies in a population remain constant from generation to generation, the population is said to be in **genetic equilibrium,** or **Hardy-Weinberg equilibrium.** At genetic equilibrium, there is no evolution. In order for equilibrium to occur, the factors that normally change gene frequencies do not occur. Thus, the following conditions hold:

1. **All traits are selectively neutral (no natural selection).**

2. **Mutations do not occur.**

3. **The population must be isolated from other populations (no gene flow).**

4. **The population is large (no genetic drift).**

5. **Mating is random.**

Genetic equilibrium is determined by evaluating the following values:

1. Allele frequencies for each allele (p, q)

2. Frequency of homozygotes (p^2, q^2)

3. Frequency of heterozygotes ($pq + qp = 2pq$)

Also, the following two equations hold:

1. $p + q = 1$ (all alleles sum to 100%)

2. $p^2 + 2pq + q^2 = 1$ (all individuals sum to 100%)

As an example, suppose a plant population consists of 84% plants with red flowers and 16% with white flowers. Assume the red allele (R) is dominant and the white allele (r) is recessive. Using the above notation and converting percentages to decimals:

$$q^2 = 0.16 = \text{white flowered plants } (rr \text{ trait})$$
$$p^2 + 2pq = 0.84 = \text{red flowered plants } (RR \text{ and } Rr \text{ trait})$$

To determine the allele frequency of the white flower allele, calculate q by finding the square root of q^2.

$$q = \sqrt{0.16} = 0.4$$

Since $p + q = 1$, p must equal 0.6.

You can also determine the frequency (or percentages) of individuals with the homozygous dominant and heterozygous condition.

$$2pq = (2)(0.6)(.4) = 0.48 \text{ or } 48\% = \text{heterozygotes}$$

$$p^2 = (0.6)(0.6) = 0.36 \text{ or } 36\% = \text{homozygotes dominant}$$

In most natural populations, the conditions of Hardy-Weinberg equilibrium are not obeyed. However, the Hardy-Weinberg calculations serve as a starting point that reveal how allele frequencies are changing, which equilibrium conditions are being violated, and what mechanisms are driving the evolution of a population.

Speciation

A **species** is usually defined as a group of individuals capable of interbreeding. **Speciation,** the formation of new species, occurs by the following processes, as illustrated in Figure 8-2.

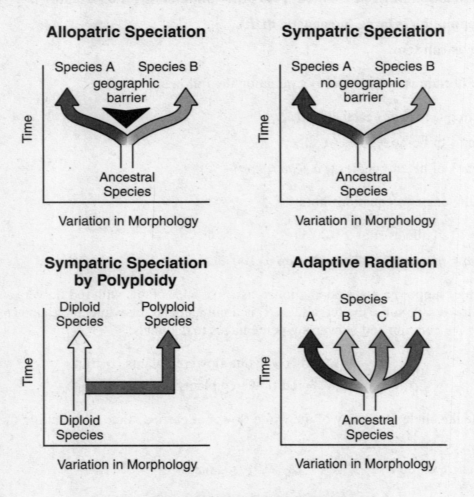

Processes of Speciation

Figure 8-2

1. **Allopatric speciation** begins when a population is divided by a geographic barrier so that interbreeding between the two resulting populations is prevented. Common barriers include mountain ranges or rivers, but any region that excludes vital resources, such as a region devoid of water, a burned area devoid of food, or an area covered with volcanic lava, can act as a barrier because individuals cannot survive its crossing. Once reproductively

isolated by the barrier, gene frequencies in the two populations can diverge due to natural selection (the environments may be slightly different), mutation, or genetic drift. If the gene pools sufficiently diverge, then interbreeding between the populations will not occur if the barrier is removed. As a result, new species have formed.

2. **Sympatric speciation** is the formation of new species without the presence of a geographic barrier. This may happen in several different ways, as follows:

   - **Balanced polymorphism** among subpopulations may lead to speciation. Suppose, for example, a population of insects possesses a polymorphism for color. Each color provides a camouflage to a different substrate, and if not camouflaged, the insect is eaten. Under these circumstances, only insects with the same color can associate and mate. Thus, similarly colored insects are reproductively isolated from other subpopulations, and their gene pools diverge as in allopatric speciation.

   - **Polyploidy** is the possession of more than the normal two sets of chromosomes found in diploid ($2n$) cells. Polyploidy often occurs in plants (and occasionally animals) where triploid ($3n$), tetraploid ($4n$), and higher ploidy chromosome numbers are found. Polyploidy occurs as a result of nondisjunction of all chromosomes during meiosis, producing two viable diploid gametes and two sterile gametes with no chromosomes. A tetraploid zygote can be established when a diploid sperm fertilizes a diploid egg. Since normal meiosis in the tetraploid individual will continue to produce diploid gametes, reproductive isolation with other individuals in the population (and thus speciation) occurs immediately in a single generation.

   - **Hybridization** occurs when two distinctly different forms of a species (or closely related species that are normally reproductively isolated) mate and produce progeny along a geographic boundary called a **hybrid zone.** In some cases, the genetic variation of the hybrids is greater than that of either parent and permits the population of hybrids to evolve adaptations to environmental conditions in the hybrid zone beyond the range of either parent. Exposed to different selection pressures, the hybrids eventually diverge from both parent populations.

3. **Adaptive radiation** is the relatively rapid evolution of many species from a single ancestor. It occurs when the ancestral species colonizes an area where diverse geographic or ecological conditions are available for colonization. Variants of the ancestral species diverge as populations specialize for each set of conditions.

   - The marsupials of Australia began with the colonization and subsequent adaptive radiation of a single ancestral species.

   - The fourteen species of Darwin's finches on the Galapagos Islands evolved from a single ancestral South American mainland species.

Maintaining Reproductive Isolation

If species are not physically separated by a geographic barrier, various mechanisms commonly exist to maintain reproductive isolation and prevent gene flow. These mechanisms may appear randomly (genetic drift) or may be the result of natural selection.

There are two categories of isolating mechanisms. The first category, **prezygotic isolating mechanisms,** consists of mechanisms that prevent fertilization.

1. **Habitat isolation** occurs when species do not encounter one another.

2. **Temporal isolation** occurs when species mate or flower during different seasons or at different times of the day.

3. **Behavioral isolation** occurs when a species does not recognize another species as a mating partner because it does not perform the correct courtship rituals, display the proper visual signals, sing the correct mating songs, or release the proper chemicals (scents, or pheromones).

4. **Mechanical isolation** occurs when male and female genitalia are structurally incompatible or when flower structures select for different pollinators.

5. **Gametic isolation** occurs when male gametes do not survive in the environment of the female gamete (such as in internal fertilization) or when female gametes do not recognize male gametes.

The second category, **postzygotic isolating mechanisms,** consists of mechanisms that prevent the formation of fertile progeny.

6. **Hybrid inviability** occurs when the zygote fails to develop properly and aborts, or dies before reaching reproductive maturity.

7. **Hybrid sterility** occurs when hybrids become functional adults, but are reproductively sterile (eggs or sperm are nonexistent or dysfunctional). The mule, a sterile offspring of a donkey and a horse, is a sterile hybrid.

8. **Hybrid breakdown** occurs when hybrids produce offspring that have reduced viability or fertility.

Patterns of Evolution

The evolution of species is often categorized into the following four patterns (Figure 8-3):

1. **Divergent evolution** describes two or more species that originate from a common ancestor. This may happen as a result of allopatric or sympatric speciation or by adaptive radiation.

2. **Convergent evolution** describes two unrelated species that share similar traits. The similarities arise, not because the species share a common ancestor, but because each species has independently adapted to similar ecological conditions or lifestyles. The traits that resemble one another are called **analogous** traits.

   - Sharks, porpoises, and penguins have torpedo-shaped bodies with peripheral fins. These traits arise as a result of adaptations to aquatic life and not because these animals inherited the traits from a recent, common ancestor.

   - The eyes of squids and vertebrates are physically and functionally similar. However, these animals do not share a recent common ancestor. That the eyes in these two groups of animals originate from different tissues during embryological development confirms that they have evolved independently.

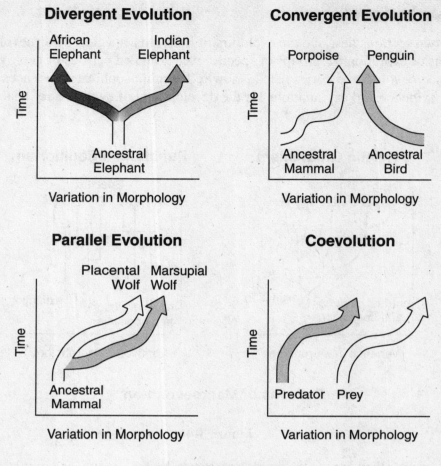

Patterns of Evolution

Figure 8-3

3. **Parallel evolution** describes two related species or two related lineages that have made similar evolutionary changes after their divergence from a common ancestor.

   - Species from two groups of mammals, the marsupial mammals and the placental mammals, have independently evolved similar adaptations when ancestors encountered comparable environments.

4. **Coevolution** is the tit-for-tat evolution of one species in response to new adaptations that appear in another species. Suppose a prey species gains an adaptation that allows it to escape its predator. Although most of the predators will fail to catch prey, some variants in the predator population will be successful. Selection favors these successful variants and subsequent evolution results in new adaptations in the predator species.

   - Coevolution occurs between predator and prey, plants and plant-eating insects, pollinators and flowering plants, pathogens and the immune systems of animals.

Macroevolution

The previous two sections describe the evolution of individual species. **Macroevolution** describes patterns of evolution for groups of species over extended periods of geologic time. The two distinct macroevolution theories listed below reflect philosophical differences in interpretations of fossil evidence and explanations for the development of evolutionary history (Figure 8-4).

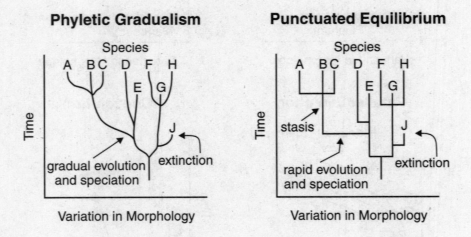

Patterns of Macroevolution

Figure 8-4

1. **Phyletic gradualism** argues that evolution occurs by the gradual accumulation of small changes. Individual speciation events or major changes in lineages occur over long periods of geologic time. Fossil evidence provides snapshots of the evolutionary process, revealing only major changes in groups of organisms. That intermediate stages of evolution are not represented by fossils merely testifies to the incompleteness of the available fossil record.

2. **Punctuated equilibrium** argues that evolutionary history consists of geologically long periods of stasis with little or no evolution, interrupted, or "punctuated," by geologically short periods of rapid evolution. The fossil history, then, should consist of fossils mostly from the extended periods of stasis with few, if any, fossils available from the short bursts of evolution. Thus, in this theory, the absence of fossils revealing intermediate stages of evolution is considered data that confirms rapid evolutionary events.

The Origin of Life

A topic related to evolution is the study of how life began, or **chemical evolution.** This kind of evolution describes the processes that are believed to have contributed to the formation of the first living things. The **heterotroph theory** for the origin of life proposes that the first cells were **heterotrophs,** organisms incapable of making their own food. The steps hypothesized to have led to the first primitive cell and the subsequent steps that led to more complex living cells are outlined below with supporting information.

1. **The earth and its atmosphere formed.**

   • The primordial atmosphere originated from outgassing of the molten interior of the planet (through volcanos) and consisted of CO, CO_2, H_2, N_2, H_2O, S, HCl (hydrochloric acid), and HCN (hydrogen cyanide), but little or no O_2.

2. **The primordial seas formed.**

   • As the earth cooled, gases condensed to produce primordial seas consisting of water and minerals.

3. **Complex molecules were synthesized.**

   • Energy catalyzed the formation of organic molecules from inorganic molecules. An organic "soup" formed.

   • Energy was provided mostly by ultraviolet light (UV), but also lightning, radioactivity, and heat.

   • Complex molecules included acetic acid, formaldehyde, and amino acids. These kinds of molecules would later serve as monomers, or unit building blocks, for the synthesis of polymers.

   • **A. I. Oparin** and **J. B. S. Haldane** independently theorized that simple molecules were able to form only because oxygen was absent. As a very reactive molecule, oxygen, had it been present, would have prevented the formation of organic molecules by supplanting most reactants in chemical reactions.

   • **Stanley Miller** tested the theories of Oparin and Haldane by simulating an experiment under primordial conditions. He applied electric sparks to simple gases (but no oxygen) connected to a flask of heated water. After one week, the water contained various organic molecules including amino acids.

4. **Polymers and self-replicating molecules were synthesized.**

   • Monomers combined to form polymers. Some of these reactions may have occurred by dehydration condensation, in which polymers formed from monomers by the removal of water molecules.

   • **Proteinoids** are abiotically produced polypeptides. They can be experimentally produced by allowing amino acids to dehydrate on hot, dry substrates.

5. **Organic molecules were concentrated and isolated into protobionts.**

   • **Protobionts** were the precursors of cells. They were able to carry out chemical reactions enclosed within a border across which materials can be exchanged, but were unable to reproduce. Borders formed in the same manner as hydrophobic molecules aggregate to form membranes (as phospholipids form plasma membranes).

   • **Microspheres** and **coacervates** are experimentally (and abiotically) produced protobionts that have some selectively permeable qualities.

6. **Primitive heterotrophic prokaryotes formed.**

   - **Heterotrophs** are living organisms that obtain energy by consuming organic substances. Pathogenic bacteria, for example, are heterotrophic prokaryotes.

   - The organic "soup" was a source of organic material for heterotrophic cells. As these cells reproduced, competition for organic material increased. Natural selection would favor those heterotrophs most successful at obtaining food.

7. **Primitive autotrophic prokaryotes were formed.**

   - As a result of mutation, a heterotroph gained the ability to produce its own food. As an **autotroph,** this cell would be highly successful.

   - Autotrophs manufacture their own organic compounds using light energy or energy from inorganic substances. Cyanobacteria (photosynthetic bacteria), for example, are autotrophic prokaryotes that obtain energy and manufacture organic compounds by photosynthesis.

8. **Oxygen and the ozone layer formed and abiotic chemical evolution ended.**

   - As a by-product of the photosynthetic activity of autotrophs, oxygen was released and accumulated in the atmosphere. The interaction of UV light and oxygen produced the ozone layer.

   - As a result of the formation of the ozone layer, incoming UV light was absorbed, preventing it from reaching the surface of the earth. Thus, the major source of energy for the abiotic synthesis of organic molecules and primitive cells was terminated.

9. **Eukaryotes formed (endosymbiotic theory).**

   - According to **endosymbiotic theory,** eukaryotic cells originated from a mutually beneficial association (symbiosis) among various kinds of prokaryotes. Specifically, mitochondria, chloroplasts, and other organelles established residence inside another prokaryote, producing a eukaryote.

There is considerable evidence for the endosymbiotic theory. A sample of that evidence follows:

1. Mitochondria and chloroplasts possess their own DNA. The DNA is circular and "naked" (without proteins) as is the DNA of bacteria and cyanobacteria.

2. Ribosomes of mitochondria and chloroplasts resemble those of bacteria and cyanobacteria, with respect to size and nucleotide sequence.

3. Mitochondria and chloroplasts reproduce independently of their eukaryotic host cell by a process similar to the binary fission of bacteria.

4. The thylakoid membranes of chloroplasts resemble the photosynthetic membranes of cyanobacteria.

Sample Questions and Answers

Multiple-Choice Questions

Directions: Each of the following questions or statements is followed by five possible answers or sentence completions. Choose the one best answer or sentence completion.

1. Which of the following was most responsible for ending chemical evolution?

   A. Natural selection

   B. Heterotrophic prokaryotes

   C. Photosynthesis

   D. Viruses

   E. The absence of oxygen in the atmosphere

2. Which of the following generates the formation of adaptations?

   A. Genetic drift

   B. Mutations

   C. Gene flow

   D. Sexual reproduction

   E. Natural selection

3. The B blood-type allele probably originated in Asia and subsequently spread to Europe and other regions of the world. This is an example of

   A. artificial selection

   B. natural selection

   C. genetic drift

   D. gene flow

   E. sexual reproduction

4. The appearance of a new mutation is

   A. a random event

   B. the result of natural selection

   C. the result of artificial selection

   D. the result of sexual reproduction

   E. usually a beneficial event

5. Which of the following is an example of sexual selection?

   A. Dark-colored peppered moths in London at the beginning of the industrial revolution

   B. The mane of a lion

   C. Insecticide resistance in insects

   D. Darwin's finches in the Galapagos Islands

   E. The ability of certain insects to avoid harm when consuming toxic plants.

6. A population consists of 9% white sheep and 91% black sheep. What is the frequency of the black-wool allele if the black-wool allele is dominant and the white-wool allele is recessive?

A. 0.09

B. 0.3

C. 0.42

D. 0.49

E. 0.7

7. After test-cross experiments, it was determined that the frequencies of homozygous dominant, heterozygous, and homozygous recessive individuals for a particular trait were 32%, 64%, and 4% respectively. The dominant and recessive allele frequencies

A. are 0.2 and 0.8, respectively

B. are 0.32 and 0.68, respectively

C. are 0.36 and 0.64, respectively

D. are $\sqrt{0.32}$ and $1 - \sqrt{0.32}$, respectively

E. cannot be determined because the population is not in Hardy-Weinberg equilibrium

8. *Cepaea nemoralis* is a land snail. Individual snails have shells with zero to five dark bands on a yellow, pink, or dark brown background. The various shell patterns could have occurred by all of the following EXCEPT:

A. convergent evolution

B. natural selection

C. a balanced polymorphism

D. chance

E. mutations

9. All of the following are homologous structures EXCEPT:

A. a bat wing

B. a bird wing

C. a butterfly wing

D. a human arm

E. a penguin flipper

Questions 10–14

Use the following key for the next five questions. Each answer in the key may be used once, more than once, or not at all.

A. Bottleneck

B. Adaptive radiation

C. Directional selection

D. Sexual reproduction

E. Sympatric speciation

10. Because of human predation, the sizes of and genetic variation in populations of most whale species are declining.

11. Progeny possess new combinations of alleles every generation.

12. Many strains of *Mycobacterium tuberculosis,* the bacterium that causes tuberculosis, are resistant to standard drug therapy.

13. There are more than 750,000 named species of insects inhabiting a wide range of habitats.

14. A recently introduced species of seed-eating birds occupies an island where small and large seeds are available. Beak size in the bird population varies from small to large, allowing some birds to be more successful at eating small seeds, while others are more successful at eating large seeds. Birds with intermediate beak size must exert additional effort to eat seeds.

15. All of the following are examples of evolution EXCEPT:

A. mutations in an individual

B. changes in an allele frequency in a population

C. changes in an allele frequency in a species

D. divergence of a species into two species

E. adaptive radiation

Answers to Multiple-Choice Questions

1. **C.** Chemical evolution was able to occur because highly reactive oxygen was not present. The production of oxygen from photosynthesis ended abiotic synthesis because oxygen interfered with the abiotic chemical reactions. Also, the oxygen interacted with UV light to form the ozone layer, which absorbed most incoming UV, the major energy source for abiotic reactions.

2. **E.** Only natural selection generates adaptations. Changes in gene frequencies from other factors may contribute to increases in fitness but not because they produce adaptations. For example, mutations may introduce a new allele, but the allele will lead to an adaptation only if it increases in the population as a result of natural selection.

3. **D.** Gene flow is the increase in allele frequencies due to transfer from other populations.

4. **A.** Mutations occur randomly and are usually harmful. Whether or not the mutation increases or decreases in frequency in the population is the result of natural selection, genetic drift, gene flow, or nonrandom mating.

5. **B.** Only male lions have a mane. Differences in appearance between males and females (sexual dimorphisms) not directly required for reproduction are usually the result of sexual selection.

6. **E.** The information given in the question is summarized as follows:

$$q^2 = 0.09 = \text{white sheep (homozygous recessives)}$$

$$p^2 + 2pq = 0.91 = \text{black sheep (homozygous dominants and heterozygotes)}$$

Then, calculate

$$q = 0.3$$

$$p = 1 - q = 0.7 \text{ (since } p + q = 1\text{)}$$

7. **E.** This population is not in Hardy-Weinberg equilibrium. The values given for p^2, $2pq$, and q^2 correctly total 1. Calculating the value of q from q^2 gives $q = \sqrt{0.04}$ or 0.2, and the value of p from p^2 gives $p = \sqrt{0.32}$, which is approximately 0.57. The sum of these *calculated* values for p and q gives 0.77. Since $p + q$ *must* equal 1 (there are only two alleles and their frequencies must total 1), the population cannot be in equilibrium. This can be caused by the nonrandom nature of a test cross, as a population in equilibrium must be mating randomly.

8. **A.** The maintenance of various patterned shells in the snail population is an example of a balanced polymorphism. It may be (and there is good evidence that it is) maintained by natural selection, genetic drift (chance), mutations and other factors as well. Convergent evolution does not apply here because it refers to two or more species not of common ancestral origin that share similar traits. This question deals with phenotypic variation within a single species.

9. **C.** Structures in different species are homologous because they have been inherited from a common ancestor. Insects (butterflies) are not closely related to the other listed animals. Mammals (bats and humans) and birds (birds and penguins) are related by descent from an early reptile.

10. **A.** A bottleneck occurs when population size precipitously falls. Surviving individuals may possess only a limited amount of the total genetic variation present previously. In addition, the effect of genetic drift intensifies when populations are small.

11. **D.** A consequence of sexual reproduction is that crossing over during prophase I of meiosis, mixing of maternal and paternal chromosomes, and random union of gametes produce new combinations of alleles in every generation. Except for identical twins, no two individuals will ever have exactly the same genetic makeup.

12. **C.** As a result of genetic variation, there will be some bacteria that are resistant to antibiotics. Extensive use of antibiotics kills bacteria that are susceptible, but resistant variants survive and reproduce. After many generations of (directional) selection for resistant bacteria, most surviving bacteria are antibiotic resistant.

13. **B.** The variety of insects and their range of habitat and ecological influence is an example of adaptive radiation on a grand scale.

14. **E.** Because there are only small and large seeds, there is disruptive selection for birds with small and large beaks. Given sufficient time, two species will emerge where only one existed before. Since no geographic barrier is present, speciation is sympatric.

15. **A.** Evolution does not occur for an individual. Only groups of individuals (of the same species) evolve.

Free-Response Questions

Free-response questions on the AP exam may require you to provide information from a narrow area of biology, or they may consist of parts that require you to assemble information from diverse areas of biology. The questions that follow are typical of either an entire AP exam question or merely that part of a question that is related to this section.

Directions: Answer the questions below as completely and as thoroughly as possible. Answer the question in essay form (NOT outline form), using complete sentences. You may use diagrams to supplement your answers, but a diagram alone without appropriate discussion is inadequate.

1. Explain how evolution occurs.

2. Describe the process of speciation. Include a discussion of mechanisms that maintain reproductive isolation.

3. Discuss each of the following as they relate to speciation. Give examples.

   (a.) Geographic barriers

   (b.) Adaptive radiation

   (c.) Polyploidy

   (d.) Sexual selection

4. Discuss Darwin's theory of natural selection.

5. Discuss how each of the following influenced the origin of living organisms.

   (a.) Primordial atmosphere

   (b.) Photosynthesis

   (c.) Oxygen and the ozone layer

   (d.) Endosymbiotic theory

Some Typical Answers to Free-Response Questions

Question 1

Evolution occurs when allele frequencies change from generation to generation in a group of interbreeding organisms. There are five mechanisms that result in changes in allele frequency. Natural selection, proposed by Darwin, is the differential survival and reproduction of individuals as a result of their interaction with the environment. As Darwin stated, natural selection is the survival of the fittest. Since there is considerable variation in traits among individuals in a population, individuals who possess advantageous traits survive and leave more offspring. Evolution occurs because alleles will increase in frequencies if they produce traits that improve an individual's survival in the environment.

Genetic drift is another mechanism that causes allele frequencies to change. Genetic drift describes random changes in allele frequencies. This is especially influential in evolution when populations are small. When a population bottleneck occurs as a result of some catastrophic event (flood, epidemic, ice age), the small surviving population may change due to genetic drift. A founder population may also be subject to the effects of genetic drift. For example, if a small group of individuals becomes separated from the mother population (perhaps by emigration), the allele frequencies of the founder group may differ from the mother population by chance.

Allele frequencies may also change if emigrating or immigrating individuals bring new alleles or change the proportion of alleles in the population. Transferring alleles between populations in this manner is called gene flow.

Mutations may also add alleles to the gene pool. Whereas most variation originates from new combinations of existing alleles, only mutations introduce new alleles.

Nonrandom mating may also contribute to changes in allele frequencies. Nonrandom mating increases the frequencies of alleles for traits that occur among the mating individuals. For example, in sexual selection, allele frequencies increase if they produce traits that give individuals a better chance of obtaining a mate. Traits that help males win contests or traits that make them more attractive to females have a selective advantage. Inbreeding is another form of nonrandom mating.

Microevolution, discussed above, describes changes in populations or individual species. In contrast, macroevolution describes changes in groups of species over extended periods of geologic time. Two patterns are observed. In phyletic gradualism, evolution occurs gradually through accumulations of successive microevolutionary events. In contrast, punctuated equilibrium describes bursts of rapid evolution that interrupt long periods of no evolutionary change (stasis). In phyletic gradualism, the lack of intermediate fossil forms suggests an incomplete fossil record. For punctuated equilibrium, the lack of intermediate fossil forms is evidence for stasis.

This question is so broad that nearly everything in this chapter would be appropriate material for the answer. The answer given, however, answers the basic question of how evolution occurs at the population level (microevolution), and how it occurs at higher group levels (macroevolution). Time permitting, examples for each of the microevolutionary mechanisms should be given. Also, selection and speciation could be discussed in more detail.

Question 2

Question 2 is more specific than question 1. For question 2, you would describe (and give examples for) the various mechanisms through which speciation occurs (allopatric and sympatric speciation and adaptive radiation) and the means by which closely related species maintain reproductive isolation. A detailed answer would include a description of the different kinds of selection and other causes of changes in gene frequencies that could cause populations to diverge.

Question 3

Speciation is the formation of one or more new species from an existing species.

(a.) Allopatric speciation occurs when a geographic barrier, such as a river or mountain range, divides the existing population into two populations. Separated in this manner, the two populations are reproductively isolated and gene flow does not occur. As a result, changes in allele frequencies in one population may not occur in the other population. If the environmental conditions vary between the two populations, natural selection may favor different traits in the two populations. Genetic drift may also cause differences in allele frequencies, either because of the founder effect, or because either (or both) new populations are small. In these two cases, allele frequencies are strongly influenced by chance (genetic drift). Also, mutations in one population may introduce new alleles absent in the other population, thus providing new variation upon which natural selection can act.

(b.) Adaptive radiation occurs when a population is introduced to an area where many geographic or ecological conditions are available. When the introduced species enters the various new habitats, selection pressures will vary with habitat. For example, in colder habitats, larger animals may be favored (for insulation). In a habitat with many fruit-producing plants, fruit-eating abilities among the animals may be favored. Adaptive radiation occurs among plants as well. For example, in a rain forest habitat, individual plants that have adaptations to wet conditions are favored, whereas in dry regions, plants with water conservation adaptations (thick cuticles, perhaps) are favored.

Darwin's finches are a model for adaptive radiation. These 14 species of finches inhabit the Galapagos Islands, a group of isolated islands off the coast of South America. Descendants from a single mainland species spread to the various islands where different ecological regions were available for colonization. The bodies of water between the islands provided a barrier that maintained isolation and led to geographic speciation. The finches on each island (and sometimes in different regions of the same island) survived if they possessed advantageous alleles that allowed them to outcompete other individuals. The ability to obtain food, an important characteristic for survival, led to specialization in sizes and shapes of beaks. As a result of natural selection, the 14 species are each adapted for obtaining different kinds of food (seeds, fruit, nectar, insects) and different sizes of food.

(c.) Polyploidy is the possession of one or more extra sets of chromosomes. As a result of nondisjunction during meiosis, gametes (sperm and eggs) have double the normal number of chromosomes. When a sperm produced in this manner fertilizes a similarly produced egg, the resulting diploid zygote also contains twice the normal number of chromosomes. The result is a polyploid individual. When this new individual undergoes a normal meiosis, gametes will contain twice the number of chromosomes (like its parent) and will be able to fertilize only similarly produced gametes. Thus, the polyploid individual and its progeny are reproductively isolated from the original population. The result is a speciation event occurring in a single generation. Polyploidy is common among plants and rare in animals.

(d.) Sexual selection is the differential mating of males within a species. Only males that win contests with other males or possess features that are attractive to females are able to mate. As a result, traits that improve a male's success in these two areas carry a selective advantage. Sexual selection results in attributes that improve success in contests (such as horns, antlers, large size, or increased musculature) or traits that are attractive to females (such as good nest-building ability, large territories, or long or colorful feathers as in peacocks and birds of paradise). Although sexual selection may change allele frequencies over time and result in new traits, speciation (the formation of a new species) does not necessarily occur.

Question 3 is the most specific of the first three questions. It asks you to discuss specific mechanisms of speciation. Note the example of Darwin's finches for adaptive radiation.

Question 4

This is a specific question about natural selection. In your discussion, use the same arguments Darwin used as presented earlier in the review part of this section. Be sure to use these important words in your discussion: variation, heritability, selection, adaptation, and fitness.

Question 5

Each part of this question corresponds to a major step leading to the origin of life and to eukaryotic cells. See the discussion on the origin of life presented earlier in this section for specific information. Be sure to separate your answers into paragraphs corresponding to each part of the question, each labeled with the appropriate letter.

Review

In **taxonomy,** organisms are classified into categories called **taxa** (singular, **taxon**). A **species** is given a name consisting of a species name and a **genus** (plural, **genera**) name. For example, the domesticated dog is categorized into the genus *Canis* and is given the name *Canis familiaris.* Closely related animals are grouped in the same genus. Thus, the wolf, *Canis lupis,* and the coyote, *Canis latrans,* share the same genus with the domesticated dog. Genera that share related features are grouped in a **family.** Related families, in turn, are grouped in **orders,** which are grouped successively in **classes, phyla** (singular, **phylum**) (or **divisions** for fungi and plants), and finally, **kingdoms.** A good way to remember the successional order of taxa is to remember the phrase "Kings Play Chess On Fine Green Sand," in which each word gives the first letter of each taxon from kingdom to species.

To prepare for the AP exam, you should not be concerned with knowing which organism is placed into which taxon. Rather, you need to know the important characteristics that define a particular taxon. These are the characteristics used to put a particular organism into a particular taxon and thus describe features that are common to all the organisms within a taxon. A major goal of classification is to organize taxa on the basis of **phylogeny,** or evolutionary relationships. Thus, by knowing the characteristics that define organisms within a taxon, you are aware of the evolutionary relationships among these organisms. The study of the evolutionary relationships among organisms is called **systematics.**

Five kingdoms are currently used to categorize all organisms. The characteristics of each of these kingdoms, and important taxa within these kingdoms, are described below.

Kingdom Monera

The single, distinguishing characteristic of organisms in the kingdom Monera is that they are **prokaryotes.** As prokaryotes, they lack nuclei and the various organelles of eukaryotes. Prokaryotes possess a single "naked" chromosome consisting of a single DNA molecule without the proteins found in eukaryotes. Some prokaryotes have **plasmids,** small circular DNA molecules, in addition to the major chromosome. The cell walls of most prokaryotes contain **peptidoglycans,** a polysaccharide modified with polypeptides. In contrast, the cell walls of plants contain cellulose.

Flagella, when present in monerans, consist of the globular protein **flagellin** arranged in helical chains (not tubulin arranged in 9 + 2 microtubule arrays as in eukaryotes). Prokaryotes without flagella move by a corkscrew motion, while still others may exhibit a gliding motion through slimy material that they secrete.

It is difficult to classify prokaryotes on the basis of phylogeny because the prokaryotes origi-nated so long ago that features characteristic of closely related groups may no longer be dis-tinct. It is apparent that many features have evolved independently in unrelated groups. In addition, transformation, the uptake of free DNA, and transduction, the transport of DNA by viruses, may have scrambled the genomes of unrelated prokaryotes.

Currently, many prokaryotes are organized by their mode of nutrition, that is, how they metab-olize resources, as follows:

1. **Autotrophs** manufacture their own organic compounds. To do this, **photoautotrophs** use light energy (as in photosynthesis) and **chemoautotrophs** use energy obtained from inor-ganic substances (as in chemosynthesis). Examples of inorganic substances used by chemoautotrophs are hydrogen sulfide (H_2S), ammonia (NH_3), and other nitrogen com-pounds (NO_2^-, NO_3^-).

2. **Heterotrophs** must obtain their energy by consuming organic substances produced by au-totrophs. Some heterotrophic bacteria are **parasites,** obtaining their energy from the living tissues of a host. Others are **saprobes** (or **saprophytes**), obtaining their energy from dead, decaying matter. Since saprobes contribute to the decay of organic matter, they are called **decomposers.**

Another feature important in describing prokaryotes is their ability to survive in the presence or absence of oxygen. **Obligate aerobes** must have oxygen to live, while **obligate anaerobes** can survive only in the absence of oxygen. A **facultative anaerobe** grows in the presence of oxy-gen but, when oxygen is absent, can switch to an anaerobic metabolism.

Molecular analysis has revealed two distinct groups within the Monera, the **eubacteria** ("true" bacteria) and the **archaebacteria.**

Archaebacteria are distinguished by these three major features:

1. Their cell walls lack peptidoglycans.
2. Their ribosomes are more similar to ribosomes of eukaryotes than to those of eubacteria.
3. Their plasma membranes contain lipids that differ from those found in the plasma mem-branes of all other organisms.

There are three groups of archaebacteria, as follows:

1. **Methanogens** are anaerobic, heterotrophic bacteria that produce methane (CH_4). They live in mud, swamps, and the guts of cows, humans, termites, and other animals.

2. **Extreme halophiles** ("salt lovers") live in environments with high concentrations of salt. They are found in salt lakes, such as the Great Salt Lake and the Dead Sea, or in salted foods, where they can cause spoilage. Most are aerobic and heterotrophic, while others are anaerobic and photosynthetic with the pigment **bacteriorhodopsin.**

3. **Thermoacidophiles** ("heat and acid lovers") live in hot (60° C to 80° C) and acid (pH 2 to 4) environments. They are found in mineral springs, such as in Yellowstone National Park, or in thermal volcanic vents on ocean floors. They are chemoautotrophs, using H_2S as their source of energy.

Various features are used to categorize the eubacteria, as follows:

1. The principal means by which the eubacteria are categorized is by their mode of nutrition, or how they metabolize resources.

2. Some eubacteria are distinguished by their ability to produce **endospores,** resistant bodies that contain the genetic material and a small amount of cytoplasm surrounded by a durable wall.

3. Eubacteria are distinguished by their means of motility, whether by flagella, gliding, or corkscrew motion. When flagella are present, they can be apical or posterior, or they can completely cover the cell.

4. Bacteria are classified into one of three shapes: **cocci** (spherical), **bacilli** (rod shaped), and **spirilla** (spirals).

5. The cell wall distinguishes two broad groups of bacteria. Bacteria that stain positive with the **Gram stain technique** have a thick peptidoglycan cell wall, while Gram-negative bacteria have a thin peptidoglycan wall covered with a layer of lipopolysaccharides.

Some of the more common groups of bacteria follow:

1. **Cyanobacteria** are photosynthetic, using chlorophyll *a* to capture light energy, splitting H_2O, and releasing O_2 as do plants. They also contain accessory pigments called **phycobilins.** Some have specialized cells called **heterocysts** that produce **nitrogen-fixing** enzymes. When nitrogen is fixed, inorganic, unreactive nitrogen gas is converted into ammonia (NH_3), which can then be used for making nitrogen-containing amino acids and nucleotides. The cyanobacteria were formerly referred to as blue-green "algae." However, that nomenclature has been abandoned, since cyanobacteria are prokaryotes, while the algae are eukaryotes.

2. **Chemosynthetic bacteria** are autotrophs. Some of these are called **nitrifying** bacteria because they convert nitrite (NO_2^-) to nitrate (NO_3^-).

3. **Nitrogen-fixing bacteria** are heterotrophs that fix nitrogen. Many of these bacteria have **mutualistic** relationships with plants; that is, both the bacteria and the host plant benefit from an interdependent relationship. The bacteria live in **nodules,** specialized structures in plant roots.

4. **Spirochetes** are coiled bacteria that move with a corkscrew motion. Their flagella are internal, positioned within the layers of the cell wall.

Kingdom Protista

Organisms in this kingdom may be algaelike, animallike, funguslike, unicellular, or multicellular. In many cases, the evolutionary relationships among the various groups are either very weak, poorly understood, or both. Thus, this kingdom is artificial and is used more for convenience than to present actual evolutionary relationships. Features shared by two or more groups may represent **convergent evolution;** that is, the features arose among the groups independently. Nevertheless, the groupings given below present this varied kingdom with a degree of organization that will help you remember them.

Algaelike (or plant-like) members of the Protista all obtain energy by photosynthesis. All have chlorophyll *a* but may have various other chlorophylls and different accessory pigments. The main features used to categorize them are their chlorophylls and accessory pigments, the form of carbohydrate used to store energy, the number of flagella (if present), and the makeup of the cell walls. Some distinguishing characteristics of the phyla follow:

1. **Euglenophyta,** or euglenoids, have one to three flagella at their apical (leading) end. Instead of a cellulose cell wall, they have thin, protein strips called **pellicles** that wrap over their cell membranes. They can become heterotrophic in the absence of light. Some have an **eyespot** that permits **phototaxis,** the ability to move in response to light.

2. **Dinoflagellata,** or dinoflagellates, have two flagella. One flagellum is posterior, while the second flagellum is transverse and rests in an encircling mid groove perpendicular to the first flagellum. Some of these are bioluminescent. Others produce nerve toxins that concentrate in filter-feeding shellfish, which then cause illness in humans when eaten.

3. **Chrysophyta,** or golden algae, are golden yellow and have one or two apical flagella.

4. **Bacillariophyta,** or diatoms, have **tests** (shells) that consist of silica (SiO_2).

5. **Chlorophyta,** or green algae, have both chlorophyll *a* and *b,* have cellulose cell walls, and store their carbohydrates as starch. There is considerable variation in sexuality. For example, some species have **isogamous** gametes, where both sperm and eggs are motile and equal in size, while in others, the gametes are **anisogamous,** where the sperm and egg differ in size. In still others, the gametes are **oogamous,** where a large egg cell remains with the parent and is fertilized by a small, motile sperm. In addition, there are examples of trends toward multicellularity. In one group of closely related species, there is a succession from unicellular organisms (*Chlamydomonas*), to colonies of four to thirty-two cells (*Gonium* and *Pandorina*), to a colony with hundreds of cells (*Volvox*). Because of these various characteristics and evolutionary trends, the Chlorophyta are believed to be the ancestors of plants.

6. **Phaeophyta,** or brown algae, are multicellular and have flagellated sperm cells. Some brown algae are giant seaweeds, or kelps.

7. **Rhodophyta,** or red algae, contain red accessory pigments called **phycobilins.** They are multicellular, and their gametes do not have flagella.

The **protozoa,** or **animal-like** protists, are heterotrophs. They consume either living cells (thus being predatory or parasitic) or dead organic matter. Some important phyla follow:

1. **Rhizopoda** are amoebas that move by extensions of their cell body called **pseudopodia.** Pseudopodia encircle food and absorb it by phagocytosis.

2. **Foraminifera,** or forams, have tests usually made of calcium carbonate. Many ancient marine sediments consisting of certain foram tests are good indicators of underlying oil deposits.

3. **Zoomastigophora,** or zooflagellates, are flagellated protozoa. Some mutualistic species digest cellulose in the guts of termites. Others are parasites, such as *Trypanosoma,* which is transmitted by the tsetse fly and causes African sleeping sickness in humans.

4. **Sporozoa** are parasites of animals. They have no physical means of motility. However, they form spores which are dispersed by one or more hosts that participate in the completion of their life cycles. The sporozoan that causes malaria, for example, spends part of its life cycle in mosquitos and part in humans.

5. **Ciliophora** are distinguished by their cilia, which they use for moving and other functions. Because of specialized structures, such as mouths, anal pores, contractile vacuoles (for water balance), two kinds of nuclei (one large macronucleus and several small micronuclei), and other features, they are perhaps the most complex of all cells. *Paramecium* is this phylum's most notable member.

The **fungus-like** protists resemble fungi because they form either filaments or spore-bearing bodies similar to the fungi.

1. **Acrasiomycota,** the **cellular slime molds,** exhibit both funguslike and protozoalike characteristics during their life cycle. Spores germinate into amoebas which feed on bacteria. When food sources are depleted, the amoebas aggregate into a single unit, which migrates as a slug. The individual cells of the slug then mobilize to form a stalk with a capsule at the top similar to the spore-bearing bodies of many fungi. Spores are then released, which repeat the cycle when they germinate. The stimulus for aggregation is **cyclic AMP** (cAMP), which is secreted by the amoebas that experience food deprivation first.

2. **Myxomycota,** the **plasmodial slime molds,** grow as a single, spreading mass (or **plasmodium**) feeding on decaying vegetation. When food becomes unavailable or when the environment desiccates (dries up), stalks bearing spore capsules form. Haploid spores released from the capsule germinate into haploid amoeboid or flagellated cells, which fuse to form a diploid cell. The diploid cell grows into the spreading plasmodium.

3. **Oomycota** include the water molds, downy mildews, and white rusts. They are either parasites or saprobes. They are much like fungi in that they form filaments (**hyphae**) which secret enzymes that digest the surrounding substances. The breakdown products of digestion are then absorbed. The filaments of the Oomycota lack **septa,** or **cross walls,** which in many of the true fungi partition the filaments into compartments. Because they lack septa, they are **coenocytic,** containing many nuclei within a single cell. Also, the cell walls of the Oomycota are made of cellulose, rather than the chitin found in the true fungi.

Kingdom Fungi

Fungi grow as filaments called **hyphae** (singular, **hypha**). A mass of hyphae is called **mycelium** (plural, **mycelia**). Some fungi have **septa** (singular, **septum**), or cross walls, which divide the filament into compartments containing a single nucleus. When filaments lack septa, they are multinucleate, or **coenocytic.** The cell walls of fungi consist of **chitin,** a nitrogen-containing polysaccharide.

Fungi are either parasites or saprobes, absorbing the breakdown products from the action of digestive enzymes that they secrete. Many parasitic fungi have hyphae called **haustoria** that penetrate their host.

Fungi are dominantly haploid, but most form temporary diploid structures for sexual reproduction. The following stages occur during sexual reproduction.

1. **Plasmogamy** is the fusing of cells from two different fungal strains to produce a single cell with nuclei from both strains. A pair of haploid nuclei, one from each strain, is called a **dikaryon.** A hypha containing a dikaryon is called a **dikaryotic** hypha.

2. **Karyogamy** is the fusing of the two haploid nuclei of a dikaryon to form a single diploid nucleus.

3. **Meiosis** of the diploid nucleus restores the haploid condition. Daughter cells develop into haploid spores, which germinate and form haploid hyphae.

Fungi reproduce asexually by various means, including **fragmentation** (the breaking up of hyphae), **budding** (the pinching off of a small hyphal outgrowth), and **asexual spores.** Two kinds of asexual spores are described below:

1. **Sporangiospores** are produced in saclike capsules called **sporangia** (singular, **sporangium**) that are each borne on a stalk called a **sporangiophore.**

2. **Conidia** (singular, **conidium**) are formed at the tips of specialized hyphae, not enclosed inside sacs. Hyphae bearing conidia are called **conidiophores.**

The fungi form three natural groups based on sexual reproduction. Three additional groups are artificial. Depending upon the classification scheme, the groups are considered either divisions (and bear the "-mycota" suffix) or classes ("-mycete" suffix). As a result, division and class names are often used interchangeably (Zygomycota and zygomycetes, for example).

1. **Zygomycota** lack septa, except when filaments border reproductive filaments. Zygomycetes reproduce sexually by fusion of hyphae from different strains, followed by plasmogamy, karyogamy, and meiosis. Haploid **zygospores** are produced, which germinate into new hyphae. Bread mold is a typical zygomycete.

2. **Ascomycota** have septa and reproduce sexually by producing haploid **ascospores.** After plasmogamy of hyphae from unlike strains, a dikaryotic hypha produces more filaments by mitosis. Karyogamy and meiosis subsequently occur in terminal hyphal cells producing four haploid cells. These four cells divide by mitosis to produce *eight* haploid ascospores in a sac called an **ascus** (plural, **asci**). In many ascomycetes, the asci are grouped together into a specialized fruiting body, the **ascocarp.** The ascomycetes include yeasts, powdery mildews, and truffles.

3. **Basidiomycota** have septa and reproduce sexually by producing haploid **basidiospores.** Plasmogamy between two unlike hyphae is followed by mitosis and the growth of dikaryotic hyphae to form a fruiting body called a **basidiocarp.** A mushroom, for example, is a basidiocarp. Karyogamy occurs in terminal hyphal cells called **basidia** (singular, **basidium**), followed by meiosis and the production of *four* haploid basidiospores.

4. **Deuteromycota,** or imperfect fungi, is an artificial group comprising fungi for which no sexual reproductive cycle has been observed. *Penicillium,* from which penicillin is obtained, is a deuteromycete.

5. **Lichens** are mutualistic associations between fungi and algae. The algae, which is usually a chlorophyta or cyanobacteria, provides sugar from photosynthesis. Nitrogen compounds are also provided if the algae is nitrogen-fixing. The fungus, which is most often an as-comycete, provides water and protection from the environment. Some fungi produce pigments that shield algae from ultraviolet radiation or excess light, or toxic substances that discourage algae consumption by grazers.

6. **Mycorrhizae** are mutualistic associations between fungi and roots of plants. The plant provides sugars to the fungus, while the fungus increases the ability of the roots to absorb water and minerals, especially phosphorus.

Kingdom Plantae

In order to survive the transition from water to land, it was necessary for plants to make adaptations for obtaining water and to prevent its loss by desiccation (drying out). Water was also required to provide a medium for the fertilization of eggs by flagellated sperm. In addition, once plants emerged from the protective cover of water, genetic material was more susceptible to damage by ultraviolet radiation. The following list summarizes the major plant adaptations for survival on land.

1. Except for the primitive division Bryophyta (mosses), the dominant generation of all plants is the diploid sporophyte generation. A diploid structure is more apt to survive genetic damage because two copies of each chromosome allow recessive mutations to be masked.

2. All plants possess a **cuticle,** a waxy covering on aerial parts that reduces desiccation.

3. The development of a vascular system in plants further reduced their dependency on water. Without a vascular system, all cells must be reasonably close to water. A vascular system reduced this dependency by providing a system for water to be distributed throughout the plant. Once cells were relieved of their dependency upon water, tissues specialized for specific tasks evolved. True leaves developed as centers for photosynthesis, true stems developed to provide a framework to support leaves, and true roots developed to obtain water and anchor the plant. Two groups of vascular tissues evolved, **xylem** and **phloem.** Xylem is specialized for water transport, and phloem is specialized for sugar transport.

4. In the more primitive plant divisions, flagellated sperm require water to swim to the eggs. In the more advanced divisions (Coniferophyta and Anthophyta), the sperm, packaged as pollen, are adapted for delivery by wind or animals.

5. In the most advanced division, the Anthophyta, the gametophytes are enclosed (and thus protected) inside an **ovary.**

6. Plants of the Coniferophyta and Anthophyta have developed adaptations to seasonal variations in the availability of water and light. For example, some trees are **deciduous;** that is, they shed their leaves to minimize water loss during slow-growing (or dormant) seasons. In contrast, desert annuals will germinate, grow, flower, and produce seeds within brief growing periods in response to a spring rain.

A list of the major plant divisions follows. Of particular importance is how each division shows an increasingly greater adaptation to survival on land.

1. **Bryophyta** are the mosses, liverworts, and hornworts. Gametes are produced in protective structures called **gametangia** on the surface of the gametophytes, the dominant haploid stage of the life cycle of bryophytes. The male gametangium, or **antheridium** (plural, **antheridia**), produces flagellated sperm that swim through water to fertilize the eggs produced by the female gametangium, or **archegonium** (plural, **archegonia**). The resulting zygote grows into a diploid structure, still connected to the gametophyte. In mosses, this structure is a stalk bearing a capsule which contains haploid spores produced by meiosis. The spores are dispersed by wind, germinate, and grow into haploid gametophytes. Since bryophytes lack the specialized vascular tissues xylem and phloem, they do not have true roots, true stems, or true leaves. Thus, bryophytes must remain small, and water must be readily available for absorption through surface tissues and as a transport medium for sperm.

The following divisions of plants are informally categorized as **tracheophytes,** or **vascular plants,** because they possess xylem and phloem. As a result, they have true roots, true stems, and true leaves. The **Lycophyta**, **Sphenophyta**, and **Pterophyta** all produce spores that germinate into small gametophytes. Like the bryophytes, the gametophytes produce antheridia and archegonia, which produce sperm and eggs, respectively. The flagellated sperm swim to the archegonia to fertilize the eggs. Successful fertilization produces a diploid zygote which grows into the sporophyte. Unlike the bryophytes, however, the sporophyte is the dominant generation.

2. **Lycophyta** include two groups of plants. One group, now extinct, consisted of woody trees that were dominant in the forests of the Carboniferous period, about 300 million years ago. The second, extant, group consists of tropical **epiphytes,** plants that live on other plants, and small herbaceous plants. Many of the herbaceous plants are called club mosses because of their club-shaped, spore-bearing cones, or **strobili.**

3. **Sphenophyta** include extinct woody trees common during the Carboniferous period and extant herbaceous plants called **horsetails.** Horsetails have hollow, ribbed stems that are jointed at **nodes.** The nodes occur at intervals along the stem and produce small, scalelike leaves and, in some species, branches. The bushy branches give the appearance of a horsetail. The stems, branches, and leaves are green and photosynthetic and have a rough texture due to the presence of silica (silicon dioxide, SiO_2). Strobili bear the spores.

4. **Pterophyta** are the ferns. Clusters of sporangia called **sori** (singular, **sorus**) develop on the undersurface of fern fronds. The sporangia undergo meiosis and produce the spores.

The next two plant divisions produce seeds. In addition, two kinds of spores are produced, male spores and female spores. Structures relating to the production of these spores are prefixed with "micro" and "macro," respectively. Thus, the **microsporangia** produce the **microspores** (male spores), and the **macrosporangia** produce the **macrospores** (female spores). A summary of reproduction in seed plants follows:

- The microsporangium produces numerous **microspore mother cells,** which divide by meiosis to produce four haploid cells, the microspores. The microspores mature into **pollen grains.** A pollen grain represents the male gametophyte generation. The pollen grain further divides into three cells (in flowering plants) or four cells (in conifers). One of these cells is a **vegetative,** or **tube,** cell that controls the growth of the pollen tube. Other cells become the sperm cells.

- The megasporangium, called the **nucellus,** produces a **megaspore mother cell,** which divides by meiosis to produce four haploid cells. One of these cells survives to become the megaspore and represents the female gametophyte generation. The megaspore divides by mitosis to produce one egg (in flowering plants) or two eggs (in conifers). Other accessory cells, in addition to the eggs, may also be produced. One to two tissue layers called **integuments** surround the megasporangium. The integuments, nucellus, and megaspore daughter cells are collectively called the **ovule.** An opening through the integuments for pollen access to the egg is called the **micropyle.**

- When a pollen grain contacts the megasporangium, the tube cell directs the growth of a **pollen tube** through the micropyle and toward the egg. After fertilization by the sperm cells, the zygote divides to form an embryo, the beginning of the sporophyte generation. The integuments develop into the seed coat.

There are two groups of seed plants, as follows:

5. **Coniferophyta** are the familiar conifers (literally, "cone-bearing"). They include pines, firs, spruces, junipers, redwoods, cedars, and others. The male and female reproductive structures are borne in pollen-bearing male cones and ovule-bearing female cones. The conifers, together with several other minor divisions (not discussed here), make up a group informally called the **gymnosperms.** The term gymnosperms (literally, "naked-seeds") refers to seeds produced in unprotected megaspores near the surface of the reproductive structure. Fertilization and seed development is lengthy, requiring one to three years.

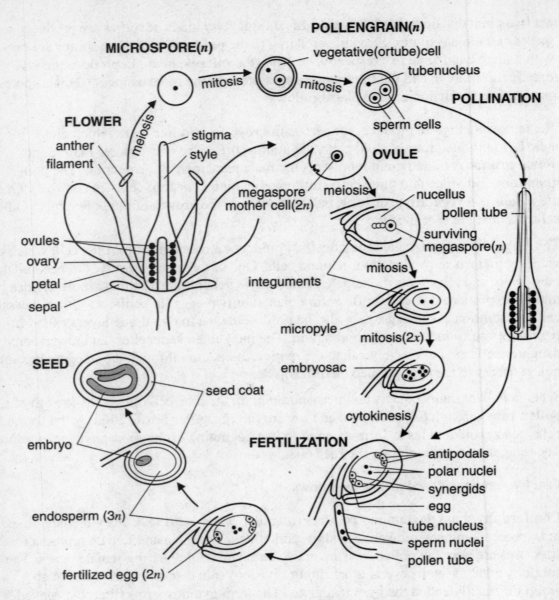

Reproduction in Angiosperms

Figure 9-1

6. **Anthophyta,** or **angiosperms,** consist of the flowering plants. Major parts of the flower (Figure 9-1) are as follows:

- The **carpel** (or **pistil**) is the female reproductive structure and consists of three parts: an egg-bearing **ovary,** a **style,** and a **stigma.**

- The **stamen** is the male reproductive structure and consists of a pollen-bearing **anther** and its stalk, the **filament.**

- **Petals,** and sometimes **sepals,** function to attract pollinators.

The flower is a major evolutionary advancement for the following reasons:

- The flower is a special adaptation to attract **pollinators,** such as insects and birds.

- The ovules are protected inside an **ovary.**

- The ovary develops into a **fruit** which fosters the dispersal of seeds by wind, insects, birds, mammals, and other animals.

Details of fertilization typical in many angiosperms are as follows (Figure 9-1):

- Pollen lands on the sticky stigma. A pollen tube, an elongating cell that contains the **vegetative nucleus** (or **tube nucleus**) grows down the style toward an ovule. There are two sperm cells inside the pollen tube.

- Ovules within the ovary consist of a megaspore mother cell surrounded by the nucellus and integuments. The megaspore mother cell divides by meiosis to produce four haploid cells, the megaspores. One surviving megaspore divides (three times) by mitosis to produce eight nuclei. Six of the nuclei undergo cytokinesis and form plasma membranes. The result is an **embryo sac.** At the micropyle end of the embryo sac are three cells, an **egg** cell and two **synergids.** At the end opposite the micropyle are three **antipodal cells.** In the middle are two haploid nuclei, the **polar nuclei.**

- When the pollen tube enters the embryo sac through the micropyle, one sperm cell fertilizes the egg, forming a diploid zygote. The nucleus of the second sperm cell fuses with both polar nuclei, forming a triploid nucleus. The triploid nucleus divides by mitosis to produce the **endosperm,** which provides nourishment for subsequent development of the embryo and seedling. The fertilization of the egg and the polar nuclei each by a separate sperm nucleus is called **double fertilization.**

Other evolutionary advancements among the angiosperms, including more specialized vascular tissues and numerous variations in habit and growth, developed to advance survival in a variety of environmental conditions.

The characteristics of the divisions of the plant kingdom are summarized in Table 9-1. Additional detail with respect to plant structure, transport, reproduction, and development is given in the section on plants.

Table 9-1					
Division	**Common Name**	**Dominant Generation**	**Fluid Transport**	**Sperm Transport**	**Dispersal Unit**
Bryophyta	mosses	gametophyte	nonvascular	flagellated sperm	spores
Lycophyta	club mosses	sporophyte	vascular	flagellated sperm	spores
Sphenophyta	horsetails	sporophyte	vascular	flagellated sperm	spores
Pterophyta	ferns	sporophyte	vascular	flagellated sperm	spores
Coniferophyta	conifers	sporophyte	vascular	wind-dispersed pollen	seeds
Anthophyta	flowering plants	sporophyte	vascular	wind- or animal-dispersed pollen	seeds

Kingdom Animalia

Although the animal kingdom is extremely diverse, its members share a number of characteristics, as follows:

1. All animals are multicellular.
2. All animals are heterotrophic.
3. The dominant generation in the life cycle of animals is the diploid generation.
4. Most animals are motile during at least some part of their life cycle.
5. Most animals undergo a period of embryonic development during which two or three layers of tissues form.

The diversity of animals originates from variations in the following characteristics:

1. **Tissue complexity.** Most animals, collectively called the **eumetazoa,** have closely functioning cells organized into tissues. Two (**diploblastic**) or three (**triploblastic**) layers of tissue called germ layers may be present. The three germ layers, the ectoderm, mesoderm, and endoderm (outer, middle, and inner layers, respectively), develop into various organs during embryonic development. In another group of animals, the **parazoa,** cells are not organized into true tissues, and organs do not develop.

2. **Body symmetry.** Animals have either **radial symmetry** or **bilateral symmetry.** In radial symmetry, organisms have only one orientation, front and back (or top and bottom). They display a circular body pattern. Organisms with bilateral symmetry have a top (**dorsal** side), bottom (**ventral** side), head (**anterior** end), and tail (**posterior** end).

3. **Cephalization.** In animals with bilateral symmetry, there is a progressively greater increase in nerve tissue concentration at the anterior end (head) as organisms increase in complexity. For example, brains have developed with accessory sensory organs for seeing, smelling, tasting, and feeling (antennae).

4. **Gastrovascular cavity.** Gastrovascular cavities, or **guts,** are areas where food is digested. If they have one opening, they are saclike, and the types of processes that can occur are limited. Two openings designate a **digestive tract,** allowing specialized activities to occur as food travels from beginning to end.

5. **Coelom.** During the embryonic development in more advanced animals, a cavity called a coelom develops from tissue derived from the mesoderm germ layer. The fluid-filled coelom cushions the internal organs and allows for their expansion and contraction. **Acoelomate** animals lack a coelom, while **pseudocoelomate** animals have a cavity that is not completely lined by mesoderm-derived tissue.

6. **Segmentation.** Many animals, such as insects and certain worms, have segmented body parts. In some cases the body parts are the same and repeat, while in other cases, the body parts are modified and adopt specialized functions.

7. **Protostomes** and **deuterostomes.** During the early development of the zygote, cell divisions, or **cleavages,** take place in an orderly fashion. Specific cleavage patterns emerge that result in the development of particular embryonic features. Two markedly different developmental patterns occur producing two groups of animals, the protostomes and deuterostomes. Three major differences between these two groups are evident as described below and outlined in Table 9-2.

- Early cleavages either are at a slight angle (spiral cleavage) or are parallel (radial cleavage) to the vertical axis of the embryo.

- When the embryo is configured as a sphere of cells, there is an infolding in the sphere that forms an internal cavity called the **archenteron.** The opening to the archenteron becomes either the mouth or the anus.

- The coelum can develop either from a splitting of the mesodermal tissue at each side of the archenteron or directly from outpouching in the wall of the archenteron.

Table 9-2		
Characteristic	*Protostome*	*Deuterostome*
Early cleavages	slight angle (spiral cleavage)	straight down (radial cleavage)
First infolding of archenteron forms	mouth	anus
Coelum develops from	split in tissue at sides of archenteron	outpouching of archenteron wall

A list of animal phyla with short descriptions follows. Major evolutionary trends are summarized in Table 9-3.

1. **Porifera** are the sponges. They feed by filtering water drawn through the sponge wall by flagellated cells called **choanocytes.** Water exits through an opening called the **osculum.** Choanocytes pass the food to **amoebocytes,** which wander between the two cell layers of the sponge wall, digesting and distributing nutrients. The sponge wall contains **spicules,** skeletal needles made from either $CaCO_3$ or SiO_2. Since the cells of the Porifera are not organized in a coordinated fashion to form tissues, they are classified with the parazoa.

2. **Cnidaria** include hydrozoans, jellyfish, sea anemones, and corals. There are two body forms. One is the **medusa,** a floating, umbrella-shaped body with dangling tentacles typical of jellyfish. The second is the **polyp,** a sessile, cylinder-shaped body with rising tentacles typical of sea anemones. The medusa is much like an upside-down polyp. In some Cnidaria, the medusa and polyp body forms alternate between the two stages of their life cycle.

3. **Platyhelminthes** consist of three kinds of acoelomate **flatworms. Free-living flatworms,** such as planarians, are carnivores or scavengers that live in marine or freshwater. **Flukes** are internal animal parasites or external animal parasites that suck tissue fluids or blood. **Tapeworms** are internal parasites that often live in the digestive tract of vertebrates. The tapeworms appear segmented, but since the segments, called **proglottids,** develop secondarily for reproduction and function independently, the tapeworm is not considered a true segmented animal. Tapeworms do not have a digestive tract themselves, as they need only absorb the predigested food around them. Other Platyhelminthes, however, have a saclike gut.

4. **Nematoda** are **roundworms.** They have pseudocoelomate bodies with a complete digestive tract. Many nematodes are free-living soil dwellers that help decompose and recycle nutrients. One species of roundworms, ingested from incompletely cooked meat, causes trichinosis in humans.

5. **Rotifera** are rotifers. Although many are microscopic, they are multicellular, with specialized organs enclosed in a pseudocoelom, and have a complete digestive tract. They are filter-feeders, drawing water and food into the mouth by the beating action of cilia.

6. **Mollusca** include snails, bivalves, octopuses, and squids. Most mollusks have shells. Bivalves, such as clams and mussels, have a shell that has two parts. In squids, the shell is reduced and internal, and in octopuses, the shell is absent entirely. Mollusks have coelomate bodies with a complete digestive tract. Octopuses have a highly developed nervous system with a large and complex brain.

7. **Annelida** are segmented worms. They include the leeches, earthworms, and polychaete worms. Leeches are either predators of small animals or blood-sucking parasites. They have two suckers at opposite ends of their bodies that are used for attachment and movement. Polychaete worms are mostly marine and, as a group, exhibit a variety of lifestyles, including tube building, crawling, burrowing, and swimming.

8. **Arthropoda** include spiders, insects, crustaceans, and various related organisms. They have jointed appendages, a well-developed nervous system, specialization of body segments, and an exoskeleton made of chitin. There are two kinds of life cycles among the arthropods. Some arthropods are born as **nymphs,** or small versions of the adult, and change shape gradually as they grow to adult size and proportions. Other arthropods are born as **larvae,** maggots specialized for eating. When they reach a certain size, they enclose themselves within a **pupa** (cocoon) and undergo a dramatic change in body form, a process called **metamorphosis.** They emerge from their pupae as adults, specialized for dispersal and reproduction.

9. **Echinodermata** include sea stars, sea urchins, and sand dollars. They are coelomate deuterostomes and usually have a complete digestive tract. Although adult echinoderms have bodies with radial symmetry, some features are bilateral, as are the body shapes of their larvae. Ancestors of echinoderms are believed to have been bilateral.

10. **Chordata** consist of animals that exhibit the following four main features. In many cases, these features are temporary, appearing only during embryonic development.

- A **notochord** provides a dorsal, flexible rod that functions as a support. In most chordates, the notochord is replaced by bone during development.

- A **dorsal hollow nerve cord** forms the basis of the nervous system. In some chordates, the nerve cord becomes the brain and spinal cord.

- **Pharyngeal gill slits** provide channels across the pharynx (a muscular structure at the beginning of the digestive tract) to the outside of the body. In some chordates, the slits become gills for oxygen exchange or filter feeding, while in others, the slits disappear during embryonic development.

- A **muscular tail** extends beyond the digestive tract. In many chordates, such as humans, the tail is lost during embryonic development.

There are two groups of chordates, the **invertebrate** chordates, which include the lancelets and the tunicates, and the **vertebrate** chordates, which include sharks, fish, amphibians, reptiles, birds, and mammals. Vertebrate chordates are characterized by a series of bones, the **vertebrae**, that enclose the spinal cord.

Table 9-3							
Phylum	*Common Name*	*Tissue Complexity*	*Germ Layers*	*Body Symmetry*	*Gut Openings*	*Coelom*	*Embryonic Development*
Porifera	sponges	parazoa	–	none	0*	–	–
Cnidaria	jellyfish, corals	eumetazoa	2	radial	1	–	–
Platyhelminthes	flatworms	eumetazoa	3	bilateral	1	acoelomate	–
Nematoda	roundworms	eumetazoa	3	bilateral	2	pseudo-coelomate	–
Rotifera	rotifers	eumetazoa	3	bilateral	2	pseudo-coelomate	–
Mollusca	clams, snails, octopuses	eumetazoa	3	bilateral	2	coelomate	protostome
Annelida	segmented worms	eumetazoa	3	bilateral	2	coelomate	protostome
Arthropoda	insects, spiders, crustaceans	eumetazoa	3	bilateral	2	coelomate	protostome
Echinodermata	sea stars, sea urchins	eumetazoa	3	radial	2	coelomate	deuterostome
Chordata	vertebrates	eumetazoa	3	bilateral	2	coelomate	deuterostome

* Amoebocytes carry out digestion.
– Characteristic does not apply to this phylum.

Sample Questions and Answers

Multiple-Choice Questions

Directions: Each of the following questions or statements is followed by five possible answers or sentence completions. Choose the one best answer or sentence completion.

1. Which of the following taxa contains organisms that are most distantly related?

   A. Order

   B. Class

   C. Genus

   D. Family

   E. Species

2. Prokaryotes differ from eukaryotes by all of the following characteristics EXCEPT:

   A. kinds of nucleotides in their DNA

   B. structure of their flagella

   C. structure of their ribosomes

   D. structure of their chromosomes

   E. methods of cell division

Questions 3–7

Use the following key for the next five questions. Each answer in the key may be used once, more than once, or not at all.

   A. Saprobic bacteria

   B. Parasitic bacteria

   C. Nitrogen-fixing bacteria

   D. Nitrifying bacteria

   E. Purple sulfur bacteria

3. Bacteria that convert NO_2^- to NO_3^-

4. Bacteria that synthesize NH_3

5. Autotrophic bacteria that use H_2S as their source of electrons to manufacture organic compounds

6. Heterotrophic bacteria that obtain energy from dead, organic matter

7. Heterotrophic bacteria that obtain energy from living tissues in hosts

8. All of the following are examples of substances found in bacteria EXCEPT:

   A. peptidoglycans

   B. flagellin

   C. bacteriorhodopsin

   D. chitin

   E. phycobilins

9. All of the following groups of organisms are photosynthetic EXCEPT:

   A. cyanobacteria

   B. diatoms

   C. dinoflagellates

   D. Foraminifera

   E. Phaeophyta

10. Which of the following groups of organisms lack motility?

    A. Cellular slime molds

    B. Ciliophora

    C. Dinoflagellates

    D. Euglenoids

    E. Sporozoa

11. All of the following are examples of mutualism EXCEPT:

    A. lichens

    B. mycorrhizae

    C. nitrogen-fixing bacteria in nodules

    D. plasmodial slime molds

    E. zooflagellates that live in the guts of termites

12. Asexual reproduction in fungi is carried out by

    A. conidia

    B. dikaryotic hyphae

    C. ascospores

    D. basidiospores

    E. zygospores

13. In plants, male gametes are produced by the

    A. ovary

    B. pistil

    C. antheridium

    D. archegonium

    E. sporophyte

14. The function of the endosperm in angiosperms is to provide

    A. nourishment for the pollen

    B. nourishment for the developing embryo

    C. material for fruit development

    D. material for the seed coat

    E. a reward for animal pollinators

15. Angiosperms differ from all other plants because

    A. they produce a pollen tube

    B. they produce wind-dispersed pollen

    C. the sporophyte generation is dominant

    D. they use animals to disperse their seeds

    E. they produce fruits

16. A body cavity completely surrounded by tissue derived from the mesoderm that provides cushioning for internal organs is called

    A. an archenteron

    B. a coelom

    C. a pseudocoelom

    D. a gastrovascular cavity

    E. a pharynx

17. The deuterostomes differ from protostomes in all of the following respects EXCEPT:

    A. early cleavages of the zygote

    B. ultimate function of the opening to the archenteron

    C. number of germ layers in the developing embryo

    D. embryonic origin of the mouth

    E. embryonic origin of the coelom

18. Roundworms have all of the following characteristics EXCEPT:

    A. a pseudocoelom

    B. bilateral symmetry

    C. a mesoderm germ layer

    D. an ectoderm germ layer

    E. a notochord

19. A characteristic common to all chordates that is lacking in other animal groups is

    A. the appearance of pharyngeal gill slits

    B. the presence of three germ layers

    C. the presence of vertebrae

    D. a true coelom

    E. the embryonic appearance of an archenteron

Answers to Multiple-Choice Questions

1. **B.** A class contains closely related orders, which, in turn, contain closely related families. A family contains closely related genera, and a genus contains very closely related species. Since a class contains many different genera, some of which may be closely related (within the same family) or some of which may be distantly related (in different families or even different orders), it contains organisms at least some of which may be very distantly related. However, there must be some general characteristic shared by all organisms in a class that allows them to be grouped at the class level.

2. **A.** Both prokaryotes and eukaryotes use the same four nucleotides (adenine, cytosine, guanine, and thymine) to construct DNA. In contrast, the flagella of prokaryotes are made of the globular protein flagellin, whereas those of eukaryotes are made of the protein tubulin. Ribosomes of prokaryotes differ structurally from those of eukaryotes. (Ribosomes of archaebacteria resemble those of eukaryotes more than they do those of eubacteria, but they differ nonetheless.) Prokaryotic chromosomes lack the proteins associated with those of eukaryotes. Furthermore, prokaryotes divide by binary fission, whereas eukaryotes divide by mitosis followed by cytokinesis.

3. **D.** The conversion of nitrite (NO_2^-) to nitrate (NO_3^-) is performed by nitrifying bacteria.

4. **C.** Nitrogen-fixing bacteria convert nitrogen gas (N_2) to ammonia (NH_3).

5. **E.** Photosynthetic, purple sulfur bacteria split H_2S to obtain electrons and H^+ for noncyclic photophosphorylation. When H_2S is split, sulfur (S) is produced. This is analogous to the splitting of H_2O during photosynthesis by cyanobacteria, algae, and plants, which produces O_2 as an end product.

6. **A.** Saprobic bacteria are decomposers, obtaining energy from the breakdown of dead organic material.

7. **B.** Parasites live on or in the tissues of living organisms, obtaining nutrition from their tissues.

8. **D.** Chitin is a polysaccharide found in the exoskeleton of arthropods and in the cell walls of fungi. Peptidoglycans are found in the cell walls of many bacteria. Flagellin is the protein of bacterial flagella. Bacteriorhodopsin is a photosynthetic pigment found in the extreme halophiles. Phycobilins are photosynthetic pigments found in cyanobacteria (as well as in red algae).

9. **D.** Foraminifera are heterotrophic (animal-like) protists.

10. **E.** The Sporozoa have no means of motility. They are parasites that are transferred among hosts by the activities of the hosts.

11. **D.** All are examples of mutualism except for the plasmodial slime molds. Lichens and mycorrhizae are mutualistic relationships between fungi and plants. Nitrogen-fixing bacteria are also mutualistic with plants. The digestion of cellulose (wood) in termites is actually carried out by the action of zooflagellates (and spirochete and other bacteria).

12. **A.** Conidia are asexual spores produced by mitosis in the haploid hyphae of many fungi. Ascospores, basidiospores, and zygospores are sexual spores produced by meiosis following karyogamy in ascomycetes, basidiomycetes, and zygomycetes, respectively. Dikaryotic hyphae have unfused nuclei from two strains and subsequently undergo karyogamy followed by meiosis and the production of sexual spores.

13. **C.** The antheridia on the gametophyte generation of bryophytes, Lycophyta, Sphenophyta, and Pterophyta produce male gametes (sperm). Female gametes are produced in archegonia. The sporophyte generation produces spores, not gametes. In flowering plants, the pistil contains an ovary which contains the female gametes.

14. **B.** The endosperm is storage material in the seed that provides nourishment to the developing embryo during and after germination.

15. **E.** Only angiosperms produce fruits, which originate from ovarian tissue. Characteristics given in all the other answers are shared with many gymnosperms and some other phyla.

16. **B.** The coelom provides cushion as well as allowing for expansion and contraction of internal organs (such as the lungs and stomach). The pseudocoelom is not completely surrounded by tissue derived from the mesoderm.

17. **C.** Both deuterostomes and protostomes have three germ layers.

18. **E.** Only members of the phylum Chordata have notochords. Roundworms are in the phylum Nematoda.

19. **A.** Pharyngeal gill slits appear only in chordates. All eumetazoa possess three germ layers and develop an archenteron. A true coelom is shared with other phyla, such as Echinodermata and Arthropoda. Not all chordates have vertebrae (only the vertebrates do).

Free-Response Questions

Free-response questions on the AP exam may require you to provide information from a narrow area of biology, or they may consist of parts that require you to assemble information from diverse areas of biology. The questions that follow are typical of either an entire AP exam question or merely that part of a question that is related to this section.

Directions: Answer the questions below as completely and as thoroughly as possible. Answer the question in essay form (NOT outline form), using complete sentences. You may use diagrams to supplement your answers, but a diagram alone without appropriate discussion is inadequate.

1. Discuss the adaptations in plants that contribute to their success in a terrestrial environment in reference to each of the following.

   (a.) Desiccation

   (b.) Distribution of water throughout the plant

   (c.) Reproduction

2. Justify the establishment of five kingdoms.

3. Describe the attributes used in the phylogenetic classification of animals.

4. Describe the processes of pollination and fertilization in flowering plants.

Some Typical Answers to Free-Response Questions

Question 1

(a.) To reduce desiccation, plants have a cuticle, a waxy covering on stems and leaves. The stomata, however, are openings through the cuticle and epidermis that allow gas exchange for photosynthesis and respiration. In order to reduce transpiration, guard cells close the stomata when water loss is excessive. More advanced plants that occupy hot or dry environments have stomata that are sunken, that is, recessed below the surface of the leaf. This reduces transpiration by reducing the movement of air over the stomatal opening.

In order to conserve water, deciduous plants drop their leaves during seasons when growth is limited by environmental conditions (for example, short day length during winters). By losing their leaves, evaporative surface area is reduced. The same result is accomplished by some plants that have adapted to hot or dry conditions by producing small leaves.

Some plants reduce water loss by physiological means. In C_4 plants, for example, stomata are open for a shorter period of time, and in CAM plants, stomata are only open at night.

(b.) As the most primitive plants, mosses (and other bryophytes) are small because they are unable to effectively transport water. All cells must be close to the surface of the moss, and the moss can grow only in a wet habitat. More advanced plants possess a vascular system that consists of xylem, specialized tissue for the transport of water, and phloem, specialized tissue for the transport of carbohydrates. In addition, various parts of the plant are specialized for particular activities. Roots are an adaptation for obtaining water from the soil, whereas stems are specialized for transporting water to the leaves, which are specialized for photosynthesis.

(c.) In aquatic environments, flagellated sperm can swim to the egg. Similarly, primitive land plants were limited to wet environments as long as their sperm were flagellated. In conifers and flowering plants, sperm are packaged into pollen, allowing wind and animal pollination. Once delivered, pollen grows pollen tubes. The sperm within the tube then travel to the egg through the pollen tube.

Note that in the first part of this answer, both anatomical and physiological adaptations are cited. Needless to say, do this whenever you can. Remember, however, that there is a maximum number of points for each part of the question. Be sure that you give an answer for each part.

Question 2

The kingdom Monera is different from all other kingdoms because monerans are prokaryotic. Prokaryotic cells are unique because they lack a nuclear membrane, have chromosomes that lack proteins of eukaryotic cells, have flagella that are made from flagellin, and lack the eukaryotic organelles.

Organisms in the kingdom Fungi are grouped because all are heterotrophs and contain chitin in their cell walls. They all reproduce by forming spores which develop into hyphae without embryonic development. They obtain nutrition by extracellular digestion.

Plants are multicellular autotrophic organisms that perform photosynthesis with chlorophylls *a* and *b* and carotenoids in specialized organelles called chloroplasts. Carbohydrates are stored as starch or used as cellulose in cell walls.

Kingdom Animalia consists of organisms that are multicellular heterotrophs. All animals develop from a diploid embryo.

The kingdom Protista consists of organisms that do not fit in any of the other kingdoms. They are all eukaryotes and may have animal-like, plant-like or fungi-like characteristics. Most are unicellular.

This is a more difficult question than it appears. The kingdom Protista, for example, is essentially arbitrary in that it consists of organisms that do not fit into the other four kingdoms. In addition, biologists continue to uncover new information that suggests that some organisms be moved from one kingdom to another or that new kingdoms be created. Recent evidence for changes comes from comparisons of genome, mitochondria, and chloroplast DNA and ribosome structure among different organisms.

Question 3

To answer this question, you should discuss the seven characteristics given in this section that describe the origins of variation in animals.

Question 4

The male reproductive structure in the flower is the stamen. It consists of the anther, or pollen-bearing body, and the filament, or stalk that supports the anther. The pistil is the female reproductive structure. The carpel, or bottom portion of the pistil, contains the ovules. The style is a slender extension from the carpel and ends at the sticky tip, or stigma.

In the anther, pollen grains are produced by meiotic divisions of microspore mother cells. Each meiotic division produces four haploid microspores. Each microspore divides twice by mitosis to produce two cells inside a third cell. The two inside cells are sperm cells, and the outer cell is the tube cell, which forms the pollen tube after pollination.

In the ovary, megaspore mother cells divide by meiosis to produce four haploid megaspores. One megaspore contains most of the cytoplasm and survives, while the remaining three die. The one surviving megaspore then divides three times by mitosis, producing eight haploid nuclei in an embryo sac. One end of the embryo sac has an opening, the micropyle. At the micropyle end of the embryo sac, the egg, formed from one of the eight nuclei, is surrounded by two synergids, cells formed from two other nuclei. At the other end of the embryo sac, three nuclei form the antipodal cells. The remaining two nuclei, called polar nuclei, remain in the center of the embryo sac and do not form cell membranes (no cytokinesis occurs).

Pollination is the process of transferring pollen from the anther to the stigma of a flower. In flowering plants, this may be accomplished by wind, water, or animals. For example, when insects in search of pollen or nectar visit flowers, pollen grains adhere to their bodies. Subsequently, the pollen grains are transferred to the stigma of other flowers visited by the insects.

After pollination occurs, the tube nucleus of the pollen grain initiates pollen tube growth. The tube grows down the style and through the micropyle. Once inside the embryo sac, one sperm cell fertilizes the egg. The zygote formed becomes the embryo. The second sperm cell merges with the two polar nuclei to form a triploid cell. The triploid cell divides to form the endosperm, a tissue in the seed that will supply nutrients to the developing embryo. Since two fertilizations occur, one of the egg and the other of the polar nuclei, this process is called double fertilization.

After fertilization, the outer layers of the embryo sac, the integuments, form the seed coat, and the ovary enlarges and develops into a fruit.

Review

Of all the plants in the plant kingdom, the AP exam puts a special emphasis on the structure and physiology of *vascular* plants, especially the seed plants. The structural variety and the various physiological mechanisms in these plants are the subject of this section.

The seed plants include the **gymnosperms** (conifers) and the **angiosperms** (flowering plants). The angiosperms are divided into two classes, the **dicotyledons** (**dicots**) and the **monocotyledons** (**monocots**). Differences between these two classes are summarized in Table 10-1.

Table 10-1			
Characteristic	*Description*	*Dicots*	*Monocots*
Cotyledons	storage tissue that provides nutrition to the developing seedling	2 cotyledons	1 cotyledon
Leaf venation	the pattern of veins in leaves	netted (a branching pattern)	parallel
Flower parts	numbers of petals, sepals, stamens, and other flower parts	in 4's, 5's or multiples thereof	in 3's or multiples thereof
Vascular bundles	arrangement of bundles of vascular tissue (xylem and phloem) in stems	organized in a circle	scattered
Root	form of root	taproot (a large single root)	fibrous system (a cluster of many fine roots)

Plant Tissues

Plant tissues form three distinct major groups, as follows:

1. **Ground tissues** include three basic kinds of cells that differ mostly by the nature of their cell walls.

   • **Parenchyma** cells, the most common component of ground tissue, have thin walls and serve various functions including storage, photosynthesis, and secretion.

- **Collenchyma** cells, which have thick but flexible cells walls, serve mechanical support functions.

- **Sclerenchyma** cells, with thicker walls than collenchyma, also provide mechanical support functions.

2. **Dermal tissue** consists of epidermis cells that cover the outside of plant parts, guard cells that surround stomata, and various specialized surface cells such as hair cells, stinging cells, and glandular cells. In aerial portions of the plant, the epidermal cells secret a waxy protective substance, the **cuticle.**

3. **Vascular tissue** consists of two major kinds of tissues, **xylem** and **phloem.** The two usually occur together to form **vascular bundles.**

- **Xylem** functions in the conduction of water and minerals and also provides mechanical support. In addition to the **primary cell wall** that all plants have, xylem cells have a **secondary cell wall** that gives them additional strength. Sometimes, the walls of xylem cells have **pits,** or places where the secondary cell wall is absent. Most xylem cells are *dead* at maturity, that is, they are essentially cell walls, completely lacking cellular components, and contain only the material being transported. There are two kinds of xylem cells, **tracheids** and **vessel members** (or **vessel elements**). In tracheids, which are long and tapered, water passes from one tracheid to another through pits on the overlapping tapered ends of the cells. Vessel members are shorter and wider than tracheids, and have less or no taper at their ends. A column of vessel members is called a **vessel.** Water passes from one vessel member to the next through areas devoid of *both* primary and secondary cell walls. These areas are called **perforations** and are literally holes between cells. Because of the perforations, water movement through vessel members is more efficient than through tracheids. As a result, vessels are considered a more evolutionarily advanced feature. They are found most prominently among the flowering plants.

- **Phloem** functions in the conduction of sugars. Phloem is made up of cells called **sieve-tube members** (or **sieve-tube elements**) that form fluid-conducting columns called **sieve tubes.** Unlike mature xylem cells, sieve-tube members are *living* at maturity, although they lack nuclei and ribosomes. **Pores** on the end walls of sieve-tube members form **sieve plates,** areas where the cytoplasm of one cell makes contact with that of the next cell. Sieve tubes are associated with **companion cells,** living parenchyma cells that lie adjacent to each sieve-tube member. Companion cells, connected to adjacent sieve-tube members by thin tubes of cytoplasm called **plasmodesmata,** maintain physiological support to the nuclei-lacking sieve-tube members.

The Seed

A seed consists of an **embryo,** a **seed coat,** and some kind of storage material. The major storage material may be **endosperm** or **cotyledons.** Cotyledons are formed by using (digesting) the storage material in the endosperm. In dicots, such as peas, there are two fleshy cotyledons. Most of what you see when you look at the two halves of a pea seed are the two cotyledons (the remainder is a small embryo). In many monocots, such as corn, most of the storage tissue is endosperm, with a single cotyledon that functions to transfer nutrients from the endosperm to the embryo.

The embryo consists of the following parts:

1. The top portion of the embryo, the **epicotyl,** becomes the shoot tip.

2. Often attached to the epicotyl are young leaves usually called the **plumule.** (Sometimes the plumule refers to both the leaves *and* epicotyl.)

3. Below the epicotyl and attached to the cotyledons is the **hypocotyl.** It becomes the young shoot.

4. In some embryos, a **radicle** develops below the hypocotyl. The radicle develops into the root.

5. In many monocots, a sheath called the **coleoptile** surrounds and protects the epicotyl. In a developing young plant, the coleoptile emerges first, appearing as a leaf. The first true leaves, however, emerge from the plumule within the coleoptile.

Germination and Development

After a seed reaches maturity, it remains **dormant** until specific environmental cues are encountered. The most important environmental cue is water. Others may include specific temperatures (cold or warm), light, or seed coat damage (for example, by fire or by the action of enzymes from the digestive tracts of animals). In some cases, there may be a required dormancy period, during which germination will not occur, regardless of the presence of external environmental cues.

Germination begins with the imbibition (absorption) of water. The water initiates the activity of various enzymes, which activate biochemical processes including respiration. In addition, imbibed water causes the seed to swell and the seed coat to crack. The growing tips of the radicle produce roots that anchor the seedling. Elongation of the hypocotyl follows, producing a young shoot.

In the young seedling, growth occurs at the tips of roots and shoots, called **apical meristems.** These are areas of actively dividing, or **meristematic,** cells. This kind of growth, typical in seedlings and young plants, is called **primary growth.**

The growth of a root can be divided into areas based on the activity of its cells. The root tip, or **root cap,** protects the apical meristem behind it. The dividing cells of the apical meristem form the **zone of cell division.** Newly formed cells absorb water and elongate, forming the next region, the **zone of elongation.** Since elongation actually makes the root tip get longer, this zone is technically responsible for our perception of growth. Behind this zone is the **zone of maturation** (or differentiation). Here, cells mature into xylem, phloem, parenchyma, or epidermal cells. Root hairs may form as extensions of epidermal cells. Except for the absence of a root cap, similar regions of growth occur at the growing tips of shoots.

Primary Growth Versus Secondary Growth

Most monocots and some dicots experience growth only at the apical meristems. This kind of growth is called **primary growth,** and the tissues produced are **primary tissues.** Thus, **primary xylem** and **primary phloem** refer to vascular tissues originating from apical meristem growth.

Other plants, like conifers and the woody dicots, undergo **secondary growth** in addition to primary growth. Whereas primary growth extends the plant in the vertical direction, secondary growth increases the girth, or lateral dimension (to the side) and is the origin of **woody** plant tissues. Secondary growth occurs at two **lateral meristems,** the **vascular cambium** and the **cork cambium.** These cells are meristematic, capable of dividing and producing new cells throughout the lifetime of the plant. The tissues that originate from the vascular cambium are the **secondary xylem** and the **secondary phloem.** The cork cambium gives rise to **periderm,** the protective material that lines the outside of woody plants.

Primary Structure of Roots

Primary growth in roots leads to the formation of the following specialized tissues, as seen in cross section, moving from the outside of the root to the center (Figure 10-1).

1. **Epidermis** lines the outside surface of the root. In the zone of maturation, epidermal cells produce **root hairs,** which increase the absorptive surface of the roots. As the zone of maturation ages, root hairs die. New epidermal cells from the zone of elongation, however, become the new zone of maturation as they form root hairs. Thus, roots must constantly grow to provide new root hairs for the absorption of water. Older epidermis functions to protect the root.

2. The **cortex** makes up the bulk of the root. Its main function is the storage of starch. The cortex often contains numerous intercellular spaces, providing aeration of cells for respiration.

3. The **endodermis** is a ring of tightly packed cells at the innermost portion of the cortex. The adjoining cell walls between cells contain a fatty substance called **suberin** that creates a water-impenetrable barrier called the **casparian strip.** As a result of the casparian strip, all water passing through the endodermis must pass through the endodermal cells and not between the cells. In this way, the endodermal cells control the movement of water into the center of the root (where the vascular tissue resides) and prevent water movement back out to the cortex.

4. The **vascular cylinder,** or **stele,** makes up the tissues inside the endodermis. The outer part of the vascular cylinder consists of one to several layers of cells called the **pericycle,** from which lateral roots arise. Inside the pericycle is the vascular tissue. In a typical *dicot,* **xylem** cells fill the center of the vascular cylinder. In cross section, the pattern of xylem cells appears as a central hub with lobes. The **phloem** cells (sieve-tube members and companion cells) occupy the regions between lobes of the xylem core. In some *monocots,* groups of xylem cells alternate with groups of phloem cells in a ring that encircles a central tissue area called the **pith.**

Dicot Root

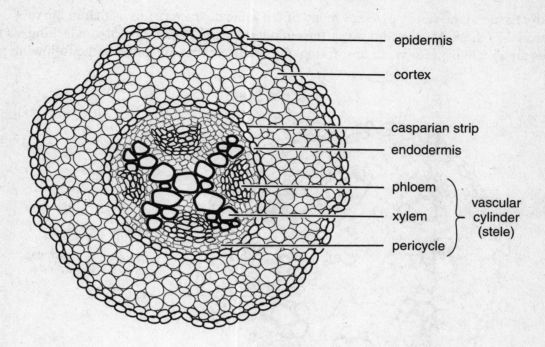

epidermis

cortex

casparian strip

endodermis

phloem
xylem   vascular
                cylinder
                (stele)
pericycle

Monocot Root

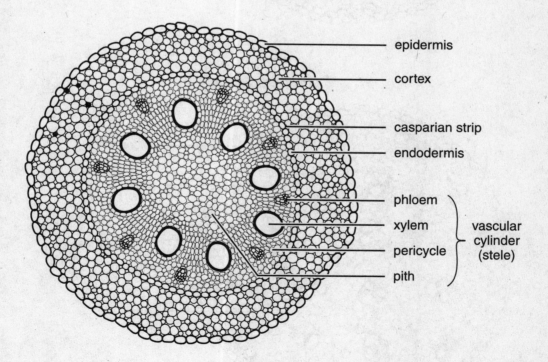

epidermis

cortex

casparian strip

endodermis

phloem
xylem   vascular
                cylinder
pericycle   (stele)
pith

Figure 10-1

Primary Structure of Stems

Primary tissue in the stem possesses many of the same characteristics as that in the root (Figure 10-2). In most cases, however, the endodermis and casparian strip are lacking, as these tissues are specialized for water absorption. Other differences are noted in the following points.

Dicot Stem

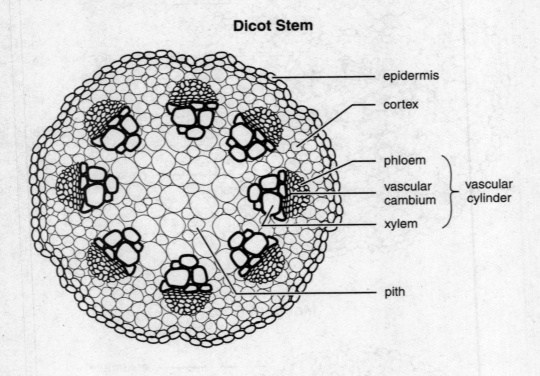

Monocot Stem

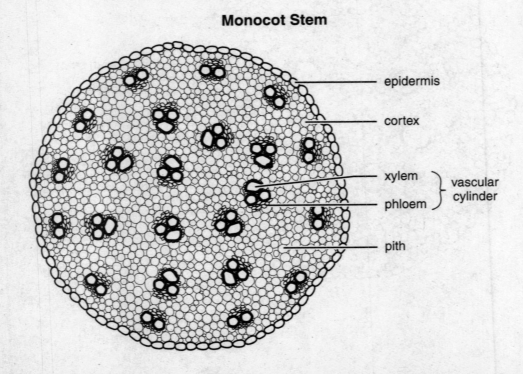

Figure 10-2

1. The **epidermis** contains epidermal cells covered with a waxy (fatty) substance called **cutin.** The cutin forms a protective layer called the **cuticle.** Other epidermal cells include various specialized cells such as guard cells and stinging cells.

2. The **cortex** consists of the various ground tissue types that lie between the epidermis and the vascular cylinder. Many of these contain chloroplasts.

3. The **vascular cylinder** consists of **xylem, phloem,** and **pith.** The arrangement of xylem and phloem varies with species. In many *conifers* and *dicots,* the xylem and phloem are grouped in bundles which ring a central pith region. The phloem is arranged on the outside of each bundle, while the xylem occupies the inside. In addition, a single layer of cells between the xylem and phloem may remain undifferentiated and later become the **vascular cambium.** In many *monocots,* the xylem and phloem bundles are scattered throughout a mass of ground tissue.

Secondary Structure of Stems and Roots

The **vascular cambium** originates between the xylem and phloem and becomes a cylinder of tissue that extends the length of the stem and root. Secondary growth in a stem is illustrated in Figure 10-3. The cambium layer is meristematic, producing new cells on both the inside and outside of the cambium cylinder. Cells on the inside differentiate into **secondary xylem** cells; those on the outside differentiate into **secondary phloem** cells. Over the years, secondary xylem accumulates and increases the girth of the stem and root. In addition, new secondary phloem is added yearly to the outside of the cambium layer. As a result, tissues beyond the secondary phloem are pushed outward as the xylem increases in girth. These outside tissues, which include the primary tissues (such as the epidermis and cortex), break apart as they expand and are eventually shed (sloughed off) as they separate from the stem or root.

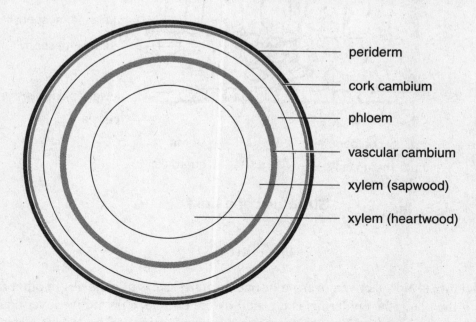

Secondary Structure of Stems and Roots

Figure 10-3

In order to replace the shed epidermis with a new protective covering, new cells called the **periderm** are produced by the **cork cambium.** The periderm consists of protective cork cells impregnated with suberin. In stems of most dicots and conifers, the cork cambium originates from the cortex just inside the epidermis; in roots, it originates from the pericycle.

Each year, new layers of secondary xylem are produced by the vascular cambium. Recall that xylem tissue, which is the actual **wood** of a plant, is dead at maturity. However, only xylem produced during the more recent years remains active in the transport of water. This xylem is referred to as **sapwood.** Older xylem, located toward the center of the stem, is called **heartwood** and functions only as support.

In many environments, conditions vary during the year, creating seasons during which plants alternate growth with dormancy. During periods of growth, the vascular cambium is actively dividing, and as the season draws to an end, divisions and growth slow and gradually come to an end. When the next season begins, the vascular cambium begins dividing again. The alternation of growth and dormancy produces **annual rings** in the secondary xylem tissue. These rings can be used to determine the age of a tree. Since the size of the rings is related to the amount of water available during the year, rings can also provide a rainfall history for the region.

Structure of the Leaf

A typical leaf is illustrated in Figure 10-4. A list of its features follows.

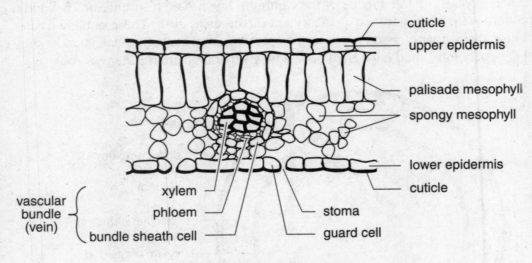

Structure of a Leaf

Figure 10-4

1. The **epidermis** is a protective covering of one or more layers of cells. As in other aerial portions of the plant, the epidermis is covered by the **cuticle,** a protective layer consisting of the waxy material **cutin.** The cuticle reduces **transpiration,** or the loss of water through evaporation. Specialized epidermal cells may bear trichomes (hairs, scales, glands, and other cell outgrowths).

2. **The palisade mesophyll** consists of parenchyma cells equipped with numerous chloroplasts and large surface areas, specializations for photosynthesis. Photosynthesis in leaves occurs primarily in this tissue. The parenchyma cells are usually tightly packed in one or more layers at the upper surface but can occur at both surfaces in leaves of plants adapted to dry habitats.

3. The **spongy mesophyll** consists of parenchyma cells loosely arranged below the palisade mesophyll. The numerous intercellular spaces provide air chambers that provide CO_2 to photosynthesizing cells (and O_2 to respiring cells).

4. **Guard cells** are specialized epidermal cells that control the opening and closing of **stomata.** Stomata are openings in the epidermis that allow gas exchange between the inside of the leaf and the external environment.

5. **Vascular bundles** consist of xylem and phloem tissues. Xylem delivers water for photosynthesis, while phloem transports sugars and other carbohydrate by-products of photosynthesis to other areas of the plant. There are usually specialized mesophyll cells called bundle sheath cells that surround the vascular bundles in such a way that no vascular tissue is exposed to intercellular spaces. In this way, air bubbles cannot enter vessels where they could impede the movement of water. In addition, bundle sheath cells provide the anaerobic environment for CO_2 fixation in C_4 plants.

Transport of Water

Water and dissolved minerals enter the roots through root hairs by osmosis. There are two pathways by which the water moves toward the center of the root, as follows.

1. Water moves through *cell walls* from one cell to another without ever entering the cells. This pathway is called the **apoplast** and consists of the "nonliving" portion of cells.

2. Water moves from one cell to another through the **symplast,** or "living" portion of cells. In this pathway, it moves from the cytoplasm of one cell to the cytoplasm of the next through **plasmodesmata,** small tubes that connect the cytoplasm of adjacent cells.

When water reaches the endodermis, it can continue into the vascular cylinder only through the symplast pathway. The apoplast pathway is blocked by the suberin that permeates the casparian strip. The endodermal cells allow water to enter the stele (vascular cylinder) but are selective as to which minerals are allowed to enter. For example, potassium (K^+), an essential mineral, is allowed to pass, while sodium (Na^+), common in soils but unused in plants, is blocked. Once through the endodermis, water and minerals continue by the apoplast pathway to the xylem. The xylem tissue, consisting of tracheids and vessels, is the major conducting mechanism of the plant.

Three mechanisms are involved in the movement of water and dissolved minerals in plants. These mechanisms are described in the following points:

1. **Osmosis.** Water moves from the soil through the root and into xylem cells by osmosis. A concentration gradient between the soil and the root is maintained in two ways—by the continuous movement of water out of the root by xylem and by the higher mineral

concentration inside the stele maintained by the selective passage of ions through the endodermis. To a certain extent, the movement of water into the root by this concentration gradient forces water up the xylem. This osmotic force, called **root pressure,** can be seen as **guttation,** the formation of small droplets of sap (water and minerals) on the ends of leaves of grasses and small herbs in the early morning. Under most environmental conditions, however, the forces generated by root pressure are too small to have a major effect on the movement of water in plants, especially large plants such as trees.

2. **Capillary action. Capillary action** or **capillarity,** is the rise of liquids in narrow tubes. It also contributes to the movement of water up xylem. Capillary action results from the forces of **adhesion** (molecular attraction between *unlike* substances) between the water and the capillary tube (a tube with a narrow bore). These forces combine to pull water up the sides of the tube. As a result, a **meniscus,** or crescent-shaped surface, forms at the top of the water column. In active xylem cells, however, water forms a continuous column without menisci. Thus, the effect of capillary action is minimal, confined to minute cavities in the cellulose microfibrils of the cell wall.

3. **Cohesion-tension theory.** Although root pressure and capillary action may make minor contributions to water movement under special conditions, most water movement through xylem is explained by **cohesion-tension theory.** The major concepts of this theory are as follows:

   - **Transpiration,** the evaporation of water from plants, removes water from leaves, causing a **negative pressure,** or **tension,** to develop within the leaves and xylem tissue.

   - **Cohesion** between water molecules produces a single, polymerlike column of water from roots to leaves. Cohesion is the molecular attraction between *like* substances. In water, cohesion results from the polarity of water molecules, which causes hydrogen bonding to occur between adjacent water molecules. As a result, the water molecules within a series of xylem cells (vessels or tracheids) behave as a single, polymerlike molecule.

   - **Bulk flow** of water through xylem cells occurs as water molecules evaporate from the leaf surface. When a water molecule is lost from a leaf by transpiration, it pulls up behind it an entire column of water molecules. In this way, water moves by bulk flow through the xylem by a pulling action generated by transpiration. Since transpiration is caused by the heating action of the sun, the sun, then, is the driving force for the ascent of sap through plants.

Control of Stomata

The opening and closing of the stomata influence gas exchange, transpiration, the ascent of sap, and photosynthesis. When stomata are closed, H_2O and CO_2 are not available, and photosynthesis cannot occur. In contrast, when stomata are open, CO_2 can enter the leaf, and water is delivered by the pulling action of transpiration, but the plant risks desiccation from excessive transpiration. A mechanism that controls the opening and closing of stomata must, therefore, balance these two states and provide a means to optimize photosynthesis while minimizing transpiration.

Each stoma is surrounded by two **guard cells.** The cell walls of guard cells are not of uniform thickness. Instead, the cell wall that borders the stomata is thicker than the rest of the cell wall. In addition, the cellulose microfibrils are arranged radially, that is, they encircle the guard cell from the stoma side to the outside. When water diffuses into a guard cell, the guard cell expands. But because of the nonuniform and radially constructed cell wall, the expansion is distorted in such a way that most of the expansion is realized by the bulging out of the thinner wall, the wall away from the stoma. The overall effect is to produce two kidney-shaped guard cells that create an opening, the stoma, between them. When water diffuses out of the guard cells, the kidney shape collapses and the stoma closes. The opening and closing of the stomata, then, is controlled by the movement of water into and out of the guard cells.

Many factors seem to be involved in the mechanism that controls opening and closing of stomata. The following observations have been made:

1. Stomata close when temperatures are high. This reduces loss of water (but shuts down photosynthesis).

2. Stomata open when CO_2 concentrations are low inside the leaf. This allows active photosynthesis, since CO_2 is required.

3. Stomata close at night and open during the day. This may be in response to CO_2 fluctuations caused by photosynthesis. During daylight hours, CO_2 is low because it is used by photosynthesis, but at night, CO_2 levels are high because of respiration.

4. Stomatal opening is accompanied by a diffusion of potassium ions (K^+) into the guard cells (from surrounding subsidiary cells). An increase in K^+ creates a gradient for the movement of water into the guard cell, which, in turn, results in guard cell expansion and the opening of the stomata.

5. When K^+ enter a guard cell, they create an unbalanced charge state. In some plants, the charge is balanced by the movement of chloride ions (Cl^-) into the guard cells along with the K^+. In other plants, H^+ are pumped out of the cell. The H^+ originate from the ionization of various organic substances within the cell.

Transport of Sugars

Translocation is the movement of carbohydrates through phloem from a **source,** such as leaves, to a **sink,** a site of carbohydrate utilization. Translocation is described by the **pressure-flow** hypothesis, as follows:

1. **Sugars enter sieve-tube members.** Soluble carbohydrates, such as fructose and sucrose, move from a site of production, such as the palisade mesophyll, to sieve-tube members by active transport. This develops a concentration of solutes (dissolved substances, sugars in this case) in the sieve-tube members at the source that is higher than that at the sink (a root, for example).

2. **Water enters sieve-tube members.** As a result of the movement of solutes into the sieve-tube members, the concentration of water inside the cell becomes less than in the area outside the cell. As a result, water diffuses into these cells, moving down the water concentration gradient.

3. **Pressure in sieve-tube members at the source moves water and sugars to sieve-tube members at the sink through sieve tubes.** When water enters the sieve-tube members in the leaves (or other source), pressure builds up because the rigid cell wall does not expand. As a result, water and sugars move by bulk flow through sieve tubes (through sieve plates between sieve-tube members).

4. **Pressure is reduced in sieve-tube members at the sink as sugars are removed for utilization by nearby cells.** As water and sugars move by bulk flow from source to sink, pressure begins to build at the sink. However, a sink is an area where carbohydrates are being utilized. Thus, sugars are removed from the sieve-tube members (by active transport), which increases the concentration of water within the sieve-tube members. Water then diffuses out of the cell (moving down the water concentration gradient), relieving the pressure.

There is a physiologically important result when sugars are stored as starches. Starch is essentially insoluble in water. Thus, any cell can act as a sink if it removes soluble sugars from its cytoplasm by converting them to starch. Doing so would have the same effect as breaking down the sugars for energy. Similarly, any cell can act as a source if it breaks down starch into soluble glucose molecules. For example, when photosynthesis activity is low (during nights or cold winters), roots in plants can act as a sugar source when stored starches are broken down to sugars.

Plant Hormones

Hormones are substances that are produced by specialized cells in one part of an organism that influence the physiology of cells located elsewhere. They are small molecules, capable of passing through cell walls, that affect the division, growth (elongation), or differentiation of the cells. Very small quantities of hormones are required to alter cell physiology. However, the specific effect of a hormone depends upon the particular hormone, its concentration, the target cell, and the presence or absence of other hormones. A description of the five classes of plant hormones follows:

1. **Auxin,** or **IAA** (indoleacetic acid), promotes plant growth by facilitating the elongation of developing cells. Auxin does this by increasing the concentration of H^+ in primary cell walls, which, in turn, loosens cellulose fibers which increase cell wall plasticity. In response, turgor pressure causes the cell wall to expand, thus generating growth. Auxin is produced at the tips of shoots and roots, where, in concert with other hormones, it influences plant responses to light (**phototropism**) and gravity (**geotropism**). In addition, auxin is active in leaves, fruits, and germinating seeds. Structurally, auxin is a modified tryptophan amino acid. After synthesis from tryptophan, it is *actively* transported (using ATP) from cell to cell in a specific direction (**polar transport**), by means of a chemiosmotic process.

2. **Gibberellins** are a group of plant hormones that, like auxin, promotes cell growth. The more than 60 various related gibberellins are abbreviated GA1, GA2, GA3, etc., for **gibberellic acid.** They are synthesized in young leaves, roots, and seeds but are often transported to other parts of the plant. For example, gibberellins produced in the roots and

transported to shoot tips interact with auxins to stimulate shoot growth. Gibberellins are also involved in the promotion of fruit development and of seed germination, and the inhibition of aging in leaves. High concentrations of GA can cause the rapid elongation of stems (called **bolting**). For example, bolting occurs in rice plants when a fungus that produces GA attacks the plant.

3. **Cytokinins** are a group of hormones that stimulate cytokinesis (cell division). Structurally, they are variations of the nitrogen base adenine. They include naturally occurring **zeatin** and artificially produced **kinetin.** Cytokinins are produced in roots (and perhaps elsewhere) and are transported throughout the plant. They have a variety of effects depending upon the target organ and, sometimes, the presence (and concentration) of auxin. In addition to stimulating cell division, cytokinins influence the direction of organ development (organogenesis). For example, the relative amounts of cytokinins and auxin determine whether roots or shoots will develop. Cytokinins stimulate the growth of lateral buds, thus weakening **apical dominance** (the dominant growth of the apical meristem). Cytokinins have been found to delay **senescence** (aging) of leaves and are often sprayed on cut flowers and fruit to prolong their usefulness.

4. **Ethylene** ($H_2C = CH_2$) is a gas that promotes the ripening of fruit. During the later stages of fruit development, ethylene gas fills the intercellular air spaces within the fruit and stimulates its ripening. Ethylene is also involved in stimulating the production of flowers. In addition, ethylene (in combination with auxin) inhibits the elongation of roots, stems, and leaves and influences **leaf abscission,** the aging and dropping of leaves.

5. **Abscisic acid** (ABA) is a growth inhibiter. In buds, it delays growth and causes the formation of scales in preparation for overwintering. In many species of plants, ABA maintains dormancy in seeds. Dormancy in these seeds is broken by an increase in gibberellins or by other mechanisms that respond to environmental cues such as temperature or light. In some desert species, seed dormancy is overcome by the leaching of ABA from seeds by rains. Although ABA is named for the process of abscission, its influence on the abscission of leaves, flowers, and fruits is controversial.

Plant Responses to Stimuli

Since plants are anchored by their roots, they cannot move in response to environmental stimuli. Instead, they change their growth pattern. A growth pattern in response to an environmental stimulus is called a **tropism.** Three tropisms are described below:

1. **Phototropism,** the response to light, is achieved by the action of the hormone auxin. The process is described as follows:

   - Auxin is produced in the apical meristem, moves downward by *active transport* into the zone of elongation, and generates growth by stimulating elongation.

   - When all sides of the apical meristem are equally illuminated, growth of the stem is uniform and the stem grows straight.

   - When the stem is *unequally* illuminated, auxin moves downward into the zone of elongation but concentrates on the *shady* side of the stem. Auxin that would have normally accumulated on the sunny side ends up on the shady side.

- The higher concentration of auxin in the shady side of the stem causes *differential growth;* that is, since auxin generates growth by stimulating elongation, the *shady side grows more* than the sunny side. When the shady side grows more than the sunny side, the stem bends toward the light.

2. **Gravitropism** (or **geotropism**), the response to gravity by stems and roots, is not well understood. In general, both auxin and gibberellins are involved, but their action depends on their relative concentrations and the target organ (root or stem). The role of auxin appears to agree with the following:

   - If a *stem* is horizontal, auxin produced at the apical meristem moves down the stem and concentrates on its lower side. Since auxin stimulates cell elongation, growth of the lower side is greater than that of the upper side, and the stem bends upward as it grows.

   - If a *root* is horizontal, auxin is produced at the apical meristem (root tip), moves up the roots, and, as in stems, concentrates on the lower side of the root. However, in roots, auxin *inhibits* growth. This is because concentrations of auxin are higher in roots than in stems.

Dissolved ions, auxins, gibberellins, and other hormones do not respond to gravity. They remain evenly distributed in a solution, regardless of the presence or directional pull of gravity. Therefore, auxins do not concentrate in the lower parts of stems or roots in *direct* response to gravity. Starch, on the other hand, is insoluble in water and does respond to gravity. It is believed that specialized starch-storing plastids called **statoliths,** which settle at the lower ends of cells, somehow influence the direction of auxin movement.

3. **Thigmotropism** is a response to touch. When vines and other climbing plants contact some object, they respond by wrapping around it. The mechanism for this kind of differential growth is not well understood.

Photoperiodism

Photoperiodism is the response of plants to changes in the **photoperiod,** or the relative length of daylight and night. To respond to changes in the photoperiod, plants maintain a **circadian rhythm,** a clock that measures the length of daylight and night. The mechanism is **endogenous**; that is, it is an internal clock that continues to keep time (although less accurately) even if external cues are absent. External cues, such as dawn and dusk, reset the clock to maintain accuracy.

The mechanism for maintaining the circadian rhythm is not well understood. **Phytochrome,** a protein modified with a light-absorbing chromophore, seems to be involved. There are two forms of phytochrome, P_r (or P_{660}) and P_{fr} (or P_{730}), depending upon which wavelengths of light the phytochrome absorbs, red (wavelength 660 nm) or far-red (730 nm). The two forms are photoreversible; that is, when P_r is exposed to red light, it is converted to P_{fr}; when P_{fr} is exposed to far-red light, it is converted back to P_r. The following observations have been made for many plants:

1. **P_{fr} appears to reset the circadian-rhythm clock.** P_{fr} is the active form of phytochrome and appears to maintain photoperiod accuracy by resetting the circadian-rhythm clock.

2. **P_r is the form of phytochrome synthesized in plant cells.** P_r is synthesized in the leaves of plants.

3. **P_r and P_{fr} are in equilibrium during daylight.** During daylight, P_r is converted to P_{fr}, since red light is present in sunlight. Some far-red light is also present in sunlight, so some of the P_{fr} is converted back into P_r. In this manner, an equilibrium between the two forms of phytochrome is maintained during *daylight*.

4. **P_r accumulates at night.** At night, the levels of P_{fr} drop. This is because there is no sunlight to make the conversion from P_r to P_{fr}. Also, P_{fr} breaks down faster than P_r, and in some plants, P_{fr} is metabolically converted back into P_r. Furthermore, the cell continues to make P_r at night. Thus, P_r accumulates at *night*.

5. **At daybreak, light rapidly converts the accumulated P_r to P_{fr}.** An equilibrium between P_r and P_{fr} is again attained.

6. **Night length is responsible for resetting the circadian-rhythm clock.** If daylight is interrupted with a brief dark period, there is no effect on the circadian-rhythm clock. In contrast, flashes of red or far-red light during the night period can reset the clock. If a plant is exposed to a flash of red light during the night, P_r is converted back to P_{fr}, a shorter night period is measured, and the circadian rhythm is reset. If a flash of far-red light follows the red light, then the effect of the red light is reversed, and the night length is restored to the night length in effect before the far-red flash. In a series of alternating flashes of red and far-red light, only the last flash affects the perception of night length. Thus, red light shortens the night length and far-red restores the night length.

Many flowering plants initiate flowering in response to changes in the photoperiod. Flowering plants can be divided into three groups, as follows:

1. **Long-day** plants flower in the spring and early summer when daylight is *increasing*.

2. **Short-day** plants flower in late summer and early fall when daylight is *decreasing*. These plants flower when daylight is *less than* a critical length (or when night *exceeds* a critical length).

3. **Day-neutral** plants do not flower in response to daylight changes. Some other cue, such as temperature or water, triggers flowering.

When the photoperiod is such that flowering is initiated, it is believed that a flowering hormone is produced. This hormone, called **florigen,** has yet to be isolated, although there is considerable experimental evidence that it is produced.

Phytochrome also seems to be involved in other light-related functions. For example, many seeds require a minimum exposure to light before germinating. The phytochrome system detects changes in the amount of light, and when the critical exposure is exceeded (and when other factors, such as water, are present), production of gibberellins (or destruction of abscisic acid) begins. Germination follows.

By measuring the red to far-red light ratio, the phytochrome system evaluates the quality of light reaching the plant. In this manner, it is able to determine shade from sun. As a result, it can stimulate growth when a shade-intolerant plant is suddenly shaded by other plants.

Sample Questions and Answers

Multiple-Choice Questions

Directions: Each of the following questions or statements is followed by five possible answers or sentence completions. Choose the one best answer or sentence completion.

1. Which of the following is dead at functional maturity?

   A. Companion cell

   B. Guard cell

   C. Palisade mesophyll

   D. Sieve-tube members

   E. Vessel member

2. Most growth takes place in terminal shoots and roots in

   A. the zone of cell division

   B. the zone of elongation

   C. the zone of maturation

   D. meristematic cells

   E. vascular cambium

3. A plant with a fibrous root system, leaves with parallel venation, and a seed with a single cotyledon is probably a

   A. corn plant

   B. fern

   C. fir tree

   D. pine tree

   E. pea plant

4. All of the following are true about the vascular cambium EXCEPT:

   A. It increases the girth of plants.

   B. It produces secondary xylem.

   C. It produces secondary phloem.

   D. It produces bark in woody plants.

   E. It occurs in the stem and in the root.

5. Root hairs occur on

   A. epidermal cells in the zone of cell division

   B. epidermal cells in the zone of maturation

   C. parenchyma cells in the zone of elongation

   D. parenchyma cells in the zone of maturation

   E. cells of the root cap

6. A tree was girdled by completely removing a ring of bark from its entire circumference to a depth to, but not including, the sapwood. This would most likely result in an inability to

   A. transport water to leaves

   B. transport water to roots

   C. transport carbohydrates to roots

   D. carry on photosynthesis

   E. obtain water from the surrounding soil

7. Which of the following contributes most to the movement of water through xylem?

   A.   Capillary action

   B.   Carbohydrate utilization in cells that act as sinks

   C.   Plasmodesmata in sieve plates

   D.   Root pressure

   E.   Transpiration

8. All of the following contribute to flowering mechanisms EXCEPT:

   A.   photoperiodism

   B.   phytochrome

   C.   length of night or day light

   D.   chlorophyll

   E.   florigen

9. During the middle of the night, a flowering plant was exposed to a sequence of red and far-red light in the following order: red, far-red, red. All of the following are true EXCEPT:

   A.   The active form of phytochrome is P_{fr}.

   B.   High levels of P_{fr} would exist at the end of the sequence.

   C.   Low levels of P_r would exist at the end of the sequence.

   D.   In short-day plants, flowering would be induced.

   E.   In day-neutral plants, flowering would not be affected.

10. All of the following are true about growth rings in trees EXCEPT:

   A.   Growth rings can be used to measure the age of trees in temperate regions.

   B.   Growth rings are caused by variations in the growth of xylem tissue.

   C.   Growth rings in nonwoody plants provide a history of precipitation during the life of the plants.

   D.   Variations in growth rings represent variations in tree growth from one year to the next.

   E.   The size of the growth rings is influenced by precipitation, light, and temperature.

11. All of the following are found in both roots and stems EXCEPT:

   A.   casparian strip

   B.   primary phloem

   C.   primary xylem

   D.   secondary xylem

   E.   vascular cambium

12. When stomata are open in C_3 plants, one would likely find

   A.   it is night

   B.   the guard cells are relaxed

   C.   the environment is excessively hot and dry

   D.   a low concentration of K^+ in the guard cells

   E.   low CO_2 levels in the leaf

13. Ripening of fruit is promoted by

    A. abscisic acid

    B. cytokinins

    C. ethylene

    D. gibberellins

    E. indoleacetic acid

14. All of the following occur in a phototropic response EXCEPT:

    A. Shoots bend toward light.

    B. Auxin is produced at the shoot tip and diffuses down the stem.

    C. Auxin accumulates on the shady side of the shoot.

    D. Auxin transport is unidirectional.

    E. The movement of auxin down a stem is by active transport.

15. In C_4 plants, most carbon fixation occurs in which of the following?

    A. Epidermis

    B. Spongy mesophyll

    C. Palisade mesophyll

    D. Xylem

    E. Bundle sheath cells

Answers to Multiple-Choice Questions

1. E. Functioning xylem tissue, both vessel members and tracheids, consists only of cell walls. There is no cell membrane, nucleus, cytoplasm, or other cellular material present.

2. B. Cells expand in the zone of elongation, the area behind shoot and root tips where water is absorbed. The expansion of cells is responsible for growth. The zone of cell division, meristematic cells, and vascular cambium are all sites of cell division. However, the formation of two cells from a parent cell does not result in a larger volume until water is absorbed and elongation takes place.

3. A. The characteristics described in the question are those of a monocot. Among the answers, only corn is a monocot.

4. D. The cork cambium produces the bark, or periderm, of woody plants.

5. B. Root hairs are produced as extensions of epidermal cells as they mature. If they were to form on younger epidermal cells, on cells in the zone of cell division or on cells in the zone of elongation, they could be damaged when the root elongated.

6. C. Girdling, or removing the bark of a tree in this manner, removes the phloem tissue. As a result, carbohydrates, which are transported through the phloem, cannot reach the roots. The sapwood, or active xylem, however, is left intact. Thus, water transport is not affected.

7. E. Transpiration is the driving force for the cohesion-tension mechanism responsible for the movement of water through xylem. Capillary action and root pressure contribute little, if at all, to water movement. Carbohydrate utilization and plasmodesmata refer to the movement of sugars through phloem.

8. D. Chlorophyll is not known to be involved in flowering.

9. D. The last light to which the plants were exposed makes the final conversion between P_r and P_{fr}. Since red light was used last, all of the P_r is converted to P_{fr}, a shorter night period is measured, and the circadian clock is reset. Short-day plants are unaffected, but flowering in long-day plants (short-night plants) is induced.

10. C. Nonwoody plants do not have growth rings because secondary xylem (woody tissue) is not produced. In woody plants, however, growth rings are present and reveal a history of precipitation. Growth rings also reveal other environmental conditions such as temperature, light, and length of growing season. The physiological health of the tree, as influenced by disease, for example, may also be revealed in growth rings.

11. A. The casparian strip, a waterproof lining created by the waxy material suberin, occurs only in roots. Suberin permeates the cell walls between adjacent cells of the endodermis, thereby preventing water movement into or out of the vascular cylinder by the apoplastic pathway.

12. E. CO_2 levels are relatively low in leaves when photosynthesis is active, which, in C_3 plants, occurs only during the day and when the stomata are open. At night or when day-time environmental conditions are severe (hot and dry), stomata close, photosynthesis stops, and CO_2 levels increase as a result of respiration. In CAM plants, however, stomata are closed during the day, but photosynthesis proceeds because CO_2 is supplied by the metabolic conversion of malic acid to CO_2 (and PEP).

13. C. The plant hormone ethylene is a gas that promotes ripening of fruit. Fruit is often picked green (unripened) and artificially ripened with ethylene before it is delivered to markets.

14. B. Although auxin is produced at the apical meristem (the tip of the shoot), it does not move down the stem by diffusion, but rather by active transport, as indicated in answer **E.**

15. E. In C_4 plants, carbon fixation (by the Calvin-Benson cycle) occurs in the bundle sheath cells. In C_3 plants, most carbon fixation occurs in the palisade mesophyll.

Free-Response Questions

Free-response questions on the AP exam may require you to provide information from a narrow area of biology, or they may consist of parts that require you to assemble information from diverse areas of biology. The questions that follow are typical of either an entire AP exam question or merely that part of a question that is related to this section.

Directions: Answer the questions below as completely and as thoroughly as possible. Answer the question in essay form (NOT outline form), using complete sentences. You may use diagrams to supplement your answers, but a diagram alone without appropriate discussion is inadequate.

1. Describe the movement of water into roots and from roots to leaves.

2. Describe the various reactions of plants to light.

Some Typical Answers to Free-Response Questions

Question 1

Water enters roots through root hairs, hairlike extensions of newly matured epidermal cells that increase the absorptive surface area of roots. In many cases, mycorrhizae, a mutualistic relationship between the plant roots and fungi, further increases surface area and aids in the absorption of water and minerals. Once inside the root, water moves toward the center by moving from one cell to the next through plasmodesmata (symplastic pathway) or through the cell walls (apoplastic pathway). At the endodermis, however, water must move through the symplast because the suberin-containing casparian strip prevents movement through or between cell walls. After traversing the endodermis, water enters the xylem. The xylem consists of either tracheids, vessel elements, or both, which are dead cells at maturity that provide a tube through which water moves to the leaves and other plant parts. Water in the leaves is used for photosynthesis or is lost by transpiration.

There are three mechanisms that move water through a plant. Osmosis develops root pressure and moves water through the cortex of the root and into the vascular cylinder. Capillary action is responsible for a limited amount of water lift in the xylem tubes. Most water movement, however, is explained by the cohesion-tension theory. In this mechanism, tension is developed when water is pulled up a column by the transpiration of water through stomata. An entire column of water moves as a unit because of the cohesion of water molecules that results from hydrogen bonding. The driving force for this mechanism is the sun.

Question 2

Plants have numerous reactions to light, including phototropism (auxin), photoperiodism in flowering and budding (phytochrome), and seed germination (phytochrome, gibberellins, and abscisic acid). You should describe the mechanisms of as many of these as you can.

Animal Structure and Function

Review

Animals are complex systems of cells working in a coordinated fashion to monitor changing external conditions while maintaining a constant internal environment. To accomplish these tasks, animal cells are organized into systems that are specialized for particular functions. This section focuses on the structure of these various systems and how they accomplish particular tasks.

Cells are organized in the following ways:

1. **Tissues** are groups of similar cells performing a common function. Animal tissues are organized into four general categories:

   - **Epithelial** tissue (outer skin layers and internal protective coverings)
   - **Connective** tissue (bone, cartilage, blood)
   - **Nervous** tissue
   - **Muscle** tissue

2. An **organ** is a group of different kinds of tissues functioning together to perform a particular activity. For example, the heart consists of tissues from all four categories functioning together to pump blood through the body.

3. An **organ system** is two or more organs working together to accomplish a particular task. For example, the digestive system involves the coordinated activities of many organs, including the mouth, stomach, small and large intestines, pancreas, and liver.

The function of many animal systems is to contribute toward **homeostasis**, or the maintenance of stable, internal conditions within narrow limits. In many cases, stable conditions are maintained by **negative feedback**. In negative feedback, a sensing mechanism (a **receptor**) detects a change in conditions beyond specific limits. A control center, or **integrator** (often the brain), evaluates the change and activates a second mechanism (an **effector**) to correct the condition. Conditions are constantly monitored by receptors and evaluated by the control center. When the control center determines that conditions have returned to normal, corrective action is discontinued. Thus, in *negative* feedback, the original condition is canceled, or negated, so that conditions are returned to normal. Compare this with positive feedback, in which an action intensifies a condition so that it is driven further beyond normal limits. Such positive feedback is uncommon but does occur during childbirth (labor contractions), lactation (where milk production increases in response to an increase in nursing), and sexual orgasm.

Thermoregulation

Animals can be loosely grouped into two groups based upon how body temperature is maintained:

1. **Ectotherms** are animals that obtain body heat from their environment. Since their temperatures often vary with the temperature of their environment, they are sometimes referred to as **poikilotherms** ("changing temperature"). Examples include most invertebrates, amphibians, reptiles, and fish. Because many of these animals may feel cold to the touch they are called "cold-blooded" animals, but many land-dwelling ectotherms can exceed ambient temperatures by basking in the sun.

2. **Endotherms** are animals that generate their own body heat. They are also referred to as **homeotherms** because they maintain a constant internal temperature or as "warm-blooded" because their temperature is relatively warm compared to ectotherms.

Animals regulate their body temperatures by employing the following mechanisms:

1. **Cooling by evaporation.** Many animals lose heat by sweating. Since changing from a liquid to gaseous state requires energy (an endergonic reaction), body heat is removed when water vaporizes. Evaporative heat loss also occurs from the respiratory tract, a cooling process employed when animals pant.

2. **Warming by metabolism.** Muscle contraction and other metabolic activities generate heat. For example, shivering warms animals from the heat generated by muscle contractions.

3. **Adjusting surface area to regulate temperature.** The extremities of bodies (arms, hands, feet, ears) add considerable surface area to the body. By changing the volume of blood that flows to these areas by vasodilation or vasoconstriction (increasing or decreasing the diameter of blood vessels), heat can be lost or conserved. In hot environments, for example, elephants and jackrabbits *increase* blood flow to their large ears to reduce body temperature. In contrast, animals in cold environments *reduce* blood flow to their ears, hands, and feet to conserve heat. In addition, when blood moves through vessels toward an extremity, it flows adjacent to blood moving away from that extremity. In this example of **countercurrent exchange,** heat conduction from the warm blood to the returning cold blood is redirected to internal parts of the body before reaching the extremity.

In addition, all animals have various behavioral, physiological, or anatomical adaptations that increase their ability to survive in a particular environment. To survive cold temperatures, for example, some animals hibernate, while others have hair, feathers, or blubber. Some animals avoid heat by merely moving from sun to shade, while others restrict their activity to nights.

The Respiratory System

Animal cells require O_2 for aerobic respiration. If cells are not directly exposed to the outside environment, then some mechanism must provide gas exchange to internal cells, delivering O_2 and removing waste CO_2. The movement of gases into and out of the entire organism is called

respiration. (This term, respiration, is also used to describe *cellular* respiration, the process of producing ATP within the mitochondria of cells.) The following gas exchange mechanisms are found in animals:

1. **Direct with environment.** Some animals are small enough to allow gas exchange directly with the outside environment. Many of these animals, such as the Platyhelminthes (flatworms), typically have large surface areas, and every cell either is exposed to the outside environment or is close enough that gases are available by diffusion through adjacent cells. In larger animals, such as the Annelida (segmented worms), gas exchange through the skin is augmented by a distribution system (a circulatory system) just inside the skin.

2. **Gills.** Gills are *evaginated* structures, or outgrowths from the body, that create a large surface area over which gas exchange occurs. Inside the gills, a circulatory system removes the oxygen and delivers waste CO_2. In some animals, such as polychaete worms (Annelida), the gills are *external* and unprotected. In other animals, the gills are *internal* and protected. In fish, for example, water enters the mouth, passes over the gills, and exits through the gill cover, or **operculum. Countercurrent exchange** between the opposing movements of water and the underlying blood through blood vessels maximizes the diffusion of O_2 into the blood and CO_2 into the water.

3. **Tracheae.** Insects have chitin-lined tubes, or **tracheae,** that permeate their bodies. Oxygen enters (or CO_2 exits) the tracheae through openings called **spiracles**; diffusion occurs across moistened tracheal endings.

4. **Lungs. Lungs** are *invaginated* structures, or cavities within the body of the animal. **Book lungs,** occurring in many spiders, are stacks of flattened membranes enclosed in an internal chamber.

Gas exchange in humans occurs as follows:

1. **Nose, pharynx, larynx.** Air enters the nose and passes through the nasal cavity, **pharynx,** and **larynx.** The larynx ("voice box") contains the vocal cords.

2. **Trachea.** After passing through the larynx, air enters the **trachea,** a cartilage-lined tube. When the animal is swallowing, a special flap called the **epiglottis** covers the trachea, preventing the entrance of solid and liquid material.

3. **Bronchi, bronchioles.** The trachea branches into two **bronchi** (singular, **bronchus**), which enter the lungs and then branch repeatedly, forming narrower tubes called **bronchioles.**

4. **Alveolus.** Each bronchiole branch ends in a small sac called an **alveolus** (plural, **alveoli**). Each alveolus is densely surrounded by blood-carrying capillaries.

5. **Diffusion between alveolar chambers and blood.** Gas exchange occurs by diffusion across the moist, sac membranes of the alveoli. Oxygen diffuses into the moisture covering the membrane, through the alveolar wall, through the blood capillary wall, into the blood, and into red blood cells. Carbon dioxide diffuses in the opposite direction.

6. **Bulk flow of O_2.** The circulatory system transports O_2 throughout the body within red blood cells. Red blood cells contain hemoglobin, iron-containing proteins to which O_2 bonds.

7. **Diffusion between blood and cells.** Blood capillaries permeate the body. Oxygen diffuses out of the red blood cells, across blood capillary walls, into interstitial fluids (the fluids surrounding the cells), and across cell membranes. Carbon dioxide diffuses in the opposite direction.

8. **Bulk flow of CO_2.** Most CO_2 is transported as dissolved bicarbonate ions (HCO_3^-) in the plasma, the liquid portion of the blood. The formation of HCO_3^-, however, occurs in the red blood cells, where the formation of carbonic acid (H_2CO_3) is catalyzed by the enzyme **carbonic anhydrase,** as follows:

$$CO_2 + H_2O \rightarrow H_2CO_3 \rightarrow H^+ + HCO_3^-$$

Following their formation in the red blood cells, HCO_3^- ions diffuse back into the plasma. Some CO_2, however, does not become HCO_3^-; instead, it mixes directly with the plasma (as CO_2 gas) or binds with the amino groups of the hemoglobin molecules inside red blood cells.

9. **Bulk flow of air into and out of the lungs (mechanics of respiration).** Air is moved into and out of the lungs by changing their volume. The volume of the lungs is increased by the contraction of the **diaphragm** (a muscle under the lungs) and the **intercostal** muscles (muscles between the ribs). When the lung volume increases, the air pressure within the lungs decreases. This causes a pressure difference between the air in the lungs and the air outside the body. As a result, air rushes into the lungs by bulk flow. When the diaphragm and intercostal muscles relax, the volume of the lungs decreases, raising the pressure on the air, causing the air to rush out.

10. **Control of respiration.** Chemoreceptors in the carotid arteries (arteries that supply blood to the brain) monitor the pH of the blood. When a body is active, CO_2 production increases. When the CO_2 that enters the plasma is converted to HCO_3^- and H^+, the blood pH drops (becomes more acidic). In response, the chemoreceptors send nerve impulses to the diaphragm and intercostal muscles to increase respiratory rate. This results in a faster turnover in gas exchange, which, in turn, returns blood pH to normal. The regulation of the respiratory rate in this manner is an example of how homeostasis is maintained by negative feedback.

The Circulatory System

Large organisms require a transport system to distribute nutrients and oxygen and to remove wastes and CO_2 from cells distributed throughout the body. Two kinds of circulatory systems accomplish this internal transport.

1. **Open circulatory systems** pump blood into an internal cavity called a **hemocoel** (or cavities called **sinuses**), which bathe tissues with an oxygen- and nutrient-carrying fluid called **hemolymph.** The hemolymph returns to the pumping mechanism of the system, a **heart,** through holes called **ostia.** Open circulatory systems occur in insects and most mollusks.

2. In **closed circulatory systems,** the nutrient-, oxygen-, and waste-carrying fluid, **blood,** is *confined* to vessels. Closed circulatory systems are found among members of the phylum Annelida (earthworms, for example), certain mollusks (octopuses and squids), and vertebrates.

In the closed circulatory system of vertebrates, vessels moving *away* from the heart are called **arteries.** Arteries branch into smaller vessels, the **arterioles,** and then branch further into the smallest vessels, the **capillaries.** Gas and nutrient exchange occurs by diffusion across capillary walls into interstitial fluids and into surrounding cells. Wastes and excess interstitial fluids move in the opposite direction as they diffuse into the capillaries. The blood, now deoxygenated, remains in the capillaries and *returns* to the heart through **venules,** which merge to form larger **veins.** The heart then pumps the deoxygenated blood to the respiratory organ (gills or lungs) where arteries again branch into a capillary bed for gas exchange. The oxygenated blood then returns to the heart through veins. From here, the oxygenated blood is pumped, once again, throughout the body.

In the human heart, blood moves through the following structures, in the following order (Figure 11-1).

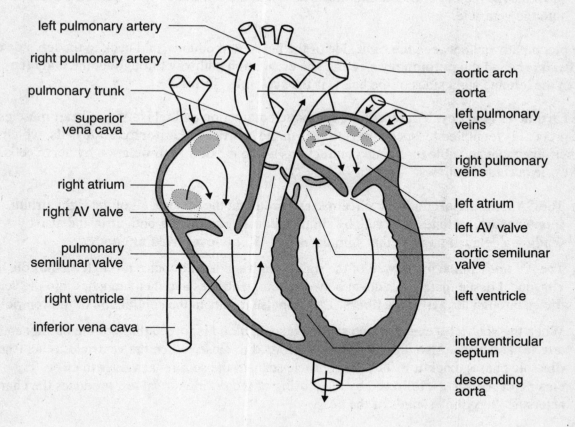

The Heart

Figure 11-1

1. **Right atrium.** *Deoxygenated* blood enters this chamber on the right side of the heart through two veins, the upper **superior vena cava** and the lower **inferior vena cava.** (Right and left refer to the right and left sides of the body.)

2. **Right ventricle.** Blood moves through the **right atrioventricular valve** (or **AV valve,** also called the **tricuspid valve**) and enters the **right ventricle.** The ventricles, with walls thicker and more muscular than those of the atria, contract and pump the blood into the **pulmonary artery,** through the **pulmonary semilunar valve,** and toward the lungs. When the ventricles *contract,* the AV valve closes and prevents blood moving backward into the atrium. When the ventricles *relax,* the semilunar valve prevents backflow from the pulmonary artery back into the ventricles.

3. **Left atrium.** After the lungs, the *oxygenated* blood returns to the left atrium through the **pulmonary veins.**

4. **Left ventricle.** Passing through the **left AV valve** (also called the mitral or bicuspid valve), the blood moves into the **left ventricle.** From here, the muscular left ventricle pumps the blood into the large artery, the **aorta,** through the **aortic semilunar valve,** and throughout the body. Similar to the valves on the right side of the heart, the left AV valve prevents movement of blood into the atrium, and the semilunar valve prevents backflow into the ventricle.

The blood pathway between the right side of the heart, to the lungs, and back to the left side of the heart is called the **pulmonary circuit.** The circulation pathway throughout the body (between the left and right sides of the heart) is the **systemic circuit.**

The **cardiac** or **heart cycle** refers to the rhythmic contraction and relaxation of heart muscles. The process is regulated by specialized tissues in the heart called **autorhythmic cells,** which are self-excitable and able to initiate contractions without external stimulation by nerve cells. The cycle occurs as follows:

1. The **SA (sinoatrial) node,** or **pacemaker,** located in the upper wall of the right atrium, spontaneously initiates the cycle by simultaneously contracting both atria and also by sending a delayed impulse that stimulates the **AV (atrioventricular) node.**

2. The **AV node** in the lower wall of the right atrium sends an impulse through the **bundle of His,** nodal tissue that passes down between both ventricles and then branches into the ventricles through the **Purkinje fibers.** This impulse results in the contraction of the ventricles.

3. When the ventricles contract (the **systole** phase), blood is forced through the pulmonary arteries and aorta. Also, the AV valves are forced to close. When the ventricles relax (the **diastole** phase), backflow into the ventricles causes the semilunar valves to close. The closing of AV valves, followed by the closing of the semilunar valves, produces the characteristic "lub-dup" sounds of the heart.

Hydrostatic pressure created by the heart forces blood to move through the arteries. As blood reaches the capillaries, however, blood pressure drops dramatically and approaches zero in the venules. Blood continues to move through the veins, *not because of the contractions of the heart,* but because of the movements of adjacent skeletal muscles which squeeze the blood vessels. Blood moves in the direction of the heart because valves in the veins prevent backflow.

Wastes and excess interstitial fluids enter the circulatory system when they diffuse into capillaries. However, not all of the interstitial fluids enter the capillaries. Instead, some interstitial fluids and wastes are returned to the circulatory system by way of the **lymphatic system,** a second network of capillaries and veins. The fluid in these lymphatic veins, called lymph, moves slowly through lymphatic vessels by the contraction of adjacent muscles. Valves in the lymphatic veins prevent backflow. Lymph returns to the blood circulatory system through two ducts located in the shoulder region. In addition to returning fluids to the circulatory system, the lymphatic system functions as a filter. **Lymph nodes,** enlarged bodies throughout the lymphatic system, act as cleaning filters and as immune response centers that defend against infection.

Blood contains the following:

1. **Red blood cells,** or **erythrocytes,** transport oxygen (attached to hemoglobin) and catalyze the conversion of CO_2 and H_2O to H_2CO_3. Mature red blood cells lack a nucleus, thereby maximizing hemoglobin content and thus their ability to transport O_2.

2. **White blood cells,** or **leukocytes,** consist of five major groups of disease-fighting cells that defend the body against infection.

3. **Platelets** are cell fragments that are involved in blood clotting. Platelets release factors that are involved in the conversion of the major clotting agent, **fibrinogen,** into its active form, **fibrin.** Threads of fibrin protein form a network that stops blood flow.

4. **Plasma** is the liquid portion of the blood that contains various dissolved substances.

The Excretory System

In general, excretory systems help maintain homeostasis in organisms by regulating water balance and by removing harmful substances.

Osmoregulation is the absorption and excretion of water and dissolved substances (solutes) so that proper water balance (and osmotic pressure) is maintained between the organism and its surroundings. Two examples follow:

1. **Marine fish.** The body of a marine fish is *hypo*osmotic with its environment—that is, it is less salty than the surrounding water. Thus, water is constantly lost by osmosis. In order to maintain their proper internal environment, marine fish constantly drink, rarely urinate, and secrete accumulated salts (that they acquire when they drink) out through their gills.

2. **Fresh water fish.** The body of a fresh water fish is *hyper*osmotic, or saltier than the surrounding water. Thus, water constantly diffuses into the fish. In response, fresh water fish rarely drink, constantly urinate, and absorb salts through their gills.

Various excretory mechanisms have evolved in animals for the purpose of osmoregulation and for the removal of toxic substances. Toxic substances include by-products of cellular metabolism, such as the nitrogen products of protein breakdown. Examples of important excretory mechanisms follow:

1. **Contractile vacuoles** are found in the cytoplasm of various protists, such as paramecia and amoebas. These vacuoles accumulate water, merge with the plasma membrane, and release the water to the environment.

2. **Flame cells** are found in various Platyhelminthes, such as planaria. The flame cells are distributed along a branched tube system that permeates the flatworm. Body fluids are filtered across the flame cells, whose internal cilia move the fluids through the tube system. Wastes (water and salts) are excreted from the tube system through pores that exit the body.

3. **Nephridia** (or **metanephridia**) occur in pairs within each segment of most annelids, such as earthworms. Interstitial fluids enter a nephridium through a ciliated opening called a **nephrostome.** Fluids are concentrated as they pass through the **collecting tubule** due to selective secretion of materials into the surrounding coelomic fluid. Blood capillaries that surround the tubule reabsorb the secreted materials. At the end of the collecting tubule, the concentrated waste materials are excreted through an **excretory pore.** Nephridia exemplify a tube-type excretory system, where body fluids are selectively filtered as they pass through the tube. Materials to be retained are secreted back into the body fluids, while concentrated wastes continue through the tube to be excreted at the far end.

4. **Malpighian tubules** occur in many arthropods, such as terrestrial insects. Tubes attached to the midsection of the digestive tract of insects (midgut) collect body fluids from the hemolymph that bathe the cells. The fluids, which include both nitrogen wastes and materials to be retained (salts and water), are deposited into the midgut. As the fluids passthrough the hindgut of the insect (along with digested food), materials to be retained pass back out though the walls of the digestive tract. Wastes continue in the tract and are excreted through the anus.

5. The vertebrate **kidney** consists of about a million individual filtering tubes called **nephrons.** Two kidneys produce waste fluids, or **urine,** which pass through ureters to the bladder for temporary storage. From the bladder, the urine is excreted through the urethra.

Individual nephrons in the human kidney consist of a tube and closely associated blood vessels (Figure 11-2). The nephron is strategically positioned in the kidney so that the tube winds from the outer portion of the kidney, the **cortex,** down through the **medulla,** then back up into the cortex, then back down through the medulla, draining into the center of the kidney, the **renal pelvis.** Details follow.

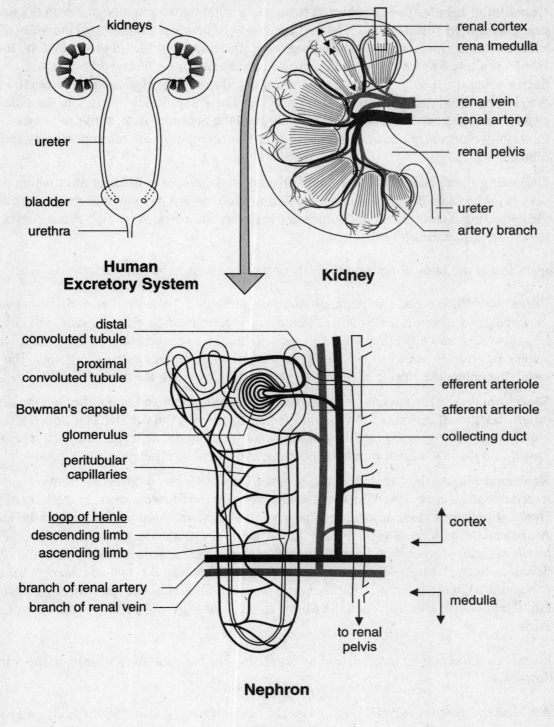

kidneys

ureter

bladder

urethra

**Human
Excretory System**

renal cortex

rena lmedulla

renal vein

renal artery

renal pelvis

ureter

artery branch

Kidney

distal
convoluted tubule

proximal
convoluted tubule

Bowman's capsule

glomerulus

peritubular
capillaries

loop of Henle
descending limb
ascending limb

branch of renal artery

branch of renal vein

efferent arteriole

afferent arteriole

collecting duct

cortex

medulla

to renal
pelvis

Nephron

Figure 11-2

1. **Bowman's capsule.** The nephron tube begins with a bulb-shaped body at one end, the
   Bowman's capsule. A branch of the renal artery (the afferent arteriole) enters into the
   Bowman's capsule, branches to form a dense ball of capillaries called the **glomerulus,**
   and then exits the capsule (efferent arteriole).

2. **Convoluted tubule.** The **convoluted tubule** is a winding tube that begins with the **proximal convoluted tubule** at the Bowman's capsule and ends with the **distal convoluted tubule** where it joins with the **collecting duct.** The middle of the tubule, called the **loop of Henle,** is shaped like a hairpin and consists of a descending and ascending limb. Surrounding the tubule is a dense network of capillaries that originate from branches of the efferent arteriole that exited the glomerulus. These capillaries merge into the renal vein as they exit the nephron. The blood flow through the nephron, then, actually passes through two capillary beds, the glomerulus and the capillary network surrounding the tubule.

3. **Collecting duct.** The distal convoluted tube empties into the **collecting duct** which descends in the same direction as the descending limb toward the center of the kidney. A single collecting duct is shared by numerous nephrons and empties into the **renal pelvis,** which, in turn, drains into the ureter.

The operation of the human nephron consists of three processes, as follows:

1. **Filtration.** When blood enters the glomerulus, pressure forces water and solutes through the capillary walls into the Bowman's capsule. Solutes include glucose, salts, vitamins, nitrogen wastes, and any other substances small enough to pass through the capillary walls. Larger substances, such as red blood cells and proteins, remain in the capillaries. The material that enters the Bowman's capsule, or filtrate, flows into the convoluted tubule.

2. **Secretion.** As the filtrate passes through the proximal tubule and, later, through the distal tubule, additional material from the interstitial fluids joins the filtrate. This added material, which originates from the capillary network surrounding the nephron, is *selectively secreted* into the convoluted tubule by both passive and active transport mechanisms.

3. **Reabsorption.** As the filtrate moves *down* the loop of Henle, it becomes more *concentrated* due to passive flow of H_2O out of the tube. As the filtrate moves *up* the loop of Henle, it becomes more *dilute* due to passive and active transport of salts out of the tubule. At the end of the loop of Henle, then, the filtrate is *not* more concentrated. Rather, the *interstitial fluids* surrounding the nephron are *more* concentrated with salts. Next, the filtrate descends through the collecting duct toward the renal pelvis. As it passes through the salts concentrated in the interstitial fluids, water passively moves out of the collecting duct and into the interstitial fluids. When the filtrate drains into the renal pelvis, it is concentrated urine.

Two hormones influence osmoregulation by regulating the concentration of salts in the urine, as follows:

1. **Antidiuretic hormone (ADH)** increases the reabsorption of water by the body and increases the concentration of salts in the urine. It does this by increasing the permeability of the *collecting duct to water.* As a result, more water diffuses out of the collecting duct as the filtrate descends into the renal pelvis.

2. **Aldosterone** increases both the reabsorption of water and the reabsorption of Na^+. It does this by increasing the permeability of the *distal convoluted tubule and collecting duct to Na^+.* As a result, more Na^+ diffuses out of this tubule and duct. Since the Na^+ increases the salt concentration outside the tubule, water passively follows.

Nitrogen forms a major waste product in animals. When amino acids and nucleic acids are broken down, they release toxic ammonia (NH_3). To rid the body of this toxin, several mechanisms have evolved, each appropriate to the habitat or survival of the animal.

1. Aquatic animals excrete NH_3 (or NH_4^+) directly into the surrounding water.

2. Mammals convert NH_3 to **urea** in their livers. Urea is significantly less toxic than NH_3 and thus requires less water to excrete in the urine.

3. Birds, insects, and many reptiles convert urea to **uric acid.** Since uric acid is mostly insoluble in water, it precipitates and forms a solid. This allows considerable water conservation by permitting the excretion of nitrogen waste as a solid. In birds, the precipitation also allows the nitrogen wastes to be securely isolated in a special sac in the egg (the **allantois**), apart from the vulnerable developing embryo.

The Digestive System

Digestion is the chemical breakdown of food into smaller molecules. In an individual cell, digestion is accomplished by **intracellular** digestion when a lysosome containing digestive enzymes merges with a food vacuole. In most animals, however, the food ingested is too large to be engulfed by individual cells. Thus, food is first digested in a **gastrovascular cavity** by **extracellular** digestion and then absorbed by individual cells.

During digestion, four different groups of molecules are commonly encountered. Each is broken down into its molecular components by specific enzymes, as follows:

1. **Starches** are broken down into glucose molecules.

2. **Proteins** are broken down into amino acids.

3. **Fats** (or **lipids**) are broken down into glycerol and fatty acids.

4. **Nucleic acids** are broken down into nucleotides.

In humans and other mammals, digestion follows the following sequence of events. In particular, note which kinds of molecules are digested (broken down) and by which enzymes. Since enzymes are specific for different bonds, only a representative few of the numerous enzymes are given.

1. **Mouth. Salivary amylase,** secreted into the mouth by the salivary glands, begins the breakdown of *starch* into maltose (a disaccharide). Chewing reduces the size of food particles, thereby increasing the surface area upon which amylase and subsequent enzymes can operate. Food is shaped into a ball, or **bolus,** and then swallowed.

2. **Pharynx.** When food is swallowed and passed into the throat, or **pharynx,** a flap of tissue, the **epiglottis,** blocks the trachea so that solid and liquid material enter only the esophagus.

3. **Esophagus.** Food moves through the esophagus, a tube leading to the stomach, by muscular contractions called **peristalsis.**

4. **Stomach.** The stomach secretes **gastric juice,** a mixture of digestive enzymes and hydrochloric acid (HCl), and serves a variety of functions, as follows:

   - *Storage.* Because of its accordionlike folds, the wall of the stomach can expand to store two to four liters of material.

   - *Mixing.* The stomach mixes the food with water and gastric juice to produce a creamy medium called **chyme.**

   - *Physical breakdown.* Muscles churn the contents of the stomach, physically breaking food down into smaller particles. In addition, HCl from the gastric juice denatures (or unfolds) proteins and loosens the cementing substances between cells of the food. Also, the HCl kills most bacteria that may accompany the food.

   - *Chemical breakdown. Proteins* are *chemically* broken down (digested) by the enzyme **pepsin.** Stomach cells producing pepsin are protected from self-digestion because they produce and secrete an inactive form, **pepsinogen.** Pepsinogen is activated into pepsin by HCl, which is produced by other stomach cells. Thus, only after pepsinogen is secreted into the stomach cavity can protein digestion begin. Once protein digestion begins, the stomach is protected by a layer of mucus secreted by still other cells in the stomach lining. Failure of the mucus to protect the stomach can lead to lesions, or **peptic ulcers.** Long believed to be caused by stress, diet, or other factors, most ulcers are now known to be caused by bacteria and can be successfully treated with antibiotics.

   - *Controlled release.* Movement of chyme into the small intestine is regulated by a valve at the end of the stomach, the **pyloric sphincter.**

5. **Small intestine.** The first twenty-five cm of the small intestine, the **duodenum,** continues the digestion of *starches* and *proteins* (which began in the mouth and stomach, respectively) as well as all remaining food types (including *fats* and *nucleotides*). Enzymes for these various processes originate from the following sources:

   - **Small intestine.** The wall of the **small intestine** is the source of various enzymes, including **proteolytic** enzymes (or **proteases,** enzymes that digest proteins, such as **aminopeptidase**), maltase and lactase (for the digestion of disaccharides), and **phosphatases** (for the digestion of nucleotides).

   - **Pancreas.** The pancreas produces various enzymes, including **trypsin** and **chymotrypsin** (proteases), **lipase** (digestion of fats), and **pancreatic amylase** (digestion of starch). These and other enzymes, packaged in an alkaline solution that serves to neutralize the HCl in the chyme, enter the duodenum through the pancreatic duct.

   - **Liver.** The liver produces bile, which functions to *emulsify* fats. Emulsification is the breaking up of fat globules into smaller fat droplets, increasing the surface area upon which fat-digesting enzymes (lipase, for example) can operate. Since bile does not chemically change anything, it is not an enzyme. Bile is also alkaline, serving to help neutralize the HCl in the chyme. The bile is stored adjacent to the liver in the **gallbladder** and flows through the bile duct where it merges with the pancreatic duct.

- The remainder of the small intestine (nearly six meters) absorbs the breakdown products of food. It is characterized by **villi** and **microvilli,** fingerlike projections of the intestinal wall that increase its total absorptive surface area. Amino acids and sugars are absorbed into blood capillaries, while most of the fatty acids and glycerol are absorbed into the lymphatic system.

6. **Large intestine.** The main function of the large intestine, or colon, is the reabsorption of water to form solid waste, or **feces.** Feces are stored at the end of the large intestine, in the **rectum,** and excreted through the **anus.** Various harmless bacteria live in the large intestine, including some that produce vitamin K, which is absorbed through the intestinal wall. At the beginning of the large intestine, there is a short branch to a dead-end pouch which bears a fingerlike projection called the appendix. Other than a possible role in the immune response, the appendix is significant only when it becomes inflamed, causing appendicitis. In herbivores, the dead-end pouch is much enlarged and is called the **cecum.** It harbors bacteria that help in the digestion of cellulose.

Hormones are involved in the digestive process. Three important hormones are described below:

1. **Gastrin** is produced by cells in the stomach lining when food reaches the stomach or when the nervous system, through smell or sight, senses the availability of food. Gastrin enters the blood stream and stimulates other cells of the stomach to produce gastric juices.

2. **Secretin** is produced by the cells lining the duodenum when food enters. Secretin stimulates the pancreas to produce bicarbonate which, when deposited into the small intestine, neutralizes the acidity of the chyme.

3. **Cholecystokinin** is produced by the small intestine to stimulate the gallbladder to release bile and the pancreas to release its enzymes.

The Nervous System

The basic structural unit of the nervous system is a nerve cell, or **neuron.** It consists of the following parts:

1. The **cell body** contains the nucleus and other cellular organelles.

2. The **dendrite** is typically a short, abundantly branched, slender extension of the cell body that *receives* stimuli.

3. The **axon** is typically a long, slender extension of the cell body that *sends* nerve impulses.

A nerve impulse begins at the tips of the dendrite branches, passes through the dendrites to the cell body, then through the axon, and finally terminates at branches of the axon.

Neurons can be classified into three general groups by their functions:

1. **Sensory neurons** (or **afferent neurons**) receive the initial stimulus. For example, sensory neurons embedded in the retina of the eye are stimulated by light, while certain sensory neurons in the hand are stimulated by touch.

2. **Motor neurons** (or **efferent neurons**) stimulate **effectors,** target cells that produce some kind of response. For example, efferent neurons may stimulate muscles (creating a movement to maintain balance or to avoid pain, for example), sweat glands (to cool the body), or cells in the stomach (to secrete gastrin in response to the smell of food, perhaps).

3. **Association neurons** (or **interneurons neurons**) are located in the spinal cord or brain and receive impulses from sensory neurons or send impulses to motor neurons. Interneurons are **integrators,** evaluating impulses for appropriate responses.

The transmission of a nerve impulse along a neuron from one end to the other occurs as a result of chemical changes across the membrane of the neuron. The membrane of an unstimulated neuron is **polarized,** that is, there is a difference in electrical charge between the outside and inside of the membrane. In particular, the *inside is negative* with respect to the outside. Polarization is established by maintaining an excess of sodium ions (Na^+) on the outside and an excess of potassium ions (K^+) on the inside. A certain amount of Na^+ and K^+ is always leaking across the membrane, but Na^+/K^+ pumps in the membrane actively restore the ions to the appropriate side. Other ions, such as large, negatively charged proteins and nucleic acids, reside inside the cell. *It is these large, negatively charged ions that contribute to the overall negative charge on the inside of the cell membrane* compared to the outside.

The following events characterize the transmission of a nerve impulse (Figure 11-3).

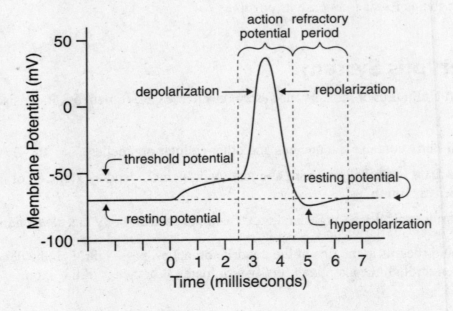

Action Potential in a Neuron

Figure 11-3

1. **Resting potential.** The resting potential describes the unstimulated, polarized state of a neuron (at about −70 millivolts).

2. **Action potential.** In response to a stimulus, **gated ion channels** in the membrane suddenly open and permit the *Na$^+$ on the outside to rush into the cell.* As the positively charged Na$^+$ rush in, the charge on the cell membrane becomes **depolarized,** or more positive on the inside (from −70 toward 0 millivolts). If the stimulus is strong enough—that is, if it is above a certain **threshold level**—more Na$^+$ gates open, increasing the inflow of Na$^+$ even more, causing an **action potential,** or complete depolarization (about +30 millivolts). This, in turn, stimulates neighboring Na$^+$ gates, further down the neuron, to open. In this manner, the action potential travels down the length of the neuron as opened Na$^+$ gates stimulate neighboring Na$^+$ gates to open. The action potential is an **all-or-nothing event**: when the stimulus fails to produce a depolarization that exceeds the threshold value, no action potential results, but when threshold potential is exceeded, complete depolarization occurs.

3. **Repolarization.** In response to the inflow of Na$^+$, another kind of gated channel opens, this time allowing the *K$^+$ on the inside to rush out of the cell.* The movement of K$^+$ out of the cell causes **repolarization** by restoring the original membrane polarization. Unlike the resting potential, however, the K$^+$ are on the outside and the Na$^+$ are on the inside. Soon after the K$^+$ gates open, the Na$^+$ gates close.

4. **Hyperpolarization.** By the time the K$^+$ gated channels close, more K$^+$ have moved out of the cell than is actually necessary to establish the original polarized potential. Thus, the membrane becomes **hyperpolarized** (about −80 millivolts).

5. **Refractory period.** With the passage of the action potential, the cell membrane is in an unusual state of affairs. The membrane is polarized, but the Na$^+$ and K$^+$ are on the wrong sides of the membrane. During this **refractory period,** the neuron will not respond to a new stimulus. To reestablish the original distribution of these ions, the Na$^+$ and K$^+$ are returned to their resting potential location by Na$^+$/K$^+$ pumps in the cell membrane. Once these ions are completely returned to their resting potential location, the neuron is ready for another stimulus.

Some neurons possess a **myelin sheath,** which consists of a series of **Schwann cells** that encircle the axon. The Schwann cells act as insulators and are separated by gaps of unsheathed axon called **nodes of Ranvier.** Instead of traveling continuously down the axon, the action potential jumps from node to node (**saltatory conduction**), thereby speeding the propagation of the impulse.

A **synapse,** or **synaptic cleft,** is the gap that separates adjacent neurons. Transmission of an impulse across a synapse, from **presynaptic cell** to **postsynaptic cell,** may be electrical or chemical. In electrical synapses, the action potential travels along the membranes of **gap junctions,** small tubes of cytoplasm that connect adjacent cells. In most animals, however, most synaptic clefts are traversed by chemicals, as follows:

1. **Calcium (Ca^{2+}) gates open.** When an action potential reaches the end of an axon, the depolarization of the membrane causes gated channels to open and allow Ca^{2+} to enter the cell.

2. **Synaptic vesicles release neurotransmitter.** The influx of Ca^{2+} into the terminal end of the axon causes **synaptic vesicles** to merge with the presynaptic membrane, releasing molecules of a chemical called a **neurotransmitter** into the synaptic cleft.

3. **Neurotransmitter binds with postsynaptic receptors.** The neurotransmitter diffuses across the synaptic cleft and binds with proteins on the postsynaptic membrane. Different proteins are receptors for different neurotransmitters.

4. **The postsynaptic membrane is excited or inhibited.** Depending upon the kind of neurotransmitter and the kind of membrane receptors, there are two possible outcomes for the postsynaptic membrane.

   - *If Na^+ gates open,* the membrane becomes depolarized and results in an **excitatory postsynaptic potential** (**EPSP**). If the threshold potential is exceeded, an action potential is generated.

   - *If K^+ gates open,* the membrane becomes more polarized (hyperpolarized) and results in an **inhibitory postsynaptic potential** (**IPSP**). As a result, it becomes more difficult to generate an action potential on this membrane.

5. **The neurotransmitter is degraded and recycled.** After the neurotransmitter binds to the postsynaptic membrane receptors, it is broken down by enzymes in the synaptic cleft. For example, a common neurotransmitter, **acetylcholine,** is broken down by **cholinesterase.** Degraded neurotransmitters are recycled by the presynaptic cell.

Some of the common neurotransmitters and the kind of activity they generate are summarized below:

1. **Acetylcholine** is commonly secreted at **neuromuscular junctions,** the gaps between motor neurons and muscle cells, where it stimulates muscles to contract. At other kinds of junctions, it typically produces an inhibitory postsynaptic potential.

2. **Epinephrine, norepinephrine, dopamine,** and **serotonin** are derived from amino acids and are mostly secreted between neurons of the central nervous system.

3. **Gamma aminobutyric acid (GABA)** is usually an inhibitory neurotransmitter among neurons in the brain.

The nervous systems of humans and other vertebrates consist of two parts, as follows:

1. The **central nervous system** (CNS) consists of the brain and spinal cord.

2. The **peripheral nervous system** consists of sensory neurons that transmit impulses *to the CNS* and motor neurons that transmit impulses *from the CNS* to effectors. The motor neuron system can be divided into two groups, as follows:

   - The **somatic nervous system** directs the contraction of skeletal muscles.

   - The **autonomic nervous system** controls the activities of organs and various involuntary muscles, such as cardiac and smooth muscles.

There are two divisions of the autonomic nervous system:

1. The **sympathetic nervous system** is involved in the stimulation of activities that prepare the body for action, such as increasing the heart rate, increasing the release of sugar from the liver into the blood, and other activities generally considered as fight-or-flight responses (responses that serve to fight off or retreat from danger).

2. The **parasympathetic nervous system** activates tranquil functions, such as stimulating the secretion of saliva or digestive enzymes into the stomach.

Generally, both sympathetic and parasympathetic systems target the same organs but often work antagonistically. For example, the sympathetic system accelerates the cardiac cycle, while the parasympathetic slows it down. Each system is stimulated as is appropriate to maintain homeostasis.

A **reflex arc** is a rapid, involuntary response to a stimulus. It consists of two or three neurons— a sensory and motor neuron and, in some reflex arcs, an interneuron. Although neurons may transmit information about the reflex response to the brain, the brain does not actually integrate the sensory and motor activities.

The Muscular System

A skeletal muscle consists of numerous muscle cells called **muscle fibers.** Muscle fibers have special terminology and distinguishing characteristics, as follows:

1. The **sarcolemma,** or plasma membrane of the muscle cell, is highly invaginated by transverse tubules (or T tubules) that permeate the cell.

2. The **sarcoplasm,** or cytoplasm of the muscle cell, contains calcium-storing **sarcoplasmic reticulum,** the specialized endoplasmic reticulum of a muscle cell.

3. Skeletal muscle cells are *multinucleate*. The nuclei lie along the periphery of the cell, forming swellings visible through the sarcolemma.

4. Nearly the entire volume of the muscle cell is filled with numerous, long **myofibrils.** Myofibrils consist of two types of filaments, as follows (Figure 11-4):

   - *Thin* filaments consist of two strands of the globular protein **actin** arranged in a double helix. Along the length of the helix are **troponin** and **tropomyosin** molecules that cover special binding sites on the actin.

   - *Thick* filaments consist of groups of the filamentous protein **myosin.** Each myosin filament forms a protruding head at one end. An array of myosin filaments possesses protruding heads at numerous positions at both ends.

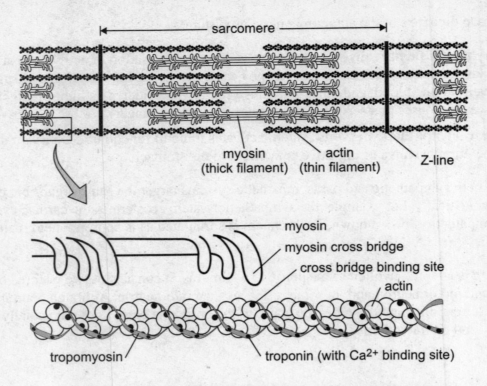

Sliding-Filament Model of Muscle Contraction

Figure 11-4

Within a myofibril, actin and myosin filaments are parallel and arranged side by side. The overlapping filaments produce a repeating pattern that gives skeletal muscle a striated appearance. Each repeating unit of the pattern, called a sarcomere, is separated by a border, or **Z-line,** to which the actin filaments are attached. The myosin filaments, with their protruding heads, are located between the actin, unattached to the Z-line.

Muscle contraction is described by the **sliding-filament model,** as follows:

1. **ATP binds to a myosin head and forms ADP + P$_i$.** When ATP binds to a myosin head, it is converted to ADP and P$_i$, which remain attached to the myosin head.

2. **Ca^{2+} exposes the binding sites on the actin filaments.** Ca^{2+} binds to the troponin molecule causing tropomyosin to expose positions on the actin filament for the attachment of myosin heads.

3. **Cross bridges between myosin heads and actin filaments form.** When attachment sites on the actin are exposed, the myosin heads bind to actin to form cross bridges.

4. **ADP and P$_i$ are released and sliding motion of actin results.** The attachment of cross bridges between myosin and actin causes the release of ADP and P$_i$. This, in turn, causes a change in shape of the myosin head, which generates a sliding movement of the actin toward the center of the sarcomere. This pulls the two Z-lines together, effectively contracting the muscle fiber.

5. **ATP causes the cross bridges to unbind.** When a new ATP molecule attaches to the myosin head, the cross bridge between the actin and myosin breaks, returning the myosin head to its unattached position.

Without the addition of a new ATP molecule, the cross bridges remain attached to the actin filaments. This is why corpses are stiff (new ATP molecules are unavailable).

Neurons form specialized synapses with muscles called **neuromuscular junctions.** Muscle contraction is stimulated through the following steps:

1. **Action potential generates release of acetylcholine.** When an action potential of a neuron reaches the neuromuscular junction, the neuron secretes the neurotransmitter acetylcholine, which diffuses across the synaptic cleft.

2. **Action potential is generated on sarcolemma and throughout the T-tubules.** Receptors on the sarcolemma initiate a depolarization event and action potential. The action potential travels along the sarcolemma throughout the transverse system of tubules.

3. **Sarcoplasmic reticulum releases Ca^{2+}.** As a result of the action potential throughout the transverse system of tubules, the sarcoplasmic reticulum releases Ca^{2+}.

4. **Myosin cross bridges form.** The Ca^{2+} released by the sarcoplasmic reticulum binds to troponin molecules on the actin helix, prompting tropomyosin molecules to expose binding sites for myosin cross-bridge formation. If ATP is available, muscle contraction begins.

Humans and other vertebrates have three kinds of muscles:

1. **Skeletal muscle** is attached to bones and causes movements of the body.

2. **Smooth muscle** lines the walls of blood vessels and the digestive tract where it serves to advance the movement of substances. Due to its arrangement of actin and myosin filaments, smooth muscle does not have the striated appearance of skeletal muscle. In addition, the sarcolemma does not form a system of transverse tubules, and as a result, contraction is controlled and relatively slow, properties appropriate for its function.

3. **Cardiac muscle** is responsible for the rhythmic contractions of the heart. Although striated, cardiac muscle differs from skeletal muscle in that it is highly branched with cells connected by gap junctions. In addition, cardiac muscle generates its own action potential, which spreads rapidly throughout muscle tissue by electrical synapses across the gap junctions.

The Immune System

The internal environment of animals provides attractive conditions for the growth of bacteria, viruses, and other organisms. Although some of these organisms can live symbiotically within animals, many either cause destruction of cells or produce toxic chemicals. To protect against these foreign invaders, humans possess three levels of defense.

The **skin** and **mucus membranes** provide a *nonspecific first line of defense* against invaders entering through the skin or through openings into the body. A nonspecific defense is not specialized for a particular invader. Rather, it is a general defense against all kinds of pathogens. The first line of defense features the following characteristics:

1. **Skin** is a physical and hostile barrier covered with oily and acidic (pH from 3 to 5) secretions from sweat glands.

2. **Antimicrobial proteins** (such as **lysozyme,** which breaks down the cell walls of bacteria) are contained in saliva, tears, and other secretions found on mucus membranes.

3. **Cilia** that line the lungs serve to sweep invaders out of the lungs.

4. **Gastric juice** of the stomach kills most microbes.

5. **Symbiotic bacteria** found in the digestive tract and the vagina outcompete many other organisms that could cause damage.

The *second line of defense* involves several nonspecific mechanisms, as follows:

1. **Phagocytes** are white blood cells (leukocytes) that engulf pathogens by phagocytosis. They include **neutrophils** and **monocytes.** Monocytes enlarge into large phagocytic cells called **macrophages.** Other white blood cells called **natural killer cells** (**NK cells**) attack abnormal body cells (such as tumors) or pathogen-infected body cells.

2. **Complement** is a group of about twenty proteins that "complement" defense reactions. These proteins help attract phagocytes to foreign cells and help destroy foreign cells by promoting cell lysis (breaking open the cell).

3. **Interferons** are substances secreted by cells invaded by viruses that stimulate neighboring cells to produce proteins that help them defend against the viruses.

4. The **inflammatory response** is a series of nonspecific events that occur in response to pathogens. When skin is damaged, for example, and bacteria or other organisms enter the body, the following events occur:

   • **Histamine** is secreted by **basophils,** white blood cells found in connective tissue.

   • **Vasodilation** (dilation of blood vessels), stimulated by histamine, increases blood supply to the damaged area and allows for easier movement of white blood cells (and other body fluids) through blood vessel walls. This also causes redness, an increase in temperature, and swelling. The increase in temperature, like a fever, may stimulate white blood cells, and they may make the environment inhospitable to pathogens.

   • **Phagocytes,** attracted to the injury by chemical gradients of complement, arrive and engulf pathogens and damaged cells.

   • **Complement** helps phagocytes engulf foreign cells, stimulate basophils to release histamine, and help lyse foreign cells.

The **immune response** is the *third line of defense*. It differs from the inflammatory response in that it targets *specific* **antigens.** An antigen is any molecule, usually a protein or polysaccharide, that can be identified as foreign. It may be a toxin (injected into the blood by the sting of an insect, for example), a part of the protein coat of a virus, or a molecule unique to the plasma membranes of bacteria, protozoa, pollen, or other foreign cells.

The **major histocompatibility complex,** or **MHC,** is the mechanism by which the immune system is able to differentiate between self and nonself cells. The MHC is a collection of glycoproteins (proteins with a carbohydrate) that exists on the membranes of all body cells. The proteins of a single individual are unique, originating from twenty genes, each with more than fifty alleles each. Thus, it is extremely unlikely that two people, except for identical twins, will possess cells with the same set of MHC molecules.

The primary agents of the immune response are **lymphocytes,** white blood cells (leukocytes) that originate in the bone marrow (like all blood cells) but concentrate in lymphatic tissues such as the lymph nodes, the thymus gland, and the spleen. The various kinds of lymphocytes are grouped as follows:

1. **B cells.** These are lymphocytes that originate *and* mature in the *bone marrow* (remember B cell for bone). B cells respond to *antigens*. The plasma membrane surface of B cells is characterized by specialized **antigen receptors** called **antibodies.** Antibodies have the following properties:

   - Antibodies are proteins.

   - Each antibody is specific to a particular antigen.

   - There are five classes of antibodies (or **immunoglobulins**): IgA, IgD, IgE, IgG, IgM. Each class is associated with a particular activity.

   - Each class of antibodies is a variation of a basic Y-shaped protein that consists of constant regions and variable regions. The variable regions are sequences of amino acids that differ among antibodies and give them specificity to antigens.

   - Antibodies inactivate antigens by binding to them. Inactivation is followed by macrophage phagocytosis. In addition, by binding to surface antigens of nonself cells, antibodies stimulate complement proteins to bring about the lysis of pathogens.

When B cells encounter antigens that specifically bind to their antibodies, the B cells proliferate, producing two kinds of daughter B cells, as follows:

   - **Plasma cells** are B cells that release their specific antibodies which then circulate through the body, binding to antigens.

   - **Memory cells** are long-lived B cells that do not release their antibodies in response to the immediate antigen invasion. Instead, the memory cells circulate in the body and respond quickly to eliminate any *subsequent* invasion by the same antigen. This mechanism provides immunity to many diseases after the first occurrence of the disease.

2. **T cells.** T cells are lymphocytes that originate in the bone marrow, but mature in the *thymus gland* (T cell for thymus). Like B cells, the plasma membranes of T cells have antigen receptors. However, these receptors are not antibodies, but recognition sites for *molecules displayed by nonself cells.* Self and nonself cells are distinguished as follows:

- The MHC markers on the plasma membrane of cells distinguish between self and nonself cells.

- When a body cell is invaded by a virus, by a foreign cell, or by any antigen, the body cell displays a combination of self and nonself markers. T cells interpret this aberrant display of markers as nonself.

- Cancer cells or tissue transplant cells, or other cells that display aberrant markers, are recognized as nonself cells by T cells.

When T cells encounter nonself cells, they divide and produce two kinds of cells, as follows:

- **Cytotoxic T cells** (or **killer T cells**) recognize and destroy nonself cells by puncturing them, thus causing them to lyse.

- **Helper T cells** stimulate the proliferation of B cells and cytotoxic T cells.

When an antigen binds to a B cell or when a nonself cell binds to a T cell, the B cell or T cell begins to divide, producing numerous daughter cells, all identical copies of the parent cell. This process is called **clonal selection,** since only the B or T cell that bears the effective antigen receptor is "selected" and reproduces to make clones, or identical copies of itself. Clonal selection results in a proliferation of B cells and T cells that will engage a specific, invading antigen.

The responses of the immune system are categorized into two kinds of reactions, as follows:

1. The **cell-mediated response** uses mostly *T cells* and responds to *any nonself cell, including cells invaded by pathogens.* When a nonself cell binds to a T cell, the T cell undergoes clonal selection, initiating the following chain of events.

   - **T cells produce cytotoxic T cells.** These cells destroy nonself cells.

   - **T cells produce helper T cells.**

   - **Helper T cells bind to macrophages.** Macrophages that have engulfed pathogens display aberrant plasma membrane markers. Helper T cells identify these marker combinations as nonself and bind to these macrophages.

   - **Helper T cells produce interleukins to stimulate a proliferation of T cells and B cells.** When helper T cells bind with macrophages, they release *interleukins,* or communication chemicals "between leukocytes." The interleukins initiate a sequence of positive-feedback events that result in the proliferation of interleukins, macrophages, helper T cells, B cells, and cytotoxic T cells.

2. The **humoral response** (or **antibody-mediated response**) involves most cells and responds to *antigens or pathogens that are circulating in the lymph or blood* ("humor" is a medieval term for body fluid). It includes the following events:

   - **B cells produce plasma cells.** The plasma cells, in turn, release antibodies that bind with antigens or antigen-bearing pathogens.

   - **B cells produce memory cells.** Memory cells provide future immunity.

- **Macrophage and helper T cells stimulate B cell production.** In many cases, the antigen will not directly stimulate the proliferation of B cells. Instead, the antigen or antigen-bearing pathogen must first be engulfed by a macrophage. T cells then bind to the macrophage in a cell-mediated response. Interleukins secreted by the helper T cells stimulate the production of B cells.

Humans have learned to supplement natural body defenses. Three important approaches follow:

1. **Antibiotics** are chemicals derived from bacteria or fungi that are harmful to other microorganisms.

2. **Vaccines** are substances that stimulate the production of memory cells. Inactivated viruses or fragments of viruses, bacteria, or other microorganisms are used as vaccines. Once memory cells are formed, the introduction of the live microorganism will stimulate a swift response by the immune system before any disease can become established.

3. **Passive immunity** is obtained by transferring antibodies from an individual who previously had a disease to a newly infected individual. Newborn infants are protected by passive immunity through the transfer of antibodies across the placenta and by antibodies in breast milk.

The Endocrine System

The endocrine system produces **hormones** that help maintain homeostasis and regulate reproduction and development. A hormone is a chemical messenger produced in one part of the body that affects target cells in another part of the body. Hormones have the following general characteristics:

1. Hormones are transported throughout the body in the blood.

2. Minute amounts of hormones can have significant influence on target cells.

3. Hormones may be steroids, peptides, or modified amino acids.

Through the various sensory neurons, the brain—and especially a portion of the forebrain, the hypothalamus—monitors the external environment and internal conditions of the body. As the master integrator of information, the brain may determine that some kind of action is necessary to maintain homeostasis or that conditions are appropriate to activate developmental changes. These actions are initiated by special **neurosecretory cells** that link the hypothalamus and the **pituitary gland,** a gland attached to the base of the hypothalamus. Neurosecretory cells are structured like neurons, but rather than secreting neurotransmitters into synapses that affect neighboring neurons, they secrete hormones into the blood. There are two halves, or lobes, of the pituitary. Their special associations with the hypothalamus are described below:

1. **Posterior pituitary.** Two hormones, **ADH (antidiuretic hormone)** and **oxytocin,** are produced by neurosecretory cells in the hypothalamus and are stored in the posterior pituitary and released as needed.

2. **Anterior pituitary. Releasing hormones** are produced by neurosecretory cells in the hypothalamus and secreted into the blood. This blood flows directly to the anterior pituitary where the releasing hormones stimulate the *release* of **tropic hormones** produced in the anterior pituitary. Tropic hormones are hormones whose target cells are other endocrine glands. Thus, they regulate hormone production by other glands.

Because the pituitary gland controls the production of hormones by many other glands, it is often referred to as the "master gland." Clearly, however, it is itself controlled by the hypothalamus. In addition, hormones from the posterior pituitary do not influence other glands, but target specific body tissues.

A summary of various important hormones, their source, and their function is given in Table 11-1.

The regulation of blood glucose concentration in the blood illustrates how the endocrine system maintains homeostasis by the action of antagonistic hormones. Among the cells of the pancreas that produce digestive enzymes, there are bundles of cells called the **islets of Langerhans**, which contain two kinds of cells, **alpha (α) cells** and **beta (β) cells**. These cells secrete hormones, as follows:

1. **Beta cells secrete insulin**. When the concentration of blood glucose rises (after eating, for example), beta cells secrete insulin into the blood. Insulin stimulates the liver and most other body cells to absorb glucose. Liver and muscle cells convert the glucose to glycogen (for storage), and adipose cells (which form a connective tissue) convert the glucose to fat. In this way, glucose concentration decreases in the blood.

2. **Alpha cells secrete glucagon**. When the concentration of blood glucose drops (during exercise, for example), alpha cells secrete glucagon into the blood. Glucagon stimulates the liver to release glucose. The glucose in the liver originates from the breakdown of glycogen and the conversion of amino acids and fatty acids into glucose.

Another example of antagonistic hormones occurs in the maintenance of Ca^+ in the blood. Parathyroid hormone (PTH) from the parathyroid glands increases Ca^{2+} in the blood by stimulating Ca^{2+} reabsorption in the kidney and Ca^{2+} release from the bones. Calcitonin from the thyroid gland has the opposite effect on the bones and kidneys.

There are two methods by which hormones are known to trigger activities in target cells, as follows:

1. The hormone (usually a steroid) diffuses through the plasma membrane, through the cytoplasm, and into the nucleus. The hormone *binds to a receptor protein in the nucleus*. The receptor protein, in turn, activates a portion of the DNA that turns on specific genes.

2. The hormone (usually a peptide) *binds to a receptor protein on the plasma membrane* of the cell (**receptor-mediated endocytosis**). The receptor protein, in turn, stimulates the production of one of the following **second messengers.**

   - **Cyclic AMP (cAMP)** is produced from ATP. Cyclic AMP, in turn, triggers an enzyme that generates specific cellular changes.

- **Inositol triphosphate (IP$_3$)** is produced from membrane phospholipids. IP$_3$, in turn, triggers the release of Ca^{2+} from the endoplasmic reticulum, which, in turn, activates enzymes that generate cellular changes.

Table 11-1			
Source	**Hormone**	**Target**	**Action**
Posterior Pituitary	ADH (antidiuretic hormone)	kidneys	increases reabsorption of water
	oxytocin	mammary glands	stimulates release of milk
Anterior Pituitary (tropic hormones)	TSH (thyroid stimulating hormone)	thyroid	secretion of T$_4$ and T$_3$
	ACTH (adrenocorticotropic hormone)	adrenal cortex	secretion of glucocorticoids
	FSH (follicle stimulating hormone)	ovary, testes	regulates oogenesis and spermatogenesis
	LH (luteinizing hormone)	ovary, testes	regulates oogenesis and spermatogenesis
Anterior Pituitary (hormones)	PRL (prolactin)	mammary glands	production of milk
	GH (growth hormone)	bone, muscle	stimulates growth
Pancreas (alpha cells)	glucagon	liver	increases blood glucose
Pancreas (beta cells)	insulin	liver, muscles, fat	lowers blood glucose
Adrenal gland (medulla)	epinephrine (adrenalin) and norepinephrine (noradrenalin)	blood vessels, liver and heart	increases blood glucose, constricts blood vessels (fight or flight response)
Adrenal gland (cortex)	glucocorticoids (e.g., cortisol)	general	increases blood glucose
	mineralocorticoids (e.g., aldosterone)	kidney	increases reabsorption of Na$^+$ and excretion of K$^+$
Thyroid	T$_4$ (thyroxin) and T$_3$ (triiodothyronine)	general	increases cellular metabolism
	calcitonin	bone	lowers blood Ca^{2+}
Parathyroid	PTH (parathyroid hormone)	bone	increases blood Ca^{2+}
Testis	testosterone	testes, general	spermatogenesis, secondary sex characteristics
Ovary	estrogen	uterus, general	menstrual cycle, secondary sex characteristics
	progesteron	uterus	menstrual cycle, pregnancy
Pineal	melatonin	body	circadian rhythms

Sample Questions and Answers

Multiple-Choice Questions

Directions: Each of the following questions or statements is followed by five possible answers or sentence completions. Choose the one best answer or sentence completion.

1. Body temperature can be increased by all of the following EXCEPT:

   A. muscle contractions

   B. drinking alcohol, which results in vasodilation

   C. increasing metabolic activity

   D. puffing up feathers or hair

   E. reducing blood flow to ears

2. All of the following are examples of countercurrent exchange EXCEPT:

   A. movement of blood through the legs of wading birds

   B. movement of blood through the fins and tails of marine mammals

   C. the loop of Henle in the nephron

   D. gas exchange in fish gills

   E. gas exchange in human lungs

3. Most carbon dioxide is transported in the blood

   A. as CO_2

   B. as HCO_3^-

   C. attached to hemoglobin

   D. attached to the membranes of erythrocytes

   E. attached to the membranes of specialized leukocytes

4. Gas diffusion in human lungs occurs across membranes of

   A. alveoli

   B. bronchi

   C. the diaphragm

   D. the larynx

   E. spiracles

5. Which of the following would normally contain blood with the least amount of oxygen?

   A. The left ventricle

   B. The left atrium

   C. The pulmonary veins

   D. The pulmonary arteries

   E. Capillaries that line the small intestine

6. Systolic blood pressure is maintained by the

   A. left atrium

   B. right atrium

   C. left ventricle

   D. right ventricle

   E. semilunar valves in the aorta

7. Which of the following is an example of an excretory mechanism?

   A. Antibodies

   B. The digestive tract

   C. Flame cells

   D. Neurosecretory cells

   E. The sarcomere

8. When the filtrate moves through the nephron, solutes

   A. become less concentrated as they move down the descending limb of the loop of Henle

   B. become less concentrated as they move up the ascending limb of the loop of Henle

   C. become less concentrated as they move down the collecting duct

   D. are most concentrated when they enter the Bowman's capsule

   E. are most concentrated when they enter the glomerulus

9. In some areas of the human circulatory system, arteries branch into capillaries, merge into veins, then branch into capillaries a second time, before merging again into veins and returning to the heart. All of the following organs are found in such double capillary bed circuits EXCEPT:

   A. the anterior pituitary gland

   B. the glomerulus

   C. the hypothalamus

   D. the liver

   E. the lungs

10. In humans, digestion occurs in all of the following locations EXCEPT:

    A. the duodenum

    B. the mouth

    C. the pancreas

    D. the small intestine

    E. the stomach

11. Which of the following is a digestive enzyme found in the stomach?

    A. Trypsin

    B. Secretin

    C. Pepsin

    D. Gastrin

    E. Bile

12. A nerve impulse is usually transmitted from a motor neuron to a muscle

    A. by acetylcholine

    B. by a hormone

    C. by an action potential

    D. by Ca^{2+}

    E. through a reflex arc

13. What occurs in neurons during the refractory period following an action potential?

   A. ATP is regenerated from ADP + P_i.

   B. Na^+ moves across the neuron membrane from outside to inside.

   C. K^+ moves across the neuron membrane from inside to outside.

   D. Na^+ on the inside and K^+ on the outside exchange places across the neuron membrane.

   E. The outside of the membrane becomes more negative with respect to the inside.

14. If only K^+ gates open on the postsynaptic membrane, then

   A. the postsynaptic membrane releases a neurotransmitter

   B. an excitatory postsynaptic potential (EPSP) is established

   C. the postsynaptic neuron is stimulated

   D. the postsynaptic neuron is inhibited

   E. Ca^{2+} is released

15. All of the following are involved in the contraction of muscle cells EXCEPT:

   A. actin

   B. cAMP

   C. myosin

   D. tropomyosin

   E. troponin

16. Which of the following is the last step leading up to muscle contraction that occurs just before a myofibril contracts?

   A. Tropomyosin exposes binding sites on actin.

   B. ATP binds to myosin.

   C. Sarcoplasmic reticulum releases Ca^{2+}.

   D. ATP is converted to ADP + Pi.

   E. Action potential travels throughout T-tubules.

17. Which of the following initiates an attack against a specific antigen or pathogen?

   A. Complement

   B. Interferon

   C. Lysozyme

   D. Macrophages

   E. Plasma cells

18. Which of the following would be activated first in response to a body cell that has been invaded by a virus?

   A. Cytotoxic T cells

   B. Natural killer cells

   C. Antibodies

   D. Macrophages

   E. Neutrophils

19. All of the following are involved in the regulation of blood glucose concentration EXCEPT:

   A. glucagon
   B. insulin
   C. the liver
   D. melatonin
   E. the pancreas

20. Which of the following results in more concentrated urine?

   A. Antidiuretic hormone
   B. Calcitonin
   C. Parathyroid hormone
   D. Prolactin
   E. Thyroxine

Answers to Multiple-Choice Questions

1. **B.** It is a myth that alcohol warms the body. As a result of vasodilation, blood flow to the extremities is increased. This may make hands and feet feel warmer temporarily, but the total surface area of blood exposed to the surroundings increases, and this results in a loss of heat. As a result, your body temperature, especially of critical internal organs, will drop.

2. **E.** Gas exchange in human lungs is not aided by countercurrent exchange. The arteries and veins in the legs of wading birds and in the fins and tails of marine mammals are closely parallel so that heat transfer from outgoing arteries to incoming veins is maximized. Similarly, the direction of blood flow through blood vessels in gills is opposite to that of the water. Also, the loop of Henle maximizes the effect of the concentration gradients in the nephron.

3. **B.** CO_2 enters erythrocytes (red blood cells), where it is converted to carbonic acid (H_2CO_3) by the enzyme carbonic anhydrase. H_2CO_3- then dissociates into H^+ and HCO_3- and diffuses back into the plasma.

4. **A.** Gas exchange occurs across the moist membranes of alveoli, small air sacs in the lungs.

5. **D.** The pulmonary arteries carry deoxygenated blood from the heart to the lungs, where it is oxygenated for transport back to the heart and throughout the body.

6. **C.** The contraction of the left ventricle pumps blood through the body and thus maintains the systolic blood pressure. When the left ventricle relaxes, diastolic blood pressure is maintained by the semilunar valve in the aorta by preventing blood movement back into the ventricle.

7. **C.** Flame cells function in the excretory system of flatworms. Be careful not to confuse excretory and digestive functions. Excretory systems maintain water balance, filter body fluids, and remove *cellular* wastes, such as nitrogen wastes (often in the form of urea). The digestive system chemically breaks down food into absorbable molecules. Feces consist mostly of undigested food and bacteria, material that never really entered any cells of the body. Technically, the digestive tract is merely a hole that passes through the body. It is separated from the body by epithelial tissue, much like skin protects the body's outer surface. In a way, it is similar to a donut—the hole that passes through the donut is not really part of the donut.

8. **B.** The concentration of solutes in the filtrate becomes greater as the filtrate descends the descending limb, then less concentrated as it ascends the ascending limb. It is most concentrated when it descends the collecting duct.

9. **E.** Double capillary beds (called portal systems) occur in the glomerulus and the capillaries that surround the loop of Henle (both in the kidney), the small intestine and liver, and the hypothalamus and the anterior pituitary gland.

10. **C.** Although the pancreas supplies digestive enzymes to the small intestine (specifically, the duodenum of the small intestine), no digestion actually takes place in the pancreas.

11. C. Pepsin splits proteins into polypeptides in the stomach. Trypsin digests proteins in the small intestine. Secretin is a *hormone* (not an enzyme) that stimulates the secretion of pancreatic enzymes into the intestine. Bile *emulsifies* fats, not digests them. Gastrin is a hormone that stimulates the secretion of pepsin and other gastric juices into the *stomach*.

12. A. Acetylcholine is the neurotransmitter that communicates a nerve impulse across the neuromuscular junction.

13. D. The Na^+/K^+ protein pumps in the membranes of neurons exchange Na^+ and K^+ so that their concentrations on each side of the membrane return to resting potential concentrations.

14. D. If K^+ gates are stimulated to open on the postsynaptic membrane, an inhibitory postsynaptic potential (IPSP) is established. This makes the membrane more polarized, and it is more difficult to establish an action potential.

15. B. Hormone receptors in certain target cells initiate cellular responses to hormones when cAMP triggers the activity of specific enzymes. It is not involved in muscle contraction.

16. A. The order of events during muscle contraction is: ATP binds to myosin heads and forms $ADP + P_i$. When a neuron stimulates a muscle, the action potential travels throughout the T-tubule invaginations, stimulating sarcoplasmic reticulum to release Ca^{2+}. The Ca^{2+} causes the tropomyosin to expose the binding sites on the actin. Once this occurs, cross bridges form between myosin and actin, ADP and P_i are released from the myosin heads, and the cross bridges cause the actin to move toward the center of the sarcomere, pulling the Z-lines together and causing the myofibril to shorten.

17. E. Plasma cells are B cells bearing specific antibodies for binding with a specific antigen.

18. A. As part of the cell-mediated immune response, cytotoxic T cells would attack the abnormal body cell first. Once the abnormal cell is lysed, nonspecific attacks by macrophages and other phagocytes would occur.

19. D. Melatonin is secreted by the pineal gland and is involved in maintaining various biorhythms.

20. A. Antidiuretic hormone (ADH), produced by the posterior pituitary, increases reabsorption of water in the kidneys, making urine more concentrated.

Free-Response Questions

Free-response questions on the AP exam may require you to provide information from a narrow area of biology, or they may consist of parts that require you to assemble information from diverse areas of biology. The questions that follow are typical of either an entire AP exam question or merely that part of a question that is related to this section.

Directions: Answer the questions below as completely and as thoroughly as possible. Answer the question in essay form (NOT outline form), using complete sentences. You may use diagrams to supplement your answers, but a diagram alone without appropriate discussion is inadequate.

---

1. Each of the following events requires the recognition of a molecule. Explain how each of the following recognition processes occurs.

    (a.) Target cells recognize hormones.

    (b.) B cells recognize antigens.

    (c.) Postsynaptic membranes recognize neurotransmitters.

2. Describe a negative feedback loop involved in the maintenance of homeostasis.

3. Describe the biochemical events associated with the transmission of nerve impulses

    (a.) along neurons

    (b.) across synapses

4. Describe the physical and biochemical events associated with the contraction of a muscle.

5. Describe the digestion and absorption of proteins, starches, and fats in humans.

6. Describe the structure and function of the human kidney. Include a description of how hormones interact with the kidney to regulate water balance.

7. (a.) Discuss how the human body responds to a virus invasion.

    (b.) What difficulties does the human body have in defending against the human immunodeficiency virus (HIV) that causes AIDS (acquired immunodeficiency syndrome)?

Some Typical Answers to Free-Response Questions

Question 1

(a.) There are two ways in which target cells recognize hormones. In cells that recognize steroid hormones, the hormone diffuses through the plasma membrane and nuclear envelope and binds with special receptor proteins in the nucleus. These receptors then activate transcription of specific genes. If the hormone is a peptide, the hormone binds to special receptor proteins on the plasma membrane surface. These receptors, in turn, trigger the conversion of ATP to cAMP, which, in turn, activates an enzyme that produces a particular cellular function.

(b.) B cells have special antigen receptors on their plasma membranes. In the production of B cells, millions of possible genetic combinations produce B cells with different kinds of receptors that will bind to different antigens. When an antigen enters the body, it will bind only to the B cell with the specific antigen receptor. When this occurs, B cells proliferate, producing plasma cells that have exactly the same antigen receptors. The antigen receptors are then released into the body fluids as antibodies, which bind and inactivate the antigens which stimulated their production.

(c.) When a neurotransmitter, such as acetylcholine, is secreted by the presynaptic membrane, it diffuses across the synaptic cleft to the postsynaptic membrane. The neurotransmitter binds to one of many specific receptor proteins on the postsynaptic membrane. Depending on the neurotransmitter and the type of postsynaptic membrane, the binding of the neurotransmitter to the receptor will cause an influx of Na^+ or an efflux of K^+, resulting in an excitatory postsynaptic potential or an inhibitory postsynaptic potential, respectively.

This question requires you to address similar mechanisms that occur in different physiological systems. This kind of question evaluates your breadth of knowledge and is often used on the AP exam.

*Note that all three answers involve receptors on the plasma membrane. If you write an introductory sentence about the role of the plasma membrane in recognition mechanisms, you **must** restate the plasma membrane's role in each and every section of the question. Since each question is scored separately, you will receive points each time you indicate that the plasma membrane is involved.*

Question 2

In physiological systems, homeostasis is often maintained by negative feedback loops. You have a choice of many mechanisms, including the following:

1. *The maintenance of blood glucose by the hormones glucagon and insulin.*

2. *The maintenance of blood Ca^{2+} by parathyroid hormone and calcitonin.*

3. *The maintenance of oxygen in the blood through monitoring of pH levels by chemorecep-tors, bicarbonate production from CO_2, and nerve stimulation of the diaphragm and inter-costal muscles to control rate of breathing.*

4. *The control of hormone production through releasing hormones from the hypothalamus and tropic hormones from the anterior pituitary.*

Questions involving feedback mechanisms are common on AP exams, both as free response and multiple choice. Additional negative feedback mechanisms are described in other sections of this book and involve the following processes:

5. *Hormone regulation of the menstrual cycle.*

6. *Regulation of population size.*

7. *The rate of an enzyme reaction (through feedback inhibition and allosteric enzymes, for example).*

8. *Gene regulation by repressible and inducible enzymes.*

Questions 3–6

These questions are "information" questions and require you only to demonstrate your knowl-edge of a particular area of human biology. They do not require you to apply this knowledge to a new situation (such as in question 7) or to synthesize information from several areas (such as in question 1). In many ways, information questions are the "easier" questions be-cause you don't have to think as much, just recall as much information as you can within the time allowed.

All of these questions, or questions very much like these, have appeared on at least one AP test in one form or another. Questions about nerve transmission and muscle contraction appear of-ten, and it is an essential part of your preparation to know these two subjects well. For a review of these and other physiological processes, see the appropriate material in this section.

Question 7

(a.) When a virus enters the body, various leukocytes (white blood cells) will recognize the virus as a foreign molecule, or antigen. Antigens circulating in body fluids stimulate the humoral immune response. Specific B cells (lymphocytes that mature in the bone marrow) that recognize an antigen proliferate (a process called clonal selection), producing two kinds of B cells: plasma cells and memory cells. The plasma cells release antibodies, proteins that bind with and inactivate antigens (the virus in this case). Memory cells provide protection against future invasions of the same virus.

In addition to the humoral immune response, nonspecific white blood cells, such as neutrophils, phagocytic macrophages, and natural killer cells, also attack the virus. They are responsible for attacking and removing antigens inactivated by antibodies.

The humoral immune response described above responds to viruses that are circulating in body fluids. If, however, some viruses infect body cells, the cell-mediated immune response is activated. A normal, uninfected cell is identified as a "self" cell by special molecular markers called the histocompatibility complex, or MHC. However, when a virus is actively replicating inside a cell (during the lytic cycle of viral reproduction), both self and nonself markers are displayed. Specific T cells (lymphocytes that mature in the thymus) recognize these markers, proliferate by clonal selection, and produce killer T cells and helper T cells. The killer T cells destroy the infected cells. Helper T cells, in cooperation with macrophages (that attack and engulf the infected cells), produce chemical signals called interleukins that stimulate the proliferation of B cells and more T cells. In addition, special proteins called complement proteins destroy the infected cells by puncturing holes in them (lysis).

(b.) HIV is different from most other viruses because it attacks helper T cells. When T cells become infected, the cell-mediated response is activated. This response stimulates the production of helper T cells, killer T cells, and B cells. As helper T cells increase in number, however, more and more of them become infected. Eventually most T cells are destroyed, allowing the proliferation of opportunistic diseases such as pneumonia and skin cancer (Kaposi's sarcoma). Eventually, these opportunistic diseases kill the infected person. In addition, some HIV may begin a lysogenic cycle in which the virus remains hidden and temporarily inactive within the DNA of the host cell. These host cells do not display nonself markers and cannot be detected as abnormal by T cells. In addition, HIV undergoes mutations, making antibodies produced earlier by the immune system obsolete.

Although most textbooks discuss the humoral and cell-mediated immune responses as if they were separate and distinct, they typically work together to combat pathogen invasions. In most cases, in fact, B cells must be stimulated by helper T cells before the B cells can mount an effective defense.

Animal Reproduction and Development

Review

The term *reproduction* describes the production of eggs and sperm and the processes leading to fertilization. The term *development* describes the sequence of events that transform a fertilized egg to a multicellular organism.

For the AP exam, you will need to know the structure and function of the human reproductive organs. This includes the formation of gametes (gametogenesis) and the role hormones play in the process. Development is covered more generally, including basic developmental characteristics of all animals, with special attention to amphibians, birds, and humans.

Characteristics That Distinguish the Sexes

In most vertebrates, especially mammals, males and females are distinguished by both primary and secondary sex characteristics. The **primary sex characteristics** are the structures directly involved in reproduction. The uterus and ovaries in females and the testes in males are examples. In contrast, **secondary sex characteristics** include such human features as body hair (pubic hair and beards, for example), distribution of muscle and fat, voice quality, and breasts. Deer antlers, lion manes, and peacock tails are examples of secondary sex characteristics in nonhumans. In general, secondary sex characteristics are used to indicate sexual maturity or sexual readiness and to attract or locate mates or are used by males to compete for females (visual displays and aggression).

Human Reproductive Anatomy

The female reproductive system consists of the following structures:

1. **Ovary.** This is the organ where **ova** (singular, **ovum**), or eggs, are produced. Each female has two ovaries.

2. **Oviduct** (or **fallopian tube**). Eggs move from the ovary to the uterus through the oviduct. There are two oviducts, one for each ovary.

3. **Uterus.** A fertilized ovum implants (attaches) on the inside wall, or **endometrium,** of the uterus. Development of the embryo occurs here until birth.

4. **Vagina.** At birth, the fetus passes through the **cervix** (an opening in the uterus), through the vagina, and out of the body.

The male reproductive system consists of the following structures:

1. **Testis** (plural, **testes**). Each of the two testes consists of **seminiferous tubules** for the production of sperm and **interstitial cells** which produce male sex hormones (testosterone and other androgens). The two testes are contained in a single sac, the **scrotum,** which hangs outside the body. The external scrotum provides a temperature of about 2° C below that of the body cavity, a condition necessary for the development of sperm.

2. **Epididymis.** This coiled tube, one attached to each testis, is the site for final maturation and storage of the sperm.

3. **Vas deferens** (plural, **vasa deferentia**). Each of these two tubes transfers sperm from one epididymis to the urethra. Sperm exit the penis through the urethra.

4. **Seminal vesicles.** During ejaculation, these two glands secrete into the vas deferens mucus (which provides a liquid medium for the sperm), fructose (which provides energy for the sperm), and prostaglandins (which stimulate uterine contractions that help sperm move into the uterus).

5. **Prostate gland.** This gland secretes a milky alkaline fluid into the urethra and serves to neutralize the acidity of urine that may still be in the urethra, as well as the acidity of the vagina.

6. **Bulbourethral glands** (or **Cowper's glands**). These two glands secrete a small amount of fluid of unknown function into the urethra.

7. **Penis.** The urethra passes through the penis and serves to transport **semen,** the fluid containing sperm and secretions, into the vagina. It also serves in the transport of urine out of the body.

Sperm are compact packages of DNA specialized for the effective delivery of the male genome. They consist of the following structures:

1. **Sperm head.** The head of the sperm contains the haploid nucleus with 23 chromosomes (in humans). At the tip of the sperm head is the **acrosome,** a lysosome containing enzymes which are used to penetrate the egg. The acrosome originates from Golgi body vesicles that fuse to form a single lysosome.

2. **Midpiece.** Opposite the acrosome, the flagellum, consisting of the typical $9 + 2$ microtubule array, emerges from the sperm head from one member of a pair of centrioles. The first part of the flagellum, the midpiece, is characterized by mitochondria that spiral around the flagellum and supply ATP for flagellar movement.

3. **Tail.** The remainder of the flagellum, behind the midpiece, is the tail. Sperm are propelled by whiplike motion of the tail and midpiece.

Gametogenesis in Humans

Gametogenesis consists of the meiotic cell divisions that produce eggs in females (**oogenesis**) and sperm in males (**spermatogenesis**).

Oogenesis begins during *embryonic development*. Fetal cells called **oogonia** divide by mitosis to produce **primary oocytes,** which then begin meiosis. All primary oocytes, however, progress only to prophase I. They remain at this stage until puberty, at which time one primary oocyte during each menstrual cycle (averaging 28 days) continues its development through the remainder of meiosis I. Development occurs within an envelope of encircling cells called a **follicle,** which protects and nourishes the developing oocyte. During the remainder of meiosis I, cytoplasm is concentrated in only one of the daughter cells (unequal cytokinesis). Thus, at the end of meiosis I, one daughter cell is the **secondary oocyte** containing most of the cytoplasm and the other daughter cell is a **polar body** with very little cytoplasm. The polar body may continue with meiosis II and divide into two daughter polar bodies, but they ultimately disintegrate. Concentrating the cytoplasm in one viable secondary oocyte (and at the end of meiosis II, one egg) assures that adequate amounts of stored food, as well as mitochondria, ribosomes, and other cytoplasmic organelles, will be available for the developing embryo. In contrast, the sperm contributes very little cytoplasm at fertilization.

Ovulation marks the release of the secondary oocyte from the follicle. If it is fertilized by a sperm as it moves through the oviduct, the secondary oocyte will begin meiosis II and produce an egg that combines with the chromosomes contributed by the sperm. The second daughter cell of meiosis II, again a polar body, disintegrates.

Spermatogenesis begins at *puberty* within the seminiferous tubules of the testes. Cells called **spermatogonia** divide by mitosis repeatedly to produce **primary spermatocytes** that begin meiosis. Meiosis I produces two **secondary spermatocytes,** which, at the end of meiosis II, become four **spermatids. Sertoli cells** in the seminiferous tubules provide nourishment to the spermatids as they differentiate into mature **sperm**. The sperm complete their development in the epididymis, where they are stored until needed.

Hormonal Control of Human Reproduction

The human female reproductive cycle is characterized by events in the ovary (**ovarian cycle**) and the uterus (**menstrual cycle**). The purpose of these cycles is to produce an egg and prepare the uterus for the implantation of the egg, should it become fertilized. The activities of the ovary and the uterus are coordinated by negative and positive feedback responses involving gonadotropin releasing hormone (GnRH) from the hypothalamus, follicle stimulating hormone (FSH) and luteinizing hormone (LH) from the anterior pituitary, and the hormones estrogen and progesterone from the follicle and corpus luteum. A description of the events follows (Figure 12-1).

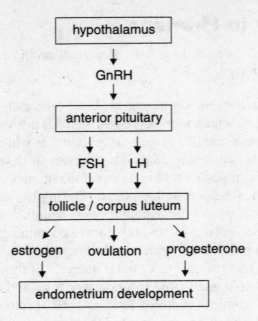

Hormones and the Female Reproductive Cycle

Figure 12-1

1. **The hypothalamus and anterior pituitary initiate the reproductive cycle.** The hypothalamus monitors the levels of estrogen and progesterone in the blood. In a *negative feedback* fashion, low levels of these hormones stimulate the hypothalamus to secrete GnRH, which, in turn, stimulates the anterior pituitary to secrete FSH and LH.

2. **The follicle develops.** FSH stimulates the development of the follicle and the egg.

3. **The follicle secretes estrogen.** FSH stimulates the secretion of estrogen from the follicle.

4. **Ovulation occurs.** *Positive feedback* from rising levels of estrogen stimulate the anterior pituitary (through GnRH from the hypothalamus) to produce a sudden midcycle surge of LH. This high level of LH triggers ovulation.

5. **The corpus luteum secretes estrogen and progesterone.** After ovulation, the follicle, now called the **corpus luteum,** continues to develop under the influence of LH and secretes both estrogen and progesterone.

6. **The endometrium thickens.** Estrogen and progesterone stimulate the development of the endometrium, the inside lining of the uterus. It thickens with nutrient-rich tissue and blood vessels in preparation for the implantation of a fertilized egg.

7. **The hypothalamus and anterior pituitary terminate the reproductive cycle.** *Negative feedback* from high levels of estrogen and progesterone cause the anterior pituitary (through the hypothalamus) to abate production of FSH and LH.

8. **The endometrium disintegrates.** In the absence of FSH and LH, the corpus luteum deteriorates. As a result, estrogen and progesterone production stops. Without estrogen and progesterone, growth of the endometrium is no longer supported, and it disintegrates, sloughing off during menstruation (flow phase of the menstrual cycle).

9. **The implanted embryo sustains the endometrium.** If implantation occurs, the implanted embryo secretes human chorionic gonadotropin (HCG) to sustain the corpus luteum. As a result, the corpus luteum will continue to produce estrogen and progesterone to maintain the endometrium. Without HCG, menstruation would begin and the embryo would abort. (Pregnancy tests check for the presence of HCG in the urine.) Later during development, HCG is replaced by progesterone secreted by the placenta. In this way, the embryo directly maintains the pregnancy.

The **menstrual cycle,** as described above, consists of the thickening of the endometrium of the uterus in preparation for implantation of a fertilized egg and the shedding of the endometrium if implantation does not occur. The **ovarian cycle** consists of three phases, as follows:

1. **Follicular phase:** the development of the egg and the secretion of estrogen from the follicle.

2. **Ovulation:** the midcycle release of the egg.

3. **Luteal phase:** the secretion of **estrogen** and **progesterone** from the **corpus luteum** after ovulation.

The male reproductive cycle is regulated by the same hormones that regulate the female reproductive cycle. In response to GnRH from the hypothalamus, the anterior pituitary in males secretes FSH and LH. (In males, LH is also called **ICSH**, interstitial cell stimulating hormone). LH stimulates the interstitial cells in the testes to produce testosterone and other male sex hormones (androgens). Under the influence of FSH and testosterone, Sertoli cells promote the development of sperm. In contrast to females, however, hormone and gamete production are constant during the reproductive life of the male.

In addition to influencing the production of sperm and eggs, testosterone and estrogen stimulate the development of the secondary sex characteristics in males and females, respectively.

Embryonic Development

There are four stages in the growth and development of animals. The first is gametogenesis, the formation of sperm and eggs. The second includes embryonic development, which begins with fertilization of the egg and continues to birth. The third stage is the process leading to reproductive maturity (puberty), and the fourth is the aging process to death. In general, the AP exam expects you to know features of only the first two developmental stages, gametogenesis and embryonic development. Gametogenesis was previously described, while a discussion of embryonic development follows.

Some animals resemble mature individuals of their species at birth, while other are physically dissimilar from the adult form. For example, tadpoles and caterpillars are larval forms of their respective adult forms, a frog and a flying insect. The larval form of a sea urchin, a pluteus, is a microscopic, free-floating animal that drifts as plankton until it attaches to a solid surface. Like other larvae, the pluteus undergoes additional development (**metamorphosis**) that transforms the larva into an adult.

In other animals, embryonic development continues until the birth of an infant that resembles the form of the adult. In mammals, the developmental period is often divided into two stages—embryonic development followed by fetal development. The **fetus** is an embryo that resembles the infant form.

Many of the events that occur during embryonic development are remarkably similar in all animals. Below, early developmental stages are described as they occur in the sea urchin. These stages are typical of development in most animals. However, some developmental events described occur only in certain groups of animals (for example, deuterostomes, chordates, amniotes, or vertebrates) or are specific to humans. These are clearly noted in the descriptions.

1. **Fertilization.** Fertilization occurs when the sperm penetrates the plasma membrane of the secondary oocyte. Fertilization is accompanied by the following steps:

   - **Recognition.** Before penetration can occur, the sperm secretes a protein that binds with special receptor molecules that reside on a glycoprotein layer surrounding the plasma membrane of the oocyte. This **vitelline layer** (or **zona pellucida** in humans) insures that fertilization occurs only between egg and sperm of the same species.

   - **Penetration.** The plasma membranes of the sperm and oocyte fuse, and the sperm nucleus enters the oocyte.

   - **Formation of the fertilization membrane.** The vitelline layer forms a fertilization membrane which blocks the entrance of additional sperm.

   - **Completion of meiosis II in the secondary oocyte.** In humans, sperm penetration triggers meiosis II in the oocyte, producing an ovum (egg) and polar body. The polar body is discharged through the plasma membrane.

   - **Fusion of nuclei and replication of DNA.** The sperm and ovum nuclei fuse, forming a zygote nucleus consisting of 23 pairs of chromosomes (in humans). Each chromosome replicates so that it consists of two identical chromatids.

2. **Cleavage.** The zygote now begins a series of **cleavage** divisions, rapid cell divisions without cell growth. As a result, each of the resulting cells, called **blastomeres,** contain substantially less cytoplasm than the original zygote. Some characteristics of early cleavages follow:

   - **Embryo polarity.** The egg has an upper, **animal pole** and a lower, **vegetal pole.** Cells formed at the vegetal pole contain more **yolk,** or stored food, because the yolk material, denser than the surrounding cytoplasm, settles to the bottom of the egg.

   - **Polar and equatorial cleavages.** Early cleavages are polar, dividing the egg into segments that stretch from pole to pole (like sections of an orange). Other cleavages are parallel with the equator (perpendicular to the polar cleavages).

- **Radial and spiral cleavages.** In deuterostomes, early cleavages are radial, forming cells at the animal and vegetal poles that are aligned together, the top cells directly above the bottom cells. In protostomes, cleavages are spiral, forming cells on top that are shifted with respect to those below them.

- **Indeterminate and determinate cleavages.** A cleavage is indeterminate if it produces blastomeres that, if separated, can individually complete normal development. In contrast, blastomeres produced by a determinate cleavage cannot develop into a complete embryo if separated from other blastomeres. Instead, their developmental program is limited to the production of definite (or determined) cells that contribute to only a part of a complete embryo. Radial cleavages of deuterostomes are usually indeterminate, while spiral cleavages of protostomes are often determinate.

3. **Morula.** Successive cleavage divisions result in a solid ball of cells called a morula.

4. **Blastula.** As cell divisions continue, liquid fills the morula and pushes the cells out to form a circular cavity surrounded by a single layer of cells. This hollow sphere of cells is called the blastula, and the cavity is the **blastocoel.**

5. **Gastrula.** Formation of the gastrula, or **gastrulation,** occurs when a group of cells invaginate (move inward) into the blastula, forming a two-layered embryo with an opening from the outside into a center cavity. The following features are associated with the gastrula.

- **Three germ layers.** A third cell layer forms between the outer and inner layers of the invaginated embryo. These three cell layers, the **ectoderm, mesoderm,** and **endoderm** (outside, middle, and inside layers, respectively) are the primary germ layers from which all subsequent tissues develop.

- **Archenteron.** The center cavity formed by gastrulation is called the archenteron. It is completely surrounded by endoderm cells.

- **Blastopore.** The opening into the archenteron is the blastopore. It becomes the mouth (in protostomes) or the anus (in deuterostomes).

6. **Extraembryonic membrane development.** In birds, reptiles, and humans, collectively called the **amniotes,** extraembryonic (outside the embryo proper) membranes develop, as follows:

- **Chorion.** The chorion is the outer membrane. In birds and reptiles it acts as a membrane for gas exchange. In mammals, the chorion implants into the endometrium. Later, the chorion, together with maternal tissue, forms the **placenta.** The placenta is a blend of maternal and embryonic tissues across which gases, nutrients, and wastes are exchanged.

- **Allantois.** The allantois begins as a sac that buds off from the archenteron. Eventually, it encircles the embryo, forming a layer below the chorion. In birds and reptiles, it initially stores waste products (in the form of uric acid). Later in development, it fuses with the chorion, and together they act as a membrane for gas exchange with blood vessels below. In mammals, the allantois transports waste products to the placenta. After subsequent development, it forms the umbilical cord, transporting gases, nutrients, and wastes between the embryo and the placenta.

- **Amnion.** The amnion, for which this group of vertebrates is named, encloses the **amniotic cavity,** a fluid-filled cavity that cushions the developing embryo much like the coelom cushions internal organs in coelomate animals.

- **Yolk sac.** In birds and reptiles, the yolk sac membrane digests the enclosed yolk. Blood vessels transfer the nutrients to the developing embryo. In placental mammals, the yolk sac is empty. Instead, nutrition is obtained through the placenta.

7. **Organogenesis.** As cells continue to divide after gastrulation, they become different from one another (cell differentiation), taking on characteristics of specific tissues and organs. This development of organs is called **organogenesis.** The formation of the following organs are characteristic of the *chordates*:

- **Notochord.** Cells along the dorsal surface of the mesoderm germ layer form the notochord, a stiff rod that provides support in lower chordates. The vertebrae of higher chordates are formed from nearby cells in the mesoderm.

- **Neural tube.** In the ectoderm layer directly above the notochord, a layer of cells forms the neural plate. The plate indents, forming the **neural groove,** then rolls up into a cylinder, the **neural tube.** The neural tube develops into the central nervous system. Additional cells roll off the top of the developing neural tube and form the **neural crest.** These cells form various tissues, including teeth, bones, and muscles of the skull, pigment cells in the skin, and other tissues.

The stages of embryonic development summarized above, from fertilization to gastrulation, are typical of a sea urchin (an echinoderm). Although these stages are general, important variations that occur among three animals commonly studied in developmental biology follow:

1. **Frog** (an amphibian)
   - **Gray crescent.** When the sperm penetrates a frog egg, a reorganization of the cytoplasm results in the appearance of a gray, crescent-shaped region, called the gray crescent. Hans Spemann, in a famous experiment, separated the cells formed during early cleavages and showed that each individual cell could develop into a normal frog only if it contained a portion of the gray crescent.

   - **Gastrulation.** During gastrulation, cells migrate over the top edge of the blastopore. The top edge, called the **dorsal lip,** forms from the same region earlier occupied by the gray crescent. The bottom and sides of the blastopore edge are called the ventral lip and lateral lips, respectively.

   - **Yolk.** The yolk material is much more extensive in the frog than in the sea urchin. Cells from the vegetal pole rich in yolk material form a **yolk plug** near the dorsal lip.

2. **Bird**
   - **Blastodisc.** The yolk of the bird egg is very large, and most of it is not involved in cleavages. Instead, the cleavages occur in a blastula that consists of a *flattened,* disk-shaped region that sits on top of the yolk. This kind of blastula is called a blastodisc.

   - **Primitive streak.** When gastrulation begins, invagination occurs along a line (rather than a circle) called the primitive streak. As cells migrate into the primitive streak, the crevice formed becomes an elongated blastopore (rather than a circular blastopore, as found in sea urchins and frogs).

3. Humans and most other mammals

- **Blastocyst.** The blastula stage, called the blastocyst, consists of two parts—an outer ring of cells, the **trophoblast,** and an inner mass of cells, the **embryonic disc.**

- **Trophoblast.** The outer ring of cells, or trophoblast, serves several functions. First, it accomplishes implantation by embedding into the endometrium of the uterus. Second, it produces **human chorionic gonadotropin (HCG)** to maintain progesterone production of the corpus luteum (which, in turn, will maintain the endometrium). Later, the trophoblast forms the **chorion,** the extraembryonic membrane that, together with maternal tissue, forms the **placenta.**

- **Embryonic disc.** Within the cavity created by the trophoblast, a bundle of cells called the **inner cell mass (ICM),** clusters at one pole and flattens into the embryonic disc. The embryonic disc is analogous to the blastodisc of birds and reptiles. A primitive streak develops, gastrulation follows, and development of the embryo and extraembryonic membranes (except the chorion) ensues.

Factors That Influence Development

Since all of the cells created during embryonic development originate from the same original zygote, they each contain copies of the same chromosomes with the same DNA sequences. What, then, causes cells to become structurally and functionally different within the same individual? Why does one cell mature into a muscle cell and another into a nerve cell? A summary of mechanisms responsible for influencing cell development and differentiation follows:

1. **Influence of the egg cytoplasm.** Cytoplasmic material is distributed unequally in the egg (or in subsequent daughter cells). The gray crescent in frogs and the yolk in bird eggs are examples. Nonuniform distribution of cytoplasm results in embryonic axes, such as the animal and vegetal poles. When cleavages divide the egg, the quality of cytoplasmic substances will vary among the daughter cells. Substances unique to certain daughter cells may influence their subsequent development.

2. **Embryonic induction.** Embryonic induction is the influence of one cell or group of cells over neighboring cells. Cells that exert this influence are called **organizers.** Cells act as organizers by secreting chemicals that diffuse among neighboring cells, influencing their development. Spemann discovered that the dorsal lip of the blastopore induced the development of the notochord in nearby cells. In particular, when a second dorsal lip was grafted into an embryo, two notochords developed. The dorsal lip functioned as an organizer.

3. **Homeotic genes.** Homeotic genes are believed to control development by turning on and off other genes that code for substances that directly affect development. *Mutant* homeotic genes in fruit flies are responsible for producing body parts in the wrong places, such as legs where antennae should be. A unique DNA segment, about 180 nucleotides long, has been found in most homeotic genes in numerous species, from fungi to humans. This gene segment, called a **homeobox,** identifies a particular class of genes that control development.

A cell in a developing embryo may contain certain substances that determine its final form and function. After a determinate cleavage, some of these substances may be absent, and as a result, the cell cannot attain some forms or functions. In various experiments, it has been demonstrated that when cells are grafted to a new position in the embryo, they may take on new forms or functions, or they may retain the form or function they were destined to have originally. The fate of a cell is said to be **determined** if its final form cannot be changed. Because cytoplasmic influences can be narrowed by each successive cell division, cells are more likely to be determined later in the developmental sequence than earlier.

By tracing the fates of cells during development, a **lineage map** can be built. A complete lineage map has been described for the nematode (roundworm) *Caenorhabditis elegans*. Every one of the 959 cells in an adult *C. elegans* can be traced back to the egg, cell division by cell division.

Sample Questions and Answers

Multiple-Choice Questions

Directions: Each of the following questions or statements is followed by five possible answers or sentence completions. Choose the one best answer or sentence completion.

1. Storage and maturation of human sperm occur in the

   A. epididymis

   B. interstitial cells

   C. seminiferous tubules

   D. Sertoli cells

   E. vas deferens

2. Oogenesis in humans begins

   A. during embryonic development

   B. at birth

   C. at puberty

   D. monthly during the menstrual cycle

   E. at fertilization

Questions 3–7

Use the following key for the next five questions. Each answer in the key may be used once, more than once, or not at all.

   A. Testosterone

   B. Progesterone

   C. Luteinizing hormone (LH)

   D. Follicle stimulating hormone (FSH)

   E. Gonadotropin releasing hormone (GnRH)

3. Stimulates the anterior pituitary gland to release hormones

4. Stimulates ovulation

5. Promotes the development of the endometrium

6. Follicles secrete this hormone.

7. Stimulates the testes to produce androgens

8. The function of the acrosome in the sperm head is to

   A. provide ATP for flagellar movements

   B. control DNA replication in the sperm

   C. store enzymes used for penetrating the egg during fertilization

   D. enclose the genetic material

   E. provide energy molecules for glycolytic reactions

Questions 9–12

Use the following key for the next four questions. Each answer in the key may be used once, more than once, or not at all.

A. Blastula (blastocyst)

B. Gastrula

C. Morula

D. Neural tube

E. Notochord

9. A solid ball of cells

10. A sphere of cells with a hollow center

11. The first stage in embryonic development in which there are three layers of cells

12. Cells from this structure migrate to other parts of the embryo and eventually form teeth and pigment cells in skin.

13. In birds and mammals, gastrulation begins at the

    A. trophoblast

    B. blastodisc

    C. blastocyst

    D. yolk

    E. primitive streak

14. Among amniotes, all of the following are extraembryonic membranes EXCEPT the

    A. allantois

    B. amnion

    C. chorion

    D. embryonic disc

    E. yolk sac

15. The dorsal lip of the blastopore induces development of the

    A. trophoblast

    B. mesoderm germ layer

    C. mouth in deuterostomes

    D. coelom

    E. notochord

Answers to Multiple-Choice Questions

1. **A.** Meiosis in the seminiferous tubules produces spermatids (immature sperm). Spermatids move to the epididymis for maturation and storage.

2. **A.** Oogenesis begins during embryonic development. However, the process is suspended at prophase I, when the production of all eggs stops. At puberty, oogenesis begins again, producing one secondary oocyte each month. At the end of meiosis I, ovulation occurs with the eruption of a secondary oocyte from the follicle. If the secondary oocyte is penetrated by a sperm (fertilization), meiosis II ensues.

3. **E.** GnRH stimulates the anterior pituitary to produce LH and FSH.

4. **C.** Ovulation from a follicle is induced by a surge in LH.

5. **B.** Progesterone (and estrogen) stimulate the thickening of the endometrium, the inside lining of the uterus.

6. **B.** Progesterone (and estrogen) are secreted by the follicle. After ovulation, progesterone and estrogen are secreted by the corpus luteum. (The follicle becomes the corpus luteum after ovulation.)

7. **C.** LH (or ICSH) stimulates interstitial cells in the testes to produce testosterone and other androgens.

8. **C.** The acrosome stores hydrolytic enzymes that allow penetration of the sperm into the vitelline layer surrounding the egg.

9. **C.** The morula is a bundle of cells shaped in the form of a sphere.

10. **A.** The blastula is an arrangement of cells around the outside of a center cavity, the blastocoel.

11. **B.** During gastrulation, cells of the blastula invaginate, moving into the blastocoel. As a result, two cell layers, the ectoderm and endoderm, form. In most animals, a third layer, the mesoderm, forms between these two layers.

12. **D.** During the formation of the neural tube (neurulation), cells roll off the top of the neural tube and form the neural crest. Cells from the neural crest migrate to various parts of the embryo to become a variety of different tissues.

13. **E.** Gastrulation begins when cells invaginate into the blastula along the primitive streak.

14. **D.** In mammals, the embryonic disc is the embryo proper—the bundle of cells that undergo gastrulation and organogenesis. The extraembryonic membranes provide support for the embryo proper.

15. **E.** By embryonic induction, the dorsal lip of the blastopore stimulates the development of the notochord.

Free-Response Questions

Free-response questions on the AP exam may require you to provide information from a narrow area of biology, or they may consist of parts that require you to assemble information from diverse areas of biology. The questions that follow are typical of either an entire AP exam question or merely that part of a question that is related to this section.

Directions: Answer the questions below as completely and as thoroughly as possible. Answer the question in essay form (NOT outline form), using complete sentences. You may use diagrams to supplement your answers, but a diagram alone without appropriate discussion is inadequate.

1. Compare and contrast sperm and egg production in humans.

2. Discuss how negative and positive feedback mechanisms regulate the ovarian and menstrual cycles. Explain how the cycles are affected if implantation of a fertilized egg occurs.

3. Discuss the embryonic development of a frog. Include each of the following.

   (a.) A description of each of the major embryonic stages

   (b.) The importance of gastrulation

   (c.) An example of embryonic induction

4. Describe mechanisms that cause differentiation during embryonic development. Describe classical experiments that have led to our understanding of these mechanisms.

Some Typical Answers to Free-Response Questions

Question 1

Compare:

Many of the hormones that regulate the production of gametes (eggs and sperm) are similar in both sexes. For both males and females, the hypothalamus monitors hormone levels in the blood and secretes gonadotropin releasing hormone (GnRH), which stimulates the anterior pituitary to produce follicle stimulating hormone (FSH) and luteinizing hormone (LH) (or interstitial cell stimulating hormone, ICSH). These hormones stimulate the gonads (testes in males, ovaries in females) to produce the gametes. In both males and females, LH stimulates the production of sex hormones, testosterone in males, and estrogen and progesterone in females. Also in both sexes, FSH stimulates the development of the gametes. In males, it does this by stimulating gametogenesis in the seminiferous tubules; in females, it does this by stimulating the development of an egg in a follicle. Positive and negative feedback loops in both males and females establish levels of hormones that maintain the constant production of sperm in males and the cyclical production of eggs in females.

Contrast:

Gametogenesis in females begins with an oogonium and ends with a single, viable egg and three nonfunctional polar bodies. By producing a single egg, most of the nutrients and cytoplasmic organelles are retained for the potential embryo. In males, each spermatogonium divides to produce four viable sperm, each containing an equal amount of cytoplasm. Gametogenesis in females begins during embryonic development, stops at prophase I at birth, and begins again at puberty, producing one egg a month until menopause. In males, gametogenesis begins at puberty and continues without interruption. In contrast to males, the female reproductive cycle also regulates the menstrual cycle, the thickening and sloughing off of the endometrium (the inner lining of the uterus). As a result, the system of feedback loops is more complex in females than in males.

Question 2

Low levels of estrogen signal the beginning of the menstrual cycle by triggering a negative feedback response. The hypothalamus (a portion of the brain involved in maintaining homeostasis) initiates the response by secreting gonadotropin releasing hormone (GnRH). GnRH, in turn, stimulates the anterior pituitary to release follicle stimulating hormone (FSH) and luteinizing hormone (LH). As part of the ovarian cycle, FSH stimulates the development of the egg within the follicle (completing meiosis I) and also stimulates the follicle to produce estrogen. In a positive feedback reaction to rising estrogen levels, the anterior pituitary secretes additional LH (after stimulation by the hypothalamus). This spike of LH in the middle of the cycle causes ovulation, the release of the egg (actually the secondary oocyte) from the follicle. After ovulation, the follicle, now called the corpus luteum, continues to produce estrogen and progesterone. These hormones regulate the menstrual cycle by stimulating the thickening of the endometrium (the inner lining of the uterus). In response to continued high levels of progesterone, a negative feedback response causes the anterior pituitary to stop production of LH and

FSH. As a result, the follicle stops producing estrogen and progesterone, and the endometrium is sloughed off.

If the egg becomes fertilized and implants into the endometrium, cells from the developing embryo secrete human chorionic gonadotropin (HCG), which induces the corpus luteum to continue production of progesterone, which, in turn, maintains the endometrium.

Both questions 1 and 2 require a discussion of the reproductive processes, but their focuses are different. In answering the first question, you need to state the similarities and differences (compare and contrast) between males and females. Details of hormone regulation alone would not address the question. In answering the second question, however, the details of hormone regulation (and feedback loops) are exactly what you need to discuss (but only for females). Note that in the answer to the first question, the two parts (compare and contrast) are clearly indicated.

Question 3

For part (a.), describe each stage in the development of a frog embryo. For part (c.), you can describe embryonic induction of the notochord by the dorsal lip of the blastopore. An answer for part (b.) follows.

(b.) During gastrulation, cells at the surface of the blastula move inward toward the center of the embryo. This causes a major rearrangement of cells. Two layers of cells result, the ectoderm and the endoderm, followed by a third layer between them, the mesoderm. These three layers are responsible for the arrangement and development of various organs throughout the body. For example, the ectoderm develops into skin and nerve tissue, the mesoderm into the reproductive organs and the lining of the coelum, and the endoderm into the linings of the respiratory and digestive tracts.

You would probably briefly describe the process of gastrulation in part (a.). You should repeat it in part (b.). Anytime there is an overlap between parts of a question, you should repeat information, where appropriate, in each part (time permitting). You may get points for a particular piece of information each time you repeat it.

Question 4

For this question, describe embryonic induction, gene regulation, and the influence of nonuniform distribution of the cytoplasm in the egg. Experiments you can cite include the dorsal lip induction of the notochord (for embryonic induction), the effect of mutant homeotic genes in fruit flies (for gene regulation), and the importance of the gray crescent (for the influence of egg cytoplasm). Also mention Hans Spemann. Past AP exams indicate that the subject of development is one of the few areas where you may need to give historical information—the names of biologists and a description of their experiments.

Animal Behavior

Review

Questions on animal behavior represent about 1% of the AP exam. This translates into a multiple-choice test section with perhaps one or two of these questions. Essay questions on animal behavior are also possible. They may take the form of an entire question or one or more parts of a larger question. This section summarizes the major concepts of **ethology,** the study of animal behavior, citing the classical behaviors and experiments (including names of famous researchers) that you will most likely need to know for the exam.

Genetic Basis of Behavior

Animal behavior can be inherited through genes (innate behavior), or it can be learned through interactions with the environment. Behavior that is influenced by genes is molded by natural selection and other evolutionary forces. As a result, most genetically based behaviors should increase the fitness, or reproductive success, of the individual. The study of behavior that seeks to explain how specific behaviors increase individual reproductive success is called **behavioral ecology.**

Kinds of Animal Behavior

Behaviors are categorized as follows:

1. **Instinct** is behavior that is innate, or inherited.

   - In mammals, care for offspring by female parents is innate.

2. **Fixed action patterns** (**FAP**) are innate behaviors that follow a regular, unvarying pattern. An FAP is initiated by a specific stimulus. Typically, the behavior is carried out to completion even if the original intent of the behavior can no longer be fulfilled.

   - When a graylag goose sees an egg outside her nest, she will methodically roll the egg back into the nest with a series of maneuvers using her beak. An egg outside the nest is the stimulus. However, she will also retrieve any object that resembles her egg, and once the FAP has begun, she will continue the retrieval motions until she has completed the motions back to the nest. Even if the egg slips away or is removed, she completes the FAP by returning an "imaginary" egg to the nest.

   - Male stickleback fish defend their territory against other males. The red belly of males is the stimulus for aggressive behavior. However, as ethologist Nikolaas Tinbergen discovered, any object with a red underside initiates the same aggressive FAP.

3. **Imprinting** is an innate program for acquiring a specific behavior only if an appropriate stimulus is experienced during a **critical period** (a limited time interval during the life of the animal). Once acquired, the behavior is irreversible.

   - Ethologist Konrad Lorenz discovered that, during the first two days of life, graylag goslings will accept any moving object as their mother. When Lorenz himself was the moving object, he was accepted as their mother for life. Any object presented after the critical period, including their real mother, was rejected.

   - Salmon hatch in freshwater streams and migrate to the ocean to feed. When they are reproductively mature, they return to their birthplace to breed, identifying the exact location of the stream. During early life, they imprinted the odors associated with their birthplace.

4. Associative learning (association) occurs when an animal recognizes (learns) that two or more events are connected. A form of associative learning called **classical conditioning** occurs when an animal performs a behavior in response to a *substitute* stimulus rather than the *normal* stimulus.

   - Dogs salivate when presented with food. Physiologist Ivan Pavlov found that if a bell were rung just before dogs were given food, they would, after repeated experiences, salivate in response to the bell ringing alone. Dogs associated the ring of the bell (the substitute stimulus) with the presentation of food (the normal stimulus).

5. Trial-and-error learning (or operant conditioning) is another form of associative learning. It occurs when an animal connects its own behavior with a particular environmental response. If the response is desirable (positive reinforcement), the animal will repeat the behavior in order to elicit the same response (for example, to receive a reward). If the response is undesirable (for example, painful), the animal will avoid the behavior. This is the basis for most animal training by humans.

   - Psychologist B. F. Skinner trained rats to push levers to obtain food or avoid painful shocks.

   Learning acquired by association can be forgotten or reversed if the performed behavior no longer elicits the expected response. The loss of an acquired behavior is called **extinction.**

6. **Habituation** is a learned behavior that allows the animal to disregard meaningless stimuli.

   - Sea anemones pull food into their mouths by withdrawing their tentacles. If the tentacles are stimulated with nonfood items (a stick, for example), the tentacles will ignore the stimulus after several futile attempts to capture the "food."

7. **Observational learning** occurs when animals copy the behavior of another animal without having experienced any prior positive reinforcement with the behavior.

   - Japanese monkeys usually remove sand from a potato by holding the potato in one hand and brushing sand away with the other hand. One monkey discovered that she could more easily brush the sand away if she held the potato in water. Through observational learning, nearly all of the other monkeys in the troop learned the behavior.

8. **Insight** occurs when an animal, exposed to a new situation and without any prior relevant experience, performs a behavior that generates a desirable outcome.

   - A chimpanzee will stack boxes so she can climb them, providing her with access to bananas previously beyond reach.

Some behaviors that appear to be learned may actually be innate behaviors that require **maturation.** For example, birds appear to "learn" to fly by trial and error or by observational learning. However, if birds are raised in isolation, they will fly on their first try if they are physically capable of flying. Thus, the ability to fly is innate but can occur only after the bird has physically matured.

In general, inherited behaviors and learning capabilities of animals have evolved because they increase individual fitness. Innate behavior, such as an FAP, improves fitness by providing a successful and dependable mechanism for the animal to perform in response to an event that, through evolution, has become *expected.* By establishing an FAP, a particular challenge need not be resolved repeatedly by every generation. In contrast, imprinting allows a certain amount of flexibility. If a mother is killed before her chick hatches, the chick will, through imprinting, choose another nearby bird for its mother (most likely of the same species).

Associative learning allows individuals to benefit from exposure to *unexpected* (or novel) repeated events. Once they form an association with the event, they can respond to the next occurrence more efficiently. Habituation allows individuals to ignore repetitive events which, from experience, they know are inconsequential. As a result, the animals can remain focused on other, more meaningful events.

Observational learning and insight provide a mechanism to learn new behaviors in response to *unexpected* events *without receiving reinforcement.* This reduces the time required for new behaviors to be acquired.

Animal Movement

Three kinds of movements are commonly found among animals:

1. **Kinesis** (plural, **kineses**) is an *undirected* (without direction) change in *speed* of an animal's movement in response to a stimulus. The animal slows down in a favorable environment or speeds up in an unfavorable environment. As a result, the animal remains longer in favorable environments.

   - When a log or rock is lifted, animals will suddenly scurry about. These movements are kineses in response to light, touch, air temperature, or other stimuli recognized as unfavorable.

2. **Taxis** (plural, **taxes**) is a *directed* movement in response to a stimulus. Movement is directed either *toward* or *away* from the stimulus. Movement toward light is called **phototaxis.**

   - Moths move toward lights at night.

   - Sharks move toward food when food odors reach them by diffusion or by bulk flow (ocean currents).

   - Female mosquitos find mammals (on which they feed) by moving toward heat.

3. **Migration** is the long-distance, seasonal movement of animals. It is usually in response to seasonal availability of food or degradation of environmental conditions (they usually occur together).

   - Whales, birds, elk, insects, and bats are examples of animals that migrate to warmer climates.

Communication in Animals

Communication in animals is commonly used in species recognition, in mating behavior, and in organizing social behavior. Communication occurs through the following mechanisms:

1. **Chemical.** Chemicals used for communication are called **pheromones.** Chemicals that cause immediate and specific behavioral changes are **releaser pheromones** (they "release," or trigger, the behavior); those that cause physiological changes are called **primer pheromones.** Some chemicals elicit responses when they are smelled; others trigger responses when they are eaten.

   - Reproductively receptive female moths attract male moths by emitting releaser pheromones into the air.

   - Ants secrete a releaser pheromone to mark trails that guide other ants to food.

   - Queen bees, queen termites, and queen ants secrete primer pheromones that are eaten by workers. The pheromone prevents development of reproductive ability.

   - Many male mammals spray urine throughout their territories (especially along their borders) to warn other animals of the same species to keep out.

2. **Visual.** Many visual displays are observed in animals during displays of aggression (agonistic behavior) or during courtship preceding reproduction.

   - Tinbergen found that various visual displays are releasers for reproductive behavior in stickleback fish. The red belly of the male fish attracts females, who adopt a head-up posture to initiate courtship. In response, males make zigzag motions. The female then follows the male to his nest and, if the nest is acceptable, enters it and deposits her eggs in response to the male's prodding on her tail. After the female leaves the nest, the male enters and fertilizes the eggs. Red bellies, head-up posture, zigzag motions, and swimming to the nest are all visual cues.

- Male sage grouse assemble into groups called **leks** in which the birds make courtship displays to solicit females. After observing the males, a female will choose one for a mate.

- Wolves make threatening gestures by staring and baring their teeth. Lowering their tails and lying on their backs are submissive behaviors.

3. **Auditory.** Sounds are commonly used to communicate over long distances, through water, and at night.

- Whales' songs produced at infrasound frequencies (below the audible range of humans) can be heard for hundreds of miles by other whales.

- Related female elephants form herds and use infrasound for greetings, for communicating danger, and for singing songs that announce reproductive readiness to solitary males who may be miles away.

- Calls of male frogs and male crickets ward off male rivals, attract females, and function in species recognition.

- Songs of male birds provide for species recognition, a display to attract mates, and a warning to other males of territorial boundaries.

4. **Tactile.** Touching is common in social bonding, infant care, grooming, and mating. Wolves greet the dominant male in the pack by licking his muzzle.

- Bees perform dances that provide information about the location of food. In most species, the dances occur inside dark hives, so the information is imparted by tactile, chemical, and auditory cues. Zoologist Karl von Frisch described two kinds of dances. When food is nearby, bees perform a *round dance,* in which the bee moves in a circle pattern. Each time she completes a circle, she turns around and repeats the pattern in the opposite direction. In the round dance, bees obtain food-location information by tasting or smelling flower or nectar scents on the dancing bee. As the distance to the food increases, the round dance develops into the *waggle dance,* a dance with a figure-eight pattern. The intersection of the two circles of the figure eight is called a straight run. When the bees dance along the straight run, they provide distance and direction information to the food. The longer the straight run, the greater the distance to the food. The larger the angle between the straight run (on a vertical honeycomb surface) and an imaginary vertical line, the greater the angle of the food source with respect to the position of the sun. While dancing along the straight run, the dancing bee vibrates its wings (buzzes) and wags its abdomen. To determine the length and angle of the straight run, the observing bees make body contact (tactile communication) with the dancing bee during her dance.

Foraging Behaviors

Numerous techniques have evolved to optimize feeding. The goal is to maximize the amount of food eaten while minimizing the energy expended to obtain it and minimizing the risks of being injured or eaten. Some foraging behaviors follow:

1. **Herds, flocks,** and **schools** provide several advantages, as follows:

   - *Concealment.* Most individuals in the flock are hidden from view.

   - *Vigilance.* In a group, individuals can trade off foraging and watching for predators. Further, it is easier to detect predators if many individuals are watching.

   - *Defense.* A group of individuals can shield their young or mob their predator.

2. **Packs** enable members to corner and successfully attack large prey.

3. **Search images** help animals find favored or plentiful food. Birds can easily find food they are accustomed to eating because they seek a specific, perhaps abbreviated, image of the target. When a new food item must be sought, additional scrutiny and thus additional time to locate the food are required until a new search image is formed. Humans commonly use search images to find a book on a bookshelf (looking for color and shape without reading the title) or to spot a police car (a black-and-white search image) in the rear view mirror.

Social Behavior

Animals may live in groups or they may be solitary. Sooner or later, however, all animals must make contact with others to reproduce. In each animal species, social behaviors have evolved that optimize individual fitness. Some patterns of interaction follow:

1. **Agonistic behavior** (aggression and submission) originates from competition for food, mates, or territory. Because most agonistic behavior is ritualized, injuries and time spent in contests are minimized.

2. **Dominance hierarchies** indicate power and status relationships between individuals in a group. Established hierarchies minimize fighting for food and mates.

   - **Pecking order** is a more or less linear order of status often used to describe dominance hierarchies in chickens.

3. **Territoriality** is the active possession and defense of the territory in which an animal lives. Territories insure their owners adequate food and a place to mate and rear their young.

4. **Altruistic behavior** is seemingly unselfish behavior that appears to reduce the fitness of the individual. It commonly occurs when an animal risks its safety in defense of another or sacrifices its reproduction to help another individual (of the same species) rear its young. However, altruistic behavior actually increases **inclusive fitness,** the fitness of the individual *plus* the fitness of relatives (who, in fact, share a percentage of identical genes with the altruist). Evolution of these behaviors occurs by **kin selection,** a form of natural selection that increases inclusive fitness.

   - Belding's ground squirrels give alarm calls (whistles) that warn other squirrels that a predator is approaching. In doing so, the squirrel risks safety by revealing her presence (an altruistic behavior) but increases the survival of other squirrels with which she lives. As it turns out, these squirrels live in groups of closely related females (daughters, mothers, sisters, and aunts). Thus, it is an example of kin selection.

- Bees live in colonies that consist of a queen and female daughters (worker bees). Since only the queen reproduces, the fitness of worker bees is zero, that is, they produce no progeny of their own. Bees are an example of a **haplodiploid** reproductive system: queens and female workers are diploid, while male bees (drones) are haploid. In the spring, males are born from unfertilized eggs. One male mates with the queen, who, in turn, stores the sperm to fertilize her eggs throughout the year. Following mating, the males are driven from the hive and die. In a normal diploid reproductive system, mother and offspring, as well as sisters, are related, on average, by only 50% of their genes. However, because half of the chromosomes of all sister bees are the same (from their haploid father), they share, on average, 75% of their genes. Thus, the inclusive fitness of a worker bee (in terms of the number of genes they contribute to the next generation) is greater if she promotes the production of sisters (by nurturing the queen) than if she were to produce offspring herself. Thus, kin selection favors sterile workers in a haplodiploid society.

Sample Questions and Answers

Multiple-Choice Questions

Directions: The following question is followed by five possible answers or sentence completions. Choose the one best answer or sentence completion.

1. All of the following may be associated with mating behavior EXCEPT:

   A. aggressive behavior

   B. releaser pheromones

   C. search image

   D. territoriality

   E. visual communication

Directions: Questions below consist of a phrase, sentence, or descriptive paragraph. Each question is preceded by five lettered choices. Select the one lettered choice that best matches the phrase, sentence, or paragraph. Each lettered choice may be used once, more than once, or not at all.

Questions 2–3

   A. Classical conditioning

   B. Imprinting

   C. Instinct

   D. Observational learning

   E. Trial-and-error learning

Wild Japanese monkeys were fed wheat that was scattered on the beach. This required the monkeys to collect that wheat one grain at a time from among the sand grains. One monkey discovered that by throwing a handful of sand and wheat into the ocean, the sand would sink and the wheat would float. She could then easily collect the wheat. Soon, other monkeys in the troop were separating the sand and the wheat in the same manner.

2. The learning technique employed when the monkey discovered she could separate the sand and wheat using water

3. The learning technique employed by other monkeys in the troop

Questions 4–7

    A. Associative learning

    B. Extinction

    C. Habituation

    D. Imprinting

    E. Maturation

4. A cat runs into the kitchen in response to the sound of a can opener.

5. As a kitten, a cat was fed canned cat food and would run into the kitchen when he heard the sound of the can opener. As an adult, the cat was fed only dry food from a bag and no longer responded to can opener sounds.

6. Some species of birds that migrate at night use the night sky as a compass. If juvenile birds are raised under an artificial night sky with no stars (or with major stars missing) for several months after hatching, they are unable to migrate in the correct direction.

7. Young sea gull chicks crouch in their nest when any bird flies overhead. Older chicks crouch only when an unfamiliar bird flies overhead.

Answers to Multiple-Choice Questions

1. **C.** A search image is associated with foraging. Aggressive behavior is exhibited in some animals when males fight for mates. Reproductively receptive female moths produce releaser pheromones that attract male moths. Possession of a territory gives males in some species exclusive access to the females in the territory. Visual communication is used during many courtship rituals (for example, leks).

2. **E.** Since the behavior was new to the troop, the first monkey to exhibit the behavior used either trial-and-error learning or insight learning. Only trial-and-error learning is listed in the key.

3. **D.** The most likely explanation of how other monkeys learned the behavior is by imitation, or observational learning.

4. **A.** The cat has associated the sound of the can opener with meal time. This is an example of classical conditioning, a form of associative learning.

5. **B.** Since the can opener (substitute stimulus) was not reinforced by the presentation of food (normal stimulus) when the cat was an adult, the conditioned response (running into the kitchen) was extinguished.

6. **D.** These juvenile birds imprint on major stars for migration orientation during a critical period that occurs during the first three months of life.

7. **C.** Habituation is the disregard for harmless, repeated stimuli.

Free-Response Questions

Free-response questions on the AP exam may require you to provide information from a narrow area of biology, or they may consist of parts that require you to assemble information from diverse areas of biology. The questions that follow are typical of either an entire AP exam question or merely that part of a question that is related to this section.

Directions: Answer the questions below as completely and as thoroughly as possible. Answer the question in essay form (NOT outline form), using complete sentences. You may use diagrams to supplement your answers, but a diagram alone without appropriate discussion is inadequate.

---

1. Define and explain how each of the following contributes to social behavior.

    a. Pecking order

    b. Territoriality

    c. Traveling in herds or packs

    d. Altruistic behavior

2. Describe each of the following animal behaviors as revealed in studies performed by the given researcher.

    a. Fixed action patterns and Nikolaas Tinbergen

    b. Imprinting and Konrad Lorenz

    c. Classical conditioning and Ivan Pavlov

    d. Bee communication and Karl von Frisch

Some Typical Answers to Free-Response Questions

Question 1

For each part of this question, you should give a definition, an explanation of how the behavior increases individual fitness, and an example. For altruistic behavior, be sure to describe how inclusive fitness is increased through kin selection.

Question 2

These four pioneers in animal behavior and their classical studies are required knowledge for the AP exam. As in the first question, be sure to define each kind of behavior, explain how the behavior benefits the animal, and give a description of the behaviors observed by each researcher.

Ecology

Review

Ecology is the study of the distribution and abundance of organisms, their interactions with other organisms, and their interactions with their physical environment.

The following terms provide a foundation for the study of ecology:

1. A **population** is a group of individuals all of the same species living in the same area. Thus, there are populations of humans, populations of black oaks, and populations of the bacteria *Streptococcus pneumoniae*.

2. A **community** is a group of populations living in the same area.

3. An **ecosystem** describes the interrelationships between the organisms in a community and their physical environment.

4. The **biosphere** is composed of all the regions of the earth that contain living things. This generally includes the top few meters of soil, the oceans and other bodies of water, and the lower ten kilometers of the atmosphere.

5. The **habitat** of an organism is the type of place where it usually lives. A description of the habitat may include other organisms that live there (often the dominant vegetation) as well as the physical and chemical characteristics of the environment (such as temperature, soil quality, or water salinity).

6. The **niche** of an organism describes all the biotic (living) and abiotic (nonliving) resources in the environment used by an organism. When an organism is said to occupy a particular niche, it means that certain resources are consumed or certain qualities of the environment are changed in some way by the presence of the organism.

Population Ecology

Population ecology is the study of the growth, abundance, and distribution of populations. Population abundance and distribution are described by the following terms:

1. The **size** of a population, symbolically represented by N, is the total number of individuals in the population.

2. The **density** of a population is the total number of individuals per area or volume occupied. There may be 100 buffalo/km^2 or 100 mosquitos/m^3.

3. **Dispersion** describes how individuals in a population are distributed. They may be clumped (like humans in cities), uniform (like trees in an orchard), or random (like trees in some forests).

4. **Age structure** is a description of the abundance of individuals of each age. It is often graphically expressed in an age structure diagram (Figure 14-1). Horizontal bars or tiers of the diagram represent the frequency of individuals in a particular age group. A vertical line down the center of each tier divides each age group into males and females. A rapidly growing population is indicated when a large proportion of the population is young. Therefore, age structure diagrams that are pyramid-shaped, with tiers larger at the base and narrower at the top, indicate rapidly growing populations. In contrast, age structure diagrams with tiers of equal width represent populations that are stable, with little or no population growth (zero population growth, or ZPG).

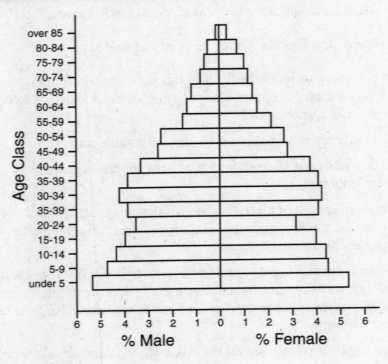

Figure 14-1

5. **Survivorship curves** describe how mortality of individuals in a species varies during their lifetimes (Figure 14-2).

- **Type I** curves describe species in which most individuals survive to middle age. After that age, mortality is high. Humans exhibit type I survivorship.

- **Type II** curves describe organisms in which the length of survivorship is random, that is, the likelihood of death is the same at any age. Many rodents and certain invertebrates (such as *Hydra*) are examples.

- **Type III** curves describe species in which most individuals die young, with only a relative few surviving to reproductive age and beyond. Type III survivorship is typical of oysters and other species that produce free-swimming larvae that make up a component of marine plankton. Only those few larvae that survive being eaten become adults.

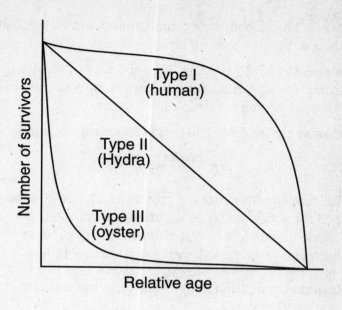

Figure 14-2

The following terms are used to describe population growth:

1. The **biotic potential** is the maximum growth rate of a population under ideal conditions, with unlimited resources and without any growth restrictions. For example, some bacteria can divide every twenty minutes. At that rate, one bacterium could give rise to over a trillion bacteria in ten hours. In contrast, elephants require nearly two years for gestation of a single infant. Even at this rate, however, after two thousand years, the weight of the descendents from two mating elephants would exceed that of the earth. The following factors contribute to the biotic potential of a species:

   - Age at reproductive maturity

   - Clutch size (number of offspring produced at each reproductive event)

   - Frequency of reproduction

   - Reproductive lifetime

   - Survivorship of offspring to reproductive maturity

2. The **carrying capacity** is the maximum number of individuals of a population that can be sustained by a particular habitat.

3. **Limiting factors** are those elements that prevent a population from attaining its biotic potential. Limiting factors are categorized into density-dependent and density-independent factors, as follows:

   - **Density-dependent** factors are those agents whose limiting effect becomes more intense as the population density increases. Examples include parasites and disease (transmission rates increase with population density), competition for resources (food, space, sunlight for photosynthesis), and the toxic effect of waste products. Also, predation is frequently density-dependent. In some animals, reproductive behavior may be abandoned when populations attain high densities. In such cases, stress may be a density-dependent limiting factor.

- **Density-independent** factors occur independently of the density of the population. Natural disasters (fires, earthquakes, volcanic eruptions) and extremes of climate (storms, frosts) are common examples.

The growth of a population can be described by the following equation:

$$r = \frac{births - deaths}{N}$$

In this equation, r is the **reproductive rate** (or **growth rate**), and N is the population size at the beginning of the interval for which the births and deaths are counted. The numerator of the equation is the net increase in individuals. If, for example, a population of size $N = 1000$ had 60 births and 10 deaths over a one-year period, then r would equal (60 - 10)/1000, or 0.05 per year.

If both sides of the equation are multiplied by N, the equation can be expressed as follows:

$$\frac{\Delta N}{\Delta t} = rN = births - deaths$$

The Greek letter delta (Δ) means "change in." Thus, $\Delta N/\Delta t$ means the change in the number of individuals in a given time interval.

When the reproductive rate, r, is maximum (the biotic potential), it is called the **intrinsic rate** of growth. Note, however, that when deaths exceed births, r will be negative, and the population size will decrease. On the other hand, when births and deaths are equal, the growth rate is zero and the population size remains constant (ZPG).

Population ecologists describe two general patterns of population growth, as follows:

1. **Exponential growth** occurs whenever the reproductive rate is greater than zero. On a graph where population size is plotted against time, a plot of exponential growth rises quickly, forming a **J-shaped** curve (Figure 14-3).

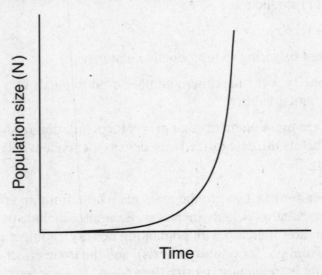

Figure 14-3

2. **Logistic growth** occurs when limiting factors restrict the size of the population to the carrying capacity of the habitat. In this case, the equation for reproductive rate given above is modified as follows:

$$\frac{\Delta N}{\Delta t} = rN\left(\frac{K-N}{K}\right)$$

K represents the carrying capacity. In logistic growth, when the size of the population increases, its reproductive rate decreases until, at carrying capacity (that is, when $N = K$), the reproductive rate is zero and the population size stabilizes. A plot of logistic growth forms an **S-shaped,** or **sigmoid, curve** (Figure 14-4).

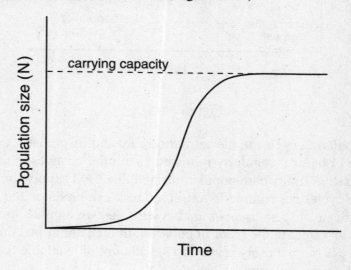

Figure 14-4

Population cycles are fluctuations in population size in response to varying effects of limiting factors. For example, since many limiting factors are density-dependent, they will have a greater effect when the population size is large as compared to when the population is small. In addition, a newly introduced population may grow exponentially beyond the carrying capacity of the habitat before limiting factors inhibit growth (Figure 14-5). When limiting factors do bring the population under control, the population size may decline to levels lower than the carrying capacity (or it may even crash to extinction). Once reduced below carrying capacity, however, limiting factors may ease, and population growth may renew. In some cases, a new carrying capacity, lower than the original, may be established (perhaps because the habitat was damaged by the excessively large population). The population may continue to fluctuate about the carrying capacity as limiting factors exert negative feedback on population growth when population size is large. When population size is small, limiting factors exert little negative feedback, and population growth renews.

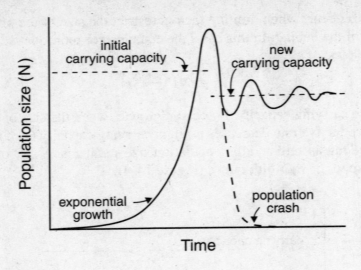

Figure 14-5

Figure 14-6 shows population cycles in the snowshoe hare and its predator the lynx. Since changes in the number of hares is regularly followed by similar changes in the number of lynx, it may appear that predation limits hare populations and that food supply limits lynx populations. Such fluctuation cycles are commonly observed between predator and prey. However, the data in Figure 14-6 indicate only an *association* between the two animals' populations, not that one population *causes* an effect in the other population. In fact, additional data suggest that population size in hares is more closely related to the amount of available food (grass), which, in turn, is determined by seasonal rainfall levels.

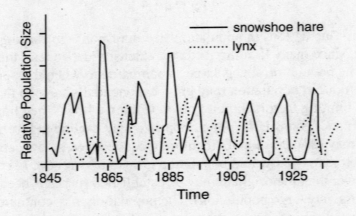

Figure 14-6

Exponential and logistic growth patterns are associated with two kinds of life-history strategies, as follows:

1. An **r-selected species** exhibits rapid growth (J-shaped curve). This type of reproductive strategy is characterized by **opportunistic species,** such as grasses and many insects, that quickly invade a habitat, quickly reproduce, and then die. They produce many offspring that are small, mature quickly, and require little, if any, parental care.

2. A **K-selected species** is one whose population size remains relatively constant (at the carrying capacity, K). Species of this type, such as humans, produce a small number of relatively large offspring that require extensive parental care until they mature. Reproduction occurs repeatedly during their lifetimes.

Human Population Growth

About a thousand years ago, the human population began exponential growth. By increasing the carrying capacity of the environment and by immigrating to previously unoccupied habitats, the following factors made exponential growth possible:

1. **Increases in food supply.** By domesticating animals and plants, humans were able to change from a hunter/gatherer lifestyle to one of agriculture. In the last hundred years, food output from agriculture was increased as a result of technological advances made during the industrial and scientific revolutions.

2. **Reduction in disease.** Advances in medicine, such as the discoveries of antibiotics, vaccines, and proper hygiene, reduced the death rate and increased the birth rate.

3. **Reduction in human wastes.** By developing water purification and sewage systems, health hazards from human wastes were reduced.

4. **Expansion of habitat.** Better housing, warmer clothing, easy access to energy (for heating, cooling, and cooking, for example) allowed humans to occupy environments that were previously unsuitable.

Community Ecology

Community ecology is concerned with the interaction of populations. One form of interaction is **interspecific competition** (competition between different species). The following concepts describe the various ways in which competition is resolved:

1. The **competitive exclusion principle (Gause's principle)**. When two species compete for exactly the same resources (or occupy the same niche), one is likely to be more successful. As a result, one species outcompetes the other, and eventually, the second species is eliminated. The competitive exclusion principle, formulated by G. F. Gause, states that no two species can sustain coexistence if they occupy the same niche.

   - Gause mixed two species of *Paramecium* that competed for the same food. One population grew more rapidly, apparently using resources more efficiently. Eventually, the second species was eliminated.

2. **Resource partitioning.** Some species coexist in spite of apparent competition for the same resources. Close study, however, reveals that they occupy slightly different niches. By pursuing slightly different resources or securing their resources in slightly different ways, individuals minimize competition and maximize success. Dividing up the resources in this manner is called resource partitioning.

   - Five species of warblers coexist in spruce trees by feeding on insects in different regions of the tree and by using different feeding behaviors to obtain the insects.

3. **Character displacement (niche shift).** As a result of resource partitioning, certain characteristics may enable individuals to obtain resources in their partitions more successfully. Selection of these characteristics (or characters) reduces competition with individuals in other partitions and leads to a divergence of features, or character displacement.

   - Two species of finches that live on two different Galapagos Islands have similar beaks, both suited for using the same food supply (seeds). On a third island, they co-exist, but due to evolution, the beak of each bird species is different. This minimizes competition by enabling each finch to feed on seeds of a different size.

4. **Realized niche.** The niche that an organism occupies in the absence of competing species is its **fundamental niche.** When competitors are present, however, one or both species may be able to coexist by occupying their **realized niches,** that part of their existence where **niche overlap** is absent, that is, where they do not compete for the same resources.

   - Under experimental conditions, one species of barnacle can live on rocks that are exposed to the full range of tides. The full range, from the lowest to the highest tide levels, is its fundamental niche. In the natural environment, however, a second species of barnacle outcompetes the first species, but only at the lower tide levels where desiccation is minimal. The first species, then, survives only in its realized niche, the higher tide levels.

Predation is another form of community interaction. In a general sense, a predator is any animal that totally or partly consumes a plant or another animal. More specifically, predators can be categorized as follows:

1. A **true predator** kills and eats another animal.

2. A **parasite** spends most (or all) of its life living on another organism (the host), obtaining nourishment from the host by feeding on its tissues. Although the host may be weakened by the parasite, the host does not usually die until the parasite has completed at least one life cycle, though usually many more.

3. A **parasitoid** is an insect that lays its eggs on a host (usually an insect or spider). After the eggs hatch, the larvae obtain nourishment by consuming the tissues of the host. The host eventually dies, but not until the larvae complete their development and begin pupation.

4. A **herbivore** is an animal that eats plants. Some herbivores, especially seed eaters (**granivores**), act like predators in that they totally consume the organism. Others animals, such as those that eat grasses (**grazers**) or leaves of other plants (**browsers**), may eat only part of the plant but may weaken it in the process.

Symbiosis is a term applied to two species that live together in close contact during a portion (or all) of their lives. A description of three forms of symbiosis follows:

1. **Mutualism** is a relationship in which both species benefit.

   - Certain acacia trees provide food and housing for ants. In exchange, the resident ants kill any insects or fungi found on the tree. In addition, the ants crop any neighboring vegetation that makes contact with the tree, thereby providing growing space and sunlight for the acacia.

- Lichens, symbiotic associations of fungi and algae, are often cited as examples of mutualism. The algae supply sugars produced from photosynthesis, and the fungi provide minerals, water, a place to attach, and protection from herbivores and ultraviolet radiation. In some cases, however, fungal hyphae invade and kill their symbiotic algae cells. For this and other reasons, some researchers consider the lichen symbiosis closer to parasitism.

2. In **commensalism,** one species benefits, while the second species is neither helped nor harmed.

   - Many birds build their nests in trees. Generally, the tree is neither helped nor harmed by the presence of the nests.

   - Egrets gather around cattle. The birds benefit because they eat the insects aroused by the grazing cattle. The cattle, however, are neither helped nor harmed.

3. In **parasitism,** the parasite benefits from the living arrangement, while the host is harmed.

   - Tapeworms live in the digestive tract of animals, stealing nutrients from their hosts.

Coevolution

In the contest between predator and prey, some prey may have unique heritable characteristics that enable them to more successfully elude predators. Similarly, some predators may have characteristics that enable them to more successfully capture prey. The natural selection of characteristics that promote the most successful predators and the most elusive prey leads to coevolution of predator and prey. In general, coevolution is the evolution of one species in response to new adaptations that appear in another species. Some important examples of coevolution follow:

1. **Secondary compounds** are toxic chemicals produced in plants that discourage would-be herbivores.

   - Tannins, commonly found in oaks, and nicotine, found in tobacco, are secondary compounds that are toxic to herbivores.

2. **Camouflage** (or **cryptic coloration**) is any color, pattern, shape, or behavior that enables an animal to blend in with its surroundings. Both prey and predator benefit from camouflage.

   - The fur of the snowshoe hare is white in winter (a camouflage in snow) and brown in summer (a camouflage against the exposed soil).

   - The larvae of certain moths are colored so that they look like bird droppings.

   - The markings on tigers and many other cats provide camouflage in a forested background. In contrast, the yellow-brown coloring of lions provides camouflage in their savanna habitat.

   - Some plants escape predation because they have the shape and color of the surrounding rocks.

3. **Aposematic coloration** (or **warning coloration**) is a conspicuous pattern or coloration of animals that warns predators that they sting, bite, taste bad, or are otherwise to be avoided.

   - Predators learn to associate the yellow and black body of bees with danger.

4. **Mimicry** occurs when two or more species resemble one another in appearance. There are two kinds of mimicry:

   - **Müllerian mimicry** occurs when several animals, all with some special defense mechanism, share the same coloration. Müllerian mimicry is an effective strategy because a single pattern, shared among several animals, is more easily learned by a predator than would be a different pattern for every animal. Thus, bees, yellow jackets, and wasps all have yellow and black body markings.

   - **Batesian mimicry** occurs when an animal without any special defense mechanism mimics the coloration of an animal that does possess a defense. For example, some defenseless flies have yellow and black markings but are avoided by predators because they resemble the warning coloration of bees.

Ecological Succession

Ecological succession is the change in the composition of species over time. The traditional view of succession describes how one community with certain species is gradually and predictably replaced by another community consisting of different species. As succession progresses, species diversity (the number of species in a community) and total biomass (the total mass of all living organisms) increase. Eventually, a final successional stage of constant species composition, called the **climax community,** is attained. The climax community persists relatively unchanged until destroyed by some catastrophic event, such as a fire.

Succession, however, is not as predictable as once thought. Successional stages may not always occur in the expected order, and the establishment of some species is apparently random, influenced by season, by climatic conditions, or by which species happens to arrive first. Furthermore, in some cases, a stable climax community is never attained because fires or other disturbances occur so frequently.

Succession occurs in some regions when climates change over thousands of years. Over shorter periods of time, succession occurs because species that make up communities alter the habitat by their presence. In both cases, the physical and biological conditions which made the habitat initially attractive to the resident species may no longer exist, and the habitat may be more favorable to new species. Some of the changes induced by resident species are listed below:

1. *Substrate texture* may change from solid rock, to sand, to fertile soil, as rock erodes and the decomposition of plants and animals occurs.

2. *Soil pH* may decrease due to the decomposition of certain organic matter, such as acidic leaves.

3. *Soil water potential,* or the ability of the soil to retain water, changes as the soil texture changes.

4. *Light* availability may change from full sunlight to partly shady, to near darkness as trees become established.

5. *Crowding,* which increases with population growth, may be unsuitable to certain species.

Succession is often described by the series of plant communities that inhabit a region over time. Animals, too, take up residence in these communities but usually in response to their attraction to the kinds of resident plants, not because of any way in which previous animals have changed the habitat. Animals do, however, affect the physical characteristics of the community by adding organic matter when they leave feces or decompose, and the biological characteristics of the community when they trample or consume plants or when they disperse seeds. But because animals are transient, their effects on succession are often difficult to determine.

The plants and animals that are first to colonize a newly exposed habitat are called **pioneer species.** They are typically opportunistic, *r*-selected species that have good dispersal capabilities, are fast growing, and produce many progeny rapidly. Many pioneer species can tolerate harsh conditions such as intense sunlight, shifting sand, rocky substrate, arid climates, or nutrient-deficient soil. For example, nutrient-deficient soils of some early successional stages harbor nitrogen-fixing bacteria or support the growth of plants whose roots support mutualistic relationships with these bacteria.

As soil, water, light, and other conditions change, *r*-selected species are gradually replaced by more stable *K*-selected species. These include perennial grasses, herbs, shrubs, and trees. Because *K*-selected species live longer, their environmental effects slow down the rate of succession. Once the climax community is established, it may remain essentially unchanged for hundreds of years.

There are two kinds of succession, as follows:

1. **Primary succession** occurs on substrates that never previously supported living things. For example, primary succession occurs on volcanic islands, on lava flows, and on rock left behind by retreating glaciers. Two examples follow:

   - *Succession on rock or lava* usually begins with the establishment of lichens. Hyphae of the fungal component of the lichen attach to rocks, the fungal mycelia hold moisture that would otherwise drain away, and the lichen secretes acids which help erode rock into soil. As soil accumulates, bacteria, protists, mosses, and fungi appear, followed by insects and other arthropods. Since the new soil is typically nutrient deficient, various nitrogen-fixing bacteria appear early. Grasses, herbs, weeds, and other *r*-selected species are established next. Depending upon local climatic conditions, *r*-selected species are eventually replaced by *K*-selected species such as perennial shrubs and trees.

   - *Succession on sand dunes* begins with the appearance of grasses adapted to taking root in shifting sands. These grasses stabilize the sand after about six years. The subsequent stages of this succession can be seen on the dunes of Lake Michigan. The stabilized sand allows the rooting of shrubs, followed by the establishment of cottonwoods. Pines and black oaks follow over the next fifty to one hundred years. Finally, the beech-maple climax community becomes established. The entire process may require a thousand years.

2. **Secondary succession** begins in habitats where communities were entirely or partially destroyed by some kind of damaging event. For example, secondary succession begins in habitats damaged by fire, floods, insect devastations, overgrazing, and forest clear-cutting and in disturbed areas such as abandoned agricultural fields, vacant lots, roadsides, and construction sites. Because these habitats previously supported life, secondary succession, unlike primary succession, begins on substrates that already bear soil. In addition, the soil contains a native seed bank. Two examples of secondary succession follow:

- *Succession on abandoned cropland* (called old-field succession) typically begins with the germination of *r*-selected species from seeds already in the soil (such as grasses and weeds). The trees that ultimately follow are region specific. In some regions of the eastern United States, pines take root next, followed by various hardwoods such as oak, hickory, and dogwood.

- *Succession in lakes and ponds* begins with a body of water, progresses to a marshlike state, then a meadow, and finally to a climax community of native vegetation. Sand and silt (carried in by a river) and decomposed vegetation contribute to the filling of the lake. Submerged vegetation is established first, followed by emergent vegetation whose leaves may cover the water surface. Grasses, sedges, rushes, and cattails take root at the perimeter of the lake. Eventually, the lake fills with sediment and vegetation and is subsequently replaced by a meadow of grasses and herbs. In many mountain regions, the meadow is replaced by shrubs and native trees, eventually becoming a part of the surrounding coniferous forest.

Ecosystems

A major goal in the study of ecosystems is to examine the production and utilization of energy. To assist in this goal, plants and animals are organized into groups called **trophic levels** that reflect their main energy source, as follows:

1. **Primary producers** are autotrophs that convert sun energy into chemical energy. They include plants, photosynthetic protists, cyanobacteria, and chemosynthetic bacteria.

2. **Primary consumers,** or herbivores, eat the primary producers.

3. **Secondary consumers,** or primary carnivores, eat the primary consumers.

4. **Tertiary consumers,** or secondary carnivores, eat the secondary consumers.

5. **Detritivores** are consumers that obtain their energy by consuming dead plants and animals (**detritus**). The smallest detritivores, called **decomposers,** include fungi and bacteria. Other detritivores include nematodes, earthworms, insects, and scavengers such as crabs, vultures, and jackals.

Ecological pyramids are used to show the relationship between trophic levels. Horizontal bars or tiers are used to represent the relative sizes of trophic levels, each represented in terms of energy (also called productivity), biomass, or numbers of organisms. The tiers are stacked upon one another in the order in which energy is transferred between levels. The result is usually a pyramid-shaped figure, although other shapes may also result. Several kinds of pyramids are illustrated in Figure 14-7.

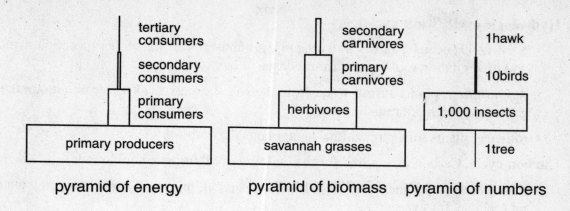

Figure 14-7

Ecological efficiency describes the proportion of energy represented at one trophic level that is transferred to the next level. The relative sizes of tiers in an energy pyramid (or pyramid of productivity) indicate the ecological efficiency of the ecosystem. On average, the efficiency is only about 10%, that is, about 10% of the productivity of one trophic level is transferred to the next level. The remaining 90% is consumed by the individual metabolic activities of each plant or animal, or is transferred to detritivores when they die.

Because ecological efficiency is so low, nearly all domestic animals used for food or work are herbivores. If a carnivore were raised for food or work, the energy required to raise and sustain it would far exceed its value in food or work. The meat consumed by the carnivore would yield a greater return by merely using it directly for human food.

Two kinds of flow charts are often used to show the flow of energy between specific organisms. The arrows used in the flow chart indicate the direction of energy flow.

1. A **food chain** is a linear flow chart of who eats whom. For example, a food chain depicting energy flow in a savanna may look like this:

$$\text{grass} \to \text{zebra} \to \text{lion} \to \text{vulture}$$

2. A **food web** is an expanded, more complete version of a food chain. It would show all of the major plants in the ecosystem, the various animals that eat the plants (such as insects, rodents, zebras, giraffes, antelopes), and the animals that eat the animals (lions, hyenas, jackals, vultures). Detritivores may also be included in the food web. Arrows point from all organisms that are eaten to the animals that eat them.

Biogeochemical Cycles

Biogeochemical cycles describe the flow of essential elements from the environment to living things and back to the environment. The following list outlines the major storage locations (reservoirs) for essential elements, the processes through which each element incorporates into terrestrial plants and animals (assimilation), and the processes through which each element returns to the environment (release).

1. **Hydrologic cycle** (water cycle).

   - *Reservoirs:* oceans, air (as water vapor), groundwater, glaciers. (Evaporation, wind, and precipitation move water from oceans to land.)

   - *Assimilation:* plants absorb water from the soil; animals drink water or eat other organisms (which are mostly water).

   - *Release:* plants transpire; animals and plants decompose.

2. **Carbon cycle.** Carbon is required for the building of all organic compounds.

   - *Reservoirs:* atmosphere (as CO_2), fossil fuels (coal, oil), peat, durable organic material (cellose, for example).

   - *Assimilation:* plants use CO_2 in photosynthesis; animals consume plants or other animals.

   - *Release:* plants and animals release CO_2 through respiration and decomposition; CO_2 is released when organic material (such as wood and fossil fuels) is burned.

3. **Nitrogen cycle.** Nitrogen is required for the manufacture of all amino acids and nucleic acids.

   - *Reservoirs:* atmosphere (N_2); soil (NH_4^+ or ammonium, NH_3 or ammonia, NO_2^- or nitrite, NO_3^- or nitrate).

   - *Assimilation:* plants absorb nitrogen either as NO_3^- or as NH_4^+; animals obtain nitrogen by eating plants or other animals. The stages in the assimilation of nitrogen are as follows:

   Nitrogen fixation: N_2 to NH_4^+ by prokaryotes (in soil and root nodules); N_2 to NO_3^- by lightning and UV radiation.

   Nitrification: NH_4^+ to NO_2^- and NO_2^- to NO_3^- by various nitrifying bacteria.

   NH_4^+ or NO_3^- to organic compounds by plant metabolism.

   - *Release:* denitrifying bacteria convert NO_3^- back to N_2 (**denitrification**); detrivorous bacteria convert organic compounds back to NH_4^+ (**ammonification**); animals excrete NH_4^+ (or NH_3), urea, or uric acid.

4. **Phosphorus cycle.** Phosphorus is required for the manufacture of ATP and all nucleic acids. Biogeochemical cycles of other minerals, such as calcium and magnesium, are similar to the phosphorus cycle.

   - *Reservoirs:* rocks. (Erosion transfers phosphorus to water and soil; sediments and rocks that accumulate on ocean floors return to the surface as a result of uplifting by geological processes.)

   - *Assimilation:* plants absorb inorganic PO_4^{3-} (phosphate) from soils; animals obtain organic phosphorus when they eat plants or other animals.

   - *Release:* plants and animals release phosphorus when they decompose; animals excrete phosphorus in their waste products.

Biomes

The biosphere is divided into regions called **biomes** that exhibit common environmental characteristics. Each biome is occupied by unique communities or ecosystems of plants and animals that share adaptations which promote survival within the biome. Following is a list of the major biomes and a summary of their characteristics:

1. **Tropical rain forests** are characterized by high temperature and heavy rainfall. The vegetation consists predominately of tall trees that branch only at their tops, forming a spreading canopy that allows little light to reach the forest floor. **Epiphytes** (plants that live commensally on other plants) and vines commonly grow on the trees, but due to lack of light, little grows on the forest floor.

2. **Savannas** are grasslands with scattered trees. Because savannas are tropical, they are subject to high temperatures. However, they receive considerably less water than rain forests.

3. **Temperate grasslands** receive less water and are subject to lower temperatures than are savannas. The North American prairie is an example.

4. **Temperate deciduous forests** occupy regions that have warm summers, cold winters, and moderate precipitation. Deciduous trees shed their leaves during the winter, an adaptation to poor growing conditions (short days and cold temperatures).

5. **Deserts** are hot and dry. Growth of annual plants is limited to short periods following rains. Other plants have adapted to the hostile conditions with leathery leaves, deciduous leaves, or leaves reduced to spines (cacti). Many animals have thick skins, conserve water by producing no urine or very concentrated urine, and restrict their activity to nights.

6. **Taigas** are characterized by coniferous forests (pines, firs, and other trees with needles for leaves). Winters are cold, and precipitation is in the form of snow.

7. **Tundras** are subject to winters so cold that the ground freezes. During the summer, the upper topsoil thaws, but the deeper soil, the **permafrost,** remains permanently frozen. During the summer, the melted topsoil supports a grassland type community consisting of grasses, sedges, and other vegetation tolerant of soggy soils.

8. **Fresh water biomes** include ponds, lakes, streams, and rivers.

9. **Marine biomes** include estuaries (where oceans meet rivers), intertidal zones (where oceans meet land), continental shelves (the relatively shallow oceans that border continents), coral reefs (masses of corals that reach the ocean surface), and the pelagic ocean (the deep oceans).

Human Impact on the Biosphere

Human activity damages the biosphere. Exponential population growth, destruction of habitats for agriculture and mining, pollution from industry and transportation, and many other activities all contribute to the damage of the environment. Some of the destructive consequences of human activity are summarized as follows:

1. **Greenhouse effect.** The burning of fossil fuels and forests increases CO_2 in the atmosphere. Increases in CO_2 cause more heat to be trapped in the earth's atmosphere. As a result, global temperatures are rising. Warmer temperatures could raise sea levels (by melting more ice) and decrease agriculture output (by affecting weather patterns).

2. **Ozone depletion.** The ozone layer forms in the upper atmosphere when UV radiation reacts with oxygen (O_2) to form ozone (O_3). The ozone absorbs UV radiation and thus prevents it from reaching the surface of the earth where it would damage the DNA of plants and animals. Various air pollutants, such as chlorofluorocarbons (CFCs), enter the upper atmosphere and break down ozone molecules. CFCs have been used as refrigerants, as propellants in aerosol sprays, and in the manufacture of plastic foams. When ozone breaks down, the ozone layer thins, allowing UV radiation to penetrate and reach the surface of the earth. Areas of major ozone thinning, called **ozone holes,** appear regularly over Antarctica, the Arctic, and northern Eurasia.

3. **Acid rain.** The burning of fossil fuels (such as coal) and other industrial processes release into the air pollutants that contain sulfur dioxide and nitrogen dioxide. When these substances react with water vapor, they produce sulfuric acid and nitric acid. When these acids return to the surface of the earth (with rain or snow), they kill plants and animals in lakes and rivers and on land.

4. **Desertification.** Overgrazing of grasslands that border deserts transform the grasslands into deserts. As a result, agricultural output decreases, or habitats available to native species are lost.

5. **Deforestation.** Clear-cutting of forests causes erosion, flooding, and changes in weather patterns. The slash-and-burn method of clearing tropical rain forests for agriculture increases atmospheric CO_2, which contributes to the greenhouse effect. Because most of the nutrients in a tropical rain forest are stored in the vegetation, burning the forest destroys the nutrients. As a result, the soil of some rain forests can support agriculture for only one or two years.

6. **Pollution.** Air pollution, water pollution, and land pollution contaminate the materials essential to life. Many pollutants do not readily degrade and remain in the environment for decades. Some toxins, such as the pesticide DDT, concentrate in plants and animals. As one organism eats another, the toxin becomes more and more concentrated, a process called **biological magnification.** Other pollution occurs in subtle ways. A lake, for example, can be polluted with runoff fertilizer or sewage. Abundant nutrients, especially phosphates, stimulate **algal blooms,** or massive growths of algae and other phytoplankton. The phytoplankton reduce oxygen supplies at night when they respire. In addition, when the algae eventually die, their bodies are consumed by detrivorous bacteria, whose growth further depletes the oxygen. The result is massive oxygen starvation for many animals, including fish and invertebrates. In the end, the lake fills with carcasses of dead animals and plants. The process of nutrient enrichment in lakes and the subsequent increase in biomass is called **eutrophication.** When the process occurs naturally, growth rates are slow and balanced. But with the influence of humans, the accelerated process often leads to the death of fish and the growth of anaerobic bacteria that produce foul-smelling gases.

7. **Reduction in species diversity.** As a result of human activities, especially the destruction of tropical rain forests and other habitats, plants and animals are apparently becoming extinct at a faster rate than the planet has ever previously experienced. If they were to survive, many of the disappearing plants could become useful to humans as medicines, foods, or industrial products.

Sample Questions and Answers

Multiple-Choice Questions

Directions: Each of the following questions or statements is followed by five possible answers or sentence completions. Choose the one best answer or sentence completion.

1. A group of interbreeding individuals occupying the same area is best called

   A. a community

   B. a population

   C. an ecosystem

   D. a society

   E. a symbiotic relationship

Questions 2–4

Questions 2–4 refer to the following age structure diagrams that represent five different populations.

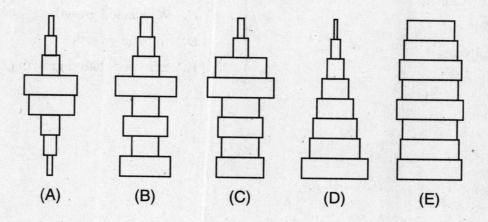

(A)   (B)   (C)   (D)   (E)

2. Which of the above populations is experiencing the fastest growth?

3. Which of the above populations is most nearly experiencing zero population growth over the time period represented by the diagram?

4. Which of the above populations is experiencing the effect of severe limiting factors?

5. All of the following populations would likely result in a uniform dispersion pattern EXCEPT:

   A. nesting penguins on a small beach

   B. territories of bears in a forest

   C. perennial shrubs (of a given species) growing in a desert habitat

   D. tropical trees (of a given species) in a tropical rain forest

   E. lions on the savanna

Questions 6–7

Questions 6–7 refer to a population of 500 that experiences 55 births and 5 deaths during a one-year period.

6. What is the reproductive rate for the population during the one-year period?

   A. 0.01/year

   B. 0.05/year

   C. 0.1/year

   D. 50/year

   E. 55/year

7. If the population maintains the current growth pattern, a plot of its growth would resemble

   A. exponential growth

   B. fluctuating growth

   C. *K*-selected growth

   D. logistic growth

   E. zero population growth (ZPG)

Questions 8–13

Use the following key for the next six questions. Each answer in the key may be used once, more than once, or not at all.

A. Character displacement

B. Commensalism

C. Mutualism

D. Batesian mimicry

E. Müllerian mimicry

8. Burr-bearing seeds that are dispersed by clinging to the fur of certain birds do not harm or help the birds.

9. The monarch and viceroy butterflies both have orange wings with the same distinctive black markings. When the monarch caterpillar feeds on milkweed, a toxic plant, it stores the toxins, making both the monarch caterpillar and butterfly unpalatable and toxic. The viceroy caterpillar feeds on nontoxic plants.

10. The mating calls of two species of frogs are different when they occupy the same island. On separate islands, the mating calls are the same.

11. Oxpeckers are birds that ride rhinoceroses and other ungulates and eat various skin parasites, such as ticks.

12. Several species of poisonous snakes bear bright colors of red, black, and yellow.

13. Several species of brightly colored, harmless snakes look like poisonous coral snakes.

14. All of the following kinds of plants or animals characterize the initial stages of succession EXCEPT:

    A. pioneer species

    B. *r*-selected species

    C. species with good dispersal ability

    D. species that can tolerate poor growing conditions

    E. species that invest large amounts of resources or time into development of progeny

15. Primary succession would occur on a

    A. meadow destroyed by flood

    B. meadow destroyed by overgrazing

    C. newly created volcanic island

    D. section of a forest destroyed by an avalanche

    E. section of a forest destroyed by fire

16. All of the following increase the concentration of CO_2 in the atmosphere EXCEPT:

    A. photosynthesis

    B. slash-and-burn clearing of tropical rain forests

    C. burning of fossil fuels

    D. burning of wood for cooking and heating

    E. burning of gasoline

17. Nitrogen becomes available to plants by all of the following processes EXCEPT:

    A. ammonification

    B. denitrification by denitrifying bacteria

    C. nitrification by nitrifying bacteria

    D. nitrogen fixation in plant nodules

    E. nitrogen fixation by soil prokaryotes

18. The transition from a tropical rain forest to a savanna is marked by fewer and fewer trees. This is most likely caused by changes in

    A. temperature

    B. rainfall

    C. the length of the growing season

    D. the average length of daylight

    E. CO_2 concentration

Question 19

Question 19 refers to the following food chain.

dinoflagellates → oysters → humans

19. In the above food chain, oysters represent

A. detritivores

B. producers

C. herbivores

D. primary carnivores

E. secondary consumers

Question 20

Question 20 refers to the following pyramid of biomass.

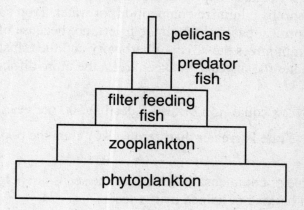

20. In which trophic level would the biological magnification of the pesticide DDT be most evident?

A. Phytoplankton

B. Zooplankton

C. Filter feeding fish

D. Predator fish

E. Pelicans

Answers to Multiple-Choice Questions

1. **B.** Since the individuals are interbreeding, they belong to a single species. A group of individuals of the same species is a population. A society is also a group of individuals of the same species, but the individuals must exhibit some form of cooperation or interdependence (social behavior).

2. **D.** An age structure diagram that is pyramid shaped with a broad base represents a population with fast growth.

3. **E.** An age structure diagram with all tiers of approximately the same width represents a population with a constant size.

4. **A.** This age structure diagram indicates high mortality rates among the older and younger generations, an indication that the weakest individuals are experiencing severe density-dependent limiting factors.

5. **E.** Lions are social animals and group in prides (or in bands of bachelor males). In contrast, the remaining answer choices are animals that are likely to be distributed in a uniform pattern, with each individual spaced equally from others. Whenever a population is subject to a limiting resource, there is likely to be competition. In order to minimize conflict, the result of competition is often to distribute the resource equally among all individuals in a population. By equally apportioning space, the penguins and bears minimize conflict. The desert shrubs minimize competition for water. Tropical trees of a single species are also uniformly spaced through the forest, not because of competition, but probably because it minimizes the effect of herbivory and the transmission of parasites and disease. The greater the distance between trees, the more difficulty herbivores have in locating a tree.

6. **C.** The rate of growth, r, equals (55 births - 5 deaths)/500 per year, or 0.1/year.

7. **A.** If the reproductive rate is greater than zero ($r > 0$), then the population is growing exponentially.

8. **B.** This is an example of commensalism because the seeds are helped (dispersal occurs) and the birds are not harmed or helped by the seeds.

9. **D.** This is an example of Batesian mimicry because the defenseless viceroy butterfly benefits by mimicking the aposematic monarch butterfly.

10. **A.** Character displacement occurs when two species compete for the same resource. In this example of frogs, that resource is mates. Those individual frogs that are best able to find mates of their own species are favored. Thus, frogs of each species that communicate with songs that promote species recognition produce more offspring. Over subsequent generations, the songs of the two species diverge until they are no longer confused.

11. **C.** Mutualism occurs when both organisms in the symbiosis benefit. In this example, the oxpeckers obtain food, and the rhinos have parasites removed.

12. **E.** Snakes are Müllerian mimics when they both look alike and possess some kind of aposematic defense (poisonous or unpalatable, for example).

13. **D.** The brightly colored, harmless snakes are Batesian mimics because they benefit from the defense mechanism of the colorful snakes they resemble.

14. E. Species that make large parental investments in their offspring, such as oak trees, whose acorns require two years to mature, or mammals that nurse their young, are *K*-selected species and are characteristic of the later stages of succession.

15. C. Primary succession occurs on newly exposed substrates, previously uninhabited by living things. All of the other choices would initiate secondary succession.

16. A. Photosynthesis removes CO_2 from the atmosphere. On the other hand, respiration adds CO_2 to the atmosphere, as does the burning of any organic fuel such as wood, coal, oil, natural gas, and gasoline.

17. B. Depending on soil conditions and plant species, plants absorb nitrogen either in the form of NH_4^+ or NO_3^-. Denitrifying by soil bacteria converts NO_3^- to gaseous N_2, a form of nitrogen that plants cannot use. The other choices describe processes that generate either NH_4^+ or NO_3^-.

18. B. The major factor responsible for the transition from rain forest to savanna is the average yearly rainfall. Because both habitats are tropical, temperatures, length of growing season, and hours of daylight are about the same.

19. C. Since the photosynthetic dinoflagellate algae are producers, the oysters are herbivores.

20. E. DDT concentrates in the pelicans because they occupy the top of the food chain. Because the pesticide results in fragile eggshells which break before incubation is completed, many pelican populations had approached extinction before DDT was banned in the U.S.

Free-Response Questions

Free-response questions on the AP exam may require you to provide information from a narrow area of biology, or they may consist of parts that require you to assemble information from diverse areas of biology. The questions that follow are typical of either an entire AP exam question or merely that part of a question that is related to this section.

Directions: Answer the questions below as completely and as thoroughly as possible. Answer the question in essay form (NOT outline form), using complete sentences. You may use diagrams to supplement your answers, but a diagram alone without appropriate discussion is inadequate.

---

1. Describe how limiting factors regulate the growth of populations.

2. (a.) Describe the process of succession for a lake as it develops into a forest.

   (b.) Compare and contrast the succession of a lake and the eutrophication of a lake polluted by fertilizer or sewage.

3. Explain how two closely related species can occupy the same habitat seemingly competing for the same kinds of resources.

4. Describe the cycling of nitrogen in an ecosystem.

Some Typical Answers to Free-Response Questions

Question 1

For this question, you should begin by describing intrinsic, exponential population growth. Describe how populations experiencing rapid growth can deplete their resources and subsequently crash to extinction. Then, discuss the different kinds of limiting factors (density-dependent and density-independent) that limit populations to logistic growth and that limit the size of populations to the carrying capacity of the habitat. Describe the interaction of predator and prey and why population sizes fluctuate around the carrying capacity. For this question, it is important that you supplement your discussion with graphs of each kind of population growth pattern because they demonstrate your ability to express and interpret data in analytical form.

Question 2

(a.) Succession describes the series of communities that occupy an area over time. If the process begins on a newly exposed surface, it is called primary succession. If it occurs on a substrate previously supporting life, such as is the case with most lakes, then it is called secondary succession. Succession occurs because each community changes the habitat in such a way that it becomes more suitable to new species. Soil, light, and other growing conditions change as each community occupies a region. The final, climax community is a stable community that remains unchanged until destroyed by some catastrophic event, such as fire. Then the process begins again.

The first community to occupy the lake consists of pioneer species with *r*-selected characteristics. These characteristics include good dispersal ability, rapid growth, and rapid reproduction of many offspring. The lake is first populated by algae and protists, then followed by rotifers, mollusks, insects, and other arthropods. Various vegetation, such as grasses, sedges, rushes, and cattails, grows at the perimeter of the lake. Submerged vegetation (growing on the lake bottom) is replaced by vegetation that emerges from the surface, perhaps covering the surface with leaves. As the plants and animals die, they add to the organic matter that fills the lake. In addition, sediment is deposited by water from streams that enter the lake. Eventually, the lake becomes marshy as it is overrun by vegetation. When, the lake is completely filled, it becomes a meadow, occupied by plants and animals that are adapted to a dry, rather than marshy, habitat. Subsequently, the meadow is invaded by shrubs and trees from the surrounding area. In a temperate mountain habitat, the climax community may be a deciduous forest consisting of oaks or maples. In colder regions, the climax community is often a coniferous forest, consisting of pines, firs, and hemlocks.

(b.) Eutrophication is the increase in inorganic nutrients and biomass of a lake. Eutrophication occurs in both unpolluted as well as polluted lakes. In the natural succession of the lake described above, eutrophication occurred slowly over a period of dozens of years (perhaps over a hundred years). As a result, changes in the chemical and physical nature of the lake allowed for the orderly change of communities, each new community suitable for the new conditions.

309

In polluted lakes, eutrophication is accelerated by effluent from sewage or fertilizer. As a result, algae growth occurs rapidly over a period of months. At high densities, algae reduce oxygen levels when they respire at night. When the algae die as shorter, winter days approach, rapidly growing aerobic bacteria that feed on the dead algae further deplete the oxygen content of the water. In the absence of oxygen, many of the plants and animals die. The bottom of the lake fills with dead organisms which, in turn, stimulate growth of anaerobic bacteria (some of which produce foul-smelling sulfur gases). In addition, the surface of the lake may become littered with dead fish.

Essay questions about succession are common on the AP exam. You may be asked to describe succession for a particular kind of habitat, as in this question, or you may be given a choice of different kinds of successions. Note that the first paragraph and the beginning of the second paragraph contain very general information that applies to all successional processes. Once you have completed the generalities, describe the successional events for the specific habitat requested. In part (b) of the question, the first paragraph makes a comparison (states that unpolluted and polluted lakes are both the result of the same eutrophication processes), and the second paragraph makes a contrast (how the rate of eutrophication is faster in a polluted lake).

Question 3

For this question you should discuss the competitive exclusion principle and how it results in resource partitioning, character displacement, and realized niches.

Question 4

Although the atmosphere consists of 80% nitrogen gas (N_2), plants can utilize nitrogen only in the form of ammonium (NH_4^+) or nitrate (NO_3^-). Nitrogen fixation, the conversion of N_2 to NH_4^+, occurs by nitrogen-fixing bacteria that live in the soil, or in the root nodules of certain plants such as legumes. In turn, nitrification occurs by certain nitrifying bacteria that convert NH_4^+ to NO_2^- (nitrite) and by other nitrifying bacteria that convert NO_2^- to NO_3^-. In addition, some N_2 is converted to NO_3^- by the action of lightning. On the other hand, denitrification occurs when denitrifying bacteria convert NO_3^- back to N_2.

From the NH_4^+ or NO_3^- absorbed, plants make amino acids and nucleic acids. When animals eat the plants (or other animals), they, in turn, obtain a form of nitrogen that they can metabolize. When animals break down proteins, they produce ammonia (NH_3). Since NH_3 is toxic, many animals, such as aquatic animals, excrete it directly. Other animals convert NH_3 to less toxic forms, such as urea (mammals) or uric acid (insects and birds). When plants and animals die, they decompose through the process of ammonification, in which bacteria convert the amino acids and other nitrogen-containing compounds to NH_4^+, which then becomes available again for plants.

The AP exam may ask you to discuss any of the biogeochemical cycles. The nitrogen cycle is the most common request. You may want to supplement your discussion with a drawing using arrows to show the various conversions of nitrogen. If you do make a drawing, however, you must still provide a complete discussion.

PART III

LABORATORY REVIEW

Review

The College Board provides twelve laboratory exercises for use in AP Biology courses. Completing these labs, or similar labs that your teacher may substitute, provides the laboratory experience typical of a first-year college course in biology. One essay question and approximately 10% of the multiple-choice questions are based on these lab exercises.

The laboratory essay question is usually one of two types:

1. **Experimental analysis.** In this type of essay question, you are given some experimental data and asked to interpret or analyze the data. The question usually includes several parts, each requesting specific interpretations of the data. In addition, you are usually asked to prepare a graphic representation of the data. Graph paper is provided. Guidelines for preparing a graph are given as follows:

2. **Experimental design.** This type of essay question asks you to design an experiment to answer specific questions about given data or an experimental situation. Guidelines for designing an experiment are given below.

Although the data or situation in both of these types of questions will be somewhat different from those you encountered in your AP labs, you will be able to draw from your AP lab experience to analyze data or design experiments.

The material in this section summarizes each of the twelve laboratory exercises with a brief description of its experimental design and conclusions. It is not intended that this material substitute for an actual laboratory experience, but to provide you with a review that will help you answer the AP biology questions.

Graphing Data

The laboratory question in the essay part of the AP exam will often ask you to create a graph using data provided in the question. Include the following in your graph:

1. **Label each axis.** Indicate on each axis what is being measured and in what unit of measurement. For example "Time (minutes)," "Distance (meters)," or "Water Loss (ml/m^2)" are appropriate labels.

2. **Provide values along each axis at regular intervals.** Select values and spacing that will allow your graph to fill as much of the graphing grid as possible.

3. **Use the *x-axis* for the independent variable and the *y-axis* for the dependent variable.** The dependent variable is the value you are measuring as a result of an independent variable imposed by the experiment. If the graph is plotting the progress of an event, then time is the independent variable and the data you collect that measure the event (such as weight change, distance traveled, or carbon dioxide released) is the dependent variable.

4. **Connect the plotted points.** Usually, straight lines are used to connect the points. Smooth curves are also used, but that usually implies knowledge about intermediate points not plotted or a mathematical equation that fits the experimental results. If the question asks you to make predictions beyond the data actually graphed, extrapolate, or extend, the plotted line with a different line form (for example, dotted or dashed).

5. **In graphs with more than one plot, identify each plot.** If you plot more than one set of data on the same graph, identify each plot with a short phrase. Alternately, you can draw the points of each plot with different symbols (for example, circles, squares, triangles) or connect the plotted points using different kinds of lines (solid line, dashed line, dash-dot line) and then identify each kind of symbol or line in a legend.

6. **Provide a title for the graph.** Your title should be brief but descriptive.

Designing an Experiment

The laboratory essay question may ask you to design an experiment to test a given hypothesis or to solve a given problem. In most cases, the question will ask you not only to design an experiment, but also to discuss expected results. Since the form of these questions can vary dramatically, it is not possible to provide a standard formula for preparing your answer. However, the following list provides important elements that you should include in your answer if they are appropriate to the question:

1. **Identify the independent and dependent variables.** The independent variable is the variable you are manipulating to see how the dependent variable changes.

   - You are investigating how the crustacean *Daphnia* responds to changes in temperature. You expose *Daphnia* to temperatures of 5°C, 10°C, 15°C, 20°C, and 30°C. You count the number of heartbeats/sec in each case. Temperature is the independent variable (you are manipulating it), and number of heartbeats/sec is the dependent variable (you observe how it changes in response to different temperatures).

   - You design an experiment to investigate the effect of exercise on pulse rate and blood pressure. The physiological conditions (independent variable, or variable you manipulate) include sitting, exercising, and recovery at various intervals following exercise. You make two kinds of measurements (two dependent variables) to evaluate the effect of the physiological conditions—pulse rate and blood pressure.

2. **Describe the experimental treatment.** The experimental treatment (or treatments) are the various values that you assign to the independent variable. The experimental treatments describe how you are manipulating the independent variable.

- In the *Daphnia* experiment, the different temperature values (5°C, 10°C, 15°C, 25°C, and 30°C) represent five experimental treatments.

- In the experiment on physiological conditions, the experimental treatments are exercise and recovery at various intervals following exercise.

3. **Identify a control treatment.** The control treatment, or control, is the independent variable at some normal or standard value. The results of the control are used for comparison with the results of the experimental treatments.

- In the *Daphnia* experiment, you choose the temperature of 20°C as the control because that is the average temperature of the pond where you obtained the culture.

- In the experiment on physiological conditions, the control is sitting, when the subject is not influenced by exercising.

4. **Use only one independent variable.** Only one independent variable can be tested at a time. If you manipulate two independent variables at the same time, you cannot determine which is responsible for the effect you measure in the dependent variable.

- In the physiological experiment, if the subject also drinks coffee in addition to exercising, you cannot determine which treatment, coffee or exercise, causes a change in blood pressure.

5. **Random sample of subjects.** You must choose the subjects for your experiments randomly. Since you cannot evaluate every *Daphnia,* you must choose a subpopulation to study. If you choose only the largest *Daphnia* to study, it is not a random sample, and you introduce another variable (size) for which you cannot account.

6. **Describe the procedure.** Describe how you will set up the experiment. Identify equipment and chemicals to be used and why you are choosing to use them. If appropriate, provide a labeled drawing of the setup.

7. **Describe expected results.** Use graphs to illustrate the expected results, if appropriate.

8. **Provide an explanation of the expected results in relation to relevant biological principles.** The results you give are your expected results. Describe the biological principles that led you to make your predictions.

- In the experiment on physiological conditions, you expect blood pressure and pulse rate to increase during exercise in order to deliver more O_2 to muscles. Muscles use the O_2 for respiration, which generates the ATP necessary for muscle contraction.

Laboratory 1: Diffusion and Osmosis

This lab provides exercises that investigate the movement of water across semipermeable membranes. You should review the processes of diffusion, osmosis, dialysis, and plasmolysis discussed in the review section on cells in this book.

In animal cells, the direction of osmosis, in or out of a cell, depends on the concentration of solutes inside and outside the plasma membrane. In plant cells, however, osmosis is also influenced by turgor pressure, the pressure of the cell wall exerted on the contents of the cell. To account for differences in both concentration and pressure, a more general term, **water potential,** is used to describe the tendency of water to move across a selectively permeable membrane. Water potential is the sum of the pressure potential (from any externally applied force) and the osmotic pressure (from the effects of solute concentration) (Figure 15-1):

$$\psi \quad = \quad \psi_p \quad + \quad \psi_\pi$$

$$\text{water potential} = \text{pressure potential} + \text{osmotic potential}$$

Figure 15-1

Water potential has the following properties:

1. Water moves across a selectively permeable membrane from an area of higher water potential to an area of lower water potential.

2. Water potential can be positive or negative. Negative water potential is called **tension.**

3. Osmotic potential results from the presence of solutes and is always negative. The higher the concentration of solutes, the smaller (or more negative) the osmotic potential.

4. Pressure potential is zero unless some force is applied, such as that applied by a cell wall.

5. Pure water at atmospheric pressure has a water potential of zero (pressure potential = 0 and osmotic potential = 0).

6. Water potential is measured in bars (1 bar is approximately equal to 1 atmosphere pressure).

Think of water potential as potential energy, the ability to do work. The water at the top of a dam has a high water potential, a high potential energy, and a large capacity for doing work, such as the ability to generate electricity as it runs downhill.

At the end of this lab, you should know the following:

1. Dialysis tubing is used to make selectively permeable bags. It will allow small molecules to pass through, such as water and monosaccharides (glucose), but not disaccharides (sucrose), polysaccharides (starch), or proteins.

2. Testape is used to test for the presence of glucose.

3. Lugol's solution is used to test for the presence of starch. Lugol's solution (iodine and potassium iodide, or IKI) is yellow brown but turns dark blue in the presence of starch.

Designing an experiment to measure water potential: The information learned in this lab can be used to determine water potential, pressure potential, or osmotic potential. For example, the concentration of solutes (osmotic potential) in a selectively permeable bag or in living tissues such as potato cores can be determined. Prepare five bags of the unknown solute or five tissue samples. Soak one of each bag or tissue sample in one of five beakers, each of which contains a different solute concentration (different osmotic potential). If the mass of a bag or tissue sample increases, then the solute concentration in the bag or tissue is hypertonic to that of the beaker. If the mass decreases, the bag content or tissue sample is hypotonic. When there is no change in mass, the bag content or tissue sample is isotonic with its surroundings and the solute concentration is equal to that of the beaker.

Laboratory 2: Enzyme Catalysis

In this lab exercise, the rate of a reaction is measured in the presence and absence of a catalyst. The catalyst, catalase, is an enzyme in cells that catalyzes the breakdown of toxic H_2O_2. The reaction is

$$2\ H_2O_2 \xrightarrow{\text{catalase}} 2\ H_2O + O_2(\text{gas})$$

Figure 15-2

At the conclusion of this lab you should know the following:

1. The rate of a reaction is determined by measuring the accumulation of one of the products or by measuring the disappearance of the substrate (reactant).

2. The rate of a reaction is the slope of the linear (straight) part of the graph that describes the accumulation of product (or decrease in substrate) as time progresses.

3. Reaction rate may be affected by temperature, pH, substrate concentration, and enzyme concentration.

Designing an experiment to determine reaction rates for an enzyme under various conditions: An experiment can be designed to determine the reaction rates for an enzyme under different conditions (such as pH, temperature, enzyme, or solute concentration). The experiment should incorporate the following:

1. Maintain constant conditions for all reaction tests. Keep substrate and enzyme concentration, pH, and temperature constant unless you are investigating the effects of these variables.

2. Stop the reaction at regular time intervals using a strong acid. Because enzymes are proteins, they are easily denatured (structurally damaged) and disabled by strong acids, such as sulfuric acid (H_2SO_4).

3. Measure the amount of substrate converted or product formed by performing a titration. In the AP lab, the amount of H_2O_2 remaining is determined by titration, that is, a burette is used to gradually add $KMnO_4$ until a pink color persists. By knowing that 2.5 molecules of H_2O_2 react with 1 molecule of $KMnO_4$, you are able to determine how much H_2O_2 remains.

4. Graph the results (with time, the independent variable, on the x-axis) and determine the reaction rate by calculating the slope of the linear portion of the plot.

Laboratory 3: Mitosis and Meiosis

As part of the review for this lab, you should read the section on cell division in this book. In particular, review the phases of mitosis and meiosis, the cell structures involved in cell division, and the similarities of and differences between plant and animal cell division.

At the conclusion of this lab you should know the following (in addition to the material in the section on cell division):

1. In plants, cells dividing by mitosis can be found at the tips of roots and shoots (called meristems). In animals, mitotically dividing cells occur in any growing tissue but are most abundant in dividing embryos (especially blastulas).

2. The length of time for each phase of mitosis can be determined by counting the number of times each phase appears under the microscope. The frequency of appearance (number of times it appears, divided by the total number of all phases, except interphase) equals the relative length of time required for each phase to complete.

3. The results of crossing over during meiosis can be readily visualized under the microscope in the asci of many ascomycete fungi. Asci are hyphae that contain eight haploid ascospores. In most ascomycetes, the asci are embedded in other hyphae that form a fruiting body. One kind of fruiting body, a **perithecium,** surrounds the asci, except for a passageway that allows for the escape of the ascospores. Sexual reproduction begins in ascomycetes when hyphae from two strains fuse. Nuclei from one strain pair with nuclei from the second strain. Subsequently, these pairs of unlike nuclei fuse (**karyogamy**) to produce diploid nuclei, which then undergo meiosis. During meiosis I, homologous chromosomes pair and separate. During meiosis II, each chromosome separates into two chromatids. At the end of meiosis, there are four daughter cells, each possessing one chromatid from each tetrad of homologous chromosomes. Each of the four daughter cells then divides by mitosis to produce two ascospores. The order of ascospores in the ascus corresponds to the chromatids. If no crossing over occurs, then each set of four adjacent ascospores represents a single parent strain and will possess the same traits. This is illustrated on the left side of Figure 15-3 for a trait that determines spore color.

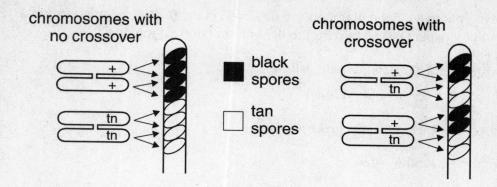

Figure 15-3

If crossing over occurs (Figure 15-3, right), then traits on two nonsister chromosomes exchange, producing alternating patterns of ascospore pairs with and without the traits included in the crossover.

Designing an experiment to determine crossover frequency: The knowledge gained in this lab exercise can be used to determine the crossover frequency in an ascomycete fungus. Include the following steps:

1. Grow two ascomycete fungal strains of the same species on a plate of nutrient enriched agar. **Perithecia** form at the interface between the two strains.

2. Under the microscope, count the number of asci that contain ascospores with crossovers and the number of asci that contain ascospores without crossovers.

3. Determine the frequency of asci with crossovers (number of asci with crossovers divided by total asci).

Laboratory 4: Plant Pigments and Photosynthesis

In the first part of this lab exercise, photosynthetic pigments are separated using the technique of paper chromatography. In this procedure, an extract from leaves is applied (spotted) near the bottom edge of a sheet of chromatography paper. The paper is then hung so that its bottom edge is just touching the chromatography solvent. As the solvent rises up the paper by capillary action, spotted pigments are carried up the paper with the solvent. Different pigments move up the paper at different rates because they differ in their ability to dissolve in the solvent and their ability to form hydrogen bonds with the cellulose in the paper. Molecules that dissolve best in the solvent and form the weakest bonds with the cellulose move up the paper the fastest. When the solvent front nearly reaches the top of the paper, the paper is removed from the solvent. Reference front (R_f) values for each pigment are then determined by calculating the ratio of the pigment migration distance to the solvent migration distance.

The following photosynthetic pigments are observed in the following order, from the top of the chromatography paper (fastest moving) to the bottom (slowest moving):

1. beta carotene, a carotenoid (pale yellow)

2. xanthophyll, a carotenoid (yellow)

3. chlorophyll *a* (green to blue green)

4. chlorophyll *b* (yellow green)

In the second part of this lab, the rate of photosynthesis is determined by the amount of dye that changes from blue to clear. The dye, DPIP, acts as an electron acceptor in place of $NADP^+$. DPIP is blue in the **oxidized** state (before accepting electrons) and is clear in the **reduced** state (after accepting electrons). The degree to which the color changes is determined by measuring the transmittance of light through the sample with a spectrophotometer. Transmittance is measured at a wavelength of 605 nm, the wavelength for which DPIP has its greatest absorbance (its darkest color).

The design of the exercise is to compare the rate of photosynthesis in four treatments, as follows:

1. A blank treatment without DPIP for calibrating the spectrophotometer.

2. A control with unboiled chloroplasts, incubated in the dark.

3. An experimental treatment with unboiled chloroplasts, incubated in the light.

4. An experimental treatment with boiled chloroplasts, incubated in the light.

For each treatment, the transmittance of a sample is measured at the beginning of the experiment, and again at five, ten, and fifteen minutes. The results are plotted on a graph with time (the independent variable) on the x-axis and percent transmittance (the dependent variable) on the y-axis. Typical results are shown below:

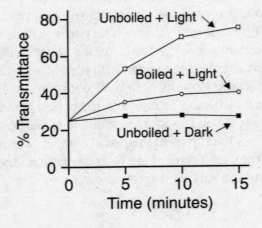

Figure 15-4

Designing an experiment to separate a group of molecules: A group of molecules (such as pigments, animo acids, or sugars) can be separated using the techniques of chromatography. The solvents and the medium (paper or silica gel) may vary with the kinds of molecules being separated. Special stains may be needed to make the separate components visible. After separation, R_f values are calculated and compared to tables of R_f values for known molecules obtained for a similar medium and solvent. If paper is used for the medium, each component can be cut from the paper, dissolved in a solvent, and further analyzed.

Designing an experiment to measure rates of photosynthesis: Light intensity, light wavelength, and temperature may each be varied to determine their effect on photosynthetic rate. Be sure to include the following in an experimental design:

1. Use DPIP as the electron acceptor. It changes from blue to clear as it is reduced.

2. Measure the change in light transmittance with a spectrophotometer set to measure transmittance at a wavelength of 605 nm.

3. Include a blank treatment with no DPIP (in which no reaction occurs) for calibrating the spectrophotometer before each measurement.

4. Include a control treatment to which the experimental treatment(s) can be compared.

5. Include one or more experimental treatments.

6. Measure the transmittance at various intervals so that photosynthetic rate can be determined.

7. Graph the results.

Laboratory 5: Cell Respiration

This lab provides a method for measuring the rate of cellular respiration. Cellular respiration is the breakdown of glucose with oxygen to produce carbon dioxide, water, and energy, as follows:

$$C_6H_{12}O_6 + O_2 \rightarrow 6CO_2 + 6H_2O + energy$$

In this lab, respiratory rate is measured in germinating peas by observing the changes in the volume of gas surrounding the peas at various time intervals. Since the volume of gas can be affected by both the consumption of O_2 and the production of CO_2, the CO_2 is removed by using potassium hydroxide (KOH). KOH reacts with CO_2 gas to produce solid K_2CO_3, as follows:

$$2KOH + CO_2 \rightarrow K_2CO_3 + H_2O$$

Since CO_2 gas is removed by its reaction with KOH, volume changes can be attributed only to the following:

1. Consumption of oxygen (due to respiration)

2. Change in temperature

3. Change in atmospheric pressure

The exercise is designed to measure respiratory rates of peas at two temperatures, 10°C and 22°C. Respirometers, consisting of vials with inserted pipettes, are used to incubate the peas and measure respiration. The following treatments are prepared:

1. An experimental treatment at 10°C, consisting of twenty-five germinating peas. Germinating peas consist of cells actively dividing and growing and exhibit a relatively high respiratory rate.

2. A control treatment at 10°C, consisting of twenty-five dry peas plus enough glass beads to yield a volume equivalent the twenty-five germinating peas in the experimental treatment. Since these peas are not germinating, the respiratory rate will be very low and will provide a comparison for the germinating peas. Since dry peas are smaller and weigh less than germinating peas (which have been soaked in water and are growing), glass beads are added to maintain equal volumes.

3. A control treatment at 10°C, consisting of enough glass beads to yield a volume equivalent to the twenty-five germinating peas. This treatment measures changes in temperature and pressure not due to respiration.

Another three treatments are prepared as above for use in a 22°C water bath. Thus, a total of six respirometers are assembled.

The six respirometers are immersed in their respective 10°C and 22°C water baths. Water in the water bath enters the pipettes and travels a short distance.

As respiration occurs, O_2 is consumed in the vials, and pressure in the vials and pipettes drops. As pressure drops, additional water from the water bath enters the pipettes. The amount of water entering can be determined by reading the ml graduations on the pipettes. This reading is a direct measurement of oxygen consumption and thus an indirect measurement of respiratory rate.

Changes in volume observed in the control treatments (beads only) represent responses to external changes in temperature and pressure. Thus, the observed increases or decreases in volume in the control treatment must be subtracted or added, respectively, to the volume changes observed for germinating peas and dry peas.

Designing an experiment to measure respiratory rates: Using the experimental design described above, respiratory rates can be determined for seeds germinating at various temperatures or for seeds that have been germinated for different lengths of time. The respiratory rate of insects can also be determined using this experimental design. Since the body size of individual insects will probably vary, volume changes in the respirometers can be plotted against insect body weight to determine the relationship between respiratory rate and insect size.

Laboratory 6: Molecular Biology

The bacterial plasmid pAMP is often used as a vector (or carrier) to transfer genes into bacteria. To insert a gene into a plasmid (or any other piece of DNA), **restriction endonucleases** (restriction enzymes) are used. A restriction enzyme cleaves a DNA molecule at a specific sequence of nucleotides, producing cuts that are usually jagged, with one strand of the DNA molecule extending beyond the second strand. If both the plasmid and the foreign DNA (with the gene of interest) are treated with the same restriction enzyme, the jagged ends, or "sticky ends," of the foreign DNA will match the sticky ends of the plasmid DNA. The foreign DNA fragment can then be bonded to the plasmid DNA by treatment with DNA ligase.

The value of using pAMP as a vector for gene transfers is that pAMP contains a gene that provides resistance to the antibiotic ampicillin. Bacteria that have successfully absorbed the plasmid, then, possess resistance to the antibiotic and can be separated from other bacteria by ampicillin treatment. Only those bacteria that have the pAMP plasmid survive the ampicillin treatment.

In the first part of this lab, the bacterial plasmid, pAMP, is transferred to *E. coli* bacteria. The following steps summarize the procedure:

1. Induce **competence** in *E. coli* bacteria by treating them with Ca^{2+} or Mg^{2+}. Bacteria are said to be competent when they are most likely to absorb DNA.

2. Facilitate the absorption of DNA by giving the bacteria a heat-shock (short pulse of heat).

3. Test for **transformation** (the absorption of foreign DNA) by treating the bacteria with ampicillin. Only transformed bacteria survive.

Designing an experiment to observe transformation and bacterial resistance: The following steps should be included:

1. Prepare two tubes of *E. coli* bacteria. One tube will be transformed with pAMP plasmids. The second will be a control.

2. Induce competence in the bacteria in both tubes by adding $CaCl_2$.

3. Transfer pAMP plasmids to one of the test tubes.

4. Induce transformation in both tubes with heat-shock.

5. After incubation (for growth), transfer bacteria from one tube to an agar plate with ampicillin and an agar plate without ampicillin. Repeat for the second tube.

Interpret the results (Table 15-1). Only bacteria transformed with pAMP plasmids can grow in the presence of ampicillin. The control tube of bacteria confirms that without pAMP, growth cannot occur in the presence of ampicillin. It also confirms that the untransformed *E. coli* are not ampicillin resistant.

Table 15-1		
	Agar Plate without Ampicillin	**Agar Plate with Ampicillin**
Tube 1: Bacteria with pAMP plasmids	growth	no growth
Tube 2: Bacteria without pAMP plasmids	growth	no growth

In the second part of this lab, DNA fragments are separated using gel electrophoresis. The steps are summarized below.

1. The DNA to be analyzed is digested (cleaved) with a restriction enzyme.

2. A tracking dye is added to the sample. This allows the leading edge of DNA migration to be observed.

3. Load the sample into a well (small hole) in the agarose gel of the electrophoresis apparatus.

4. Begin electrophoresis. The electrophoresis apparatus applies a voltage to opposite ends of the gel. The negatively charged DNA molecules migrate from the negative to the positive electrode. Turn off the apparatus when the tracking dye nears the end of the gel.

5. Immerse the gel in a dye that allows the fragments to be observed. Methylene blue is used in this exercise.

6. Record the distance each fragment has migrated from the well.

Designing an experiment to separate and identify DNA fragments: Include the following steps in an experiment to investigate the sizes of fragments produced by a restriction enzyme:

1. Prepare a sample of DNA digested with the restriction enzyme under investigation. (In this exercise, phage lambda DNA molecules are digested with *Eco*RI endonuclease.)

2. Prepare a second sample of undigested DNA for use as a control.

3. Prepare a third sample of DNA digested with a standard restriction enzyme. The fragment sizes produced by this standard are known and provide a standard against which fragment sizes produced in step 1 can be compared. (In this exercise, phage lambda DNA molecules are digested with *Hind*III endonuclease.)

4. Separate the fragments in the three preparations using gel electrophoresis. Load each preparation into a separate well.

5. Using semi-log graph paper, prepare a standard curve using the observed migration distances and known fragment sizes for the standard endonuclease. The standard curve is a plot of fragment size (base pairs) against migration distance. Since migration distance is inversely proportional to fragment size, plotting migration distance against the log of the number of base pairs produces a straight line.

6. Use the standard curve to determine the size of each fragment produced by the sample under investigation.

Laboratory 7: Genetics of *Drosophila*

In this lab, a genetics experiment is conducted using *Drosophila* fruit flies. A summary of important information for conducting these experiments follows:

1. **Life cycle.** Depending upon temperature, *D. melanogaster* requires ten to fourteen days to complete the stages from egg to adult.

   - **Eggs** hatch into larvae after about one day.

   - **Larvae** undergo three growing stages, or instars, over a four- to seven-day period. They molt (shed their skins) after the first two stages.

   - **Pupae** form after the third larval instar. A hardened outer case (cocoon) forms around the larva. Inside, a larva undergoes metamorphosis and emerges as an adult fly after five to six days.

   - **Adults** may live for several weeks. Females may begin mating ten hours after they emerge from the pupa.

2. **Sex of fruit flies.** To properly mate parents and count offspring, the sex of each fly must be recognized. The following *typical* (*but variable*) characteristics are used:

   - A female is larger than a male and has four to six solid dark stripes across the dorsal side (top) of her abdomen. The posterior end of the abdomen is somewhat pointed.

   - A male is smaller than a female and has fewer (two to three) stripes on his abdomen. The posterior end of the abdomen is rounded and heavily pigmented (as if two or three stripes have fused). A male also has a small bundle of black hairs, or sex combs, on the uppermost joint of his front legs.

3. **Virgin females.** After mating, female flies store male sperm to fertilize their eggs. To insure that the female does not use sperm from a mating that occurred before the experiment begins, only virgin, or unmated, females can be used. Since a female does not mate until ten hours after emerging from the pupa, isolating the female soon after emergence will ensure a virgin fly.

Fly mutations. The experiments cross a normal fly (wild-type) with a fly mutant for a particular trait. The following table shows the commonly used traits and mutations. Mutations are recessive if their abbreviations begin with a lowercase letter, dominant if uppercase.

		Table 15-2		
Trait	*Wild-Type*	*Mutation*	*Mutation Abbreviation*	*Chromosome*
eye color	red	white	*w*	chromosome 1 (sex-linked)
eye shape	round	bar	*Bar*	chromosome 1 (sex-linked)
wing	present	apterous (absent)	*apt*	chromosome 2
wing	normal	vestigial (reduced wings)	*vg*	chromosome 2
antennae	normal	spineless aristapedia (enlarged and shaped like a leg)	ss^a	chromosome 3
eye color	red	sepia (brown eyes)	*s*	chromosome 3

5. **Fly crosses and genetic notation.** Experiments are usually designed so that a fly homozygous for the mutant trait is crossed with a fly homozygous for the normal trait. The wild type genotype is usually denoted by "+," while the mutant type is denoted by an abbreviation for the mutation. An allele pair representing the two alleles for a gene (each on one homologue of a homologous pair of chromosomes) is separated by a diagonal. For example, a monohybrid cross between a wild-type fly and a fly homozygous for apterous wings is indicated by +/+ × *ap/ap*. The F_1 generation flies are all heterozygous for this trait, or +/*ap*.

6. χ^2 **statistical analysis.** Results of genetic crosses are evaluated using a chi-square (χ^2) statistical analysis. The purpose of this analysis is to determine how well the results of the genetic crosses fit predicted probability ratios. If the experimental results from a cross between two flies are equal to the results expected (from using a Punnett square), the χ^2 value is 0. To determine whether a nonzero value occurs by chance or because something is wrong with the experiment, a χ^2 statistical table is consulted. If chance explains 95% or more of the deviation of χ^2 from zero (a low value for χ^2), then the experimental results are acceptable. If not, the number of flies produced for each trait indicate that something other than chance is influencing the experiment. Crossing over, deleterious mutations, or nonrandom mating (perhaps some traits produce poor breeders) are factors to consider. High values of χ^2 may also result if the expected values used do not account for sex linkage or are otherwise in error.

Designing an experiment to show independent assortment of chromosomes, sex-linkage, or crossing over: To show any of these modes of inheritance, use fruit flies, and employ the following procedures:

1. To show the independent assortment of chromosomes, make a dihybrid cross using flies with two different mutations, each occurring on separate chromosomes. For example, make the cross +/+;*ap/ap* × ss^a/ss^a;+/+. If independent assortment occurs, the F_1 generation will be heterozygous for both traits, or +/ss^a;+/*ap*, and the F_2 generation will show a 9:3:3:1 distribution of traits. (Compare the cross of yellow/green, round/wrinkled peas in the section review of heredity.)

2. To show sex-linkage, make a monohybrid cross involving a sex-linked trait, such as white eyes. A white-eyed female (X^w/X^w) crossed with a wild-type (red-eyed) male (X^+/Y) will produce red-eyed females (X^+/X^w) and white-eyed males (X^w/Y). If these traits were not sex-linked, all F_1 flies, males and females, would be red-eyed ($+/w$).

3. To determine crossover frequencies, make a cross between two genes occurring on the same chromosome. Compare the F_2 generation results to those that would be obtained if the genes assorted independently (genes on different chromosomes).

Laboratory 8: Population Genetics and Evolution

This lab demonstrates genetic equilibrium and the use of the Hardy-Weinberg law to describe allele frequencies in populations. Genetic equilibrium (or Hardy-Weinberg equilibrium) occurs when frequencies of alleles remain constant from generation to generation. In particular, note the following conditions that maintain genetic equilibrium:

1. no mutation

2. no selection

3. no gene flow (no migration)

4. large populations (no genetic drift)

5. random mating

The lab compares a population that is in equilibrium to a population undergoing natural selection against the homozygous recessive condition. The following important conclusions can be made from this exercise:

1. For a population in genetic equilibrium, the allele frequencies (p, q) and the genotypic frequencies (p^2, $2pq$, q^2) remain constant (approximately) from generation to generation.

2. For a population in which natural selection eliminates individuals with the homozygous recessive condition, the frequency of the recessive allele (q) declines from generation to generation. However, the allele is not completely eliminated because it is masked in individuals with the heterozygous condition ($2pq$ individuals).

For further review of Hardy-Weinberg concepts, you should read the section on evolution in this book.

Designing an experiment to determine if a population is in genetic equilibrium: Alleles in the gene pool of a population in Hardy-Weinberg equilibrium remain constant through the generations. In addition, $p + q = 1$ and $p^2 + 2pq + q^2 = 1$. Deviations from these conditions indicate that the population is not in equilibrium, that allele frequencies are changing, and that evolution is occurring.

Laboratory 9: Transpiration

The first part of this lab demonstrates how transpiration rates vary with environmental conditions. Recall from Lab 1 that water moves from areas of higher water potential to areas of lower water potential. Movement of water through a plant is influenced by each of the following mechanisms:

1. **Osmosis.** Water enters root cells by osmosis because the water potential is higher outside the root in the surrounding soil than inside the root. Dissolved minerals contribute to a lower water potential inside the root by decreasing the osmotic pressure.

2. **Root pressure.** As water enters the xylem cells, the increase in osmotic pressure produces root pressure. Root pressure, however, causes water to move only a short distance up the stem.

3. **Transpiration.** In leaves, water moves from mesophyll cells to air spaces and then out the stomata. This occurs because the water potential is highest in the mesophyll cells and lowest in the relatively dry air outside the leaf. Evaporation of water from plant surfaces is called transpiration.

4. **Cohesion-Tension.** Cohesion (attraction of like molecules) between water molecules occurs because weak hydrogen bonds form between the polar water molecules. As a result, water acts as a continuous polymer from root to leaf. As transpiration removes molecules of water from the leaves, water molecules are pulled up from the roots. The transpirational pull of water through the xylem vessels decreases the pressure potential, resulting in negative water potential, or tension. The cohesion-tension condition produced by transpiration is the dominant mechanism for the movement of water up a stem.

The following factors affect transpiration rates:

1. **Temperature.** When the temperature of liquid water rises, the kinetic energy of the water molecules increases. As a result, the rate at which liquid water is converted to water vapor increases.

2. **Humidity.** An increase in humidity increases the water potential in the surrounding air. In response, the rate of transpiration decreases.

3. **Air movement.** Moving air removes recently evaporated water away from the leaf. As a result, the humidity and the water potential in the air around the leaf drops, and the rate of transpiration increases.

4. **Light intensity.** When light is absorbed by the leaf, some of the light energy is converted to heat. Transpiration rate increases with temperature.

On very hot or dry days, the loss of water by transpiration may exceed the rate by which water enters the roots. Under these conditions, the stomata may close to prevent wilting.

In the second part of the lab, a bean stem is prepared for microscopic study. The following plant cell types are identified. (For a complete discussion of these cell types, see the review section on plants.)

1. **Parenchyma** cells have thin walls and serve various functions including storage, photosynthesis, or secretion. Starch grains are visible in parenchyma cells serving a storage function.

2. **Collenchyma** cells have thick but flexible walls, and serve to provide flexible support. In stems, they are often located just inside the epidermis.

3. **Sclerenchyma** cells have thicker walls than collenchyma and provide rigid support. **Fibers** are specialized sclerenchyma cells located toward the outside portion of vascular bundles. They provide support to the vascular bundle and shield the phloem from insect invasion.

4. **Xylem** cells transport water. They have thick secondary walls that prevent them from collapsing under the negative pressure that develops from transpiration. There are two kinds of xylem cells, **tracheids** and **vessel members.** Both are dead at maturity.

5. **Phloem** cells transport sugars. Phloem tissue consist of two kinds of phloem cells, **sieve-tube elements** and **companion cells.** Sieve-tube elements lack nuclei. Companion cells provide physiological support for the sieve-tube elements.

6. **Dermal tissue** consists of **epidermis cells** that cover the outside of plant parts and **guard cells** that surround **stomata.**

Designing an experiment to measure the effects of environmental conditions on the rate of plant transpiration: The transpiration rate in a bean seedling can be measured directly by the methods employed in this lab. In brief, the procedures are as follows:

1. Prepare a potometer by inserting a pipette into one end of a flexible tube. Bend the flexible tube into a U shape so that the open ends of the pipette and tube are pointing up. Fill the tube and pipette completely with water and insert the stem of a freshly cut seedling into the open end of the tube. Apply petroleum jelly to seal the space between the stem of the seedling and the tube.

2. Prepare one potometer for each environmental condition to be investigated. High temperature, high humidity, bright light, or moving air are examples.

3. Prepare one additional potometer for normal conditions, a control to which the transpiration rate at extreme conditions can be compared.

4. Measure the transpiration rate by observing the change in water level in the pipette over several intervals of time.

5. Determine the total leaf surface area.

6. Determine the transpiration rate by dividing the total leaf surface area by the amount of water lost indicated by the pipette.

7. Graph the results.

329

Laboratory 10: Physiology of the Circulatory System

In the first part of this lab, blood pressure is measured in individuals subjected to various conditions. A **sphygmomanometer** is used to measure blood pressure. The blood pressure cuff is inflated so that blood flow through the brachial artery in the upper arm is stopped. As pressure in the cuff is released, a stethoscope is used to listen for the blood flow entering the brachial artery. When blood first enters the artery, snapping sounds called **sounds of Korotkoff** are generated. Blood pressure is determined as follows:

1. **Systolic blood pressure** is the blood pressure generated by the contraction of the ventricles. It can be read from the sphygmomanometer when the sounds of Korotkoff are first heard in the stethoscope.

2. **Diastolic blood pressure** is the blood pressure maintained by arterial walls between ventricular contractions. It is read from the sphygmomanometer when the sounds of Korotkoff disappear.

3. A systolic reading of 120 mm Hg and a diastolic reading of 75 is recorded as 120/75.

The following changes in blood pressure and heart rate (pulse) are observed:

1. Blood pressure and heart rate increase when the subject moves from a reclining to a standing position. The increases counteract the gravitational forces on blood movement.

2. Blood pressure and heart rate increase with increase in body activity (exercise). The increases supply additional oxygen to muscle tissue.

3. Individuals who are physically fit require less time than physically unfit individuals for blood pressure and heart rate to return to normal values after exercise. The hearts of fit individuals pump a larger volume of blood with each contraction (**stroke volume**) and deliver more O_2 to muscle tissue than that which occurs in hearts of unfit individuals. As a result, blood pressure and heart rate increases are smaller for fit individuals, and the time required to return to normal conditions is shorter than it is for unfit individuals undertaking the same amount of activity.

In the second part of this lab, the Q_{10} **value** is calculated for *Daphnia,* the water flea. The Q_{10} value measures the increase in metabolic activity resulting from a 10° C increase in body temperature in ectothermic animals. As environmental temperatures rise, body temperatures and the rates of chemical reactions and physiological processes increase. The Q_{10} value cannot be determined for endothermic animals because body temperatures remain constant regardless of environmental temperatures.

Q_{10} is determined for *Daphnia* by counting the number of heartbeats per minute at two temperatures. The following formula gives the Q_{10} value for two temperatures that differ by 10°C:

$$Q_{10} = \frac{\text{heart rate at higher temperature}}{\text{heart rate at lower temperature}}$$

Ectothermic animals use behavior to help regulate their body temperatures. Moving into the sun to get warm or burrowing into a hole to keep cool are examples. Refer to the review section on animals for a complete review of thermoregulation.

Designing an experiment to measure the effects of drugs on blood pressure: Heart rate changes in *Daphnia* can be measured in response to nicotine, alcohol, caffeine, aspirin, or other drugs by adding varying concentrations of these substances to the *Daphnia* culture fluid. Graph the results showing change in concentration (independent variable on *x*-axis) and heart rate (dependent variable on *y*-axis). Be sure to include a control measurement (drug concentration = 0).

Laboratory 11: Animal Behavior

The objective of this lab is to observe animal behavior in pillbugs (a terrestrial isopod) and fruit flies (*Drosophila melanogaster*). (An older version of this lab examined behavior in the brine shrimp, *Artemia*). Refer to the review section on animal behavior for a complete review of the various kinds of behavior.

For pillbugs, you align two petri dishes side by side with a small section of the touching walls cut away to provide a passageway between the dishes. The lab exercise manipulates substrate moisture and humidity by lining the dishes with filter papers, one damp and one dry. You then count the number of pillbugs (the dependent variable) per unit time (the independent variable) that move from one dish chamber to the other.

In the second part of the lab, you observe courtship behavior of mating fruit flies. Males and females have specific behaviors that often follow a fixed pattern. To reduce the number of variables, you should first observe these behaviors using one male and one female.

Designing an experiment to measure the effects of environmental variables on animal behavior: Select an organism and observe the organism in the absence of applied stimuli. Then, change the environment by introducing a stimulus. Only one stimulus should be applied at a time. Be sure to include the following in your experimental design.

1. One or more experimental treatments (or experimental variables).

   • Physical stimuli include moisture, temperature, light, sound, gravity, pH, and chemicals (salt, drugs, nicotine, alcohol, caffeine, aspirin, pesticides).

   • Biotic stimuli include the introduction of members of the same species (males or females) or other species (predators or prey). If members of the same species are introduce, the sex of the introduced individual may influence behavior (mating or agonistic behaviors). Multiple members of the same species may elicit social behaviors.

2. A control treatment to which the experimental treatments can be compared.

3. A graph, histogram or other graphic representation of the data.

4. An interpretation or discussion of the data.

Laboratory 12: Dissolved Oxygen and Aquatic Primary Productivity

In this lab, the amount of oxygen dissolved in natural water samples is measured and analyzed to determine the primary productivity of the sample. The amount of dissolved oxygen is dependent upon many factors, including the following:

1. **Temperature.** Dissolved oxygen concentration decreases as temperature increases.

2. **Salinity.** Dissolved oxygen concentration decreases as salt concentrations increase.

3. **Photosynthesis.** Photosynthetic activity produces oxygen and increases the amount of dissolved oxygen.

4. **Respiration.** Respiration consumes oxygen and reduces the amount of dissolved oxygen.

The primary productivity of a community is a measure of the amount of biomass produced by autotrophs through photosynthesis (or chemosynthesis) per unit of time. Primary productivity can be determined by measuring the rate at which CO_2 is consumed, O_2 is produced, or biomass is stored. In this lab, primary productivity is determined by the amount of O_2 produced. In addition, the effects of light, nitrogen, and phosphorus on primary productivity are examined.

Primary productivity can be examined with respect to the following factors. (Note that the term *rate* means *per unit time*.)

1. **Gross primary productivity** is the rate at which producers acquire chemical energy before any of this energy is used for metabolism.

2. **Net primary productivity** is the rate at which producers acquire chemical energy *less* the rate at which they consume energy through respiration.

3. **Respiratory rate** is the rate at which energy is consumed through respiration.

The following four procedures are used to determine primary productivity:

1. The **Winkler method** is used to measure dissolved oxygen using a titration technique. Titration is the process of adding a substance of known concentration to a solution containing a substance of unknown concentration until a specific reaction is completed and a color change occurs.

2. The **light and dark bottle method** is used to compare dissolved oxygen values in water samples exposed to light and dark. Three samples are required, as follows:

    - **Initial bottle.** The amount of dissolved oxygen in this sample will provide an initial value to which the remaining two samples can be compared.

    - **Light bottle.** Expose the second sample to light. After twenty-four hours, determine the amount of dissolved oxygen in the sample.

    - **Dark bottle.** Store the third sample in the dark. After twenty-four hours, determine the amount of dissolved oxygen in the sample.

3. The dissolved oxygen values determined above are used to calculate primary productivity, as follows:

- **Net primary productivity** is determined from the amount of dissolved oxygen *gained* in the sample exposed to light. The increase is calculated by subtracting the amount of dissolved oxygen in the initial bottle from the amount in the light bottle.

- **Respiratory rate** is determined from the amount of dissolved oxygen *lost* in the sample kept in the dark. The decrease is calculated by subtracting the amount of dissolved oxygen in the dark bottle from the amount in the initial bottle.

- **Gross primary productivity** is determined by summing the absolute values of the net primary productivity and the respiratory rate, or gross primary productivity = net primary productivity + respiratory rate

4. Convert dissolved oxygen values to mg C/m^3/day (where C = carbon). At standard temperature and pressure (0°C and 1 atmosphere pressure), the production of 1 ml of O_2 corresponds to an assimilation of 0.54 grams of carbon into glucose.

Designing an experiment to measure primary productivity in an aquatic community: Follow the four procedures above for determining primary productivity. You can investigate the effect of light, nutrients, pesticides, or other substances. Prepare a bottle of water for each effect you investigate and an initial bottle of water for comparison. You may also investigate the effect of varying concentrations of a particular substance. In this case, prepare additional water samples for each concentration of the substance to be examined. The effect of light intensity can be investigated by exposing additional samples to various intensities of light. Various intensities of light can be produced by using different numbers of screens to filter the light source. Varying the light in this manner can also be used to simulate different depths of water.

Sample Questions and Answers

Multiple-Choice Questions

Directions: Each of the following questions or statements is followed by five possible answers or sentence completions. Choose the one best answer or sentence completion.

1. A dialysis bag is filled with a 3% starch solution. The bag is immersed in a beaker of water containing a 1% IKI solution. All of the following observations are correct EXCEPT:

   A. When the bag is first placed in the beaker, the water potential inside the bag is negative.

   B. When the bag is first placed in the beaker, the solution in the beaker is yellow brown.

   C. The starch solution inside the bag is hypertonic relative to the solution in the beaker.

   D. After fifteen minutes, the solution in the bag turns blue.

   E. After fifteen minutes, the mass of the dialysis bag has decreased.

Questions 2–3

Five potato cores are placed in five beakers containing different concentrations of sucrose. The following graph shows the change in mass of each of the potato cores after twenty-four hours in the beakers.

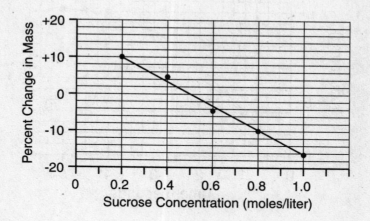

2. The water potential of the potato core can be calculated using which of the following sucrose concentrations?

   A. 0 M

   B. 0.2 M

   C. 0.4 M

   D. 0.5 M

   E. 0.10 M

3. All of the following statements are true EXCEPT:

   A. When first immersed in the beaker with 0.2 M sucrose, the water potential of cells in the potato core is more negative than that of the sucrose solution.

   B. After twenty-four hours in the beaker with 0.2 M sucrose, the pressure potential of cells in the potato core has increased.

   C. All of the sucrose solutions have a negative water potential.

   D. All of the sucrose solutions have a pressure potential equal to zero.

   E. When the net movement of water into a potato core is zero, the water potential of the potato core is zero.

Questions 4–6

Use the following graph of an enzyme-mediated reaction for the next three questions.

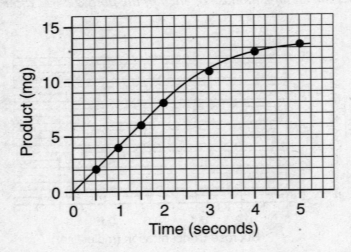

4. What is the initial rate of the reaction?

   A. 0.25 mg/sec

   B. 4 mg/sec

   C. 4.5 mg/sec

   D. 5 mg/sec

   E. 8 mg/sec

5. What will be the effect on the reaction if the enzyme is heated to 100°C before being mixed with the substrate?

   A. The reaction rate will increase.

   B. The reaction will occur at a slower rate.

   C. The reaction will not occur.

   D. The reaction rate will remain unchanged.

   E. A different reaction will occur.

6. Which of the following is LEAST likely to increase the forward rate of an enzyme-mediated reaction?

   A. An increase in the substrate concentration

   B. An increase in the enzyme concentration

   C. An increase in the product concentration

   D. An increase in pH

   E. An increase in the temperature

Question 7

The following diagram illustrates five different arrangements of ascospores all resulting from a cross between a strain homozygous for the wild type of spores (black spores) and a strain homozygous for the mutant color (tan).

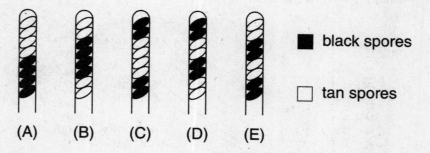

(A) (B) (C) (D) (E)

■ black spores

☐ tan spores

7. Which of the above asci contain ascospores produced during meiosis without crossing over?

8. In a paper chromatography procedure, molecules with which of the following characteristics migrate the fastest up the chromatography paper?

A. High solubility in solvent and weak hydrogen bonding to cellulose

B. High solubility in solvent and strong hydrogen bonding to cellulose

C. Low solubility in solvent and strong hydrogen bonding to cellulose

D. Low solubility in solvent and weak hydrogen bonding to cellulose

E. Insoluble in solvent

Question 9

An experiment designed to measure the rate of photosynthesis uses DPIP as a substitute for NADP⁺. Oxidized DPIP is blue, and reduced DPIP is clear. Various wavelengths of light are used to illuminate samples which contain chloroplasts, DPIP, and an appropriate buffer. The results of the experiment are shown below.

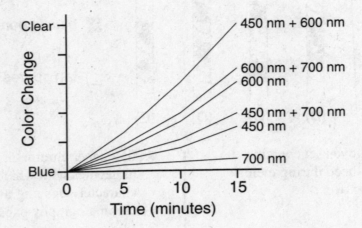

9. Which of the following is a reasonable interpretation of the results?

A. All wavelengths of light are equally absorbed and utilized during photosynthesis.

B. Blue (450 nm) is the most efficient wavelength for photosynthesis.

C. There are at least two wavelengths of light utilized during photosynthesis.

D. A blue solution indicates maximum photosynthetic activity.

E. Green light (at 525 nm) has the highest absorption efficiency.

Questions 10–11

An experiment is designed to measure the respiratory rate of crickets. Three respirometers are prepared as follows.

Table 15-3	
Respirometer	**Contents**
1	KOH, cricket weighing 2 grams
2	KOH, cricket weighing 3 grams
3	KOH

All respirometers (consisting of a jar connected to a pipette) are immersed in the same water bath. One end of the pipette is connected to the jar; the other end of the pipette is open to the surrounding water.

10. A pressure change registered by respirometer 1 or 2 may indicate any of the following EXCEPT:

A. the cricket is alive

B. a change in temperature of air inside the jar

C. a change in atmospheric pressure

D. a change in the amount of oxygen inside the jar

E. a change in the amount of CO_2 inside the jar

11. The purpose of respirometer 3 is to control for all of the following EXCEPT:

A. changes in the amount of O_2 inside the jar

B. changes in water bath temperature

C. changes in atmospheric pressure

D. changes produced by water pressure variations in the water surrounding the respirometers

E. changes in air temperature surrounding the water bath

12. Competent bacteria

A. are resistant to antibiotics

B. contain recombinant DNA

C. can be induced to accept foreign DNA

D. cannot reproduce

E. cause disease

Question 13

Question 13 refers to the following semi-log graph of results from the standard restriction enzyme used in a gel electrophoresis procedure. Phage lambda DNA molecules digested with Hind III are used as the standard.

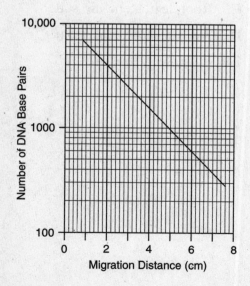

13. A fragment of phage lambda DNA produced by *Eco*RI endonuclease migrates 6 cm. If this fragment is produced during the same electrophoresis procedure as the standard shown in the graph above, how large is the fragment?

A. 150 base pairs

B. 600 base pairs

C. 800 base pairs

D. 1000 base pairs

E. 6000 base pairs

Question 14

Question 14 refers to the following diagram representing the bands produced by an elec-trophoresis procedure using DNA from four human individuals. Each DNA sample is treated with the same restriction enzyme.

Individual 1	Individual 2	Individual 3	Individual 4

14. Which of the following is a correct interpretation of the gel electrophoresis data?

    A. Individual 1 could be an offspring of individuals 3 and 4.

    B. Individual 1 could be an offspring of individuals 2 and 3.

    C. Individual 2 could be an offspring of individuals 1 and 3.

    D. Individual 3 could be an offspring of individuals 2 and 4.

    E. All four individuals could be the same person.

15. A population consists of twenty individuals of which 64% are homozygous dominant for a particular trait and the remaining individuals are all heterozygous. All of the following could explain this situation EXCEPT:

    A. Genetic drift is occurring.

    B. The recessive allele is deleterious.

    C. All homozygous recessive individuals emigrate.

    D. The population is very small.

    E. Only heterozygous individuals mate.

16. Which of the following series of terms correctly indicates the gradient of water potential from lowest water potential to highest water potential?

    A. Air, leaf, stem, root, soil

    B. Soil, root, stem, leaf, air

    C. Root, leaf, stem, air, soil

    D. Air, soil, root, leaf, stem

    E. Stem, leaf, root, soil, air

Question 17

Question 17 refers to the following graph that shows the rate of water loss for three plants. One plant is exposed to normal conditions, a second plant is exposed to high temperature, and a third plant is exposed to high humidity.

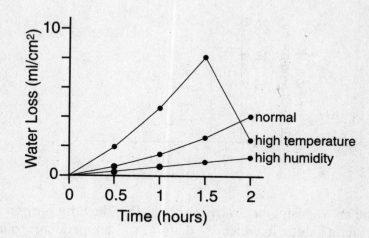

17. The sudden decrease in water loss after 1.5 hours for the plant exposed to high temperatures is probably caused by

   A. the burning of the leaves

   B. a lack of CO_2 to maintain photosynthesis

   C. a lack of O_2 to maintain photosynthesis

   D. stomatal closure

   E. the collapse of sieve-tube elements

18. A Q_{10} value of 3 in an ectothermic animal means that the metabolic rate

   A. triples when body temperature triples

   B. triples when body temperature increases by 10°C

   C. doubles when the body temperature increases by 3°C

   D. doubles when the body temperature increases by 10°C

   E. triples when the body temperature decreases by 10°C

Questions 19–20

Questions 19 and 20 refer to an experiment that allows Artemia brine shrimp to move into water with different concentrations of salt. The results of the experiment are shown in the histogram below.

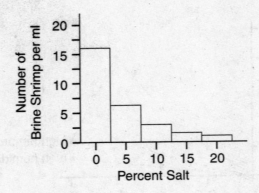

19. According to the above histogram, most brine shrimp prefer a habitat in which the salt concentration is

    A. 0%

    B. 5%

    C. 10%

    D. 15%

    E. 20%

20. *Artemia* brine shrimp are rarely found in bodies of water with salt concentrations below 5%. This is probably because

    A. the brine shrimp prefer low levels of salt concentration

    B. the brine shrimp prefer high levels of salt concentration

    C. the brine shrimp cannot survive in fresh water

    D. the brine shrimp cannot survive the temperatures found in bodies of water with fresh water or water with low salinity

    E. predators of the brine shrimp are common in fresh water and water with low salinity

21. The net primary productivity for a temperate forest was measured at 2000 mg C/m²/day. The respiratory rate of the community was determined to be 1000 mg C/m²/day. The gross primary productivity for this community is

    A. 1000 mg C/m²/day

    B. 2000 mg C/m²/day

    C. 3000 mg C/m²/day

    D. 4000 mg C/m²/day

    E. 5000 mg C/m²/day

Answers to Multiple-Choice Questions

1. E. After fifteen minutes, water will move from the beaker (higher water potential) into the bag (lower water potential), and the bag will gain weight. After fifteen minutes, the solution inside the *bag* turns blue because the IKI that diffuses into the bag mixes with the starch. When the bag is first placed in the beaker, the water potential in the bag is negative—the sum of the negative osmotic potential and a zero pressure potential (flaccid bag).

2. D. When the net movement into and out of the potato core is zero, the water potentials inside and outside the potato core are the same, and there is no change in the mass of the potato core. The concentration of the sucrose solution can be used to calculate its osmotic pressure. since the pressure potential of the sucrose solution is zero, its water potential is equal to its osmotic pressure.

3. E. When the net movement of water into a potato core is zero, the water potentials inside and outside the potato core are the same, but not zero. Because the potato core immersed in the 0.2 M sucrose solution gained weight, the water potential of its cells must have been smaller than the water potential of the sucrose solution. After twenty-four hours, water that enters the potato core in the 0.2 M sucrose solution causes the potato cells to expand and gain weight. Since the rigid cell walls cannot expand, pressure potential increases as the cell walls exert a restraining pressure on the cell contents.

4. B. The initial rate of reaction is the slope of the plotted curve at the beginning of the reaction. Since the straight line portion of the curve from 0 to 2 seconds indicates a constant rate of reaction, the slope at any point along this portion of the line will provide the initial rate. For the entire interval from 0 to 2 seconds, the slope, determined by the change in product formed divided by the change in time, is (8 mg - 0 mg)/(2 sec - 0 sec) = 4 mg/sec.

5. B. An enzyme that is heated to 100°C will be structurally damaged. The reaction will still occur, but at a much slower rate (perhaps an extremely slow rate).

6. C. Since enzyme-mediated reactions are reversible (they convert product back to substrate), increasing the concentration of the product will slow the forward direction of the reaction and accelerate the reverse reaction. Conversely, an increase in the substrate concentration will increase the forward rate of the reaction. Increasing the enzyme concentration will not slow the reaction rate but may increase it if the substrate concentration is high enough to utilize additional enzyme. An increase in pH or temperature may change the rate of reaction, but the nature of the enzyme must be known in order to determine whether the rate is increased or decreased.

7. A. The ascus containing ascospores with two groups of four adjacent ascospores of the same color results when no crossovers occur. If no crossing over takes place, the order of ascospores corresponds to each of the four chromatids of a homologous pair of chromosomes (two ascospores from each chromatid). Thus, the first four ascospores possess traits from one parent and the second four ascospores possess traits from the second parent. If crossing over occurs, traits on two nonsister chromatids will exchange, resulting in a swap of traits between one pair of ascospores and another pair.

8. A. Molecules that have strong bonding to the cellulose are held back, as are those molecules which do not dissolve well in the solvent.

9. **C.** Because the graph shows that 450 nm and 600 nm each produce a high photosynthetic rate, and together produce the highest rate, the graph indicates that the photosynthetic process depends on these two wavelengths. Although light of 450 nm does induce significant photosynthetic activity, light of 600 nm induces more. A blue solution indicates little or no photosynthesis has occurred because DPIP has not been reduced. The graph does not provide any information concerning green light or light wavelengths other than 450 nm, 600 nm, and 700 nm.

10. **E.** An increase in CO_2 gas (from respiration) cannot be detected because it immediately reacts with KOH to produce solid K_2CO_3. A live cricket will decrease the amount of O_2 gas detected by the respirometer. Changes in temperature and atmospheric pressure also cause the respirometer to register a change in volume because temperature and atmospheric pressure affect the water pressure on the pipette inlets.

11. **A.** Since there is no insect and thus no O_2 consumption in respirometer 3, the purpose of this respirometer is to control all the variables that might influence the volume changes in respirometers 1 and 2, other than O_2 consumption by insects.

12. **C.** Competence refers to a stage of rapid population growth during which bacteria are most receptive to absorbing foreign DNA.

13. **B.** The vertical line at 6 cm and the horizontal line at 600 base pairs intersect on the standard curve. On the log scale for the y-axis, each horizontal line between 100 and 1000 represents an increase of 100 base pairs.

14. **D.** This is an example of DNA fingerprinting. The DNA fragments from individual 3 can be found in *either* individuals 2 or 4. As a result, it is possible (but not certain) that individual 3 inherited his or her DNA from individuals 2 and 4. In an actual DNA fingerprinting analysis, many different restriction enzymes are used so that many different DNA fragments can be compared.

15. **E.** If only heterozygotes mate, 25% of the offspring, on average, should be homozygous recessive. Thus, this answer cannot explain the absence of homozygous recessive individuals in the population. Because the population is so small, genetic drift may be responsible. Alternately, natural selection against individuals with a deleterious homozygous recessive genotype may also explain why this genotype is absent from the population. Note, however, that the recessive allele remains in the population because it is masked by the dominant allele in heterozygous individuals. The absence of homozygous recessive individuals can also be explained if these individuals leave the population (emigrate) for another location.

16. **A.** Water potential is highest in the soil, decreases from root to leaf, and is lowest in the air. Water moves from the soil into the roots and through the plant and transpires from the leaf because water moves from the area of greatest water potential to the area of lowest water potential.

17. **D.** When water entering roots cannot adequately replace the water loss by transpiration, the stomata close to prevent wilting.

18. **B.** The Q_{10} is the ratio of the metabolic rate at one temperature to the metabolic rate at a temperature 10°C colder. A Q_{10} equal to 3 indicates that the metabolic rate triples when the body temperature increases by 10°C.

19. A. The tallest vertical bar (above 0% salt concentration) indicates the preference of the greatest number of brine shrimp.

20. E. The predators of brine shrimp cannot survive in bodies of water with high concentrations of salt. Thus, brine shrimp survive in bodies of water with a high salt concentration because predators are absent. In waters with low concentrations of salt, predators eliminate the brine shrimp.

21. C. The gross primary productivity is the sum of the net primary productivity and the respiratory rate.

Free-Response Questions

Free-response questions on the AP exam may require you to provide information from a narrow area of biology, or they may consist of parts that require you to assemble information from diverse areas of biology. The questions that follow are typical of either an entire AP exam question or merely that part of a question that is related to this section.

Directions: Answer the questions below as completely and as thoroughly as possible. Answer the question in essay form (NOT outline form), using complete sentences. You may use diagrams to supplement your answers, but a diagram alone without appropriate discussion is inadequate.

1. An experiment was conducted to measure the effect of light on photosynthetic rate. The following three treatments were evaluated:

   - Treatment I: Healthy chloroplasts exposed to light
   - Treatment II: Boiled chloroplasts exposed to light
   - Treatment III: Healthy chloroplasts incubated in darkness

   Oxidized DPIP was added to each treatment to simulate $NADP^+$. When oxidized DPIP is reduced by photosynthesis, it turns from blue to clear. The degree to which the DPIP was reduced in each treatment was determined by using a spectrophotometer. A spectrophotometer measures the amount of light that is transmitted through a sample. The spectrophotometer in this experiment was set to measure light at a wavelength of 605 nm.

   The following data were collected for the healthy chloroplasts exposed to light.

Table 15-4						
	Treatment I					
Time (minutes)	0	5	10	15	20	25
Average % transmittance (five-minute intervals)	30	45	60	70	75	78

   (a.) Construct and label a graph for the healthy chloroplasts exposed to light. On the same set of axes, draw and label two additional lines representing your prediction of the data obtained for treatments II and III.

   (b.) Justify your predicted data for treatments II and III.

   (c.) Describe the process that causes the reduction of DPIP.

2. Design an experiment to measure the effect of a drug on animal physiology. Include the following in your answer:

   (a.) A description of the animal, drug, equipment, and procedure to be used in the experiment

   (b.) A graph describing the results you would expect from your experiment

   (c.) An explanation for your expected results

Some Typical Answers to Free-Response Questions

Question 1

(a.)

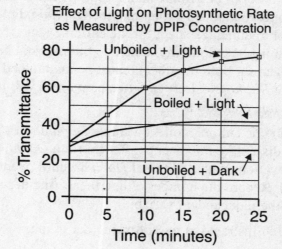

Effect of Light on Photosynthetic Rate
as Measured by DPIP Concentration

(b.) In treatment II, the chloroplasts were boiled. Boiling damages the chloroplasts, disrupting the thylakoid membranes. Also, the enzymes and photosynthetic pigments imbedded in the membranes are denatured. When these molecules lose their secondary and tertiary structures, they can no longer function properly. As a result, photosynthesis in treatment II is greatly reduced, occurring only in those few membranes which may still be intact with functioning enzymes and pigments. Only a small amount of DPIP is reduced, and the transmittance of a treatment II sample remains low (blue).

In treatment III, no DPIP is reduced because photosynthesis cannot occur in the absence of light. If photosynthesis cannot occur, electrons in the pigment systems are not reduced (energized) and thus there are no energized electrons to reduce DPIP. The DPIP remains oxidized (blue), and transmittance remains low.

(c.) When healthy chloroplasts are exposed to light, electrons of pigment molecules in photosystem II are energized (reduced). These electrons are eventually passed to the special chlorophyll a (P_{680}). Two electrons are then passed to a primary electron acceptor, the first molecule of an electron transport chain, a series of electron carriers (such as cytochromes). As the two electrons are passed from one carrier to the next, energy from the electrons is used to generate 1.5 ATP molecules (on average). At the end of the chain, the two electrons are accepted by pigment molecules in photosystem I, where they are again energized by light energy, passed to a special chlorophyll a (P_{700}), and then passed to a primary electron acceptor. The two electrons are then used to reduce NADP$^+$. With H$^+$ (from photolysis of H_2O), NADPH is formed. NADPH then supplies energy for the fixation of CO_2 during the Calvin-Benson cycle. In this experiment, DPIP is added so that the process can be visualized. As oxidized DPIP is energized by electrons from photosystem I to form reduced DPIP, DPIP turns from blue to clear.

Question 2

(a.) The experiment will measure the effect of caffeine on the heart rate of the water flea, *Daphnia*. *Daphnia* is a small aquatic crustacean whose heartbeat can be observed under a dissecting microscope. Divide the *Daphnia* into two containers. To one container (the experimental treatment), add a dilute solution of caffeine. Several dilutions may need to be separately evaluated in order to determine an appropriate caffeine dose (strong enough to cause an observable effect, but not so strong that the *Daphnia* die). The second container will serve as the control treatment. Except for the caffeine added to the experimental treatment, both treatments must be held to the same conditions. For example, water temperature and dissolved oxygen for both treatments must be maintained at the same levels. Randomly dividing one *Daphnia* culture into two containers will insure that both treatments begin with the same conditions.

After adding caffeine to one culture, collect a single *Daphnia* in a small pipette and count the heartbeats under a dissecting microscope. Repeat for a *Daphnia* from the control treatment. Repeat the observations with additional *Daphnia* until twenty *Daphnia* from each treatment are observed. Record the number of heartbeats (the dependent variable) for each of the two treatments (the independent variable).

(b.) The expected results are illustrated in the following bar graph.

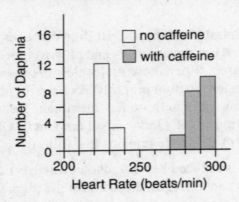

(c.) Since caffeine is a stimulant in other animal models, it should respond similarly in *Daphnia*. In other animal models (such as humans), caffeine increases heart rate, constricts blood vessels, and increases blood pressure.

This experiment could also have examined the effects of other drugs, such as alcohol (a depressant) or nicotine (a stimulant). The effects of these drugs could have been measured for humans as well. For humans, both heart rate and blood pressure could have been evaluated.

PART IV

AP BIOLOGY PRACTICE TEST

Answer Sheet for the Practice Test

(Remove This Sheet and Use It to Mark Your Answers)

Section 1
Multiple-Choice Questions

CUT HERE

1 Ⓐ Ⓑ Ⓒ Ⓓ Ⓔ	31 Ⓐ Ⓑ Ⓒ Ⓓ Ⓔ	61 Ⓐ Ⓑ Ⓒ Ⓓ Ⓔ	91 Ⓐ Ⓑ Ⓒ Ⓓ Ⓔ
2 Ⓐ Ⓑ Ⓒ Ⓓ Ⓔ	32 Ⓐ Ⓑ Ⓒ Ⓓ Ⓔ	62 Ⓐ Ⓑ Ⓒ Ⓓ Ⓔ	92 Ⓐ Ⓑ Ⓒ Ⓓ Ⓔ
3 Ⓐ Ⓑ Ⓒ Ⓓ Ⓔ	33 Ⓐ Ⓑ Ⓒ Ⓓ Ⓔ	63 Ⓐ Ⓑ Ⓒ Ⓓ Ⓔ	93 Ⓐ Ⓑ Ⓒ Ⓓ Ⓔ
4 Ⓐ Ⓑ Ⓒ Ⓓ Ⓔ	34 Ⓐ Ⓑ Ⓒ Ⓓ Ⓔ	64 Ⓐ Ⓑ Ⓒ Ⓓ Ⓔ	94 Ⓐ Ⓑ Ⓒ Ⓓ Ⓔ
5 Ⓐ Ⓑ Ⓒ Ⓓ Ⓔ	35 Ⓐ Ⓑ Ⓒ Ⓓ Ⓔ	65 Ⓐ Ⓑ Ⓒ Ⓓ Ⓔ	95 Ⓐ Ⓑ Ⓒ Ⓓ Ⓔ
6 Ⓐ Ⓑ Ⓒ Ⓓ Ⓔ	36 Ⓐ Ⓑ Ⓒ Ⓓ Ⓔ	66 Ⓐ Ⓑ Ⓒ Ⓓ Ⓔ	96 Ⓐ Ⓑ Ⓒ Ⓓ Ⓔ
7 Ⓐ Ⓑ Ⓒ Ⓓ Ⓔ	37 Ⓐ Ⓑ Ⓒ Ⓓ Ⓔ	67 Ⓐ Ⓑ Ⓒ Ⓓ Ⓔ	97 Ⓐ Ⓑ Ⓒ Ⓓ Ⓔ
8 Ⓐ Ⓑ Ⓒ Ⓓ Ⓔ	38 Ⓐ Ⓑ Ⓒ Ⓓ Ⓔ	68 Ⓐ Ⓑ Ⓒ Ⓓ Ⓔ	98 Ⓐ Ⓑ Ⓒ Ⓓ Ⓔ
9 Ⓐ Ⓑ Ⓒ Ⓓ Ⓔ	39 Ⓐ Ⓑ Ⓒ Ⓓ Ⓔ	69 Ⓐ Ⓑ Ⓒ Ⓓ Ⓔ	99 Ⓐ Ⓑ Ⓒ Ⓓ Ⓔ
10 Ⓐ Ⓑ Ⓒ Ⓓ Ⓔ	40 Ⓐ Ⓑ Ⓒ Ⓓ Ⓔ	70 Ⓐ Ⓑ Ⓒ Ⓓ Ⓔ	100 Ⓐ Ⓑ Ⓒ Ⓓ Ⓔ
11 Ⓐ Ⓑ Ⓒ Ⓓ Ⓔ	41 Ⓐ Ⓑ Ⓒ Ⓓ Ⓔ	71 Ⓐ Ⓑ Ⓒ Ⓓ Ⓔ	101 Ⓐ Ⓑ Ⓒ Ⓓ Ⓔ
12 Ⓐ Ⓑ Ⓒ Ⓓ Ⓔ	42 Ⓐ Ⓑ Ⓒ Ⓓ Ⓔ	72 Ⓐ Ⓑ Ⓒ Ⓓ Ⓔ	102 Ⓐ Ⓑ Ⓒ Ⓓ Ⓔ
13 Ⓐ Ⓑ Ⓒ Ⓓ Ⓔ	43 Ⓐ Ⓑ Ⓒ Ⓓ Ⓔ	73 Ⓐ Ⓑ Ⓒ Ⓓ Ⓔ	103 Ⓐ Ⓑ Ⓒ Ⓓ Ⓔ
14 Ⓐ Ⓑ Ⓒ Ⓓ Ⓔ	44 Ⓐ Ⓑ Ⓒ Ⓓ Ⓔ	74 Ⓐ Ⓑ Ⓒ Ⓓ Ⓔ	104 Ⓐ Ⓑ Ⓒ Ⓓ Ⓔ
15 Ⓐ Ⓑ Ⓒ Ⓓ Ⓔ	45 Ⓐ Ⓑ Ⓒ Ⓓ Ⓔ	75 Ⓐ Ⓑ Ⓒ Ⓓ Ⓔ	105 Ⓐ Ⓑ Ⓒ Ⓓ Ⓔ
16 Ⓐ Ⓑ Ⓒ Ⓓ Ⓔ	46 Ⓐ Ⓑ Ⓒ Ⓓ Ⓔ	76 Ⓐ Ⓑ Ⓒ Ⓓ Ⓔ	106 Ⓐ Ⓑ Ⓒ Ⓓ Ⓔ
17 Ⓐ Ⓑ Ⓒ Ⓓ Ⓔ	47 Ⓐ Ⓑ Ⓒ Ⓓ Ⓔ	77 Ⓐ Ⓑ Ⓒ Ⓓ Ⓔ	107 Ⓐ Ⓑ Ⓒ Ⓓ Ⓔ
18 Ⓐ Ⓑ Ⓒ Ⓓ Ⓔ	48 Ⓐ Ⓑ Ⓒ Ⓓ Ⓔ	78 Ⓐ Ⓑ Ⓒ Ⓓ Ⓔ	108 Ⓐ Ⓑ Ⓒ Ⓓ Ⓔ
19 Ⓐ Ⓑ Ⓒ Ⓓ Ⓔ	49 Ⓐ Ⓑ Ⓒ Ⓓ Ⓔ	79 Ⓐ Ⓑ Ⓒ Ⓓ Ⓔ	109 Ⓐ Ⓑ Ⓒ Ⓓ Ⓔ
20 Ⓐ Ⓑ Ⓒ Ⓓ Ⓔ	50 Ⓐ Ⓑ Ⓒ Ⓓ Ⓔ	80 Ⓐ Ⓑ Ⓒ Ⓓ Ⓔ	110 Ⓐ Ⓑ Ⓒ Ⓓ Ⓔ
21 Ⓐ Ⓑ Ⓒ Ⓓ Ⓔ	51 Ⓐ Ⓑ Ⓒ Ⓓ Ⓔ	81 Ⓐ Ⓑ Ⓒ Ⓓ Ⓔ	111 Ⓐ Ⓑ Ⓒ Ⓓ Ⓔ
22 Ⓐ Ⓑ Ⓒ Ⓓ Ⓔ	52 Ⓐ Ⓑ Ⓒ Ⓓ Ⓔ	82 Ⓐ Ⓑ Ⓒ Ⓓ Ⓔ	112 Ⓐ Ⓑ Ⓒ Ⓓ Ⓔ
23 Ⓐ Ⓑ Ⓒ Ⓓ Ⓔ	53 Ⓐ Ⓑ Ⓒ Ⓓ Ⓔ	83 Ⓐ Ⓑ Ⓒ Ⓓ Ⓔ	113 Ⓐ Ⓑ Ⓒ Ⓓ Ⓔ
24 Ⓐ Ⓑ Ⓒ Ⓓ Ⓔ	54 Ⓐ Ⓑ Ⓒ Ⓓ Ⓔ	84 Ⓐ Ⓑ Ⓒ Ⓓ Ⓔ	114 Ⓐ Ⓑ Ⓒ Ⓓ Ⓔ
25 Ⓐ Ⓑ Ⓒ Ⓓ Ⓔ	55 Ⓐ Ⓑ Ⓒ Ⓓ Ⓔ	85 Ⓐ Ⓑ Ⓒ Ⓓ Ⓔ	115 Ⓐ Ⓑ Ⓒ Ⓓ Ⓔ
26 Ⓐ Ⓑ Ⓒ Ⓓ Ⓔ	56 Ⓐ Ⓑ Ⓒ Ⓓ Ⓔ	86 Ⓐ Ⓑ Ⓒ Ⓓ Ⓔ	116 Ⓐ Ⓑ Ⓒ Ⓓ Ⓔ
27 Ⓐ Ⓑ Ⓒ Ⓓ Ⓔ	57 Ⓐ Ⓑ Ⓒ Ⓓ Ⓔ	87 Ⓐ Ⓑ Ⓒ Ⓓ Ⓔ	117 Ⓐ Ⓑ Ⓒ Ⓓ Ⓔ
28 Ⓐ Ⓑ Ⓒ Ⓓ Ⓔ	58 Ⓐ Ⓑ Ⓒ Ⓓ Ⓔ	88 Ⓐ Ⓑ Ⓒ Ⓓ Ⓔ	118 Ⓐ Ⓑ Ⓒ Ⓓ Ⓔ
29 Ⓐ Ⓑ Ⓒ Ⓓ Ⓔ	59 Ⓐ Ⓑ Ⓒ Ⓓ Ⓔ	89 Ⓐ Ⓑ Ⓒ Ⓓ Ⓔ	119 Ⓐ Ⓑ Ⓒ Ⓓ Ⓔ
30 Ⓐ Ⓑ Ⓒ Ⓓ Ⓔ	60 Ⓐ Ⓑ Ⓒ Ⓓ Ⓔ	90 Ⓐ Ⓑ Ⓒ Ⓓ Ⓔ	120 Ⓐ Ⓑ Ⓒ Ⓓ Ⓔ

Section I (Multiple-Choice Questions)

Time: 1 hour and 30 minutes

120 questions

Directions: Each of the following questions or statements is followed by five possible answers or sentence completions. Choose the one best answer or sentence completion.

1. The main function of the large intestine is the

   A. digestion of proteins

   B. digestion of carbohydrates

   C. digestion of fats

   D. absorption of water

   E. production of bile

2. ATP is required for all of the following processes EXCEPT:

   A. active transport by transport proteins

   B. facilitated diffusion

   C. microtubule movement within flagella

   D. Na$^+$/K$^+$ pump activity

   E. protein synthesis

3. DNA replication occurs during

   A. anaphase

   B. interphase

   C. metaphase

   D. prophase

   E. telophase

4. Adenine, a nitrogen base, is found in all of the following EXCEPT:

   A. RNA

   B. DNA

   C. ATP

   D. cAMP

   E. amino acids

5. The *lac* operon

   A. is found in eukaryotic cells

   B. codes for the sequence of amino acids in lactase

   C. regulates the translation of mRNA

   D. regulates transcription by turning on or off the production of a repressor protein

   E. regulates DNA replication by turning on or off the production of an inducer protein

GO ON TO THE NEXT PAGE

6. Food storage in seeds occurs in the

   A. embryo

   B. coleoptile

   C. cotyledon

   D. germ

   E. plumule

7. All of the following statements about endosperm in angiosperms are correct EXCEPT:

   A. It forms entirely from maternal tissue.

   B. It has a triploid chromosome number.

   C. It forms from a portion of the embryo sac that contains the polar nuclei.

   D. It provides nutrients for the growing embryo.

   E. It originates from a cell that is fertilized by a sperm nucleus from a pollen grain.

8. The primary function of progesterone in the menstrual cycle is to

   A. stimulate development of the egg

   B. stimulate development of the endometrium

   C. stimulate development of the corpus luteum

   D. stimulate development of the follicle

   E. trigger ovulation

9. Both viruses and prokaryotes contain

   A. nucleic acids

   B. ribosomes

   C. a plasma membrane

   D. a protein coat

   E. a peptidoglycan wall

10. A cell contains four pairs of homologous chromosomes represented by $A_1/A_2\ B_1/B_2\ C_1/C_2\ D_1/D_2$. Which of the following represents the chromosome makeup of a gamete derived from this cell?

    A. $A_1A_2B_1B_2C_1C_2D_1D_2$

    B. $B_1B_1C_1D_1$

    C. $A_1A_2B_1B_2$

    D. $A_1B_2C_2D_2$

    E. $A_1C_1C_2D_1$

11. Which of the following is an anabolic reaction?

    A. $ATP + H_2O \rightarrow ADP + P_i$

    B. Cellular respiration

    C. $Starch + n(H_2O) \rightarrow n(C_6H_{12}O_6)$

    D. $CO_2 + H_2O \rightarrow C_6H_{12}O_6 + O_2$

    E. Glycolysis

12. Which of the following is MOST responsible for the movement of water up a tall tree?

    A. Adhesion

    B. Capillary action

    C. Guttation

    D. Osmosis

    E. Sunlight

13. Which of the following statements concerning photosynthetic pigments (chlorophylls *a* and *b*, carotenes, and xanthophylls) is correct?

    A. The R_f values obtained from a chromatographic analysis are the same for these molecules.

    B. The wavelength of light absorbed is the same for these molecules.

    C. The molecules have the same molecular weight.

    D. The molecules have the same solubility in chromatography solvents.

    E. The molecules absorb energy by boosting electrons to higher energy orbitals.

14. Aphids are insects that insert their needlelike mouth parts into plants. Sometimes, fluid from the plant tissues passes entirely through the digestive tract of the aphid and emerges as a small droplet at its posterior end. The source of this liquid is probably

    A. epidermal cells

    B. phloem cells

    C. tracheids

    D. vessels

    E. xylem cells

15. In an effort to clone a human protein, material from a human cell is introduced into bacteria. Which of the following human materials are needed for this procedure?

    A. The segment of DNA coding for the protein's mRNA transcript

    B. The rRNA and tRNA used during translation of the protein

    C. The protein's mRNA transcript found in the nucleus

    D. The protein's mRNA found in the cytoplasm

    E. The introns removed from the protein's unprocessed mRNA transcript

16. Which of the following transmits nerve impulses between neurons?

    A. Cholinesterase

    B. Acetylcholine

    C. K^+

    D. Ca^{2+}

    E. Synaptonemal complex

17. All of the following characteristics are found in the phylum Arthropoda EXCEPT:

    A. body segmentation

    B. jointed appendages

    C. an exoskeleton made with chitin

    D. a true coelom

    E. a closed circulatory system

GO ON TO THE NEXT PAGE

18. Which of the following structures are found in both prokaryotic and eukaryotic cells?

    A. Cell membrane and chloroplasts

    B. DNA and ribosomes

    C. Cell walls and a nuclear envelope

    D. Flagella and endoplasmic reticulum

    E. Golgi complex and mitochondria

19. Which of the following describes a single population?

    A. A group of bacteria all of the species *Bacillus subtilis*

    B. All insects occupying three hectares of farmland

    C. An exact count of 315 animals in a fenced plot of land

    D. All the birds counted in one day by census takers in the United States

    E. All the animals and plants on an isolated island

20. All of the following are associated with an increase in the rate of breathing EXCEPT:

    A. an increase in HCO_3^- in the blood

    B. an increase in pH in the blood

    C. an increase in CO_2 in the blood

    D. moving to a higher elevation

    E. an increase in muscular activity

21. Duchenne's muscular dystrophy is inherited as a sex-linked recessive allele. From whom does a male with this disease inherit the defective allele?

    A. Only his mother

    B. Only his father

    C. The mother or the father, but not both

    D. Both the mother and the father

    E. It is impossible to determine with certainty using only the given information.

22. Which of the following is a function of the Golgi complex?

    A. Protein synthesis

    B. Ribosome synthesis

    C. DNA replication

    D. Ca^{2+} storage in muscle cells

    E. Modifying and packaging of proteins and lipids into vesicles

Questions 23–24

Over a period of 100 years, a clear mountain lake is transformed into a meadow. During the transition, various communities inhabit the area. Each community is replaced by a new community after a period of time.

23. The ecological process described in the above paragraph is an example of

    A. carrying capacity

    B. density-dependent limiting factors

    C. density-independent limiting factors

    D. succession

    E. biotic potential

24. Which of the following statements best explains why a new community is able to replace the resident community?

    A. Species in the resident community die from old age.

    B. Species in the resident community die from disease that eventually appears.

    C. Given enough time, new species able to compete for the same resources as the resident species will arrive.

    D. Species extinction is inevitable.

    E. The biotic and abiotic characteristics of the habitat change due to the influence of the resident community.

25. A transcription of the DNA sequence CCCGGAATT would produce which of the following sequences in mRNA?

    A. CCCGGAATT

    B. GGGCCTTAA

    C. AAATTCCGG

    D. UUUAACCAA

    E. GGGCCUUAA

26. Which of the following best describes the pattern of punctuated equilibrium in evolution?

    A. Speciation events occur relatively rapidly.

    B. Small changes that accumulate over long periods of time lead to the formation of a new species and the extinction of the old species.

    C. Small changes that accumulate over long periods of time lead to the divergence of one species into two or more species.

    D. Speciation occurs when random changes accumulate over long periods of time.

    E. Geographic isolation is the predominant mechanism of speciation.

GO ON TO THE NEXT PAGE

27. Elongation of cells in shoot tips of plants is promoted by

    A. abscisic acid

    B. carotenes

    C. cytokinins

    D. ethylene

    E. indoleacetic acid

28. The main function of water in photophosphorylation is to

    A. provide electrons which are energized by light energy

    B. facilitate the movement of pigments into and out of the chloroplasts

    C. provide the necessary oxygen for the photosynthetic process

    D. supply the energy required for photosynthesis

    E. maintain the integrity of the chloroplast membranes

29. Hemophilia is inherited as a sex-linked recessive trait. If a woman whose father has hemophilia marries a man without hemophilia, what is the probability that their child will be a boy with hemophilia?

    A. 0%

    B. 25%

    C. 50%

    D. 75%

    E. 100%

Question 30

Question 30 refers to the graph below that shows the progress of the reaction

$$A + B \leftrightarrow C + D$$

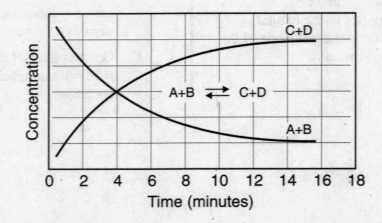

30. All of the following are correct interpretations of the progress of the reaction EXCEPT:

A. At the beginning of the reaction there is very little of substance C.

B. The reaction is in equilibrium four minutes after the reaction begins.

C. After four minutes, the concentration of substances C and D together exceeds that of A + B together.

D. When C and D react together, they convert to A and B.

E. When A and B react together, they convert to C and D.

31. A body plan with radial symmetry is found in which of the following groups?

A. Flatworms

B. Roundworms

C. Hydrozoans and jellyfish

D. Rotifers

E. Sponges

32. All of the following occur for the contraction of a motor muscle EXCEPT:

A. The sarcoplasmic reticulum releases Ca^{2+}.

B. The actin cross-bridges attach to the myosin filaments.

C. An action potential travels along the T-tubules.

D. ATP is available.

E. A neurotransmitter diffuses across the neuromuscular junction.

33. The function of the notochord is to

A. form the placenta in placental mammals

B. form the vertebrae in higher chordates

C. form the central nervous system in higher chordates

D. form the umbilical cord in placental mammals

E. provide body support in lower chordates

34. When ATP is produced in mitochondria, all of the following occur EXCEPT:

A. Water is formed from O_2, electrons, and H^+.

B. NADH is converted to $NAD^+ + H^+$.

C. Protons are pumped out of the mitochondria.

D. An electrochemical gradient is established across mitochondrial membranes.

E. A pH gradient is established across mitochondrial membranes.

35. A recessive trait appears in 81% of the individuals in a population that is in Hardy-Weinberg equilibrium. What percent of the population in the next generation is expected to be homozygous dominant?

A. 1%

B. 9%

C. 18%

D. 19%

E. 81%

GO ON TO THE NEXT PAGE

36. A plant that produces fruit, has leaves with veins branching to form a netlike pattern, and has vascular bundles in stems arranged in a circle is most likely a

    A. corn plant

    B. fern

    C. moss

    D. pea plant

    E. pine

37. Which of the following statements about the blastopore is correct?

    A. It is the opening to the archenteron.

    B. It is the opening to the blastocoel.

    C. It appears in the morula stage of embryonic development.

    D. It forms the anus in protostomes.

    E. It forms the mouth in deuterostomes.

38. Which of the following organisms would most likely be located at the bottom of a pyramid of biomass?

    A. Squid

    B. Crustaceans

    C. Seal

    D. Diatoms

    E. Sharks

39. Which of the following carries the code that determines the sequence of monomers in a protein?

    A. rRNA

    B. tRNA

    C. mRNA

    D. The large ribosome subunit

    E. DNA polymerase

40. All of the following can be found in plasma membranes of eukaryotes EXCEPT:

    A. cellulose

    B. phospholipids

    C. oligosaccharides

    D. proteins

    E. cholesterol molecules

41. Which of the following lack a true coelom?

    A. Earthworms

    B. Mammals

    C. Mollusks

    D. Roundworms

    E. Sea stars and sea urchins

42. Turner syndrome occurs in humans whose cells are missing the Y chromosome. All of the following are true about Turner syndrome EXCEPT:

    A. A Turner syndrome zygote results when a sperm missing a Y chromosome fertilizes a normal egg.

    B. A Turner syndrome zygote results when a normal sperm bearing an X chromosome fertilizes an egg missing an X chromosome.

    C. During meiosis, nondisjunction occurs to produce one of the gametes used to form the Turner syndrome zygote.

    D. Barr bodies form in the nuclei of Turner syndrome individuals.

    E. The zygote has 45 chromosomes.

43. All of the following substances pass out of the glomerulus and into the Bowman's capsule EXCEPT:

    A. proteins
    B. glucose
    C. water
    D. urea
    E. salts

44. Clown fish hide among the tentacles of sea anemones. Unlike their predators, clown fish are immune to the stinging tentacles. Thus, clown fish are protected within the sea anemones. The sea anemones are neither helped nor harmed by the presence of the clown fish. The relationship between the clown fish and the sea anemone is an example of

    A. competition
    B. commensalism
    C. mutualism
    D. parasitism
    E. predation

45. A severe storm forms a new river that divides a population of mice. After 500 years, a drought causes the river to dry up, allowing the two populations of mice to mix. Mating between mice from the two populations does not yield any offspring. This is an example of

    A. hybridization
    B. adaptive radiation
    C. balanced polymorphism
    D. sympatric speciation
    E. allopatric speciation

GO ON TO THE NEXT PAGE

46. When oxygen is unavailable, a yeast cell can obtain ATP

   A. through glycolysis

   B. by breaking down carbon dioxide

   C. through oxidative phosphorylation

   D. by substituting carbon dioxide for processes requiring oxygen

   E. by breaking down water to obtain small amounts of energy

47. Photoperiodism is regulated by which of the following substances?

   A. Anthocyanin

   B. Chlorophyll

   C. Gibberellins

   D. Phytochrome

   E. Xanthophyll

48. A bacteriophage is a

   A. bacterium that attacks viruses

   B. virus that attacks bacteria

   C. bacterium that attacks eukaryotic cells

   D. parasitic bacterium

   E. parasitic eukaryotic cell

49. Which of the following cellular bodies contain enzymes for breaking down macromolecules?

   A. Desmosomes

   B. Lysosomes

   C. Nucleosomes

   D. Peroxisomes

   E. Ribosomes

50. A young gosling follows its mother soon after birth. If a human raises the gosling from birth, the young gosling follows the human. If no animate object is nearby at birth, the gosling fails to follow its mother or a human if either are introduced several days after birth. This behavior can best be described as

   A. insight

   B. associative learning

   C. imprinting

   D. fixed action pattern

   E. trial-and-error learning

51. In most flowering plants, photosynthesis occurs in leaves primarily in

   A. cells of the spongy mesophyll

   B. cells of the palisades mesophyll

   C. epidermal cells

   D. cells of the vascular tissue

   E. bundle sheath cells

52. In peas, a dominant allele (*R*) produces a round pea shape, while a recessive allele (*r*) produces a wrinkled shape. At a second locus on a different chromosome, a dominant allele (*Y*) produces yellow-colored seeds, while a recessive allele (*y*) produces green-colored seeds. If a cross between two pea plants produces ¼ wrinkled seeds and ½ yellow seeds, which of the following represents the parental genotypes?

   A. *RRYY × rryy*

   B. *RrYy × rryy*

   C. *RrYy × Rryy*

   D. *RrYy × RrYy*

   E. *Rryy × Rryy*

53. Two sympatric species of pine trees release their pollen during different months. This is an example of

 A. habitat isolation

 B. temporal isolation

 C. behavioral isolation

 D. mechanical isolation

 E. geographic isolation

54. Kangaroo rats live in desert habitats. Which of the following physiological or behavioral adaptations increases their survival in this hot and dry environment?

 A. Frequent drinking

 B. Frequent urination

 C. Nephrons with long loops of Henle

 D. Numerous sweat glands in their skin

 E. Diurnal activity

55. During cellular respiration, ATP is generated by all of the following EXCEPT:

 A. glycolysis

 B. oxidative phosphorylation

 C. the Calvin-Benson cycle

 D. biochemical pathways occurring in the cytoplasm

 E. biochemical pathways occurring in the mitochondria

56. Which of the following is correct about diastolic blood pressure?

 A. It is generated by contraction of the ventricles.

 B. It is measured in the veins.

 C. It is the pressure determined using a sphygmomanometer that is recorded when the sounds of Korotkoff disappear.

 D. It is measured in cubic centimeters per second (cc/sec).

 E. It increases as an individual becomes more physically fit.

57. The size of a population of mice on an isolated island has remained constant for 50 years. What is the average number of offspring that each breeding pair produce during their lifetime that survive to reproductive maturity and reproduce?

 A. 0

 B. 1

 C. 2

 D. 10 to 20

 E. More than 20

58. The frequency of individuals better able to survive in a new habitat increases in a population over time. The best explanation for this is

 A. mutation

 B. natural selection

 C. genetic drift

 D. gene flow

 E. the founder effect

GO ON TO THE NEXT PAGE

59. Mature xylem tissue is characterized by

    A. companion cells
    B. dead cells
    C. plasmodesmata
    D. sieve-tube members
    E. the secretion of a cuticle

60. Which of the following is produced by the corpus luteum?

    A. Progesterone and estrogen
    B. Progesterone and follicle stimulating hormone
    C. Follicle stimulating hormone (FSH) and luteinizing hormone (LH)
    D. Estrogen and luteinizing hormone (LH)
    E. Progesterone and gonadotropin releasing hormone (GnRH)

61. All of the following are end products of the light-dependent reactions of photosynthesis EXCEPT:

    A. NADPH
    B. ATP
    C. O_2
    D. H^+
    E. $C_6H_{12}O_6$

62. An experiment to replicate the production of organic molecules in an environment similar to earth's environment before life appeared would require all of the following EXCEPT:

    A. ammonia gas
    B. carbon dioxide gas
    C. oxygen gas
    D. ultraviolet light
    E. water vapor

63. Which of the following is the dominant reaction as blood flows through the pulmonary capillaries? (Hb = hemoglobin)

    A. $H_2CO_3 \rightarrow H^+ + HCO_3$
    B. $H_2O + CO_2 \rightarrow H_2CO_3$
    C. $Hb + 4CO_2 \rightarrow Hb(CO_2)_4$
    D. $Hb(O_2)_4 \rightarrow Hb + 4O_2$
    E. $Hb + 4O_2 \rightarrow Hb(O_2)_4$

64. If A represents a dominant allele and a represents the recessive allele, what are the genotypes of parents that produce 300 progeny with the dominant trait and 100 progeny with the recessive trait?

    A. $AA \times AA$
    B. $AA \times Aa$
    C. $AA \times aa$
    D. $Aa \times aa$
    E. $Aa \times Aa$

65. Which of the following is true about the vascular cambium?

   A. The vascular cambium transports sugars.

   B. The vascular cambium transports water and solutes.

   C. Secondary growth of the vascular cambium produces xylem and phloem cells.

   D. Cells of the vascular cambium are connected by plasmodesmata.

   E. The vascular cambium constitutes the sapwood of the plant.

66. All of the following are effective in lowering body temperature in mammals EXCEPT:

   A. large ears

   B. sweating

   C. panting

   D. decreased muscular activity

   E. decreased blood flow to extremities

67. In C_3 plants, the enzyme that incorporates CO_2 into an organic molecule is

   A. helicase

   B. PEP carboxylase

   C. RuBP carboxylase

   D. carboxypeptidase

   E. pyruvate decarboxylase

68. A function of the allantois is to

   A. form the amniotic cavity

   B. fuse with the endometrium and form the placenta

   C. develop into the nervous system

   D. store food for use by the developing embryo

   E. store or dispose of wastes from the developing embryo

69. "Primers" that initiate DNA replication consist of

   A. RNA nucleotides

   B. DNA nucleotides

   C. Okazaki fragments

   D. DNA polymerase

   E. nucleosomes

70. Secondary growth in angiosperms

   A. produces woody tissue

   B. occurs in the apical meristem

   C. increases the height of a plant

   D. increases the length of roots

   E. generates root hairs

GO ON TO THE NEXT PAGE

71. Four genes, *A*, *B*, *C*, and *D*, occur on the same chromosome. Use the following crossover frequencies to determine the order of the genes on the chromosome.

Genes	Crossover Frequency
A and *D*	5%
B and *C*	15%
A and *C*	30%
C and *D*	35%
B and *D*	50%

    A. BCAD

    B. CBDA

    C. BACD

    D. CDAB

    E. CBAD

72. The products of the Krebs cycle include

    A. ATP, NADH, $FADH_2$, CO_2

    B. ATP, NAD^+, FAD, CO_2

    C. ATP, H_2O, O_2

    D. ADP, CO_2, H_2O

    E. NADH, FAD^+, CO_2

73. Which of the following correctly describes plasmids?

    A. They are composed only of RNA.

    B. They are composed of RNA and protein.

    C. They are DNA segments in the chromosomes of bacteria.

    D. They are the DNA cores of viruses.

    E. They can be transferred between bacteria during conjugation.

74. A man and a woman have blood types A and B, respectively. Both have one parent with O blood type. What is the probability that the man and woman have a child with O blood type?

    A. 0%

    B. 25%

    C. 50%

    D. 75%

    E. 100%

Directions: Questions below consist of a phrase or sentence. Each question is preceded by five lettered choices. Select the one lettered choice that best matches the phrase or sentence. Each lettered choice may be used once, more than once, or not at all.

Questions 75–76

A. Cellulose

B. Glycogen

C. Glucagon

D. Guanine

E. Phospholipid

75. A hormone involved in the maintenance of blood sugar levels

76. A nitrogen base found in DNA

Questions 77–79

A. Neurulation

B. Cleavage

C. Fertilization

D. Organogenesis

E. Gastrulation

77. Forms the morula

78. Begins the formation of the three primary germ layers

79. Begins at the primitive streak

Questions 80–83

A. Genetic drift

B. Coevolution

C. Character displacement

D. Sexual selection

E. Kin selection

80. Two species of finches living on separate islands have beaks of the same size. On one island where both species live together, beak sizes are different.

GO ON TO THE NEXT PAGE

81. In an ant colony, sterile sisters are workers who maintain the nest and provide care for their reproducing mother, the queen.

82. A devastating blizzard dramatically reduces the size of a population and results in the disappearance of several alleles from the gene pool.

83. In many animal species, males and females look different.

Question 84

Question 84 refers to the following diagram.

84. All of the following are true about the molecule above EXCEPT:

  A. The molecule releases energy and forms ADP + P_i.

  B. High-energy bonds are located at positions A and B.

  C. A polymer made of these molecules is an energy-storage molecule in cells.

  D. The molecule can provide energy for muscle contraction.

  E. Part of this molecule describes the structure of an RNA nucleotide.

Questions 85–87

Questions 85–87 refer to the following graph.

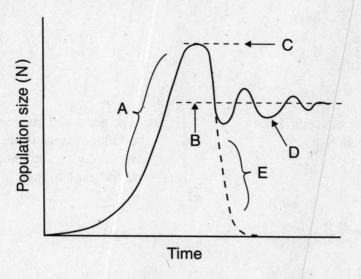

85. The closest approximation to the biotic potential of this population

86. The carrying capacity of the habitat for this population

87. The effect of density-dependent limiting factors on this population

Questions 88–89

Questions 88–89 refer to a cell with a diploid chromosome number of 8.

    A. 2

    B. 4

    C. 8

    D. 16

    E. 32

88. How many chromosomes would be present in a cell at anaphase of mitosis?

89. How many chromosomes would be present in each daughter cell at the end of telophase II of meiosis?

GO ON TO THE NEXT PAGE

Questions 90–91

A. Angiosperms

B. Ferns

C. Green algae

D. Gymnosperms

E. Mosses

90. The development of seeds is not protected inside an ovary.

91. The gametophyte generation is the dominant stage of the life cycle, and the sporophyte generation remains attached to the gametophyte.

Questions 92–93

A. Polyploidy

B. Deletion

C. Substitution

D. Frameshift mutation

E. Inversion

92. A change in the gene sequence from *ABCDEF* . . . to *ADCBEF* . . .

93. A change in the DNA sequence from *ATCAGTC* . . . to *ATCAAGTC.* . .

Directions: Questions below involve data from experiments or laboratory analyses. In each case, study the information provided. Then choose the one best answer for each question.

Questions 94–96

Questions 94–96 refer to the following diagram, where a dialysis bag, filled with a solution of sucrose and glucose, is placed in a beaker containing a solution of fructose, glucose, and sucrose. Dialysis tubing will allow fructose and glucose, but not sucrose, to pass through.

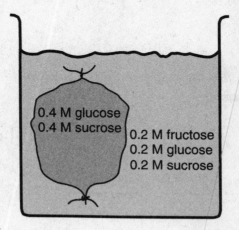

0.4 M glucose
0.4 M sucrose

0.2 M fructose
0.2 M glucose
0.2 M sucrose

94. When the dialysis bag is placed into the beaker, there will be a net movement of

  A. glucose from the dialysis bag into the beaker solution

  B. sucrose from the dialysis bag into the beaker solution

  C. fructose from the dialysis bag into the beaker solution

  D. glucose from the beaker solution into the dialysis bag

  E. sucrose from the beaker solution into the dialysis bag

95. After the dialysis bag is allowed to remain in the beaker for 24 hours,

  A. the solution inside the dialysis bag will be hypotonic relative to the solution outside the bag

  B. the concentration inside and outside the dialysis bag will be equal for each solute

  C. the volume of water in the beaker will increase

  D. the dialysis bag will become flaccid

  E. the dialysis bag will become turgid

GO ON TO THE NEXT PAGE

96. Which of the following processes occurs during the 24-hour period after the dialysis bag is put into the beaker?

   A. Diffusion and plasmolysis

   B. Facilitated diffusion and osmosis

   C. Osmosis and active transport

   D. Osmosis and dialysis

   E. Osmosis and plasmolysis

Questions 97–99

Questions 97–99 refer to the following pedigree. Filled boxes or filled circles indicate the inheritance of a biochemical disorder.

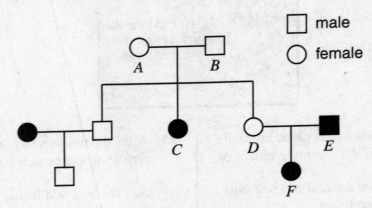

97. The disorder illustrated in the pedigree is probably inherited as

   A. an autosomal dominant allele

   B. an autosomal recessive allele

   C. an X-linked dominant allele

   D. an X-linked recessive allele

   E. a Y-linked dominant allele

98. The best explanation for the inheritance of the disorder in individual *F* is that she received

   A. an allele for the disorder only from her mother

   B. an allele for the disorder only from her father

   C. alleles for the disorder from both parents

   D. two alleles for the disorder from her mother

   E. two alleles for the disorder from her father

99. Which of the following is the probability of the disorder appearing in the next offspring from *D* and *E*?

    A. 0%

    B. 25%

    C. 50%

    D. 75%

    E. 100%

Question 100

Question 100 refers to the following diagram of a DNA segment.

$$\downarrow$$
$$5'\text{-}TCTCGACT\text{-}3'$$
$$3'\text{-}AGAGCTGA\text{-}5'$$
$$\uparrow$$

100. Arrows in the above diagram show the cleavage points for the restriction enzyme *Taq*I. Which of the following describes the correct DNA segments produced after treatment with the restriction enzyme?

    (A) two fragments: 5'-TCT   CGACT-3'
                        3'-AGAGC and TGA-5'

    (B) two fragments: 5'-TCTCGACT-3' and 3'-AGAGCTGA-5'

    (C) two fragments: 5'-TCTCGTGA-3' and 3'-AGAGCACT-5'

    (D) four fragments: 5'-TCT, 3'-AGAGC, CGACT-3', and TGA-5'

    (E) four fragments: 5'-TCTCG, ACT-3', 3'-AGAGC, and TGA-5'

GO ON TO THE NEXT PAGE

Questions 101–103

Questions 101–103 refer to the following graph that shows the changes in electrical potential across the membrane of a nerve cell during the transmission of a nerve impulse.

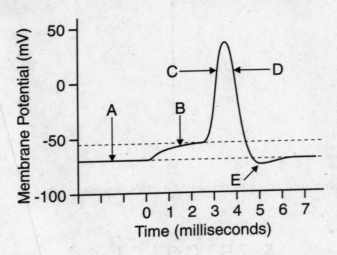

101. Refractory period

102. Resting potential of the neuron

103. Net movement of K^+ out of the neuron

Questions 104–106

Questions 104–106 refer to the following graph of an immune response.

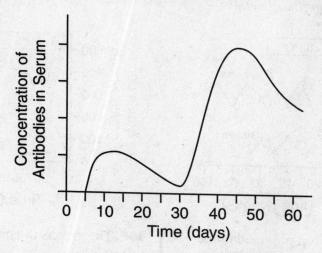

104. The action of the immune system at day 5 is most likely in response to the introduction of

    A. an antibiotic

    B. an antibody

    C. an antigen

    D. an immunoglobulin

    E. a major histocompatibility complex molecule

105. The immune response indicated at day 5 in the graph is most likely produced by the action of

    A. B cells

    B. T cells

    C. cytotoxic T cells

    D. helper T cells

    E. macrophages

106. If the immune responses at day 5 and day 30 are reactions to the same substance, the likely source of antibodies at day 30 are

    A. cytotoxic T cells

    B. erythrocytes

    C. interleukins

    D. memory cells

    E. macrophages

GO ON TO THE NEXT PAGE

Questions 107–108

Questions 107–108 refer to the following graphs that plot changes in population density for two species of Tribolium flour beetles.

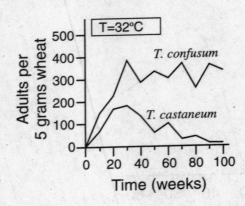

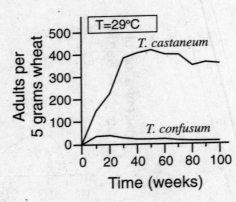

107. From the information provided in the graphs, the factor most responsible for differences in population size between *Tribolium confusum* and *T. castaneum* after 100 weeks is the

   A.   amount of flour available

   B.   more aggressive nature of *T. castaneum*

   C.   temperature

   D.   initial population size of *T. castaneum*

   E.   initial population size of *T. confusum*

108. The graphs illustrate the concept of

   A.   succession

   B.   competitive exclusion

   C.   commensalism

   D.   mutualism

   E.   predation

Questions 109–110

Questions 109–110 refer to the following graph that shows the relationship between CO_2 uptake by leaves and the concentrations of O_2 and CO_2 in growth chambers.

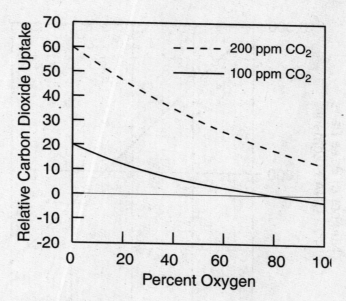

109. According to the graph, relative CO_2 uptake increases as O_2 concentration decreases. This can best be explained by which of the following?

   A. O_2 is not necessary for photosynthesis.

   B. As O_2 concentration decreases, CO_2 increases.

   C. As O_2 concentration increases, CO_2 decreases.

   D. O_2 competes with CO_2 for RuBP carboxylase activity.

   E. A higher concentration of O_2 causes an increase in the relative CO_2 uptake.

110. In the graph above, a relative CO_2 uptake less than zero is an indication that

   A. more CO_2 is being consumed in the leaf than the leaf is absorbing from the growth chamber atmosphere

   B. more CO_2 is being absorbed from the growth chamber atmosphere than is needed by the leaf

   C. the plant is a C_4 plant

   D. the plant is a CAM plant

   E. cellular respiration is taking place in the leaf cells

GO ON TO THE NEXT PAGE

Questions 111–112

Questions 111–112 refer to the following semilog graph of results from a gel electrophoresis procedure.

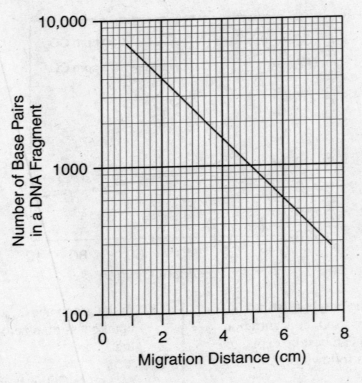

111. What is the relationship between migration distance and DNA fragment size?

    A. Migration distance is independent of DNA fragment size.

    B. Longer DNA fragments travel a greater distance than shorter fragments.

    C. Migration distance is inversely proportional to the fragment size.

    D. Migration distance is directly proportional to the fragment size.

    E. The heavier the fragment size, the greater the migration distance.

112. According to the graph, approximately how far will a DNA fragment with 3000 base pairs travel on the gel?

    A. 1.0 cm

    B. 2.0 cm

    C. 2.3 cm

    D. 2.6 cm

    E. 5.0 cm

Question 113

DNA material from each of four individuals was treated with a restriction enzyme. The products were separated using gel electrophoresis. The results, which show relative migration distances for DNA fragments from each individual, are given below.

Individual 1   Individual 2   Individual 3   Individual 4

113. Which of the following is a correct interpretation of the gel electrophoresis data?

A. All four individuals could be the same person.

B. Individual 3 could be an offspring of individuals 2 and 4.

C. Individual 2 could be an offspring of individuals 1 and 3.

D. Individual 1 could be an offspring of individuals 2 and 3.

E. Individual 1 could be an offspring of individuals 3 and 4.

GO ON TO THE NEXT PAGE

Questions 114–117

Questions 114–117 refer to the following experiment:

An experiment was conducted to determine if light and chloroplasts are necessary for photosynthesis. To detect photosynthesis, DPIP, an electron acceptor, was used. DPIP is blue in its oxidized state but turns clear when reduced. That is, when electrons from photosynthesis are transferred to DPIP, the blue solution (oxidized DPIP) turns clear (reduced DPIP). A spectrophotometer measures the degree to which the blue solution becomes clear. (The clearer the solution, the greater its transmittance.) Assume that the ability of DPIP to accept electrons is not affected by heat.

Three groups, each containing four solutions, were tested in the experiment. All solutions contained chloroplasts and DPIP. Four solutions in the first group were each exposed to light for 0, 5, 10, and 15 minutes, respectively. Four solutions in the second group were each kept in darkness for 0, 5, 10, and 15 minutes, respectively. Four solutions in the third group were each boiled before being exposed to light for 0, 5, 10, and 15 minutes, respectively. The graph below shows the results of the experiment.

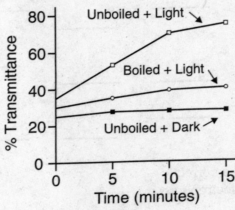

114. It is reasonable to conclude from the data in the graph that the percent transmittance for boiled solutions remained low because

    A. DPIP was inactivated by boiling

    B. the spectrophotometer was set to the wrong frequency of light

    C. chloroplasts were inactivated by boiling

    D. either DPIP, or chloroplasts, or both were inactivated by boiling

    E. the solutions became clear

115. From the data in the graph, it is reasonable to conclude that

    A. neither light nor chloroplasts are required for photosynthesis

    B. only light is required for photosynthesis

    C. only chloroplasts are required for photosynthesis

    D. both light and chloroplasts are required for photosynthesis

    E. the amount of light produced increases with time

116. Which of the following is correct?

A.   It is reasonable to conclude that light absorbance is maximum at 400 nm.

B.   It is reasonable to conclude that light absorbance is maximum at 500 nm.

C.   It is reasonable to conclude that light absorbance is maximum at 600 nm.

D.   It is reasonable to conclude that light absorbance is maximum at 700 nm.

E.   The frequency for maximum light absorbance cannot be determined from the data provided.

117. The dependent variable measured in this experiment is the

A.   percent transmittance through the solutions

B.   time exposed to light

C.   amount of photosynthesis taking place

D.   presence or absence of chloroplasts

E.   frequency of light to which the solutions were exposed

Questions 118–120

Questions 118–120 refer to the following graphs. The graphs present the frequency of size classes for mandible lengths for two species of ants at site A and two species of ants at site B.

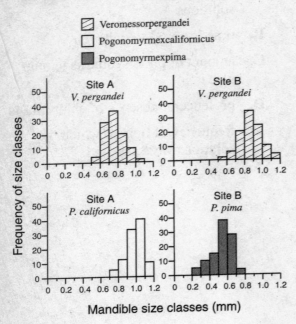

119. According to the data given in the graphs, which of the following statements is correct?

    A. The distribution of mandible size for *V. pergandei* differs between Site A and Site B.

    B. The distribution of mandible size for *P. pima* differs between Site A and Site B.

    C. The distribution of mandible size for *P. californicus* differs between Site A and Site B.

    D. The distribution of mandible size for *P. californicus* is about the same at both sites A and B.

    E. *V. pergandei* exists only at site A.

118. According to these data, the most common size class of mandibles among ants of the species *P. pima* is

    A. 0.4–0.5 mm

    B. 0.5–0.6 mm

    C. 0.6–0.7 mm

    D. 0.7–0.8 mm

    E. 1.0– 1.1 mm

120. The data in the graphs best represent the concept of

    A. succession

    B. competitive exclusion

    C. character displacement

    D. mutualism

    E. intraspecific competition

IF YOU FINISH BEFORE TIME IS CALLED, CHECK YOUR WORK ON THIS SECTION ONLY. DO NOT WORK ON ANY OTHER SECTION IN THE TEST.

Section II (Free-Response Questions)

Time: 1 hour and 30 minutes

4 questions

Directions: Answer the questions below as completely and as thoroughly as time permits. Answer the questions in essay form (NOT outline form), using complete sentences. You may use diagrams to supplement your answers, but a diagram alone without appropriate discussion is inadequate.

Use a black or blue ink pen to write your answers. To save time, you may correct errors by crossing out rather than by erasing.

Answer all four questions. Since each question has equal weight, you should allocate your time so that you spend approximately 22 minutes on each question.

1. The results below are measurements of dissolved oxygen obtained from water samples collected at various depths in a fresh-water lake. Temperatures of samples do not differ significantly.

Table 16-1				
Depth (meters)	Daytime Measurements (ml O$_2$/L)		Nighttime Measurements (ml O$_2$/L)	
	8 A.M.	4 P.M.	8 P.M.	4 A.M.
0	6.0	18.0	16.0	8.0
0.5	4.0	14.0	13.0	6.0
1	3.0	11.0	10.0	4.0
2	2.0	7.0	6.0	1.0
2.5	1.0	5.0	5.0	0.5

(a.) Using the graph grid provided, draw a graph showing how the amount of oxygen gained during the period from 8 A.M. to 4 P.M. varies with the depth of the collected sample. On the same set of axes, draw a graph showing how the amount of oxygen lost during the period from 8 P.M. to 4 A.M. varies with the depth of the collected sample.

GO ON TO THE NEXT PAGE

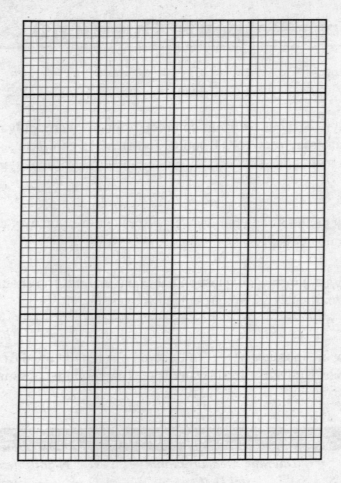

(b.) Calculate the gross productivity, net productivity, and respiratory rate for the water sample collected *at the lake surface*. Use the following formulas:

$$\text{gross productivity} = \frac{\text{daytime O}_2 \text{ increase}}{\text{time}} + \frac{\text{nighttime O}_2 \text{ decrease}}{\text{time}}$$

$$\text{net productivity} = \frac{\text{daytime O}_2 \text{ increase}}{\text{time}}$$

$$\text{respiration rate} = \frac{\text{nighttime O}_2 \text{ decrease}}{\text{time}}$$

(c.) Account for differences in oxygen levels between daytime and nighttime measurements made at the same lake depth.

(d.) Account for differences in oxygen levels measured at different lake depths.

2. Photosynthesis is a biochemical pathway in plants that converts light energy to chemical energy.

   (a.) Describe the light reactions of photosynthesis.

   (b.) Describe the process of CO_2 fixation in C_3 plants.

   (c.) Describe how CO_2 fixation differs in C_4 plants. Describe the benefits of the C_4 pathway as compared to those of the C_3 pathway.

3. Discuss how each of the following contributes to evolutionary change.

   (a.) A geographic barrier

   (b.) Nonrandom mating

   (c.) Polyploidy

   (d.) Genetic drift

4. Discuss how each of the following affects or contributes to the process of contraction in a striated muscle.

   (a.) Acetylcholine

   (b.) O_2

   (c.) Ca^{2+}

   (d.) A decrease in the pH of the blood

IF YOU FINISH BEFORE TIME IS CALLED, CHECK YOUR WORK ON THIS SECTION ONLY. DO NOT WORK ON ANY OTHER SECTION IN THE TEST.

STOP

Answer Key for the Practice Test

Section I (Multiple-Choice Questions)

1. D		29. B	
2. B		30. B	
3. B		31. C	
4. E		32. B	
5. D		33. E	
6. C		34. C	
7. A		35. A	
8. B		36. D	
9. A		37. A	
10. D		38. D	
11. D		39. C	
12. E		40. A	
13. E		41. D	
14. B		42. D	
15. D		43. A	
16. B		44. B	
17. E		45. E	
18. B		46. A	
19. A		47. D	
20. B		48. B	
21. A		49. B	
22. E		50. C	
23. D		51. B	
24. E		52. C	
25. E		53. B	
26. A		54. C	
27. E		55. C	
28. A		56. C	

57. C
58. B
59. B
60. A
61. E
62. C
63. E
64. E
65. C
66. E
67. C
68. E
69. A
70. A
71. A
72. A
73. E
74. B
75. C
76. D
77. B
78. E
79. E
80. C
81. E
82. A
83. D
84. C
85. A
86. B
87. D
88. D
89. B

90. D
91. E
92. E
93. D
94. A
95. E
96. D
97. B
98. C
99. C
100. A
101. E
102. A
103. D
104. C
105. A
106. D
107. C
108. B
109. D
110. E
111. C
112. D
113. C
114. C
115. D
116. E
117. A
118. B
119. A
120. C

Section II (Free-Response Questions)

Guidelines for scoring your essay answers begin following the answers and explanations for the practice test.

Scoring Your Practice Test

Section I (Multiple-Choice Questions)

Number of questions you answered correctly: _____ × 1 = _____
Number of questions you answered wrong: _____ × ¼ = -_____*
Number of questions you left unanswered: _____ × 0 = __0__
TOTAL for Section 1 (0–120 points): = _____**
(subtract number wrong from number correct)

*Round to nearest whole number.
**If less than zero, enter zero.

Section II (Free-Response Questions)

Score for essay 1 (0–10 points): _____
Score for essay 2 (0–10 points): _____
Score for essay 3 (0–10 points): _____
Score for essay 4 (0–10 points): _____
TOTAL for Section II (0–40 points): _____

Combined Score (Sections I + II)

Total for Section I (from above): _____ × 0.75 = _____
(60% of 150 points = 90 points maximum)
Total for Section II (from above): _____ × 1.5 = _____
(40% of 150 points = 60 points maximum)
COMBINED SCORE (add Sections I and II): _____
(0-150 points)

Probable AP Grade	
Combined Score	AP Grade
94–150	5
73–93	4
54–72	3
34–53	2
0–33	1

Answers and Explanations for The Practice Test

Section I (Multiple-Choice Questions)

1. **D.** The main function of the large intestine is the absorption of water to form feces.

2. **B.** Facilitated diffusion is passive transport (transport with no energy expended) that occurs by specialized transport proteins in plasma membranes. Active transport requires energy (ATP).

3. **B.** DNA replication generates a second chromatid for each chromosome during interphase (specifically, the S phase of the cell cycle).

4. **E.** Adenine is not found in amino acids. However, it is the nitrogen base found in RNA, DNA, ATP, ADP, AMP, and cAMP (cyclic AMP).

5. **D.** The *lac* operon in bacteria regulates gene expression by turning on or off the production of a repressor protein. The repressor protein, in turn, occupies the operator region of the operon, blocking transcription of the structural gene for lactase. When the sugar lactose is available, it inactivates the repressor protein, thereby allowing transcription of the structural gene for lactase. Lactase is then produced, and lactose digestion proceeds.

6. **C.** Food storage in seeds occurs in either the cotyledons or the endosperm.

7. **A.** The endosperm, a nutrient storage tissue in seeds, forms from the union of the two polar nuclei in the embryo sac with one of the sperm nuclei. Thus, the endosperm is triploid (*3n*), and has both a maternal and paternal origin.

8. **B.** Progesterone (and estrogen) stimulate the thickening of the endometrium in preparation for implantation of a fertilized egg.

9. **A.** Viruses contain either RNA or DNA, and bacteria contain both. Only viruses have a protein coat. Prokaryotes, but not viruses, have ribosomes and a plasma membrane. Most prokaryotes have a cell wall made from peptidoglycan.

10. **D.** A pair of homologous chromosomes contributes one homologue to each haploid daughter cell. For example, the homologous pair A_1/A_2 contributes A_1 to one gamete, and A_2 to a second gamete. When each of the four pairs of chromosomes contributes one homologue, each gamete has one homologue of each homologous pair.

11. **D.** A metabolic reaction that synthesizes smaller molecules into larger molecules is anabolic. Answer **D** describes the process of photosynthesis in which glucose, $C_6H_{12}O_6$, is assembled. The remaining answer choices describe catabolic reactions where molecules are broken into smaller molecules.

12. **E.** The sun is the driving force for transpiration. The tension in xylem tissues generated by transpiration causes water molecules, held together by cohesion (from hydrogen bonding), to rise.

13. **E.** Photosynthetic pigments absorb light energy by boosting ("exciting") electrons to orbitals of higher potential energy. Because the pigment molecules have different molecular structures, they have different molecular weights and different solubilities in solvents. In a

chromatographic analysis, R_f values (which indicate the relative distance of pigment migration in a solvent front) differ because each pigment interacts differently with the solvent and the chromatography media (paper or gel).

14. **B.** Aphids feed on sugar solutions which are transported through the phloem. The transport of sugar through phloem, according to the pressure-flow hypothesis, occurs by bulk flow forced forward by hydrostatic pressure. Because of this pressure, fluid is forced entirely through the aphid's digestive tract.

15. **D.** The processed mRNA found in the cytoplasm codes directly for the protein. However, the unprocessed mRNA transcript found in the nucleus contains introns that interfere with translation. Similarly, if the protein's DNA segment is introduced into bacteria, the mRNA produced from the DNA will contain introns that the bacteria will be unable to remove.

16. **B.** Acetylcholine is one of several neurotransmitters that transmit action potentials across synaptic gaps. Others include norepinephrine, dopamine, and serotonin.

17. **E.** Arthropods have an open circulatory system. All arthropods have body segmentation, jointed appendages, a true coelom, and an exoskeleton made with chitin.

18. **B.** Both prokaryotes and eukaryotes have DNA and ribosomes. All prokaryotes lack endoplasmic reticulum, Golgi complexes, mitochondria, chloroplasts, and nuclear envelopes. In addition, the structure of prokaryotic cell walls (when present) and flagella differ markedly from eukaryotes.

19. **A.** A population is a group of organisms all of the same species.

20. **B.** Chemoreceptors in the carotid arteries monitor the pH of the blood. When CO_2 dissolves in the blood, it forms HCO_3^- and H^+, *decreasing* the blood's pH. When the blood becomes more acidic (a decrease in pH), respiratory rate increases.

21. **A.** Since the disease is inherited as a sex-linked recessive, the male must be $X^n Y$, where N = normal and n = muscular dystrophy. Since he can inherit the Y chromosome only from his father, the X^n chromosome is inherited from his mother.

22. **E.** The Golgi complex modifies proteins by changing their length or by adding lipids to them to form glycoproteins. The products are packaged into vesicles, some of which remain in the cell as storage vessels, while others merge with the cell membrane for export during exocytosis.

23. **D.** Succession is the change in composition of communities over time. Because the lake occupies a region previously occupied by living things, the process is termed secondary succession. In an area devoid of previous habitation by living things, such as on a newly formed volcanic island or newly exposed granite after a glacier retreat, the process is termed primary succession.

24. **E.** When a community occupies a region, it changes it in some way. For example, soil character, light availability, or the density of organisms may change. After a period of time, the features that originally made the area a successful habitat for the resident community no longer prevail. Instead, the habitat is more suitable for other species. When this occurs, the resident species cannot compete with immigrant species that are more competitive under the new environmental conditions.

25. E. During transcription, the C, G, A, and T nucleotides of the DNA base-pair with G, C, U, and A nucleotides, respectively, for the RNA.

26. A. In punctuated equilibrium, evolutionary history consists of geologically long periods of little or no evolution, interrupted by short periods of rapid evolution. In contrast, gradual accumulations of small evolutionary events over long periods of geologic time depict the pattern of phyletic gradualism.

27. E. Indoleacetic acid, an auxin, stimulates growth in most plant tissues by increasing cell wall plasticity. When cell walls are relaxed in this way, water entering by osmosis causes the cell to elongate.

28. A. Photolysis of water provides electrons which are energized by light energy in photosystems I and II.

29. B. The woman is a carrier ($X^N X^n$) because she inherits the allele for hemophilia (n) from her father ($X^n Y$). The progeny of a carrier woman and a normal man ($X^N Y$) are $\frac{1}{4} X^N X^N$ + $\frac{1}{4} X^N X^n$ + $\frac{1}{4} X^N Y$ + $\frac{1}{4} X^n Y$.

30. B. At the fourteen-minute mark (not the four-minute mark), when the concentrations of A + B and C + D remain constant, the reaction has reached equilibrium. At this point, the rate at which A + B converts to C + D is equal to the rate that C + D converts to A + B.

31. C. Members of the phylum Cnidaria, which includes hydrozoans, jellyfish, and sea anemones, have radial symmetry.

32. B. The thick protein filaments of myosin form cross-bridges that attach to the thin filament of actin protein.

33. E. The notochord is a stiff rod that provides body support in lower chordates. In higher chordates, the notochord disappears during development. Nearby cells in the mesoderm layer form the vertebrae. The central nervous system develops from the neural tube that forms from the ectoderm.

34. C. Protons are pumped from the matrix to the outer compartment of the mitochondria (the intermembrane space between the cristae membrane and the outer mitochondrial membrane). As a result, H^+ concentration increases in the outer compartment, creating a pH and electrochemical gradient.

35. A. Since $q^2 = .81$, then $q = 0.9$, and $p = 1 - q = 0.1$ and $p^2 = 0.01$, or 1%. These frequencies will continue as long as the population is in Hardy-Weinberg equilibrium.

36. D. The plant description given in the question is that of a pea plant, a dicot angiosperm. In contrast, a monocot plant, such as a corn plant, would have leaves with parallel veins and vascular bundles scattered in the stems. Ferns, mosses, and pines do not produce fruit.

37. A. The blastopore, formed during gastrulation, is the opening to the archenteron. In deuterostomes, it develops into the anus, while in protostomes, it develops into the mouth.

38. D. The bottom tier of a pyramid is always occupied by a producer. Diatoms are algae upon which primary consumers, such as crustaceans, feed. In turn, secondary consumers, such as squid, feed on the primary consumers. At the top of the pyramid are the top carnivores (sharks, in this question).

39. C. Three consecutive RNA nucleotides on the mRNA (a codon) code for a particular amino acid. A series of codons, then, determines the amino acid sequence of a protein.

40. A. Cellulose is the major constituent in the cell walls of plants and many fungi. The plasma membrane consists mostly of proteins and cholesterol molecules embedded in a phospholipid bilayer (fluid-mosaic model). Recognition proteins have oligosaccharides attached to them.

41. D. Roundworms (nematodes) have a pseudocoelom.

42. D. Since Turner syndrome individuals have only one X chromosome, a Barr body (an inactive second X chromosome) does not form. Turner syndrome results when nondisjunction produces a gamete missing a sex chromosome. The union of this gamete with a normal egg or sperm bearing an X chromosome produces a Turner syndrome zygote.

43. A. Proteins are too large to pass through the capillary walls and into the Bowman's capsule.

44. B. Commensalism occurs when one species benefits from a living relationship with another species but the second species is neither helped nor harmed by the first species.

45. E. Allopatric speciation may occur when reproductive isolation results from a geographic barrier. A new species emerges when the two populations of mice are unable to successfully interbreed after the barrier is removed.

46. A. When oxygen is absent, yeasts perform fermentation. Fermentation regenerates the NAD^+ (from NADH) needed for glycolysis. Glycolysis produces a net of 2 ATP. If O_2 is present, oxidative photophosphorylation in aerobic respiration regenerates the NAD^+.

47. D. Two forms of phytochromes, P_r (P_{660}) and P_{fr} (P_{730}), are involved. The amount of P_r that accumulates at night measures the length of night, and indirectly, the length of daytime.

48. B. A bacteriophage is a virus that attacks bacteria.

49. B. Lysosomes contain enzymes that digest food and cellular debris.

50. C. Imprinting is a form of innate behavior in which a specific behavior is acquired only if an appropriate stimulus is provided during a limited period of time (critical period). Goslings and other birds will follow the first moving object they see after birth. At the end of the critical period of about two days, however, the ability to imprint is lost.

51. B. Cells of the palisade mesophyll are specialized for photosynthesis. In C_4 plants, the Calvin-Benson cycle pathway of photosynthesis occurs in the bundle sheath cells, but C_4 plants are relatively rare, making up less than 0.4% of all flowering plants.

52. C. $Rr \times Rr$ produces 3/4 round and ¼ wrinkled seeds, and $Yy \times yy$ produces ½ yellow and ½ green. Thus, $RrYy \times Rryy$ produces the ¼ wrinkled and ½ yellow.

53. B. Temporal isolation occurs when two species reproduce at different times.

54. C. Water conservation is achieved by concentrating the urine. The long loop of Henle allows for a very high concentration of solutes in the interstitial fluids surrounding the collecting duct of the nephron. As a result, more water leaves the collecting duct, concentrating the urine as much as three times that of humans. Water is also conserved by reducing evaporation (no sweat glands in skin, narrow nasal passage, and nocturnal activity).

Answers

55. **C.** The Calvin-Benson cycle occurs in photosynthesis, not respiration. Glycolysis generates ATP in the cytoplasm, while oxidative phosphorylation and the Krebs cycle generate ATP in the mitochondria.

56. **C.** When one takes blood pressure with a sphygmomanometer, the sounds of Korotkoff (tapping sounds) are heard in the arteries as the cuff pressure is deflated. Systolic and diastolic pressures are indicated when the sounds of Korotkoff begin and end, respectively. Diastolic pressure is the pressure of blood in the arteries when the ventricles are relaxed. It is measured in mm Hg.

57. **C.** Because the population size remains constant, each breeding pair must leave two offspring, replacing the two parents that produce them.

58. **B.** Natural selection promotes traits (adaptations) that increase an individual's ability to survive and reproduce in its environment.

59. **B.** Mature xylem cells are dead. Companion cells, sieve-tube members, and plasmodesmata are associated with phloem cells. Epidermal cells secrete a cuticle.

60. **A.** FSH and LH are produced by the anterior pituitary, and GnRH is produced by the hypothalamus.

61. **E.** Glucose, $C_6H_{12}O_6$, is the end-product of the Calvin-Benson cycle ("dark reaction").

62. **C.** Little or no oxygen gas was present in the primordial atmosphere.

63. **E.** Blood travels to the lungs through the pulmonary artery, flows through the lungs within the pulmonary capillaries, and returns to the heart through the pulmonary veins. Oxygen molecules in the lungs pass through the capillary walls and enter the red blood cells. Inside the red blood cells, an O_2 attaches to each of the four hemoglobin chains of a single hemoglobin molecule. While oxygen enters the blood stream, CO_2 passes out into alveoli of the lungs. This latter process can be described as $HCO_3^- + H^+ \rightarrow H_2CO_3 \rightarrow CO_2 + H_2O$.

64. **E.** $Aa \times Aa$ produces $\frac{1}{4} AA + \frac{1}{2} Aa + \frac{1}{4} aa$. Thus, 75% (both the AA and Aa genotypes) express the dominant trait and 25% express the recessive trait (aa).

65. **C.** The vascular cambium forms a cylinder of tissue through stems and roots. On the inside of the cylinder, cell divisions produce secondary xylem cells. On the outside of the cylinder, secondary phloem cells are produced. Sugar transport and plasmodesmata are associated with phloem cells. Water and solute transport occur in xylem cells. Secondary xylem tissue that is actively transporting water and solutes makes up the sapwood.

66. **E.** Decreasing blood flow to the extremities *increases* internal body temperature and is a physiological response to cold.

67. **C.** RuBP carboxylase (rubisco) is the enzyme that catalyzes the reaction of CO_2 and RuBP to form PGA (phosphoglycerate).

68. **E.** The allantois is a layer, below the chorion, that encircles the early embryo. During early development, in birds and reptiles, it stores waste products; in mammals it transports wastes to the placenta.

69. **A.** Short segments of RNA nucleotides begin each new DNA complementary segment. Subsequently, the RNA nucleotides are replaced with DNA nucleotides.

70. A. Secondary growth produces woody tissue and increases the girth of a plant. Primary growth occurs in the apical meristem and results in increases in the height of the plant or the length of its roots.

71. A. To map this chromosome, draw a horizontal line with about 15 tick marks. Since the crossover frequencies are in increments of 5%, let each tick mark represent a crossover frequency of 5%. Begin the map by writing an A and D on adjacent tick marks (5%). Use these two genes to map other genes. For example, for the AC frequency, write a C at 6 ticks (30%) to the right and 6 ticks to the left of A. Then check the CD frequency to see which C matches correctly with D. When the map is completed, the gene order should be BCAD or the reverse, DACB. If your first map sequence is not listed in the answer choices, reverse the order and check again.

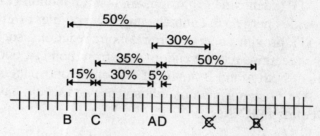

72. A. ATP, NADH, FADH$_2$, and CO$_2$ are produced. The NADH and FADH$_2$ subsequently generate additional ATP in oxidative phosphorylation.

73. E. Plasmids are small, circular segments of DNA in bacteria that exist separately from the bacterial chromosome. They can be transferred between bacteria during conjugation.

74. B. Since both parents have a mother with O blood type, the genotypes of the parents are AO and BO. The probability of having a child with genotype OO is 25% (AO × BO → ¼ AB + ¼ AO + ¼ BO + ¼ OO).

75. C. Glucagon is a hormone secreted by the pancreas that stimulates the liver to break down glycogen into glucose (glycogen hydrolysis) and to release the glucose into the blood.

76. D. Guanine, along with thymine, cytosine, and adenine, are the nitrogen bases that, together with ribose and phosphate, make up nucleotides. Nucleotides are the building blocks of DNA.

77. B. Cleavage describes the rapid cell divisions that begin during the early stages of development. There is very little cell growth between cleavage divisions so that the total volume of the resulting cells is about the same as the original zygote.

78. E. The invagination process of gastrulation produces a gastrula with two germ layers, the ectoderm and the endoderm. Subsequently, the third layer, or mesoderm, forms between these two other layers.

79. E. Gastrulation in birds and most mammals begins with invagination at the primitive streak.

80. C. Interspecific competition results in resource partitioning and character displacement.

Answers

81. **E.** Kin selection occurs when individuals contribute to the survival and reproductive efforts of relatives. By increasing the number of offspring among their relatives, individuals increase the frequency of their own genes in the next generation because relatives share a portion of their genes. By supporting the reproductive effort of the queen, female workers contribute to an increase of the frequency of their genes among sisters.

82. **A.** Genetic drift (random change in allele frequencies) may heavily impact a small population. When a population size is dramatically reduced (a bottleneck), some alleles may be randomly lost.

83. **D.** Sexual selection leads to sexual dimorphism, or differences between males and females.

84. **C.** This molecule, ATP (adenosine triphosphate), is not a monomer component in any polymer used to provide energy. (In contrast, starch, a polymer of glucose, is an energy-storage molecule.) ATP provides energy for metabolic reactions, such as muscle contraction. Most metabolic reactions require energy only from bond A, but some reactions require the breaking of both A and B bonds. If two of the phosphates were removed, this molecule would be AMP (adenosine monophosphate) and would have the same structure as the adenine nucleotide in RNA.

85. **A.** The biotic potential is the maximum growth rate of a population under ideal conditions. This high growth rate often occurs when a small number of individuals begins a new population. When population size is small, there is little competition, and resources are relatively unlimited.

86. **B.** The maximum population size that can be maintained by the habitat is the carrying capacity.

87. **D.** The effects of density-dependent limiting factors, such as competition for food or predation, increase when the population size is large and decrease when the population size is smaller. The result is a fluctuation of the population size around the carrying capacity of the habitat.

88. **D.** At anaphase, the cell contains 16 chromosomes, each consisting of a single chromatid. After cytokinesis, each daughter cell contains 8 chromosomes, each consisting of a single chromatid.

89. **B.** At the end of telophase II, each daughter cell has 4 chromosomes, each consisting of a single chromatid.

90. **D.** The seeds of gymnosperms (conifers) are often called "naked" seeds because they do not develop inside a protective ovary as they do in the angiosperms (flowering plants).

91. **E.** Sperm and egg are produced by the haploid gametophyte, the dominant, leafy form of the moss. After fertilization, the diploid zygote grows out of the gametophyte. In ferns, the sporophyte also grows out of the gametophyte, but the sporophyte stage is dominant.

92. **E.** An inversion occurs when the sequence of a series of genes is reversed.

93. **D.** A frameshift mutation occurs when a nucleotide is inserted into or deleted from the DNA. A frameshift mutation causes all the subsequent nucleotides beyond the insertion or deletion to be displaced one position.

94. A. Glucose will move from the area of higher concentration inside the dialysis bag to a lower concentration outside the bag. There will also be a net movement of fructose into the dialysis bag. Sucrose cannot pass through the membrane.

95. E. After 24 hours, glucose and fructose will diffuse through the dialysis tubing until equilibrium is reached. Since sucrose will remain in the dialysis bag, there will be a higher concentration of solutes inside the bag (the solution in the dialysis bag will be hypertonic relative to the outside). As a result, the dialysis bag becomes turgid as water moves in.

96. D. Osmosis (movement of water) occurs because there is a net movement of water into the dialysis bag. Dialysis (movement of solutes) occurs because there is a net movement of glucose out of the dialysis bag and a net movement of fructose into the bag. These processes are also examples of diffusion. Plasmolysis, the net movement of water *out* of a *cell,* does not occur. Similarly, active transport and facilitated diffusion occur only with specialized proteins in cell membranes.

97. B. Because both parents (*A* and *B*) lack the disorder and one child has the disorder, the best explanation for the inheritance is an autosomal recessive allele. In this case, both parents are heterozygous for the trait and daughter *C* is homozygous recessive ($Nn \times Nn \rightarrow nn$).

98. C. Since the trait is inherited as an autosomal recessive allele, father *E* is homozygous recessive (*nn*). To inherit the disorder, child *F* (*nn*) must inherit an allele from mother *D* as well. Thus, mother *D,* who does not have the disorder, must be *Nn.*

99. C. The probability of the next offspring having the disorder is ½ because $Nn \times nn \rightarrow$ ½ *Nn* (normal) + ½ *nn* (disorder). Note that the probability of inheriting a trait from one set of parents is the same for each offspring and is not influenced by traits inherited by other offspring.

100. A. After treatment with the restriction enzyme, the DNA molecule is cleaved into two double-strand pieces, each bearing a "sticky end" of unpaired nucleotides.

101. E. During the refractory period, Na^+ and K^+ are restored to their normal concentrations inside and outside the plasma membrane by the Na^+/K^+ pump. During this time, the neuron cannot respond to a new stimulus.

102. A. The resting potential is the potential across the plasma membrane of the neuron when no nerve impulse is being transmitted.

103. D. During this phase of the action potential, K^+ is moving out of the neuron. During the previous phase, indicated by B and C, there is a net movement of Na^+ into the neuron.

104. C. An antigen is any substance identified as foreign to the body. Antibody production at day 5 is in response to an antigen.

105. A. Antibodies are produced by B cells.

106. D. When B cells encounter an antigen, they divide, and produce two kinds of daughter B cells—plasma cells and memory cells. Plasma cells release antibodies immediately, but memory cells circulate in the blood for years. When an antigen is introduced into the body a second time, antibodies from the memory cells respond to the antigens immediately.

107. C. The independent variable that differs between the two graphs is the temperature. In the warmer environment, *Tribolium castaneum* outcompetes *T. confusum*. In the cooler environment, the reverse occurs.

108. B. The competitive exclusion principle states that when two species compete for the same resources, one species will eliminate the other. Which species survives depends upon the realized niches of each species, as well as environmental conditions.

109. D. RuBP carboxylase fixes O_2 as well as CO_2. The Calvin-Benson cycle occurs when CO_2 is combined with RuBP. When O_2 combines with RuBP, photorespiration occurs. As O_2 concentration increases, more O_2 and less CO_2 is fixed.

110. E. A CO_2 uptake of less than zero means that CO_2 is being released. This occurs when the CO_2 concentration is so low that photosynthesis cannot be supported and cellular respiration begins.

111. C. The longest (or largest) fragment sizes travel the shortest distance on the gel. Thus, the relationship between fragment size and migration distance is inversely proportional.

112. D. On the log scale for the *y*-axis, each horizontal line between 100 and 1000 represents an increase of 100 base pairs. Between lines 1000 and 10,000, each horizontal line represents an increase of 1000 base pairs. Thus, the second line above the 1000 line represents 3000 base pairs. On the arithmetic scale for the *x*-axis, each vertical line represents an increment of 0.2 cm.

113. C. This is an example of DNA fingerprinting. The DNA fragments from individual 2 can be found in *either* individuals 1 or 3. As a result, it is possible (but not certain) that individual 2 inherited his DNA from individuals 1 and 3. In an actual DNA fingerprinting analysis, many different restriction enzymes are used so that many different DNA fragments can be compared.

114. C. Because solutions with unboiled chloroplasts reduce DPIP and boiled chloroplasts reduce very little DPIP, then boiling changes the ability of the solutions to carry out photosynthesis or measure photosynthesis. One of the two ingredients in the solutions, DPIP, is not affected by heat (given in the introductory paragraph). Thus, you can conclude that chloroplasts (the second ingredient) are damaged during boiling.

115. D. Since boiled solutions and dark-exposed solutions reduce very little DPIP, while solutions with intact chloroplasts exposed to light reduce a considerable amount of DPIP, you can conclude that both light and chloroplasts are required to reduce DPIP. Since reduction of DPIP indicates that photosynthesis is occurring, you can also conclude that light and chloroplasts are required for photosynthesis.

116. E. No data are provided concerning the relationship between light frequency and light absorbance. To determine the light absorbance spectrum, measurements of absorbance (100% − transmittance) must be made at various frequencies.

117. A. The dependent variable is the condition that can vary as a result of the independent and controlled variables imposed by the experiment. In this case, the dependent variable is the percent transmittance. The independent variables, which are the conditions under study, are different for each of the three treatments—the presence or absence of light and the presence or absence of healthy chloroplasts. Other variables that could affect the results of the experiment are held constant for each treatment. Such variables are called controlled variables.

In this question, controlled variables include the frequency of light to which the solutions are exposed, the frequency of light at which transmittance is measured, and the length of time solutions are exposed to light (0, 5, 10, and 15 minutes for all three treatments).

118. B. Only one graph describes *P. pima*. The tallest bar is the 0.5–0.6 mm size class.

119. A. Mandible size distributions for *V. pergandei* are provided for two sites. The distribution at site B is skewed to the right compared with the distribution at site A. Distributions for species *P. pima* and *P. californicus* are described only for a single site. The data do not give the size distribution for *P. californicus* at site B, or even if *P. californicus* exists at site B.

120. C. Character displacement is a character change that minimizes niche overlap. In order to minimize interspecific competition with *P. californicus* at site A, there is selection against individuals of *V. pergandei* that have longer mandible sizes. In order to minimize interspecific competition with *P. pima* at site B, there is selection against individuals of *V. pergandei* that have shorter mandible sizes.

Section II (Free-Response Questions)

Scoring Standards for the Essay Questions

To score your essay answers, award your essay points using the standards given below. For each item listed below that matches the content and vocabulary of a statement or explanation in your essay, add the indicated number of points to your essay score (to the maximum allowed for each section). Scores for each essay question range from 0 to 10 points.

Question 1 (10 points maximum)

   (a.) graph (3 points maximum)

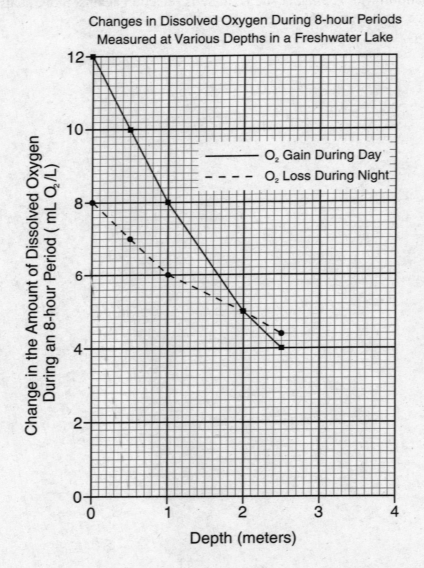

Changes in Dissolved Oxygen During 8-hour Periods
Measured at Various Depths in a Freshwater Lake

1 pt: Dissolved oxygen concentration (dependent variable) is displayed on the y-axis and depth (independent variable) is displayed on the x-axis.

1 pt: Axes are properly labeled and scaled.

1 pt: Both plots are correctly drawn.

1 pt: Each plot is identified with a label or in a legend.

1 pt: A title is given to the graph.

(b.) calculations (*3 points maximum*)

1 pt: Calculations for dissolved oxygen rates for day and night use values for samples collected at the surface (a depth of 0 meters). For day values, 6.0 and 18.0 are used, and for night values, 16.0 and 8.0 are used.

1 pt: Gross productivity correctly calculated—12/8 + 8/8 = 2.5 ml O_2/L/hr.

1 pt: Net productivity correctly calculated—12/8 = 1.5 ml O_2/L/hr.

1 pt: Respiration rate correctly calculated—8/8 = 1 ml O_2/L/hr.

(c.) differences in dissolved oxygen levels between day and night (*3 points maximum*)

1 pt: During the day, photosynthesis in plants produces O_2.

1 pt: During the day and night, respiration consumes O_2.

1 pt: Respiration during the night occurs in both plants and animals.

(d.) differences in dissolved oxygen levels at different depths (*3 points maximum*)

1 pt: At lower depths, the attenuation of light results in reduced photosynthetic activity (or, at lower depths, fewer plants are able to carry out photosynthesis because of reduced levels of light).

1 pt: At lower depths, less oxygen is available for animals to carry out respiration.

1 pt: Less food (plants and animals) is available to animals at lower depths because most plants live closer to the surface.

Question 2 (10 points maximum)

(a.) light reactions of photosynthesis (*4 points maximum*)

1 pt: Light energy is absorbed by photosystems.

1 pt: Light energy is transferred to electrons.

1 pt: Electrons provide energy for phosphorylation of ADP to ATP.

1 pt: Photolysis of water provides electrons that become energized by the photosystems.

1 pt: Energized electrons combine with $NADP^+$ and H^+ to form NADPH.

1 pt: Any additional information about the biochemical details of the light reactions, such as a description of the differences in photosystems I and II, electron transport chain mechanism, chemiosmotic theory, chloroplast structure, etc. (*maximum 1 point*).

(b.) CO_2 fixation in C_3 plants (*4 points maximum*)

   1 pt: CO_2 combines with RuBP to form PGA.

   1 pt: Rubisco is the enzyme that catalyzes the first step (CO_2 + RuBP).

   1 pt: Energy from ATP and NADPH is used for CO_2 fixation.

   1 pt: PGAL (or glucose or carbohydrates) are produced by one cycle of the CO_2 fixation pathway.

   1 pt: Calvin-Benson (or Calvin) is the name of the CO_2 fixation pathway.

   1 pt: Any additional information about the biochemical details of the Calvin-Benson cycle, such as names of intermediate molecules, the regeneration of RuBP, or numbers of molecules used, or a diagram that provides this information (*maximum 1 point*).

(c.) C_4 photosynthesis (*4 points maximum*)

   1 pt: CO_2 combines with PEP.

   1 pt: The enzyme PEP carboxylase fixes CO_2.

   1 pt: After fixation, the carbon from CO_2 is transported to bundle sheath cells where the Calvin-Benson cycle begins.

   1 pt: The enzyme that fixes CO_2 during C_3 photosynthesis (or Rubisco) also fixes O_2. The enzyme that fixes CO_2 during C_4 photosynthesis (or PEP carboxylase) does not fix O_2.

   1 pt: In C_3 photosynthesis, O_2 reduces the efficiency of CO_2 fixation (or leads to photorespiration).

   1 pt: Any additional information about the biochemical details of C_4 photosynthesis, such as names of intermediate molecules (OAA, malate, etc.) or the specialized nature of C_4 leaves (*maximum 1 point*).

Question 3 (10 points maximum)

(a.) a geographic barrier (*3 points maximum*)

   1 pt: A geographic barrier may be a mountain, river, desert, or other physical barrier (that prevents gene flow).

   1 pt: A geographic barrier results in reproductive isolation.

   1 pt: A geographic barrier prevents gene flow.

   1 pt: A geographic barrier allows two populations to undergo different selection pressures (natural selection) and may lead to the development of different adaptations.

   1 pt: Mutations or genetic drift in one population may not occur in the second population.

   1 pt: A geographic barrier may lead to speciation (allopatric speciation).

(b.) nonrandom mating (*3 points maximum*)

1 pt: Nonrandom mating occurs when mates are chosen based on their particular traits.

1 pt: Inbreeding and sexual selection are examples of nonrandom mating.

1 pt: Inbreeding reduces genetic variability.

1 pt: Sexual selection leads to competition among males (and the evolution of sexual dimorphism) and the appearance of traits such as antlers and large body size.

1 pt: Sexual selection can lead to evolution of male traits that are attractive to females (colorful feathers, mating behaviors).

(c.) polyploidy (*3 points maximum*)

1 pt: Polyploidy occurs as a result of nondisjunction of meiotically dividing cells (cells that produce gametes).

1 pt: Polyploidy results in gametes that have twice the usual number of chromosomes.

1 pt: Polyploidy results in individuals with twice the number of chromosomes.

1 pt: Polyploidy occurs mostly in plants.

1 pt: A polyploid event produces a daughter population that is reproductively isolated (a new species).

(d.) genetic drift (*3 points maximum*)

1 pt: Genetic drift is a random change in allele frequencies (a change due to chance).

1 pt: Founder effect is an example (explanation required) of genetic drift.

1 pt: A population bottleneck is an example (explanation required) of genetic drift.

1 pt: Genetic drift is more likely to occur in small populations.

(e.) One additional point may be awarded in any section where one of the following appears:

1 pt: Evolutionary change results when allele frequencies change over time.

1 pt: Microevolution describes changes in populations or species from generation to generation.

Question 4 (10 points maximum)

(a.) acetylcholine (*2 points maximum*)

1 pt: Acetylcholine is a neurotransmitter at neuromuscular junctions.

1 pt: Acetylcholine initiates action potential on plasma membrane (sarcolemma) of muscle.

1 pt: Action potential travels along transverse tubules (or T-system).

(b.) O_2 (*3 points maximum*)

   1 pt: O_2 is necessary for respiration.

   1 pt: Respiration provides ATP.

   1 pt: O_2 is stored in myoglobin in muscle cells.

   1 pt: Any additional information about the biochemical details of cellular respiration (*1 point maximum*).

   1 pt: ATP binds to myosin heads, releasing ADP and P_i.

   1 pt: ATP causes myosin heads to unbind from actin.

(c.) Ca^{2+} (*3 points maximum*)

   1 pt: Ca^{2+} initiates muscle contraction.

   1 pt: Ca^{2+} is released from sarcoplasmic reticulum.

   1 pt: Ca^{2+} causes myosin cross bridges to attach to actin.

   1 pt: Ca^{2+} binds to troponin causing tropomyosin to expose binding sites on actin.

   1 pt: Ca^{2+} withdrawal from cytoplasm terminates muscle contraction.

(d.)   a decrease in the pH of the blood (*3 points maximum*)

   1 pt: Blood pH decreases as CO_2 from respiration is released.

   1 pt: CO_2 reacts in plasma to form HCO_3^- (bicarbonate ions) and H^+.

   1 pt: $CO_2 + H_2O \rightarrow H_2CO_3 \rightarrow H^+ + HCO_3^-$

   1 pt: Carbonic anhydrase in red blood cells catalyzes CO_2 reaction to form HCO_3^-.

   1 pt: Chemoreceptors in carotid arteries increase respiratory rate.